TUNISIAN TALES

THE 1ST PARACHUTE BRIGADE IN NORTH AFRICA 1942–43

Niall Cherry

Helion & Company Ltd

Helion & Company Limited
26 Willow Road
Solihull
West Midlands
B91 1UE
England
Tel. 0121 705 3393
Fax 0121 711 4075
Email: info@helion.co.uk
Website: www.helion.co.uk
Twitter @helionbooks
Blog http://blog.helion.co.uk/

Published by Helion & Company 2011. This paperback reprint 2015.

Designed and typeset by Farr out Publications, Wokingham, Berkshire
Cover designed by Farr out Publications, Wokingham, Berkshire
Printed by Lightning Source Ltd, Milton Keynes, Buckinghamshire

ISBN 978-1-910777-39-8

British Library Cataloguing-in-Publication Data.
A catalogue record for this book is available from the British Library.

Cover illustrations: Front cover – Three officers of the 2nd Parachute Battalion – left to right are Captain R. Stark, Lieutenant J. Brayley and Major R. Ashford. This photo was taken in the Beja area days before Major Ashford was killed. (Airborne Assault Duxford). Rear cover – Sergeant M. Lewis, 2nd Parachute Battalion, beside the memorial at the Tamera Valley. Note the non-uniform trousers! (Airborne Assault Duxford).

For details of other military history titles published by Helion & Company Limited contact the above address, or visit our website: http://www.helion.co.uk.

We always welcome receiving book proposals from prospective authors.

Contents

List of Illustrations

List of Maps

List of Abbreviations

A&SH	Argyll & Sutherland Highlanders
AAG	Assistant Adjutant General
ACC	Army Catering Corps
ADC	Army Dental Corps
ADMS	Assistant Director Medical Services
ADS	Advance Dressing Station
AFV	Armoured Fighting Vehicle
AXP	Ambulance Exchange Point
BEM	British Empire Medal
CB	Companion of the Most Honourable Order of the Bath
CF	Chaplain to the Forces
CIGS	Chief of the Imperial General Staff
CLS	Central Landing School
CP	Command Post
CRA	Commander Royal Artillery
CRE	Commander Royal Engineers
CSM	Company Sergeant Major
CWGC	Commonwealth War Graves Commission
DAAQMG	Deputy Assistant Adjutant and Quartermaster General
DADMS	Deputy Assistant Director Medical Services
DAQMG	Deputy Assistant Quartermaster General
DCM	Distinguished Conduct Medal
DFC	Distinguished Flying Cross
DS	Dressing Station
DSO	Distinguished Service Order
DZ	Drop Zone
FA	Field Ambulance
FDL	Forward Defence Line
FOO	Forward Observation Officer
FST	Field Surgical Team
FSU	Field Service Unit
GD	General Duties
GOC	General Officer Commanding
GS	General Supply
GSO	General Staff Officer. Could have various grades, e.g. GSO2 or General Staff Officer (Grade 2), ranked as a major
GSW	Gunshot Wound
HE	High Explosive
HQ	Headquarters
i/c	In Command
IO	Intelligence Officer

JAG	Judge Advocate General
L of C	Lines of Communication
LF	Lancashire Fusiliers
LMG	Light Machine Gun
LO	Liaison Officer
MC	Military Cross
MDS	Main Dressing Station
MG	Machine Gun
MI	Medical Inspection
MiD	Mention in Despatches
MM	Military Medal
MO	Medical Officer
MT	Motor Transport
NAAFI	Navy, Army & Air Force Institutes
NCO	Non-Commissioned Officer
NKG	No Known Grave
NO	Nursing Orderly
OC	Officer Commanding
OP	Observation Post
OR	Other Rank
ORA	Operating Room Assistant
PFA	Parachute Field Ambulance
PJI	Parachute Jump Instructor
POW	Prisoner of War
PRI	President of the Regimental Institute
PT	Physical Training
QM	Quartermaster
QMS	Quartermaster Sergeant
RA	Royal Artillery
RAF	Royal Air Force
RAMC	Royal Army Medical Corps
RAP	Regimental Aid Post
RASC	Royal Army Service Corps
RE	Royal Engineers
RMO	Regimental Medical Officer
RN	Royal Navy
RNVR	Royal Naval Volunteer Reserve
RPO	Regimental Pay Office
RSM	Regimental Sergeant Major
RTU	Returned To Unit
RV	Rendezvous
RZ	Type of German static-line parachute
SAA	Small Arms Ammunition
TA	Territorial Army
TCG	Troop Carrier Group
TCV	Troop Carrying Vehicle

TD	Territorial Decoration
WO	Warrant Officer *or* War Office, dependent on context

Foreword

Since becoming curator of Airborne Assault – The Museum of the Parachute Regiment and Airborne Forces, one area that has intrigued me has been the operations of the 1st Parachute Brigade in Tunisia.

This is particularly well detailed in the archives but has, surprisingly, attracted little coverage in the wider historical community, with later operations in Normandy, Arnhem and the Rhine Crossing being the most covered. It was with great pleasure, therefore, that I learned of Niall's plans to research and write an in-depth study on this very subject. I was also honoured that Niall entrusted the foreword to me.

The campaign in North Africa during 1942 to 1943 acted as a proving ground for British Airborne Forces and unleashed this new form of British soldier on an unsuspecting Axis army. These men were not tied to old tactics and ideas but were bound by the ethos of their training and were volunteers to a man. Thankfully, Niall also covers this initial establishment and training in this comprehensive work, incorporating archive material, orders and notes alongside the recollections of those involved.

Whilst earlier raids into mainland Europe, as detailed in Niall's earlier work – Striking Back: Britain's Airborne and Commando Raids 1940-1942 – had demonstrated the potential of Airborne Forces it was to be in Tunisia that they would earn their fearsome reputation and cement their place in the history of the British Army.

Indeed, in Tunisia the 1st Parachute Brigade would earn the title 'Red Devils', given out of respect by the Germans – an action, at that time, they did not do for any other unit. From the Brigade's point of view it justified their intense training and also selection of men required to wear the maroon beret and to the War Office, back home, it clearly demonstrated that Churchill's call for an Airborne Force was fully justified.

In this study Niall covers each operation in Tunisia and includes details and stories of the men involved, the casualties and even reports at the time on how equipment was performing. For a study on Airborne Forces in North Africa this is the definitive account of this intense campaign.

Jonathan Baker
Curator
Airborne Assault – The Museum of the Parachute Regiment and Airborne Forces
Duxford
October 2010

Introduction

I think I first became aware of the conflict that took place between 1939 and 1945 when I was a schoolboy and watched films such as *The Battle of Britain* and *A Bridge Too Far*. I also remember watching *The World at War* TV series and learning of the campaign in North Africa. Of the fighting in North Africa I suppose by far the greater emphasis has been on the Western Desert and many people seem to be unaware that there was fighting in Tunisia.

Even more people seem to be unaware that the 1st Parachute Brigade was present in this theatre. I first heard about their campaign when I interviewed a number of medics for my first book *Red Berets and Red Crosses*. Indeed, several veterans said that the fighting in Tunisia, and particularly at the Djebel Mansour, was the hardest time in the war for them, even worse than Arnhem. After my airborne medics book came out I have followed this up with books on Gallipoli, Loos and the early airborne and commando raids of the Second World War. This last mentioned book was my second for Helion and just before it was published Duncan, the owner of Helion, asked me what I was doing next? My immediate answer was that I was thinking of covering the 1st Parachute Brigade in North Africa as there was very little coverage out there. Duncan once again willingly agreed to my choice of subject, even though I hadn't written a word or done any research! I think it is fair to say that whilst the Tunisian campaign has been touched upon in many of the general histories of the Parachute Regiment and Airborne Forces, no one book has been entirely focused on the subject. Perhaps this is because the campaign was virtually fought in secret and as one of the unit commanders commented, "Throughout, nobody but the enemy knew we were fighting. Our presence in the forefront of the battle was not divulged and no reporters were allowed."

Another factor is perhaps that due to the distance and lack of focus the airborne events of 1942 and 1943 go unnoticed. To the best of my knowledge only one veteran's tour has ever taken place, which was in 1984 – compare this to the number of times veterans and supporters travel to Normandy and Arnhem. The leader of the 1984 pilgrimage, Major Dickson, wrote, "I don't think anyone has given the Tunisian campaign its fair place in history ... Because it was really the first time we invaded and took the war to the enemy. It was the forerunner of all the operations that went on through the Mediterranean, Sicily, Anzio, Salerno and so on from which the lessons were learnt which helped to make the invasion of Europe in 1944 such a success. I think that it has never been given the just reward that it deserved. Very few really understand the conditions and the ferocity of the Tunisian battles because so relatively few people took part – they did not have the glamour of other battles." These few lines sum it up most admirably in my view.

As is usual in these circumstances I received help from a number of sources. Firstly, I would like to thank my gang of research assistants, notably John Howes, Steve Sowerby and Kevin Barnes. A special mention must also go to my daughter Claire, who helped with research at Airborne Assault at Duxford, and my other daughter Sarah for inputting words into the computer for the draft manuscript. I must also include my long-suffering wife Deborah in this, as in 2007, when looking for a sunshine holiday for the family, whilst I was thinking of Spain to keep them all happy, she looked through the brochure and suggested Tunisia without realising the significance of this destination to the airborne warrior.

Moral support was received from two good friends, Frog Barlow and Doc Hughes. Frog gets a mention in despatches for services over and above the call of duty for dragging me into a gay bar in Arnhem where they seemed to know him, even though he claimed he'd never been there before! The Doc, as usual, gave practical advice over several beers and curries in Solihull and made me aware of JJ's Memorial Fund, of which I am now a volunteer helper and intend to donate a proportion of any royalties from this book to the fund. JJ's Memorial Fund was set up by Jeff Doherty in memory of his son, Private Jeff 'JJ' Doherty or 'Doc' as he was known to his brothers in 2nd Battalion, The Parachute Regiment, after he was killed in an ambush in Afghanistan on 12th June 2008. It was two days after his 20th birthday. Their aim is to raise money to support paratroopers wounded in action and supporting the families of those who are killed. I would urge you to visit their website www.jjsmemorialfund.org.

I sell wristbands for JJ's which are in the wonderful colour of maroon and have the words 'Airborne Forever' on them, suggested donation £2.

Wallace Mckie and James Macrae also receive my thanks for letting me look at their Alistair Pearson archive, most of which emanated from the great man himself, and for supplying photographs. Michael Pine-Coffin deserves my deep thanks for allowing us to use some of the unique photographs taken by his Grandfather R.G. Pine-Coffin in the UK and North Africa in 1942 and 1943.

A special word of thanks to Jon Baker, the curator of Airborne Assault for agreeing to write the foreword and also for letting me rape and pillage the North African archive and photograph collection. Thanks also to the other team members, Tom Lusby and Becks Skinner, for their help, although I think they are trying to get their pound of flesh out of me now!

John Howes gets another mention and also my eternal thanks for researching the war diaries of the units of the 1st Parachute Brigade from North Africa at the National Archives. The team is also grateful to the staff of the Imperial War Museum for their help at the Sound Archive, Department of Documents and Photograph Archive. Crown Copyright material from the National Archives is reproduced with their permission.

I think that just about covers it for now!

Utrinque Paratus and *Airborne Forever*.

1

Birth of an idea

It is probably fair to say that whilst the idea of dropping troops from aircraft was first thought of in the Great War, it failed to literally get off the ground due to a shortage or lack of suitable aircraft. After the end of the Great War nobody really had much appetite for the armed forces and in many respects they were left to wither on the vine.

However, not every army was sitting on its hands and the first major army to take on board the concept of airborne warfare was the Soviet Red Army. Indeed it is recorded that in their 1930 summer manoeuvres the Red Army had successfully dropped a small force by parachute and captured an 'enemy' HQ. The aircraft used for this was the Tupolev ANT-6, a large four-engined, fixed-undercarriage plane. There was an exit hatch on top of the fuselage and braving the aircraft's slipstream, men had to clamber down to the wing before dropping off and pulling their own ripcord to deploy their parachute as soon as they were clear of the aircraft.

The Russian manoeuvres of 1935 and 1936 were attended by military observers from most of the major powers including Britain and Germany. The effect in these two countries is interesting. The British Army observers seem to have been unimpressed and even though they witnessed successful heavy drops of light tanks, field guns and armoured cars, one said, "Such novelties would not have a great deal of influence on the future course of war." On his return to Moscow the German Military Attaché sent an immediate top-secret signal to Berlin saying that he had seen a revolutionary transformation in the technique of war. In October 1935 orders were issued which led to the formation of the first German parachute battalion, with the intention of forming a future parachute corps. It should be noted here that the German airborne forces were part of the Luftwaffe, the air arm rather than the army, as was the case with British airborne forces. In January 1936 a parachute training school was set up, aircraft allocated to it and production of a suitable glider was started. This glider had the stipulation that it could carry 10 men but cost no more than 10 parachutes. After 1936 the Russians changed to static-line parachutes.

Soon after arriving in France in September 1939 the British Expeditionary Force (BEF) settled down to what became known as the 'Phoney War', with very little activity on either side. Indeed the winter of 1939/1940 was one of the worst on record. All of this inactivity changed in the early morning of 10th May 1940 when the German armed forces swung into action. As well as the Luftwaffe bombing airfields in France, German tanks and infantry unleashed a massive offensive through Belgium and Holland.

In May 1940 the BEF consisted of 10 divisions and was concentrated mainly in the northern part of France, in areas that would have been familiar to the BEF of 1914. Together with French and Belgian troops the Allies were able to field 53 divisions. Arrayed against them were 72 German divisions. In spite of these large numbers the fighting over the coming weeks was to be dominated by just 10 German armoured divisions. Indeed the coast of France was reached on 21st May by armoured troops.

Amongst all these operations, the use of German airborne forces on 10th May was significant, notably against the Belgium fort at Eben-Emael. The main body of them were to be used in Holland to capture vital bridges at Rotterdam, Dordrecht and Moerdijk, which carried the main road into the south of Holland over the lower Rhine. The remaining troops were to be used in Belgium by seizing bridges over the Albert Canal near Maastricht. A key point in the Belgian defences here was a modern fortress at Eben-Emael. It was intended to land gliders on top of the fort and destroy the gun emplacements by using a new 'secret weapon'- a hollow charge. A hollow charge was a specially shaped explosive that looked like a small beehive and directed the explosive charge into a concentrated force. This meant it was able to blow a hole through concrete and steel up to 12 inches thick, depending on the weight of explosives.

The fort at Eben-Emael, which was situated on a plateau overlooking the Albert Canal, was manned by about 1200 Belgian soldiers and covered an area about half a mile wide by three-quarters of a mile long. There was a 50-yard drop on the canal side and wide anti-tank ditches had been dug on the others. The gun emplacements had a mixture of 75mm and 120 mm guns together with many machine gun posts. In spite of these static defences, none of the gun casemates were protected by surface trenches, and no defensive precautions had been placed on the large flat open top surface of the fort. Obviously no-one on the Belgian side thought an air assault was likely, indeed there was only one small anti-aircraft battery in the vicinity. The Germans had obviously spotted this weak link. Eleven gliders containing 86 men were to take part in the operation, which was timed to start at 0525, five minutes before German troops crossed the Belgian border. Other parties of German airborne forces were to capture three bridges over the Albert Canal – in all around 450 men. The planning had been greatly helped by aerial photographs of the fort, one of which showed Belgian soldiers playing football on top of the fort, which meant there should be no mines up there!

Although the fort held out in places for nearly 24 hours the majority of the casemates had been put out of action and did not really hinder the German attack. This operation showed that a small group of determined men could attack a much larger objective and succeed. The German tactic of landing right on top of the target with the element of shock and surprise proved its worth, even if heavy casualties might result. The German casualties were six men killed and twenty wounded. The German High Command had estimated they would have taken 6000 casualties in a 'conventional' attack. Of the three bridges over the Albert Canal, two were captured intact, and within a few hours the Panzer divisions were pouring over them and into the heart of Belgium. Fewer than 500 troops in 42 gliders had opened the way for the defeat of the Belgian Army and led to the evacuation of the BEF, mainly through the port and beaches around Dunkirk.

After the withdrawal from Dunkirk, in the summer of 1940 Britain was in the grip of 'invasion fever' and every day people expected to see fleets of German transport aircraft disgorging large numbers of paratroopers over southern England. Fortunately, for a variety of reasons, this never happened, but in the interim Britain was intending to fight back.

In early June the Royal Air Force had taken the decision to set up a parachute training school at Ringway airfield near Manchester. This is now Manchester International Airport, and I suspect few people travelling through there today realise its significant place in the history of the airborne forces nor its contribution to the war effort. With typical RAF logic it was decided to call it the Central Landing School (CLS) and its first commander was Squadron Leader L. Strange. Within a few days a Major J. Rock from the Royal Engineers was sent there to implement 'the military organisation of British airborne forces'. It was decided that Physical Training Instructors would be ideal candidates to train men in parachuting and nine men from the Army Physical Training Corps and fourteen from the RAF Physical Education branch were posted in.

On 22nd June 1940 Churchill penned a memo to General Sir Hastings Ismail, head of the Military Wing of the War Cabinet Secretariat, stating "We ought to have a corps of at least 5,000 parachute troops, including a proportion of Australians, New Zealanders and Canadians, together with some trustworthy people from Norway and France. Advantage of the summer must be taken to train these troops, who can nonetheless play their part meanwhile as shock troops in home defence. Pray let me have a note from the War Office on the subject."

The real problem now was that the services were being asked to do in a few weeks what the Germans had undertaken over several years. The RAF grudgingly 'gave' six virtually obsolete Whitley bombers and a thousand parachutes. The civil aerodrome at Ringway was chosen, probably because it would be unlikely to suffer much from German interference. Then in late June/early July it was decided to send one of the newly-formed commando units to be converted to the parachute role, and No 2 Commando was selected. This unit was moved to Knutsford in Cheshire, not far from Ringway, and on 3rd July Lieutenant Colonel C. Jackson from the Royal Tank Regiment arrived to take command of this unit.

The RAF were not exactly overjoyed at their new role and it is probably fair to say that they did not make the best use of the summer. Indeed, in an Air Staff paper dated 12th August 1940, the following comment is contained: "We are beginning to incline to the view that dropping troops from the air by parachute is a clumsy and obsolescent method and that there are far more important possibilities in gliders. The Germans made excellent use of their parachute troops in the Low Countries by exploiting surprise, and by virtue of the fact that they had practically no opposition. But it seems to us at least possible that this may be the last time that parachute troops are used on a serious scale in major operations." The report continued by outlining the difficulties encountered since June in training the first five hundred let alone five thousand.

On 9th July 1940 B and C Troops of No 2 Commando started to arrive at Ringway. To an RSM they must have looked a strange bunch, nearly every Regiment and Corps was represented. They kept their parent formations' dress, so there was a mixture of berets, sidecaps, glengarries and tam o'shanters and a multiplicity of cap badges. However, there were several common bonds – every man was a volunteer, had a desire to hit back at Hitler, and guts. It appears that apart from an interview no other selection procedures took place. This would all change over the coming months. Before the training started a suitable drop zone had to be found – eventually Tatton Park, just a few miles away, was selected. All commanders in the area were told that friendly paratroopers would be landing in the area and were not to be shot at while descending. The threat of invasion was still a very present one and as previously explained the country was in the grip of parachutist fever.

The parachutes sent to Ringway were of a slightly bigger diameter (28 feet) than the normal aircrew one of 22 feet. This had been found to give a softer landing than the aircrew version, I suppose the logic being a smaller diameter was easier to fit either inside a cockpit or the fuselage of an aircraft. A paratrooper would be expected to go straight into action whereas aircrew would either be in captivity or go back to their base for tea. The CLS reported they were ready to carry out the first descents on 13th July by the instructors at Ringway. In these early days it was all a matter of trial and error. Pre-war stuntmen had carried out descents by climbing out onto the wing of biplane aircraft, and while holding on to a strut, had released the canopy. The canopy filled up with air from the aircraft's slipstream and they were then pulled off the wing. This became known as the 'pull-off' method.

After the realisation that the pull-off method was unsatisfactory, a hole was cut in the floor of the Whitley and trainees now started to exit through this. Over the coming weeks and months many new techniques were learnt and improved upon at Ringway but this success was not without cost as several trainees died as a result of parachute malfunctions and other accidents. Indeed the first casualty of parachute training occurred on 25th July 1940, when T/175282 Driver Ralph Evans of the Royal Army Service Corps became entangled in his rigging lines and fell to his death. He is now buried at Walton-on-Thames in St Mary's Churchyard. Training was stopped whilst an investigation was carried out and it became clear that the cause was the way the parachute deployed from its pack.

A few words for the uninitiated about the deployment of parachutes and their attachment to the jumper … The Germans also used a static-line parachute called the RZ. This had a single-point anchor point in the middle of the back, which had the disadvantage that the parachute could not be steered and all landings became forward ones, hence the rubber kneepads often worn by German paratroopers. The British used a two-point attachment with webbing risers at the shoulders which at least meant that the parachute could be steered by pulling down on the appropriate riser. All parachute harnesses also had a couple of straps that went between the legs and could be painful if these straps were not fastened correctly when the parachute deployed.

The parachutes used by the Germans and Russians were similar to those used at Ringway, in that the static line first pulled the canopy from the pack followed by the rigging lines. However, if the jumper made a bad exit, which could lead to his body turning or twisting in the slipstream, he risked becoming entangled in the rigging lines, or, as one RAF parachute jumping instructor said at Brize Norton in the 1980s whilst on ground training, "Come out of the aircraft like that and you'll be turning somersaults down the side of the aircraft counting every rivet as you go past."

Training was suspended after the death of Driver Evans whilst trials using dummies were carried out, which again led to several more failures. The two parachute manufacturers, Irvin and GQ, were asked to advise, and between themselves and the CLS a hybrid design was decided upon. This consisted of an Irvin parachute in a GQ bag, which had the subtle difference of letting the parachute pack itself break away from the wearer's back as he left the aircraft. It was of course still attached to the static line and then the aircraft; as the jumper continued to fall away from the aircraft, his momentum first pulled his webbing risers and then his rigging lines out of the pack. Finally, when these were fully deployed, the canopy itself came out of the bag, attached to the static line by a length of string. This piece of string, being a weak link, broke under the weight of the jumper and in theory the canopy was then deployed with negligible chance of a

Senior officers being shown the glider arm of 11th Special Air Service Battalion in December 1940. (Imperial War Museum)

jumper becoming entangled in his own rigging lines. This became known as the X series of parachutes and was the standard parachute for the rest of the war, and indeed up until the 1960s.

This is not to say that the method worked 100%, as during trials of the new system a canopy became entangled in the tail wheel of a Whitley. Perhaps Rock and the staff of the CLS briefly made the decision to stop jumping from Whitleys. Perhaps they had been looking enviously at other parachuting aircraft such as the German Junkers Ju 52, which had a door in the side of the aircraft. Jumping through a hole in the bottom of the aircraft was obviously running the risk of something catching on the tail wheel. The top RAF officer at the CLS, Squadron Leader L. Strange, is reported to have commented, "The Whitley fuselage is dark and gloomy with its hole in the middle, and is bad for the nerves. The sight of other men disappearing through the hole is an unpleasant one, and the prospect of scraping one's face on the other side is not encouraging."

Another RAF officer commented, "Most of the men were of a good type and were a loss to the Commando. The majority got to the edge of the hole in the aircraft before refusing. Four men fainted in the aircraft, while a number jumped in a state of collapse having forced themselves to do so by sheer willpower."

On 31st August 1940 Churchill was informed that with the current resources the figure of 5,000 parachute troops would not be reached for another 12 months.

The RAF pointed out that owing to the need to expand the bombing force, there could be no question of having resources solely dedicated to dropping parachute troops. It saw it as an alternative role for the heavy bomber squadrons. It also pointed out the need to train parachutists in the same aircraft that would be used on operations. The only aircraft with the necessary range to reach Europe at this stage was the Whitley.

A decision was taken in November to change the name of No 2 Commando to the 11th Special Air Service Battalion and to encompass all types of airborne warfare. They were ordered to form a glider wing and a parachute wing.

In September 1940 a report was sent to Churchill which outlined the RAF's view of the deployment of airborne forces. The main points of this report were as follows:

(a) There appeared to be three types of raid for which airborne troops might be used:-
   (i) A raid on a selected position, to be followed by the evacuation of the raiding force by air.
   (ii) A raid to be followed by evacuation by sea.
   (iii) The dropping of parachutists as saboteurs, pure and simple.

(b) For the first two roles the best method would be to use a small force of parachutists, who would be followed by a larger body landing from gliders.

(c) For any particular operation about 1,000 men would be required, of whom 100 would be parachutists, and 900 glider-borne. To enable more than one raid to be carried out, plans are being made to train three such forces by the spring of 1941, plus 200 parachute saboteurs.

(d) The total airborne force envisaged, therefore, was:-
   500 parachute troops.
   2,700 glider-borne troops.
   360 glider pilots to fly the glider-borne troops.

To secure the RAF's continued involvement in airborne forces a concession was made, which was probably dismissed as insignificant at the time, but had far-reaching effects in 1944. The RAF requested and got approval for the landing and dropping zones for any future operations to be selected by them. Although there was of course in the coming years the usual horse-trading, the RAF had the final word on the zones. If the Army didn't like those selected it was a case of "tough luck, old boy, you'll just have to get on with those selected." As a student of the Arnhem battle in September 1944 it is easy to lay the blame for the failure of the plan on the distance from the ultimate objective of the dropping and landing zones. However many people are not aware of the decision agreed to by the Army earlier in the war and so it is wrong to solely blame the RAF.

It was expected that the 500 parachute troops would be trained by the spring of 1941, however the plans for an increase in this number were vague. The only equipment they could carry was small arms and no trials had been undertaken as to how to provide support weapons.

Apart from the notional 'glider wing' of 11th Special Air Service Battalion no other units had been nominated to provide the glider-borne forces. It was felt better to provide them when the gliders themselves were ready. To back this up plans had been drawn up for the design and manufacture of four types of gliders as follows:

(i) An eight-seater, later named the Hotspur. Originally intended to go on operations, it later became the standard training aircraft for aspiring glider pilots. It had the advantage that it could be towed by a relatively small aircraft.

(ii) A medium glider, the Horsa, able to carry cargo or up to 25 passengers.

(iii) A slightly smaller medium glider able to carry 15 passengers, called the Hengist. This was planned purely as an insurance policy should the Horsa prove unsuitable.
(iv) A heavy glider able to carry heavy cargos including a light tank or 40 passengers. This subsequently became known as the Hamilcar.

In the light of the somewhat hazardous nature of parachuting, officers were allowed an extra four shillings (£0.20) a day and other ranks two shillings (£0.10) a day parachute pay. This was allowed after the completion of three jumps, when they would also qualify for parachute wings. This allowance was later changed to two shillings a day (£0.10) for everyone. The number of qualifying jumps also increased to seven.

Fortunately for Britain the expected German invasion in 1940 never materialised and Churchill insisted that the fight be taken to the Germans. In practice this meant mainly the commando forces undertaking pinprick raids against the northern coast of France and later the Channel Islands. To put it politely these raids were not really well executed and the method of getting the men to and from their objectives was not really satisfactory. However, with the formation of a 'Combined Operations' department it was hoped things would improve.

It was not easy in these early months to maintain morale and motivation; many people had volunteered to join the new units to get to grips with the enemy and nothing seemed to be happening. The number of troops asking to go back to their parent units was on the increase and minor cases of ill-discipline were occurring. However, as often occurred during the struggle, Churchill was unhappy with the lack of progress and wanted action. Perhaps more importantly Britain was virtually fighting alone and wanted to show to the outside world that she was still capable of fighting back. In early 1941 the only real theatre that any fighting was taking place was in North Africa, where British and Commonwealth troops were fighting the Italians, although the Italians were also involved in Albania fighting the Greeks. It was felt that the Italian forces were being supported logistically through the ports of Taranto, Brindisi and Bari. As well as supporting the troops in North Africa an operation against the Italians would be good for propaganda purposes but had to be cost-effective in terms of the effort expended.

As early as June 1940 it had been suggested to the Air Ministry by a British engineering firm (in fact one of their board members, Mr W.G. Ardley of George Kent and Sons) that destroying a vital aqueduct in southern Italy might wreak havoc with the water supply to a large part of that area. This does, to some extent, mirror the idea of Barnes Wallis and his plans to disrupt the German steel industry by hindering their supply of water. This suggestion contained the information that the aqueduct was part of a extensive pipeline system supplying around two million people in the areas around the towns of Bari, Brindisi, Taranto and Foggia. The aqueduct in question was near a small hilltop town called Calitri, and as it crossed a small river called the Tragino, it was known as the Tragino Aqueduct. This area was part of the Apennine Mountains region.

Perhaps it's necessary to give a few words here about the water system in this area of Italy to provide some background information. It is probably fair to say that the idea of a system of aqueducts dated back to about 1868 when a junior Italian Government engineer suggested a canal taking water from the head of the river Sele (about 1,300 feet above sea level) and transferring it south of Taranto. Initial surveying of the route took place in 1901 and construction started a few years later on 150 miles of the main canal/route from the Sele to a place called Villa Castelli approximately halfway between the towns of Taranto and Brindisi. The design of the system called for many tunnels to go through mountains as well as soft ground and aqueducts to cross valleys where the depths of the valleys were not too excessive. Where there were deep valleys a system of siphons was employed. This was vital to the entire network. The siphon design provided the technical breakthrough that allowed the system to work in conjunction with the use of reinforced concrete pipes (which allowed for the reduction of the operating pressure to 5.3 atmospheres). In total there were 68 miles of tunnels and 77 bridges, some up to 690 feet long. The bridges were either constructed using a masonry arch design (for use on wide valleys) or in reinforced concrete (narrow valleys). The flow rate of the water through the aqueducts was between 3 to 4 feet per second. The control of the flow of water was critical to the management of the system and this is where a British firm played a part. Towards the end of the 1920s and in the early 1930s the entire system was completed. George Kent and Sons had begun business in 1838 as mechanical engineers and specialised in flume and metering systems. They had supplied the flow metering and measuring system to the Italians and as such would have known the actual operating volumes of water. Ardley had suggested the Tragino Aqueduct as a suitable target, although it took a few months for the military to get their heads around the idea.

A planning meeting was held at the Air Ministry in December 1940, which, although stating it to be a suitable target, deemed it not feasible to attack with bombers. An important reason would probably have been the distance to the target. It was therefore decided to hand it over to Admiral Keyes and his Combined Operations HQ.

A further meeting was held at Combined Operations HQ on 12th December 1940, at which, amongst others, a Colonel J. Davidson (late Chief Engineer to the Metropolitan Water Board) and Mr W. Ardley were present. The meeting considered the likely effects of blowing up the aqueduct and the effect on the Italian war effort. It concluded that if all the necessary pipes, concrete mixers and labour were available, then 10% of the original flow might be got across the valley by D+14, 20% by D+21 and 40% to 50% after 30 days. These numbers were based on day and night working. The meeting minuted that if the RAF could follow up with a bombing raid then it would obviously delay the work

The only ground photograph available to the planners for Colossus was this one, taken in 1928 when the aqueduct was being built. The huts were used by the construction workers and were not there in 1941. (Airborne Assault Duxford)

even more. However, it was considered that there was no reason to abandon the plan even if the RAF did not want to carry out a later attack. Subsequent discussions also suggested that if the water supply to the towns of Bari, Brindisi and Taranto could be interrupted this would reduce their fire-fighting capacity. This might lead to greater bombing damage should raids be launched. Also it might possibly affect the morale and motivation of the civilians in these towns, which were all important in the logistical tail in support of Italian operations in North Africa and Greece.

As a double banker the idea of attacking the Tragino Aqueduct was handed over to Major Gubbins of SO2 (otherwise known as the people responsible for Irregular Warfare in Europe – later known as the Special Operations Executive). They reported back on 2nd January 1941 that they did not have the resources in terms of equipment or explosives to carry out this attack let alone have the time to prepare, train and transport people for such a job. According to some records they were asked to supply two interpreters. So, the ball went back to Combined Operations.

After assessing their options it was decided to accept the target and in January 1941 Operation Colossus came into being. The decision was taken to give the 11th SAS Battalion the chance to take part, probably because they had done nothing so far and it would be an ideal opportunity to test this new arm.

The plan called for a party from 11th SAS to first go to Malta by air and then mount the operation from there. It was proposed to spare eight Whitley bombers for the operation, six to carry the men and two to carry out a bombing raid on the railway yards at Foggia. It was hoped that the Italians would believe that all eight aircraft were going to bomb Foggia. After destroying the aqueduct the raiding party was to make its way on foot to the west coast of Italy where they would be picked up by a Royal Navy submarine.

With the benefit of hindsight this does seem a risky venture as up to the end of 1940 the maximum number of men dropped simultaneously from Whitleys was 20 on Salisbury Plain. Now it was envisaged to drop nearly 40 in enemy territory after a long approach flight.

After several months training both in soldiering, parachuting and commando skills, the morale of the unit was starting to fall. Then in the middle of January 1941 a rumour started going round that "something was going to happen soon". At a parade of the whole unit at Cliffe House in Knutsford, the CO, Lieutenant Colonel Jackson, informed them that a top-secret operation involving a long-range penetration into enemy territory was being planned. He also said that it was unlikely that any arrangements for the evacuation of the assault party could be guaranteed and capture by the enemy was highly likely. It was also revealed that although the party would be dressed in normal army uniforms, it was possible they might be regarded as secret agents and treated as such. He ended his address by calling for volunteers for a dangerous mission – it is reported that every single man on the parade of around 500 stepped forward. L/Corporal Harry Pexton was present on this parade and recalls:

> The Colonel had the whole unit paraded on Shaw Heath in Knutsford and said something like the following: "Now this is serious, I'm being told there is something coming up, and I'll need some volunteers." By that time everyone was feeling pretty browned off, fully trained with nothing much exciting to do. So when he asked for

volunteers everyone stepped forward. It was as it turned out up to Colonel Jackson to decide who should go.

Obviously Lieutenant Colonel Jackson now had a tough decision who to pick. Jackson decided that the unit's second-in-command, Major T.A.G. Pritchard, originally from the Royal Welch Fusiliers, would lead the operation. As the ultimate aim of the operation was blowing something up a number of Royal Engineers would have to be included and Captain G. Daly was selected as the chief engineer. From this first decision the other officers were chosen as follows:

To command the three infantry sections:

Captain C. Lea, originally from the Lancashire Fusiliers

Lieutenant A. Deane-Drummond, originally from the Royal Signals

Second Lieutenant A. Jowett, originally from the Highland Light Infantry

To act as the assistant demolition officer:

Second Lieutenant G. Paterson from the Royal Engineers

These six officers were all told to select 'five good men' to take part in Operation Colossus, but with the provision that half of the party had to be Royal Engineers. One officer and two men were selected as reserves. An additional man from 11th SAS Battalion, a Private Nicol Nastri, was added to the party as he could speak Italian.

Those selected to take part became known as X Troop. and after much training around the Ringway area, they first were flown to Malta. Here they carried out their last-minute preparations before the operation took place on the night of 10th February 1941. Eight Whitleys took part in the operation, six carried six paratroopers and a small bomb load each, while the remaining two just carried bombs. The plan called for all aircraft to bomb Foggia in the hope that if the Italians did detect eight aircraft, it was deemed a small bombing raid and not an airborne operation. As it turned out one man went sick in a Whitley on the runway at Malta and so 35 men actually took part in Operation Colossus. Without going into too much detail, even though not all the men and supplies were dropped in the correct place, the aqueduct was blown up. Over the coming days all the men of X Troop were captured *en route* to their supposed pick up point with a submarine (it had been recalled due to one of the Whitleys crash-landing in the estuary they were meant to be picked up from). The damage caused was far less than that expected in the pre-planning meetings and was repaired within 3 days.

Operation Colossus: A Balance Sheet

So, what can be said about the first British parachute raid of the Second World War?

In purely strategic terms the raid achieved little as the aqueduct was repaired within about 3 days, well before any local reservoirs ran dry. It also failed in the aim of affecting the Italian war effort in North Africa or Albania. However the tactical effects of the raid were far-reaching. Much effort in the days after the 10th February 1941 were spent in looking for the parachutists, and the Italians were unsure for many days if everyone had been rounded up. In the spin of the time the Italian propaganda machine told the public that the raid had been a total failure. However, the Italian Government considered it to be a serious threat and with there being the possibility of more raids, new security measures were introduced. Additional soldiers were posted to dams, bridges, power stations and other likely targets the length and breadth of Italy. Lieutenant Deane-Drummond commented that, "The raid had a profound psychological effect upon the Italians. It was a slap in the face for Italian pride. It meant that troops were brought from the front to be on guard duty all over Italy protecting bridges and other vital installations." So it can be said that the small force of 35 was able to punch well above their weight and certainly caused problems with a lasting effect.

Additionally, once details of the raid had been released in Britain it gave a fillip to morale and encouraged more men to volunteer for the airborne forces. There was initial caution about the raid from the War Office due to the lack of news and the photographic evidence. Indeed, in his report of 13th February, Wing Commander Norman, who had gone along as an observer, commented that either the raid had been expected and X Troop had been captured immediately on landing, or that the aqueduct had been of a different construction to that thought and could not be destroyed with the explosives taken.

Fortunately he was wrong on both counts, as on 24th February 1941, information was received via the American Embassy that the raid had achieved some success. Colonel Fiske from this embassy was able to report back via the Rome correspondent of the *Chicago Daily News* who was expelled from Rome in early March. Definite confirmation came from a coded message in one of Major Pritchard's letters home. Then in August 1942 a first-hand account came from Lieutenant Deane-Drummond when he arrived back in the UK after his successful escape.

Like the somewhat ineffective commando raid on Guernsey in 1940, Operation Colossus provided valuable information on what to do and what not to do. Perhaps the most important learning was the need for proper reconnaissance, especially using aerial photographs. The methods of dropping the containers also came under scrutiny. It is perhaps no surprise that within months paratroopers were jumping with their own weapons and equipment rather than relying on containers.

In February 1941 the Russian-German non-aggression pact was still intact and America was still not involved in the war – Britain was virtually on her own. Operation Colossus showed that in the dark days of 1941 Britain was willing to strike back at the Axis powers.

2

The Brigade takes shape

During the summer of 1940 Churchill had stated that he wanted to see a corps of around 5,000 parachute troops, although by the summer of 1941 this idea was still in its infancy, with only the 11th Special Air Service Battalion on the order of battle. Whilst the Tragino Aqueduct raid had gone a little way to keeping this somewhat rebellious gang in check by June 1941 things were starting to go wrong again. Churchill, for one, was unhappy with the lack of progress towards his goal of 5,000 and it is fair to say there were less than 500 parachute troops trained by then. There were many reasons for this, some of which have been touched on before, but a study of the records of the Army and the RAF do not paint a good picture. There were certainly difficulties between the two services which probably have a great deal to do with the slow growth in numbers.

From the middle of January until May 1941 draft proposals between the Air Ministry and the War Office continued to ping-pong between the two establishments. The War Office stated that they considered that the development of airborne forces should be based on the principle that the Army would present their requirements for airborne forces to the Air Force, who would do what they could to meet them. The Air Ministry countered by generally agreeing with the Army proposals and asking them to draw up a paper recommending the action required for raising the airborne forces, and that any questions and answers not agreed by the Ministries should be left to the decision of the Chiefs of Staff. They also asked the War Office to suggest the requirements for an airborne establishment in the UK which could look after research, development and training for the Home Forces, as distinct for any requirements for offensive operations overseas. The Air Ministry was also an advocate of airlanding troops, as it seemed to economise on the number of aircraft required and had the advantage of landing in tactical groups and with heavier equipment.

On 26th May 1941 Winston Churchill visited the Central Landing Establishment at RAF Ringway and could have been forgiven for being depressed at the lack of progress made. Whilst there he was 'treated' to the spectacle of a parachute and glider demonstration. This probably left him in no doubt as to the lack of progress towards his idea of a 'Corps of 5,000 men'. A formation of six Whitleys dropped 60 men, there was a glider landing of five sailplanes and a fly past by one Hotspur. It is reported that around 800 men had been trained as parachutists but the numbers who could be dropped was limited by the number of aircraft available, which was small.

On his return to London Churchill asked urgently for the latest proposals for increasing the size of the airborne forces together with a timetable for achieving this.

On 20th May 1941 the Germans once again used airborne troops to spearhead an invasion, this time in the Mediterranean at Crete. Churchill wrote another memo towards the end of May asking for a progress report and this seemed to galvanise things into action.

Fortunately this joint memorandum was now almost finished and on 31st May 1942 the Chiefs of Staff submitted it to the Prime Minister. The main points in this joint paper, which Churchill accepted, can be summarised as follows:

(a) Airborne forces could only be used successfully in localities where air superiority had been firmly established and where the flow of reinforcements could be assured. It was impossible to foresee these conditions in the immediate future, but by the middle of 1942 airborne forces might be required.

(b) The existing 500 parachutists were picked volunteers. The policy to date had been to keep this body up to strength and to train, in addition, a limited number of parachutists, among whom were special agents chosen from Polish and French soldiers in the country. There would be no difficulty in raising further British volunteers, and expanding the present parachutists' training organisation to an output of 400 a month. This would produce some 5,000 British parachutists by May 1942. If these were required earlier a considerable expansion in both personnel and material would be necessary, but the programme would be assisted by the institution of a parachute school in the Middle East or India.

(c) In future all Wellingtons were to be modified for parachuting. It was hoped that by spring 1943 there would be an additional ten squadrons of transport aircraft, with a total air-transported lift of about 3,000 men, which would also be suitable for parachuting.

(d) The 25-seater operational glider, which could also carry some supporting weapons and light cars, was in the prototype stage. Production was expected to begin not earlier than January 1942 and the total would carry approximately a brigade and ancillary troops without armoured fighting vehicles, or Bren carriers, on one operation, with no reserves. The intention was to place an order for a further 400 gliders in India as soon as possible. It might be possible to increase output later.

(e) The tank-carrying glider was in the 'mock-up' stage. At the most optimistic estimate, the delivery of a sufficient number to carry a squadron of light tanks would probably not be before November 1942.

(f) For the future, Army requirements were: -

    (i) One brigade of parachute troops to be located at Home, and one in the Middle East with the necessary transport aircraft. The strength of each brigade would be approximately 2,400 men.

    (ii) Sufficient gliders to carry two airlanding brigades, each approximately 5,000 strong, including ancillaries and armoured fighting vehicles. One airlanding brigade would be stationed at Home and one in the Middle East, with their glider pilots and tug aircraft.

    (iii) Sufficient transport aircraft to lift an airlanding brigade in an air transported role, both at Home and in the Middle East.

(g) The provision of the Army requirements would make considerable inroads on Bomber Command and might involve crews and aircraft being absent from bomber operations for as long as two months. It would also mean reserving up to five airfields exclusively for airborne operations and the setting aside of a considerable amount of motor transport for moving gliders.

(h) The Chiefs of Staffs agreed to the existing programme for airborne forces and this was to be pressed on as fast as possible. With regard to the additional Army requirements, and in particular to the provision of a large number of transport aircraft, this raised the question as to how far the building up of Army support as a whole, of which airborne forces were only a part, was to be allowed to interfere with the expansion of the main Royal Air Force effort. They proposed to submit their views on this subject separately.

Thus there was now a kind of agreement, and as can be seen, it was intended for the one parachute unit, the 11th Special Air Service Battalion, to be expanded into a parachute brigade as soon as possible. Staff wallahs started looking into the problems and machinery to bring this to fruition. Close behind was the authorisation by the CIGS to authorise the raising of a brigade headquarters, four parachute battalions, a signal section and one air troop of Royal Engineers. The raising of other support units such as medical, artillery and transport although approved would be left on the back burner for a while.

The immediate problems the staff came up with related to the following:

(a) The method by which the new units would be formed.
(b) The terms of service, with special reference to the continuance of subsidence allowance, the right of return to parent units after six months and the rate of parachute pay.
(c) Training and the means of co-operation with the Central Landing Establishment.
(d) A timed programme for raising the new units.
(e) Questions of accommodation.

It is worth adding here that the men of 11th Special Air Service Battalion were living in 'digs' with a variety of landlords in the Knutsford area. This was a carry-over from their Commando days, when it was felt that putting the Commandos in barracks would be an unnecessary administrative burden. However, it was now felt that for the 11th this should not be allowed to continue. The reasons for this were that the lack of cooks was hampering their operational efficiency, and accommodation was becoming increasingly difficult to find and a drain on the civilian rationing system. Personnel of the new brigade, therefore, were not to be granted a special subsidence allowance but were to be accommodated and fed in normal barracks.

The option of a volunteer returning to their parent unit after six months' parachuting service was also withdrawn and the new terms included no fixed period of service with a parachute unit. It was decided that parachuting pay would be 4 shillings a day for an officer and 2 shillings a day for other ranks, subject to the discretion of the unit commander and on completion of three jumps. This low number of three was reluctantly agreed upon due to the limited number that could be reasonably undertaken in the near future with the few aircraft available.

It was further agreed that it would be more economical to carry out all the parachute training at RAF Ringway at the Central Landing Establishment. The course was designed to last three weeks and the capacity at Ringway would be 100 new trainees a week. This was hoped to meet an operational readiness date for a three-battalion brigade by March 1942. For the time being it was decided to leave the formation of a fourth battalion on the back burner.

The decision to form the brigade was announced on 31st August 1941 and the 1st Parachute Brigade HQ came into being on 15th September 1941. The first brigade commander was Richard Gale. It is believed he was spotted by General Sir Alan Brooke during an inspection of the unit Gale commanded in 1941 and noted as a possible future brigade commander. Here a few details of his career up to 1941.

Richard 'Windy' Gale was born in London on the 25th July 1896. His father hailed from Hull, in Yorkshire, but had ventured to Australia in search of adventure, and it was here that he met and married Richard's mother, who was half English and half Irish. They had returned to England for the birth, but quickly found themselves back in Australia, and it was here that Richard spent the first eight years of his life. Two years in New Zealand followed, but in 1906 the family returned to England on a permanent basis. Richard was educated at Aldenham School, but he did not excel academically; he later reflected that he was firmly in the category of "could do better if he tried". He was, however, an avid reader, "I read anything I could lay my hands on, including Disraeli's *Vivian Grey*, which stimulated my imagination. I loved and still love the Classics and found in *The Iliad* a type of beauty and adventure that had a strong appeal." It was always his intention to become an officer in the British Army, however his lack of scholarly success barred the preferred route, via Woolwich. Instead, Gale left school in July 1913, and, with some reluctance, embarked upon a career in the City. He freely confessed, "I was a bit of a dreamer, building castles in the air, a delight I have never given up, for they are the only castles one can live in and perhaps they give an impulse when life becomes dreary and slow." The dream of a military career was not gone, because the Great War was but a year away.

With the call to arms in August 1914, Gale was only too delighted to abandon the day job and apply to join the London Territorials. He was, however, rejected on the grounds that City living had taken a toll on his fitness. Such was the sense of patriotic duty that flooded the nation at the outbreak of war, Gale was bitterly disappointed to be denied a chance to join in. A young lady, not pausing to consider Gale's predicament, passed him in the street and pinned a white feather to him, the symbol of cowardice. He was not so easily dissuaded, however, and took it upon himself to attend physical training classes after work. This paid dividends, and by the summer of 1915 he was attending the Royal Military College, Sandhurst. Such was the desperate shortage of manpower on the Western Front, the training regime was necessarily brief, and on the 22nd December of that year, Gale was commissioned, as he had requested, into the Worcestershire Regiment. Gale's boyish enthusiasm, however, was soon dented when he found that the half-hearted training regime of the holding battalion that he had joined was not at all to his liking. He had taken an interest in the machine gun, the new weapon of war, and in March 1916 was posted to the Machine Gun Training Centre, Grantham. Gale had assumed that he was attending a mere course, but instead he found himself seconded to the Machine Gun Corps.

Eager to get into the War, Gale was posted to France in the summer of 1916 and joined the 164th Machine Gun Company of the 55th West Lancashire Division. With this unit he was soon involved in the terrible fighting on the Battle of the Somme and later served on the Ypres Salient, where he and his men endured gas attacks and the terrible winter of early 1917. Here he took part in the highly successful attack on Wijtschate Ridge on the 7th June 1917, but was not involved in the subsequent Passchendaele massacre due to being on leave, during which he was diagnosed with pyorrhoea and spent a short time in hospital. Suffering from mental and physical exhaustion, he was sent on a month's sick leave. Upon his return to France, on the 1st January 1918, Gale was posted to the 42nd East Lancashire Division and commanded a section of the 126th Machine Gun Company. With this unit he took part in defending against the German offensive along the Somme River in March 1918. Here, Gale and his men were almost cut off when German infantry infiltrated all around them during the dark, but silently they were able to withdraw to a second line of defence from where their guns helped to cut down the German attacks on the following day. In the final months of the War, Gale was promoted to Captain and he played his part in the advance towards, and over, the Hindenburg Line.

Gale emerged from the Great War unscathed, though there had been numerous incidents which he had been fortunate to survive. On the Somme in 1916, soon after his arrival at the front, a shell had exploded amongst his party, killing several people and leaving the young Lieutenant Gale uninjured but spattered with blood and human remains. He had, earlier, been slightly unnerved at the sight and smell of a German corpse, the first dead body that he had ever seen, but this explosion in his trench curiously removed any fear of the enemy shells from his shoulders. At Ypres, a German machine gunner opened fire on Gale and his batman as he was in the process of setting up firing positions for the night. A bullet struck Gale's webbing but did not inflict an injury, however his batman was wounded. Later, Gale's replacement batman was killed by a shell as he was in the process of cooking a meal for his officer. Once again, Gale miraculously escaped, but the shock of seeing the horrendously mutilated remains of his faithful batman proved too much for him and he wept as he tried to wrap the body in a blanket. His company commander noted the fragile state that Gale was in and took him out of the line for a period of rest, a comfort which returned him to his original self. Gale later wrote, "I really think he saved me from completely going off my rocker."

Gale was firmly of the view that the military was where he wished to stay. In September 1919, not wishing to be exposed to the tedium that came with a posting in England, he left for India with the 12th Battalion The Machine Gun Corps. In 1920, Gale's company was posted to the North West Frontier where the Third Anglo-Afghan War was being fought. A year later, the Machine Gun Corps was disbanded and Gale was returned to the Worcestershire Regiment and their 3rd Battalion, stationed at Fyzabad. In 1922, this battalion was disbanded and Gale transferred to the Machine Gun School in India. In January 1928, however, he returned to the 1st Worcestershires before being posted to The Indian Staff College. In 1934 he was appointed Brigade Major to the Ferozepore Brigade, with whom he remained until January 1936, when after in excess of sixteen years absence, he returned to England.

Captain Gale was posted to the 2nd Battalion The Duke of Cornwall's Light Infantry, stationed at Blackdown. A year later he was with the War Office, where he was responsible for all training publications, an appointment that kept him well abreast of all new tactical innovations. In December 1938, Gale was made GSO 2 to the SD(P) section of the General Staff, a small group of planners who ascertained the feasibility of war plans, beginning with the aftermath of the Munich Crisis through to the declaration of war in September 1939 and the shipment of the British Expeditionary Force to France. In April 1940, the shoddy and hastily improvised Allied landings in Norway

Brigadier R. Gale inspects the 1st Parachute Battalion with its new commander, Lieutenant Colonel E. Down, at Ringway in September 1941. (Airborne Assault Duxford)

took place, an operation in which Gale was only peripherally involved as the chairman of the Inter-Services Executive Planning Staff. Gradually, Gale grew weary of his desk job as a "Whitehall Warrior" and was keen to return to the field. As a Lieutenant Colonel on the 1st January 1941, he was given command of the 2nd/5th Battalion The Leicestershire Regiment. Nine months later, Gale left the regular infantry and, promoted to Brigadier, was transferred to the Airborne Forces and given the task of raising and commanding the 1st Parachute Brigade.

Another question was what to do with the 11th Special Air Service Battalion. One school of thought was that it should be disbanded and its members spread across the units of the planned 1st Parachute Brigade. It was however, spared this fate after a new CO, Lieutenant Colonel E. Down, was posted in and oversaw a radical shake up of the unit which saved it from disbandment, although they did receive a new name in September 1941 – the 1st Parachute Battalion. This occurred on the same day (15th September) that the 1st Parachute Brigade officially came into existence. The other two units for this new Brigade, the 2nd and 3rd Parachute Battalions, began forming at Hardwick Hall near Chesterfield in Derbyshire. An advance party of administrators had been sent here to oversee these two units' formation. They were meant to be formed up by 1st October and then have a month's training before parachute training for the thousand or so volunteers was to start on 1st November 1941. However, much to the chagrin of many a member of the new 1st Parachute Battalion, they were told they would now have to live in barracks and move to Bulford on Salisbury Plain.

Officially Gale had been ordered to disband the 11th SAS Battalion and distribute the men amongst the other battalions of the brigade. It was felt that apart from a troop of about 50 ex-Guardsmen under a Guards officer, the unit was badly disciplined. It was thought that when the new CO, Lieutenant Colonel Down, gave the men the option of staying in the brigade and giving up the 'Commando' privilege of living in digs and foregoing parachuting, he might lose a large number of expensively highly trained men. However, the powers that be reckoned without the inspiring leadership of Down and nearly 90% of the men volunteered to accept the new conditions. Gale was impressed and he decided to ignore his previous orders and renamed them the 1st Parachute Battalion.

At first Down was hated, nicknamed 'Dracula', and his early talks to the unit were greeted with boos and shouts. But gradually he won the men over by the force of his personality and by the time he left in July 1942 the battalion would have followed him anywhere.

As well as Lieutenant Colonel Down, Lieutenant Colonel E. Flavell was appointed to command the 2nd Battalion and Lieutenant Colonel G. Lathbury the 3rd Battalion. With regard to Brigade HQ, Major Bromley-Martin was posted in from the 1st Battalion as Brigade Major and Captain J. Squirrel was Staff Captain. These new units were formed on a basis of three rifle companies, a support company and a headquarter company. These units were also slightly different in that the sections in the rifle platoons were commanded by a sergeant rather than the normal corporal.

So where were all these new recruits to come from? The ball was set rolling by a further communication from the AAG (Assistant Adjutant General) branch at the War Office on 28th August 1941 entitled 'Urgent Memo Re: Formation of Two Additional Airborne Battalions', which was addressed to all units then serving in the UK.

Urgent Memorandum

Date 28th August 1941

Subject Formation of two additional Air Service Battalions.

1. It has been decided to form two additional Air Service battalions forthwith.
2. Volunteers are required.
   Officers. Any infantry officers.
   Other Ranks. From all field force infantry, rifle and machine gun battalions, in Great Britain.
3. Conditions of service are as follows:-
   (i) All personnel now volunteering will be normally rationed and accommodated and will not draw any special allowances.
   (ii) Personnel will volunteer on no fixed terms of service and without any right to return to their former units.
   (iii) Parachute Pay at the rate of 4/- per day for Officers; 2/- per day for Other Ranks; may be granted at the discretion of the Commanding Officer after the performance of a minimum of three drops.
   (iv) Personnel of Air Service Units may be returned to former units if found unsuitable under authority of the Brigade Commander.
4. Physical standards required for parachutists are laid down in an ACI which is in course of publication. Advanced copy is attached at Appendix A.
   No volunteers with glasses will be considered.
5. Volunteers must be first class fighting soldiers and show keenness, intelligence and initiative and must be men of first class character only.
   A high standard of individual weapon training is essential. Men must be able to shoot off right shoulder.
6. Return of volunteers as under to reach War Office (AG17) by 13th September 1941.

Officers Nominal roll showing:-

Name, Substantive or War Substantive Rank. Any Acting or Temporary Rank. Age. Unit.

Officers of the rank of Captain to have qualified at a Company Commanders' Course.

Two Subaltern Officers required as Signalling Officers.

Two Subaltern Officers required as Mortar Officers.

Other Ranks. Numbers of volunteers by ranks and units.

Summary of WO and NCO ranks required for each battalion:-
WO's 4
Sergeants 47
Corporals 39
Lance-Corporals27
NCOs submitted must be recommended for promotion to next higher rank.

7. In order that no unit may be unduly depleted maximum of 10 Other Ranks only permitted to volunteer from any one unit.
8. Detailed instructions with regard to postings will be issued in due course.

Appendix A – Standards of Fitness for SAS Training.

1. Personnel selected for parachute training will not be below 22 years nor more than 32 years of age and will be medically examined to ensure that they comply with the standards noted below.
   The age limit may be relaxed in exceptional circumstances, e.g. Officers and NCOs, but there must be no relaxation of the standards of physical fitness in these cases.
2. Height – any height applicable to the man's arm of the service.
3. Weight – without clothes is not to exceed 196 lbs and must correlate normally with the height.
4. Visual standards – the visual acuity must not be below 6/12 in each eye without glasses and personnel must have normal or colour defective safe colour vision. Visual acuity and colour vision will be tested at the nearest Military Ophthalmic Centre.
5. Hearing standards – the acuity of hearing must comply with Hearing Standard 2, i.e. the man standing with his back to the examiner and using both ears must be able to hear a forced whisper from 10 feet away.
   No man with otorrhoea or a perforation of an ear drum will be accepted and the eustachian tubes must be patent.
6. Dental standard – there must be eight sound or repairable teeth (including two molars) in the upper jaw, in good functional opposition to corresponding teeth in the lower jaw.
7. General – at the medical examination special care will be taken to ascertain that the circulatory system is normal; that there are no disabilities of limbs, especially of the bones and joints, present; and that in all other respects the man is fit for army medical category A1.

The two new COs had already been selected and it was up to them to choose their officers, similar to the way the officers for the Commandos had been done in 1940. So with a core of officers the men who had answered the appeal started to arrive at Hardwick Hall. One of those officers who saw the notice in September 1941 was Martin Willcock. He recalled:

On the 8th September 1941 I saw that volunteers were required for the Airborne Forces (parachute duties) and so I put my name down, having looked through the minimum health requirements.

On the 26th September 1941 I received a telegram instructing me to report to Hobart House in London at 10.00 hours for an interview on the 27th. On that afternoon I was interviewed by a Lieutenant Colonel Flavell, who I later found out was selecting subalterns for his 2nd Parachute Battalion which was being formed and he was commanding. I had no idea how I fared. In the adjacent room another Lieutenant Colonel was selecting his subalterns for the 3rd Battalion. I like to think that I picked the right room to be interviewed in.

I returned to my unit and on the 29th I heard that I had been accepted, and then events moved at a bewildering speed. I was instructed to report the next day to the 2nd Parachute Battalion at Hardwick Hall Camp near Chesterfield. I got on the train at St Pancras and met up with two other subalterns and whilst rather naturally our conversation was a little guarded, when we all got out at Chesterfield it was obvious where we were all heading.

On the morning of the 1st October the CO spoke to all of us, six subalterns and about 20 NCOs were detailed to go on a parachute course at Ringway starting that afternoon! It didn't give us much time to think about things. We arrived at Ringway about 4.00 and started to settle in. The next morning there was a delay for our first training session in the gym as Mass was being said for a Pole who had been killed three days before! I rang my mother to tell her what I was doing, and for the first and only time in my life she hung up on me!

The next seven days were taken up with PT, talks, films and synthetic training. We expected to make our first balloon jump the next day but this was cancelled due to the weather. The following day was full of hopes and disappointments. After breakfast we were told during PT that we would be jumping by balloon. So a quick change and out to Tatton by bus, only to be told it was cancelled and that we might make our first jump from a Whitley – and so back to Ringway where we waited and hoped. There was no decision till after lunch when we put our parachutes on and were all set. Again it was cancelled on account of the wind. We waited until about 4.30 when we changed into PT clothes and got on parade – only to be told we would be jumping after all. So we changed once again, put on our harnesses and waited. One stick went and when the plane returned we marched out full of hope. On arrival at the plane all was cancelled – the plane was U/S.

Next day, Saturday the 11th, after morning PT we were told once again we would be jumping. We hurriedly changed, collected our chutes, formed up and got into the plane. We took off and circled over Tatton. I was Number 4. It must be the real thing this time! Numbers 1 and 2 jumped and we waited expectantly – and then we got the wash out signal! It did not seem possible to be so near to jumping and then not to do it! And so we returned and carried on with normal training. I forget now why, on this occasion, jumping was stopped but I expect it was on account of the wind. Sunday was a day of rest and so Peter Naoumoff and I walked to Wilmslow Church for the Harvest Festival Service.

On Monday the 13th of October we went to Tatton Park and did two balloon jumps. We had been warned that we would drop about 180 feet before the canopy fully develops and this takes about two seconds. On my first jump I distinctly remembering thinking to myself "It's about time this bloody thing opened!" – which of course it did – and in due course I landed quite safely. The second jump was even easier and I landed on my feet. I thought "this is a piece of cake", that afternoon taught me otherwise. The man I most admired was an NCO whose name I do not remember – he refused the first time but went up a second time and had to be pushed out. He also had to be pushed out on his third attempt and after that he was all right and I believe he got his wings. After lunch we returned to Ringway to make our first Whitley jump. I was Number 1 in the third plane and in my enthusiasm went too early causing some consternation in the aircraft. I landed with a bit of an oscillation and the shock of hitting the ground so hard taught me not to take jumping too lightly.

On the 14th and 15th we did two further drops without any problems that I can remember. On the 20th the news media descended on Ringway. Cameras and Newsreel cameras took pictures of us doing synthetic training from every angle. In

RAF PJIs trying to set the pace at RAF Ringway. (Imperial War Museum)

> the afternoon we did a drop for them at Tatton Park either in pairs or sticks. Later we all watched the 1st Battalion do a massed drop of about 60 men – I think every available aircraft was used. Anyway the weather was good and they took lots of photos. Some of us found ourselves in the national press a few days later.
>
> On the 21st we made two more attempts to make a further jump but the weather stopped it. On the 23rd we were issued with our wings although we had only done 6 jumps. This was because the next day we would return to Hardwick and be dropped in the Park before the assembled ranks of the 2nd and 3rd Battalions and it was felt that as we would be making our 7th and qualifying jump it would be appropriate for us to land qualified. We thought this was a nice gesture.
>
> On the 24th we fitted chutes etc. in the morning, but we were unable to go before lunch. We emplaned at 1.45 and taxied out to the take off point, but then returned as one engine was U/S. We got into another aircraft and took off about 2.25, about 25 minutes after the others. I was Number 8 and thus I was the last to land. Thus we completed our course, at least most of us. Looking back on it, it seems incredible that none of us had had any medical examination and we made our first three jumps 14 days after joining the Battalion! Guinea pigs-I suspect.

Martin Willcock certainly took an unusual route to joining and this was repeated for a lot of the early volunteer officers. Another officer who volunteered was a pre-war regular by the name of John Frost. In 1940 and 1941 he had been with his unit, the Cameronian Rifles, on beach defence duties in Suffolk. According to an account from him it was a most boring period and as part of the 15th Scottish Division felt he was earmarked for a most inactive war. He recalls:

> One evening after returning from a solitary walk the company office clerk handed me a letter marked 'Secret'. The War Office were looking for volunteers for special units, I had little idea what they were about, but wanted something better than I had at the moment. I went up to London and did really badly in the interview. I couldn't remember the name of my divisional commander or any other important detail. So I thought I'd failed and was quite glad to be back in Suffolk again. However, about ten days later I was posted to Hardwick Hall near Chesterfield. I recall it was a terrible place, hideous countryside, horrible camp, only half-built and bitterly cold, with mud everywhere. The whole atmosphere was very strange. I wasn't at all sure I'd done the right thing or could possibly compete on the physical side. Then I got caught for the Adjutant's job.

Amongst all the normal duties of an Adjutant in these two newly-forming parachute units, it was his job to allocate the newly-arrived volunteers to companies and duties which in theory they would be best suited to. However, even a relatively experienced officer like John Frost was concerned at the quality of the men arriving in his office saying they were ready to parachute and wanted to do so with the 2nd Battalion. He later recalled,

> In my humble opinion I thought around half of those I saw in my office were unsuitable for one reason or another. Some of the old commanding officers had

played the Army at their own game and when the call had come for volunteers in September 1941 had shunted off their naughty boys and misfits. Some of them had conduct sheets about six pages long. [Author's note: in spite of what it sounds like, to have even one entry on your conduct sheet is not good.] There were few good NCOs because the units were reluctant to let them go. To me it seemed that I would never be able to get the Battalion up to strength, which did not seem to be happening with the 3rd Battalion, who were also at Hardwick. Then I found out my counterpart in the 3rd Battalion had stationed a man at the entrance and told all new arrivals to report to the 3rd Battalion Guardroom. Here their RSM inspected them all and kept the best ones for himself and sent the chaff down to me! I decided to send a few men with a truck to just outside the camp and for them to pick up all the new arrivals. This worked out well for a while, till the 3rd's Adjutant sent a truck even further down the road, we then called a truce and both units started to build up fairly equally.

Early morning PT at RAF Ringway - a familiar sight to any trainee paratrooper. (Imperial War Museum)

Other people had a less formal introduction, as Hugh Levien recalled:

My personal record shows that on 4th September 1941 I travelled from Beverley in Yorkshire to Chesterfield, leaving the 10th Battalion The Queen's Own Royal West Kents. At Chesterfield railway station we were ferried to the camp at Hardwick where there were many newly-built red brick huts along partially constructed roads. As a Sergeant I was one of the first in the queue to report and was welcomed, if that is the right expression, by a Major full of jocularity, who enquired what Regiment I was from, in spite of the fact that we all had our own cap badges. He made a most offensive remark, mispronouncing the county, accompanied by an inane cackle. On being told that I had been the Intelligence Sergeant of the unit I came from, he said something like, "Oh, I think we still have a vacancy for one of those chaps in the 2nd Battalion. You had better trot down there and see how you fit in." So I followed his directions and was duly taken on in that capacity with Dicky Ashford as the Intelligence Officer.

The classic photograph of the cliff top villa and Würzburg radar dish taken on 5th December 1941 by Flight Lieutenant Tony Hill. (Airborne Assault Duxford)

Mortar Platoon 1st Parachute Battalion 1941. (Airborne Assault Duxford)

> I didn't really have any duties, and made out my own programme, which mainly consisted of joining a squad undergoing intensive PT and synthetic training under qualified parachutists. I moseyed around Battalion HQ a bit each day to make sure I kept up to date with what was going on, and after parades if I still had the price of a few pints I fairly often took the free transport provided into Chesterfield. As soon as I discovered that C Company was to be the first to go to Ringway I got myself a temporary posting to that Company.

So by fits and starts during the month of October 1941 the two new Battalions grew in number and in physical fitness, following the plan that the first 'large parachute course' would start on 2nd November. This first contingent travelled by a special train and arrived at Heald Green station on Saturday 1st November 1941. As one account put it,

> Seventeen officers, two warrant officers, twenty-two sergeants and two hundred and twenty-eight other ranks tumbled out on to the platform laughing and joking and wondering in their hearts what it was going to be like. Every man was a free volunteer, character and courage were innate in them, for not only had they shown the desire to meet and fight their King's enemies but they were willing to challenge the unknown perils of parachuting in order to hasten the day of combat. Short days and the notorious November weather would add to the difficulties. In fourteen days, if all went well, those men would be leaving Ringway after having completed their training.

As it turned out these 250 or so trainees mainly from C Company of the 2nd Battalion and A Company of the 3rd Battalion, started their training on 2nd November. On 15th November a message was sent to the War Office from Ringway that Number 1 Parachute Training Course had been successfully completed at 1330. Descents were around 500 from balloons and over 1,200 aircraft descents, some of them in front of the newly appointed 'Major-General Airborne Forces' – Major-General Browning. It can be said that it was a most successful course, with only one man not completing the course. It is also probably fair to say that the extra PT and high altitude training at Hardwick was doing its job. The ethos of this time is carried on today in the rigorous pre-parachuting course known as 'P Company' which you must pass before being allowed anywhere near an aircraft to throw yourself out of!

Over the next few weeks large courses for the men from Hardwick ran almost continuously, as the following details show:

- Number 2 Parachute Training Course, 18th to 30th November 1941, 270 successful trainees encompassing 924 balloon and 1633 aircraft descents.
- Number 3 Parachute Training Course, 5th to 15th December 1941, 270 successful trainees including 24 Poles.
- Number 4 Parachute Training Course, 17th to 25th December 1941, 209 successful trainees.

There were some trainees unable to complete their course due to various injuries and records show that in the six weeks after 1st November 39 students could be included in this category. The overall number of descents during these six weeks was 5,239 or a 0.75% failure rate, which was entirely acceptable. Within a period of about eight weeks virtually two Battalions completed their training and were ready to take part in any operations that may come their way.

In the very early days one support unit for the 1st Parachute Brigade also slowly stated to take shape. This was an engineer unit who came into life under the name of No 1 Air Troop, Royal Engineers. Again an appeal for volunteers for airborne service was sent around the engineer units and in time volunteers came forward and earned their wings.

Around Christmas 1941 a further opportunity to test the viability of the airborne forces presented itself. It was felt by military scientists that more and more RAF aircraft were being shot down as a result of information from German radar. Obviously the best thing might be to capture some of the German kit, and in late 1941, after a study of aerial reconnaissance photographs, it was felt that a new German radar had been positioned on a cliff on the northern coast of France close to a small village by the name of Bruneval, not far from Le Havre. A later photo reconnaissance flight confirmed the existence of a 'fire bowl' radar on the cliffs.

So now that a suitable target had been located by intelligence, the question was, who would be given the operation? As the location of the radar station was on the coast, it seemed an ideal opportunity for the Commandos to carry out a raid. But unlike Norway it became clear from studying aerial photographs that the coastal area was well defended. It was thought that a seaborne assault having potentially to fight its way in would give the Germans a warning and perhaps cause them to destroy the radar equipment before it could be examined. So on 8th January 1942, the Chief of Combined Operations, Admiral Lord Mountbatten, asked if a unit from the newly-formed 1st Parachute Brigade, together with support from 38 Wing of the RAF, could carry out a raid on the northern coast of France. It is perhaps worth mentioning here that the airborne forces were at last getting their needs addressed and voiced in the right places by a newly-appointed officer, Brigadier F. Browning, who was given the rank of acting Major-General and whose role in life (at least in the early months) was to be 'Major-General Airborne Forces'. He had won a DSO in the Great War and had been Adjutant at the Royal Military Academy Sandhurst in the 1920s. He may have been lacking in operational experience but he was certainly well-connected, a Grenadier Guardsman and a good man to have fighting your corner in Whitehall. Browning perhaps viewed this raid in northern France as an ideal opportunity to get some credit for the airborne forces after their unfortunate baptism in Italy in 1941. So it is said that the same day he was asked if his men could carry out this raid he accepted it. If nothing else Browning was always quick to sense an opportunity to 'empire build'.

One source claims that Browning personally selected the troops to go on this operation but this is doubtful. It seems more likely that the choice of who would go was left to the commander of the 1st Parachute Brigade, Brigadier R. Gale. The obvious choice would probably have been to use the 1st Parachute Battalion, who had previously been our old friends the 11th Special Air Service Battalion, and had been whipped into shape by their forceful commander, Lieutenant Colonel E. Down. Instead, it seems that to prove that the entire brigade was ready, he looked away from his 'oldest' unit, to his two newest ones. So the choice was narrowed down to those sub-units of the 2nd and 3rd Battalions who had been through Ringway. The reader may recall that the first large Ringway course comprised C Company from the 2nd Battalion and A Company from the 3rd. I am making an educated guess here but my theory is C Company were chosen because the majority of the men had volunteered from infantry units and not from the arms and services, as was fairly common in the early days. This meant in theory they would not need extra training in infantry tactics as perhaps a body of men mainly from such units as the Royal Artillery, Royal Signals and RASC would need.

From a trawl of the surviving records at the National Archives one of my research assistants found a document which was written in early January 1942 addressed to the HQ 1st Parachute Brigade from the HQ Airborne Division (as it was sometimes known in those early days). Part of this document stated, "You will therefore detail for this training one complete company of parachutists plus two subaltern officers and twenty ORs as first reinforcements, plus one RE officer and eleven sappers. All personnel must be fully trained in parachute jumping."

Brigadier Gale therefore nominated C Company to be the chosen ones. In early 1942, in spite of the company being all Scotsmen, its commander was an Englishman from the Royal Fusiliers, Major P. Teichman. It is fair to say that the CO of the unit, Lieutenant Colonel E Flavell, wanted a Scottish officer to be in command of a company that had a rough and tough reputation. He felt he had an ideal candidate in his current Adjutant, the previously mentioned Captain J. Frost. However John Frost was not really in a position, in early January 1942, to take up command, as Frost himself recalled:

> As I said, I got caught soon after my arrival for the Adjutant's job. With all the paperwork I had little chance to get fit or train. I thought I could get away without all the training. Came the day and I did my first jump successfully and went up

Men of C Company 2nd Parachute Battalion in training for Operation Biting, waiting to board a landing craft. Note the mixed headgear and that they all are armed with the relatively new Sten SMG. (Imperial War Museum)

immediately for the next. This time I landed awkwardly and badly damaged my knee. Ten days later, after I'd got out of hospital, I really started to get fit by going for long runs. I returned from a Scottish New Year to relinquish the Adjutancy and take over C Company, who were all Scots, from Philip Teichman. Two weeks later I was told that C Company were to move to Salisbury for special training. However, as I was not qualified, I would only be given one week at Ringway to pass and get all my jumps in. Philip took the advance party from the company down to Salisbury, and if I failed he would resume command.

It was known that the company would be based on Salisbury Plain for about six weeks undergoing a programme of special training for an undisclosed reason or objective.

In the middle part of January Frost travelled to Ringway with the threat that if he didn't complete his course within a week, he would lose the opportunity of commanding C Company. To anyone who has lived near Manchester or in the north of England, they will know that the weather can be somewhat unfavourable in January and also there are not many hours of daylight. However, when Frost started training it appears his card had been specially marked and he seemed to get preferential treatment, indeed he himself said that he heard RAF instructors talking about him and the words 'the last time'. He stated he felt this was a reference to Operation Colossus. He was allowed to do jumps with very little ground training and given priority over other attendees for places on an aircraft. Frost himself commented on the Manchester weather, "It was notoriously fickle. On the slightest provocation a smoky fog would creep across the airfield from the direction of Manchester, and a wind strong enough to dispel the fog very often made jumping unsafe."

As it turned out Frost got his jumps in on time and travelled down to Salisbury Plain to take command of C Company. Over the next few weeks, much training was carried out, most of the group being told that they were training for a demonstration for the War Cabinet. It was to be one of the first truly 'combined operations', with the RAF (using Whitley bombers) dropping the Army paratroopers in northern France and the Royal Navy bringing the force back by sea.

It must be said that the training did not always go well, with the landing craft sometimes getting stuck fast when trying to take the men of C Company off a beach. A four day window (23rd to 26th February 1942) had been identified for when the moon and tides would be favourable to carry out the operation. By this it meant there would be a full moon (for ease of finding the drop zone) and the landing craft could approach the coast on a rising tide. On Monday the 23rd February, the first probable date to go, the men checked and cleaned the weapons and stores before packing them into containers; these were to leave for the airfield at 2.00 p.m. prior to being loaded on the Whitley aircraft taking them to France. But at around 5.00 p.m., in keeping with the Army's dislocation of expectation, a message came through that due to unfavourable weather conditions the Bruneval raid, or Operation Biting, to give it it's official title, would have to be postponed for 24 hours. The evening was spent unpacking the containers.

This procedure was also repeated on the following three days, the containers being packed in the mornings, having a return trip from RAF Thruxton (the outbound airfield) and being unpacked in the evenings. Operation Biting was postponed on Tuesday, Wednesday and Thursday, this last day being the last date thought feasible for the raid before the next full moon, in March. It must have been a somewhat stressful few days being wound up and then let down. Frost himself commented,

> We are all thoroughly miserable. Each morning we brace ourselves for the venture, and each night, after a further postponement, we have time to think of all the things that go wrong, and that if we don't go on Thursday we shall have to wait for a whole month to pass before conditions may be suitable. After all, the weather in the English Channel in February and March is not inclined to be 'suitable'.

It was recorded in the orders the comment that "even if the operation is postponed from 22nd February containers must still be packed during the morning of that day as it is impossible to say until approx. 1500 hours whether the operation will take place on that day. It may be cancelled up to 2215 hours if the weather changes."

As it turned out the men of C Company awoke on the morning of Friday 27th February 1942 to a bright crisp sunny morning, with no cloud. Indeed, it was the best day they had seen for a while. Frost expected to be told to stand down for a short period and give everyone some leave. In spite of this thought the operation was on and in the late afternoon, about 5.00 p.m., Major-General Browning arrived to wish them all good luck. The 119 men travelled to RAF Thruxton and later that evening climbed aboard the 12 Whitleys for the short flight to northern France.

It is not the place here to go into a detailed account of this operation, except to say that, generally speaking, it went very well. Inevitably there were a few casualties and a few minor mishaps but the balance sheet was as follows:

- German casualties were estimated at a minimum of 40.
- Two paratroopers were killed in action.
- Seven were wounded in action.
- Six were posted missing as they had been either wounded and left behind or missed the boats.

With regards to the radar equipment liberated, the scientists got virtually everything they wanted on their shopping list except one item. These enabled the scientific community a "navigational fix in confirming the dead reckoning in the intelligence voyage into the German radar defences."

Within a couple of days Major Frost was called up to London to explain to the War Cabinet the details of the raid. The head of Combined Operations, Lord Mountbatten, was also present and this meeting probably did much to put the airborne forces on the map and guaranteed their future. Major Frost himself commented,

> The Bruneval raid came at a time when our country's fortunes were at a low ebb. Singapore had recently fallen and the German battleships had escaped up the Channel from Brest in the very teeth of everything that could be brought against them. Many people were disgruntled after a long catalogue of failures, and the success of our venture, although it was a mere flea-bite, did have the effect of making people feel we could succeed after all.
>
> One very beneficial result from our point of view was that it put airborne forces on the map. General Browning had been having difficulty in persuading people that the airborne forces could play a really useful part in the war. Despite the successes of the German airborne troops, the traditional conservatism of many Service chiefs stood in the way of experiment, very largely because our more conventional resources were already strained. Now our General was able to get some degree of priority and the Prime Minister who had initiated the formation of our parachute arm, was encouraged to ensure that we had the necessary support. It was also a feather in the cap for HQ Combined Operations.

3

Off to pastures new

Whilst the men of C Company 2nd Battalion had earned their spurs in northern France, the Brigade continued to grow in strength. The Air Troop Royal Engineers was expanded to become the 1st Parachute Squadron Royal Engineers. It was also decided that another support arm was vital for the efficiency of the brigade, and this was a medical unit. Major-General Browning took a keen interest in the organisation and development of the medical services within his command. He demanded very high standards of efficiency and frequently stressed to unit commander's the importance of the medical services.

In November 1941 Colonel A. Austin Eagger was posted to HQ Airborne Division as Assistant Director Medical Services (ADMS) and shortly afterwards Captain T.R.B. Courtney was appointed Deputy Assistant Director Medical Services (DADMS). Captain Courtney can be looked on as one of the founding fathers of the Airborne Medical Services as he took an active part in devising and making practical trials for the new equipment required for airborne operations. He was one of the first officers, certainly the first medical officer, to jump with a kit-bag tied to his leg.

In these early days there were numerous conferences as a result of these trials and proposals were put forward as to modifications to equipment and procedures, and ways to combat airsickness. Other points raised touched upon the needs for a lightweight stretcher that could be dropped by parachute, a design for a trailer that could take two stretchers and the need for a large transport aircraft that could be adapted for the medical services' use. Other problems that needed to be resolved were, for example, precise information on the size of containers that would be available for air-dropping of medical stores. It was from these conferences and discussions, and following trials and experiments, that the scale and types of equipment to enable items to be either man-packed or dropped by containers was devolved.

It was also discovered on exercise that over 80% of glider-borne troops suffered seriously from airsickness. Therefore clinical trials were held under supervision of the Medical Research Council in ways to combat this problem. It was found that hyoscine tablets were effective in about 50% of all cases in preventing airsickness. However, it should be remembered that subsequent experience on operations showed that the problem was a minor one once landing had taken place!

It would now be a good time to pause and to look at the general role of the Royal Army Medical Corps in the British Army order of battle, and the casualty evacuation chain and the general composition of a field ambulance.

The role of the RAMC in peace and war has always been the maintenance and repair of the fighting men. In the Second World War this meant that surgical teams and nursing orderlies were sent forward to the fighting zones rather than waiting in base areas for casualties to reach them, and this was especially true for the airborne units, as will be discussed later. Soldiers' morale was always that little bit higher if they knew that

On one of the practice jumps undertaken by the 3rd Parachute Battalion in 1942 in England, the pilot of the aircraft carrying Lieutenant Colonel Pine-Coffin, made, in his words "an error of judgement and put some of us out short of the Drop Zone." He landed in this churchyard. He stated there was some alarm on the descent as it seemed they might land on a headstone but the CO came down on the grass without injury. During the exercise he later climbed up the church tower to take this picture. (R. Pine-Coffin)

when wounded they would be looked after with a high level of skill and expertise. Senior ranks often speak of the devotion to duty, efficiency and self-sacrifice of all ranks of the Corps. All who served in Airborne Forces were members of a team to whom had been entrusted a great responsibility under conditions for which there was no real previous experience. They succeeded in gaining the confidence and respect of the combat units with which they served and upheld the traditions of the Corps. It should also be noted that some other ranks were Quakers and conscientious objectors who were not prepared to take life but to sacrifice theirs to save others, although these seem to have mainly served in the medical units of the 6th Airborne Division.

The British Army has always worked on a casualty evacuation chain, so that casualties are moved from the point of wounding rearwards through a number of different units

Some men of the 3rd Parachute Battalion emplaning into a Whitley for a practice jump in 1942. (R. Pine-Coffin)

where their condition is assessed, stabilised and their priority for treatment determined. Usually there were three types of casualties:

Priority 1: Casualties needing urgent resuscitation and/or surgery e.g. severe bleeding, respiratory obstruction, open chest wounds and penetrating abdominal wounds. The aim is to get these casualties on an operating table within six hours of wounding.

Priority 2: Casualties needing early surgery and possible resuscitation e.g. multiple wounds, compound fractures and large wounds of muscles. The aim is to get these casualties operated upon as soon as possible after six hours.

Priority 3: All other casualties.

The main principals of the evacuation chain are:

(a) The collection of casualties from forward units by these further back.
(b) Early first aid followed by rapid, smooth evacuation through a series of check points where the casualty's condition is checked, and steps taken to ensure their fitness to continue along the evacuation route.
(c) Ensuring that casualties reach a surgeon as soon as possible, certainly inside six hours for priority one cases. The diagram below shows the longest conventional

The casualty evacuation chain can be part summed up in the following diagram

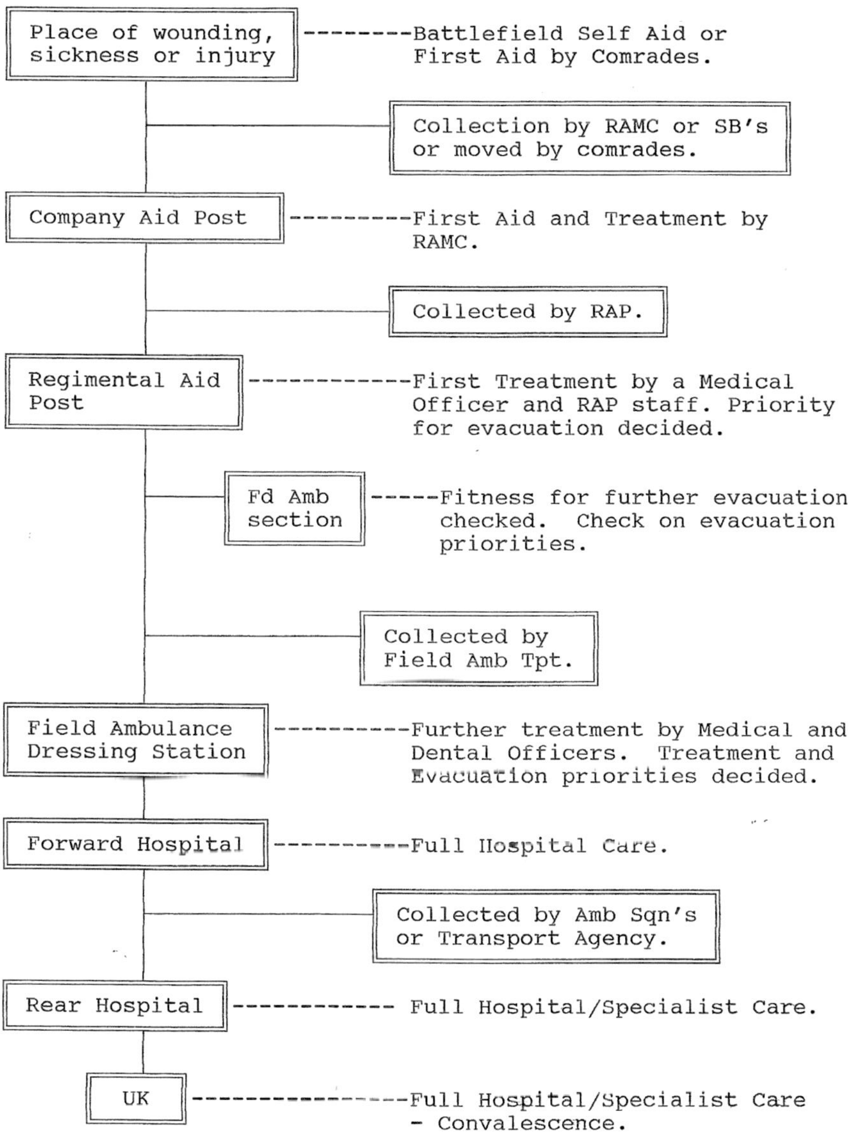

Casualty Evacuation Chain

chain. Some of the staging posts may be omitted according to the situation or the evacuation means available; for example during the Normandy campaign casualties were airlifted from dressing stations via forward landing strips direct to the UK.

The field ambulance section was not usually placed in the evacuation chain between the RAP and the DS unless there were special reasons, such as casualties having to spend a long time travelling between the RAP and DS. The role of the section would then be a staging post, where the Medical Officer would check the condition of the casualties and if necessary change the order of priority for evacuation. In airborne operations it is obvious that the medical services were faced with a situation never before experienced. Airborne operations, by their very nature, involve dropping large numbers of troops behind enemy lines and holding on until relieved by advancing ground forces, and therefore the normal evacuation chain could not operate. To compensate for this the airborne field ambulances had to be prepared to hold all casualties until evacuation was possible which, although undesirable, had on occasions to be accepted. To help overcome this difficulty extra surgical and nursing capabilities were added to the strength of these field ambulances.

The parachute field ambulance unit would (normally) consist of a headquarters and four sections, giving a total of around 180 all ranks. A breakdown of these would be as follows:

1 Headquarters:
   6 officers (commanding officer, second-in-command, two surgeons, an anaesthetist and a quartermaster).
   5 Other Ranks.
2 Four Sections:
   1 officer and 19 Other Ranks each.
3 Attached personnel:
   Royal Engineers – 1 Sapper (carpenter).
   Royal Army Service Corps – 1 officer and 51 Other Ranks.
   Army Dental Corps – 1 officer and 1 Other Rank.
   Army Physical Training Corps – 1 Other Rank.
   Army Catering Corps – 5 Other Ranks.

Volunteers were called for from all parts of the RAMC for the first parachute medical unit and so by April 1942 16 Parachute Field Ambulance RAMC was in the process of formation at Hardwick Hall. Indeed, its establishment was nearly complete except for a commanding officer. The man selected for this task was a colourful and flamboyant character, Lieutenant Colonel Malcolm MacEwan. He had been born in 1894 on the Isle of Harris, Scotland. He had served as a pre-First World War volunteer in the Ross Mountain Battery and was mobilised in 1914. Wartime service saw him in action in Gallipoli in 1915, and in 1916 he was commissioned into the Royal Artillery. Subsequently in 1917 he was in Salonika where he joined the Royal Flying Corps, first as an observer and later as a pilot. He was awarded the Distinguished Flying Cross (DFC) and was mentioned in despatches.

After the armistice in 1918 he joined in the Russian Civil War and was awarded the Order of St George (Russia) and another mention in despatches. He was demobilised in 1920 and started training to become a doctor. After qualifying he settled in Ipswich and had the rare distinction of commanding the 58th Medium Regiment RA TA. He went with his Regiment to France in January 1940 and stayed with them until their evacuation from Dunkirk. After a short period as Commander Royal Artillery Dorset Division he transferred to the RAMC.

As second-in-command of 16 Parachute Field Ambulance, Major P.R.Wheatley went to the railway station at Chesterfield to meet him and recalls an imposing figure alighting from the train in breeches and riding boots, a highly polished Sam Browne belt and an array of First World War medals including the DFC and the St George of Russia. It must have been a comedown for a gunner brigadier to be posted to a field ambulance, but this very special embryo unit needed a very special CO and Lieutenant Colonel MacEwan fitted the bill exactly. Not only for his passion for medal ribbons, which had to be spotless, was he affectionately known as 'Technicolor' but also for his colourful personality. His upright stance, his immaculate turn out, his deliberate mannerisms and carefully chosen words all inspired confidence. A strict disciplinarian, he yet had a keen sense of humour and a kindly disposition which endeared him to his men. He was a war veteran with considerable experience and a man of great courage who set a fine example. He was 47 years old when he undertook his parachute training with all the youngsters. In no time he had under his command a trained and efficient unit with extremely high morale.

The unit was allocated the number '16', which had not been used since the disbandment of 16 Field Ambulance RAMC that served on the Western Front in the Great War with the 6th Division. After the unit had undergone initial parachute training the unit's name changed to 16 (P) Field Ambulance, which later added 'Parachute' and dropped the brackets. It was during 1941 that units of the 1st Parachute Brigade started wearing distinguishing lanyards – so one was adopted by 16 Para Field Ambulance and its colours were dull cherry – the RAMC colour – and sky blue. A lanyard of these colours is still worn today by the members of the airborne RAMC. Volunteers for 16 Parachute Field Ambulance came from many different units; one was Private G.C. Stanners. He had been called up in October 1940 and was posted to 225 Field Ambulance. It didn't take long for him to work out he was in a very inefficient unit and he asked for a transfer. Upon parading before the unit's Commanding Officer, Geoff was told he could try to become a gunner in the RAF with a normal life expectancy of 2½ operations. In spite of this Geoff said he would go. So on 6th April 1942, together with five others from the unit, they travelled to Hardwick Hall, arriving in the early hours of the following day. The volunteers were ordered to be on parade at 06.00 and Geoff was one of the first three marched in front of Major Wheatley (OC Depot Unit RAMC at Hardwick Hall and 2 i/c 16 PFA). His first words were "What decided you to become a parachutist?" Geoff says he could have fallen through the floor. He replied, "Of course, I had volunteered for the RAF as an air gunner." Wheatley then replied that the list was full and "as I had been so daft to volunteer to be an air gunner they felt I would be ideal for a Parachute Field Ambulance". Major Wheatley did offer Geoff the opportunity of returning to 225 but he decided to stay. Geoff remembers quite a lot of men were returned to their units because they were not up to the required medical standards – in the early days men had to have eight teeth in the top jaw meeting eight in the bottom. However, by the end of the war volunteers with full sets of dentures were allowed in.

The first few entries in 16 PFA's war diary are as follows:

3rd April 1942 Hardwick Hall. In accordance with ADMS Airborne Division letter M/505/4 dated 1.4.1942 Major P.R. Wheatley RAMC reported to OC 2nd Parachute Battalion. Major Wheatley had travelled by road with a party of 15 ORs RAMC (including one QMS and one S/Sgt) and 5 ORs RASC from 181 Airborne Field Ambulance at Chilton Foliat. These ORs were attached to 2nd Parachute Battalion to assist in the formation of No 16 Airborne Field Ambulance and were to be returned to 181 FA when a Headquarters Staff in the new Field Ambulance was established. Four 30 cwt lorries were lent by 181 Field Ambulance.

Officer i/c RAMC Records had detailed 260 ORs RAMC to report to Hardwick Camp on 6.4.1942. Major Wheatley was ordered to select from these, men suitable for parachute training and these would be posted to 16 Field Ambulance. In the first instance all these men are to be attached to 2nd Parachute Battalion for all purposes. Officers up to War Establishment of an Airborne Field Ambulance had also been posted by AMDI.

On arrival of Major Wheatley's party accommodation had been allotted by Officer i/c Details at Hardwick Camp. Rations, pay and the drawing of accommodation stores had also been arranged.

4th April 1942. A messing store was taken over as an office and medical examination room. Seven huts were taken over in readiness for the arrival of personnel. All these premises were cleared out and necessary accommodation stores were drawn. Necessary medical apparatus was borrowed from the camp MI Room.

Postal address of New Unit arranged c/o GPO Chesterfield.

Stationmaster at Chesterfield contacted. Arrangements made that one OR should always be on station from 1730 hours on 6.4.1942 to meet men arriving and one lorry to be always waiting – an additional lorry to be sent down during rush periods.

Arrangements made with Chief Instructor for 60 of the fittest men to start PT and synthetic training on 7.4.1942 with a view to starting parachuting at Ringway on 20.4.1942. Considered that time available is insufficient to train any but the fittest by then – also there is a shortage of PT instructors. This is being remedied by DAAQMG Parachute Brigade. Final cleaning up of huts. Plans for disposal of men arriving:- meal, bath, checking of kit, medical examination, interview by CO – men to be allotted to temporary companies (which would be accommodated in separate huts) according to the following descriptions: -

A Company – men medically fit and in other respects for a parachute field ambulance. These men to start training at once.

B Company – men just below the required medical standard and those in which there is doubt as to their suitability for parachuting. These men to be carefully observed for one week.

C Company – men unfit or unsuitable for parachuting. These men to be disposed of by Officer i/c Records as soon as possible.

6th April 1942. 151 ORs arrived. 78 examined and allotted as follows: A Company 50, B Company 18 and C Company 10.

Total strength – Officers 1, ORs 171.

War Office authority received for formation of the unit as No 16 (Parachute) Field Ambulance on 3.4.1942 WO Urgent Memorandum 20/MED/965 (AMDI).

Lieutenant K.M. Wheeler (205581) RAMC reported from 223 Field Ambulance.

90 ORs arrived and all examinations and interviews completed.

66 ORs started intensive PT and training for jumping.

Strength of Companies – A 109, B 31, and C 28.

Total strength – Officers 2, ORs 188.

8th April 1942. PT class continued with some alterations of personnel – only those definitely accepted were taught in the class. Lieutenant Wheeler joined the class.

Senior NCOs employed in taking drill squads and testing men in medical knowledge and RAMC training to weed out doubtful cases.

Strength of Companies – A 122, B 22, and C 35.

Clerks selected to start office and begin to take over from men from 181 (Airlanding) Field Ambulance.

There are a large number of corporals above establishment, it will be necessary to cause many of them to revert to private.

Lieutenant A. Percival (223758) reported from 185 Field Ambulance.

Lieutenant D. Wright (218952) reported from 156 Field Ambulance.

Strength – Officers 4, ORs 121.

9th April 1942. Lieutenant Colonel M MacEwan DFC, TD, RAMC (22266) arrived and took over command of the unit from 128 Field Ambulance. Interviewing of ORs completed and provisional allotment to the War Establishment. Moved into permanent office.

In these early days things proceeded rapidly and the unit's war diary records that on 1st May Lieutenant Wright and 45 ORs completed their training at Ringway and were awarded their wings. Then on 3rd May Lieutenant Colonel MacEwan, Lieutenant Keesey, Lieutenant Percival, Lieutenant McGavin and Captain Ridler (Army Dental Corps) and 53 ORs went to Ringway to start their parachute training. By the beginning of June over 100 men had earned their wings and it can be said that the first parachute medical unit was at least on a sound footing with regards to the method of getting to war, although there was a lot work to be done on the equipment front. The CO of the unit cannot have been too happy a man during these early days because as well as injuring a leg during a jump on the 14th of May, his office was visited during the 3rd of June and a cash box containing about £50 of imprest and PRI money taken.

The administrative side of things occurred as one of the first members of 16, John Bellamy, recalls:

> …16 was to have 4 sections and 2 surgical teams and in the early days at Bulford in 1942 no-one was really sure of what was needed so the enterprising QM Lieutenant Anderson managed to persuade someone to issue the unit with two full sets of equipment, the first to the same issue scale as a light FA and the second to a

scale of a full FA. This did represent a huge amount of equipment and a novel idea was thought of. In one of the vast storerooms at Bulford the whole lot was unpacked and laid out in long lines against the walls – the light FA on one wall, the full entitlement on the other. In the space down the middle were some supply containers. Each surgical team and section was allowed four containers for their equipment. So by trial and error and repeated consultation with the section medical officers and surgeons on what was absolutely necessary, we discovered what could be packed in the space available to them. This formed the basis of what appeared to me to be a very long list but it did form the basis of the scale of equipment issued to us. It also became clear that everyone would have to carry something with him on his jump if we were to have what was needed on arrival.

The 'operational' side was not ignored, as these orders for an exercise show:

16 (Parachute) Field Ambulance Operational Instruction Number 1
Exercise Burglar
4th June 1942.
1. Object.

a) To exercise a section of a parachute field ambulance in collecting, treating and evacuating patients in a small raid.

b) To find out the most suitable equipment.

2. Map References Sheet 64.

It is assumed that enemy territory lies to the east of a bay of which the coastline runs from Heath 9086 along the road through mill to Glingsby Gate 9284. Thence along the boundary to the park westwards to road junction 915944. Then along the road to Astwith 9084.

3. Narrative.

We have learned that Hitler, Goering and Ribbentrop have hidden a personal fortune consisting of diamonds to the value of £50,000,000 in Hardwick Hall. This is guarded by a force of about 50 SS men. The German Army are not aware of the hiding place. There is however a strong force of one brigade at Glapwell 9486, and there are some troops at Rowthorn 9485.

The 16th Parachute Battalion is ordered to bring away the diamonds from Hardwick Hall and may use two companies of paratroops to do this. Landing ground chosen lies between the ponds in square 9384 and the wood in that square lying south west of the ponds.

On 5th June A Company of the Battalion will drop in 10 sticks between 09.15 and 09.30 hours. Their objective will be to secure landing ground, secure the approaches between Rowthorn and Hardwick Hall and Rowthorn and the beaches between Mill Farm and Glingsby Gate.

They will be accompanied by a Battalion MO and 4 RAMC Stretcher Bearers. These will collect casualties to a Medical Post at the Park Gate 935848.

Between 09.45 and 10.00 hours B Company of the Battalion will drop in 10 sticks and will immediately proceed to their objective at Hardwick Hall. They will be accompanied by a Senior NCO and 4 RAMC Stretcher Bearers, who will collect casualties and establish a Medical Post at road junction 928843.

Members of 16 Parachute Field Ambulance pictured at Bulford in 1942 prior to their move to North Africa. They are wearing the 1942 pattern gabardine jumping jacket. (N. Cherry)

Section 1 16 (Parachute) Field Ambulance will drop in 2 sticks at 10.00 hours.

4. Orders to Section 1 of Field Ambulance.

The Section will carry out the following tasks:-

a) Clear the landing ground of wounded to the Medical Post of A Company.

b) Set up ADS in the belt of trees alongside the track at point 927849.

c) Evacuate patients from both Medical Posts to the ADS.

d) If these tasks are completed before 11.45 hours, the Section will render assistance as may be required to Battalion Stretcher Bearers.

e) Evacuate the ADS at 12.00 hours to the beach west of the Balloon site at 922848.

5. Beach timings.

Barges will be waiting on the beach to collect the wounded and RAMC personnel between 12.10 and 12.30 hours.

6. Detail.

All infantry are imaginary except 20 stretcher cases, which will be provided by Section 2 and HQ. 30 imaginary walking wounded will be considered to pass through the Medical Posts and ADS at the same time.

MO and Stretcher Bearers of A Company will be represented by S/Sergeant Brock and first reinforcements of Section 2.

Senior NCO and Stretcher Bearers of B Company will be represented by Corporal Ralston and first reinforcements of Section 1.

Section 1 less first reinforcements will carry out the Exercise. RSM Bagg will supervise laying out of casualties and equipment.

7. Umpires.

All available officers of the unit, RSM Bagg, S/Sergeant Crane and Corporal Wallace.

The exercise was repeated on 11th June with the following changes:

Exercise Burglar will be repeated on 11/6/42 with the following modifications.
1. Personnel taking part.

No 2 Section will be the Section of the Field Ambulance taking part. The first line reinforcements will drop with the Section. No 3 Section will provide the RAMC personnel of the two infantry companies.

No's 3 and 4 Sections will provide the 20 patients.

Umpires: All available officers, RSM Bagg and S/Sergeant Crane.

2. Equipment.

As equipment is being packed by the Quartermaster only stretchers will be taken. They will be bundled up in the way they are issued when handed in at the completion of the exercise. The Section will drop 15 stretchers including 2-wheeled stretchers. Each infantry company will drop 2 stretchers.

3. Application of lessons learnt during previous exercise.

a) Battalion Stretcher Bearers must not clear the dropping zone. These wounded must be left for the Field Ambulance Section. Battalion Stretcher Bearers must push on with their companies.

b) A larger number of stretchers are being used. Any excess can be dumped near the dropping zone where they will be available if required.

c) The Medical Officer and S/Sergeant must maintain full control of the Section. They cannot do this if they overburdened with equipment.

d) Some Stretcher Bearers of the Section must start clearing the dropping zone as soon as they have picked up their stretchers and others must go straight to the collecting centre of B Company.

e) The exercise must be completed i.e. all wounded carried down to the beach. This should be timed so that the first batch of wounded arrive on the beach just before the barges are due to arrive.

There is a comment in the unit's war diary for this day – "Exercise Burglar repeated by No 2 Section. Excellent work done by the stretcher bearers and all patients evacuated to time."

So after a few weeks 'forming up' at Hardwick Hall, an advance party of Captain Young, No 1 Section (Lieutenant Wright, 19 ORs RAMC and 3 drivers RASC) and three other RASC men moved to Bulford on Salisbury Plain on 6th June 1942 where the unit was now going to be based. Soon afterwards, on the 17th June, after a movement order, the rest of the Field Ambulance headed south, the Advance Party arriving at 1730 hours and the road and rail parties at 2000 hours. Over the coming weeks and months they settled down to a tough training regime as they came to understand their new customers' requirements and to improve individual skills. Part of this training regime was outlined in a programme as follows:

16 (Parachute) Field Ambulance
Intensive Individual Training
1. Duration of course:-
4 -5 weeks

2. Daily Working Hours:-
Monday to Thursday 08.00 – 18.00 hours
Friday 08.00 – 16.00 hours
Saturday 08.00 – 12.00 hours
Sunday – Nil
N.B. Night scheme every Tuesday 23.00 hours to 06.00 hours Wednesday. Saturday afternoons and Sundays reserved for jumping. All Officers and NCOs to attend CO's lectures as follows:
Monday, Tuesday and Thursday 20.00 – 22.00 hours.

3. Duty Section.
Confined to Bulford Camp for seven days. Those men not on duty to attend all lectures. Each man to receive 15 hours driving instruction, this to be arranged between the Section Commanders and Sergeant Rowe.

4. Training Programme.
The following hours/week are allotted to the various subjects:-
First Aid, theoretical 5 hours
First Aid, practical 5 hours
Hygiene and Sanitation 3 hours
Gas 2 hours
Route March 6 hours
PT and cross country runs 5 hours
Night Scheme (compass stars) 7 hours
Field craft (concealment, map reading) 2 hours
Medical equipment 1 hour
Synthetic 1 hour
Container Drill 1 hour
Container packing 1 hour
Weapon Training 2 hours
Ceremonial Drill 1 hour
Setting up ADS 3 hours
Current Affairs 1 hour
Padre 1 hour
Total 47 hours
Commanding Officer's lectures 6 hours

Meanwhile, the three teeth battalions were eager to go on further operations – many intended ones came their way. One of these operations was a raid on Dieppe, known as Operation Rutter, that was intended to take place in early July 1942, and was seen as an opportunity for the Canadian Army to test itself against the Germans. It is recorded that when Lord Mountbatten offered Lieutenant-General Crerar, who commanded the 1st Canadian Corps, the chance to take part in a large-scale raid on Dieppe, his reply was "You bet!"

The coast of France around Dieppe has high chalk cliffs similar to that on the south coast of England, and these acted as natural defences. The task of attacking Dieppe

A picture taken during an exercise against the Home Guard in the New Forest in 1942. On the right is Lieutenant Colonel Gofton-Salmond, the CO of the 2nd Parachute Battalion, who is discussing a point of detail with Major P. Teichman. It is stated that Philip Teichman had been a barrister pre-war and so recorded things most carefully; he is possibly making such an observation in his booklet here. (R. Pine-Coffin)

itself was given to six battalions and an armoured unit from the 2nd Canadian Division. Either side of Dieppe were two German artillery positions at Berneval and Varengeville. Their guns could bring down a murderous crossfire on any approaching boats and so would have to be knocked out, otherwise the operation had the makings of a massacre. Each gun position had ten 150 mm artillery pieces with a range of ten miles. The shell fired by these guns weighed around 90 lbs.

The job of knocking out these two artillery positions was initially given to the 1st Parachute Battalion, who trained hard for the task. This however, was not the first operation to be planned for the 1st Battalion in 1942 as their then CO, Lieutenant Colonel J. Hill recalled:

> First we were going to capture Alderney and hold it for a short time. That was cancelled. Then we trained for the Dieppe raid with the Canadians on the Isle of Wight. We were going to drop on each flank and take out some German artillery positions and then be evacuated by sea, pretty similar to the Bruneval raid. Security though was abysmal; several Canadians told my chaps that the objective was Dieppe. We got as far as being loaded in the aircraft when a weather front came in

> and the operation was postponed for a month. In that time Mountbatten decided to simplify the operation by eliminating one of the weather-dependent factors, so we were out and the Commandos were given our task. I nearly had a mutiny on my hands; it was a hell of a job keeping the men happy.
>
> Our next job was to capture Ushant [Author's note – off the western Atlantic coast of France] and hold it for 48 hours, being taken off by Hunt Class destroyers. Again, we were in the aircraft at Hurn airport, with engines ticking over, when that one was cancelled! The reason – a group of American Flying Fortresses, despatched to bomb airfields supporting Ushant, got caught in a weather front, losing their way and formation. They were escorted by a squadron of Spitfires who were ordered to tail them. The Fortresses had the fuel capacity to find their way back, the Spitfires did not and were forced to land in France and as far away as Spain. I then took the battalion to Exmoor and we did an exercise with live ammunition. I then marched them back to Bulford, saying that anyone who fell out would not go on the next operation. We did the 112 miles in two and a half days, carrying sixty pounds per man. Some people failed to make it. They had to pay the price.

Taking the place of the 1st Parachute Battalion were Nos. 3 and 4 Commandos. No 3 Commando was given the job at the Berneval location while No 4 was to go to Varengeville.

The main difficulty at this time was the lack of suitable parachuting aircraft. Again, for the Dieppe raid the RAF had to borrow them from Bomber Command as there were insufficient to lift one battalion. As one writer put it "the inability of the RAF to provide aircraft was to dog the steps of all those who were trying to form and train the new force."

Air Marshal Harris, who led Bomber Command, said "parachute or glider operations are not a practical operation of war.....the weather in Europe is unsuitable for airborne operations.....airborne troops could not be employed with any material contribution to victory.....the only alternative (to using bombers to drop parachutists and tow gliders) was to set up a separate transport force." However, in spite of this indifference, a separate transport force was set up, using a variety of aircraft, ranging from the C47 Dakota from America to obsolete bombers, such as the Stirling, Halifax and Albemarle.

The arguments between the Army and the RAF continued and eventually it was put to the Prime Minister for a final decision. In spite of arguments on both sides the coin came down in favour of the airborne forces. Browning had also been appointed as 'adviser on airborne forces to Commanders-in-Chief in all theatres of war'. Whilst wearing this hat he heard that only one battalion from the 503rd United States Parachute Infantry had been earmarked to take in a campaign in North Africa, and suggested that this would be inadequate. He additionally argued that a campaign in North Africa would offer tremendous opportunities for airborne operations. The campaign was likely to be fought over great distances and during the early stages only light opposition might be encountered. The Commander-in-Chief Home Forces and then the War Office, then approved the addition of 1st Parachute Brigade to the order of battle for Operation Torch, as the invasion of Algeria was to be codenamed. The Brigade was however, looked on as a strategic unit and placed under command of the Supreme Allied Commander,

General Dwight Eisenhower. He sub-contracted them to the British 1st Army for specific operations on his say so.

As the RAF were unable to guarantee either sufficient aircraft or crews to work with the Brigade on a full time basis, the USAAF stepped into the breach and took over responsibility for operations and training. They were obviously unused to British techniques and equipment but nevertheless threw themselves into this new task. The first training drop by 60th Group of 51st Wing occurred on 9th October 1942. Regretfully different techniques used by the Americans had not quite been mastered and three men were killed in parachuting accidents out of the 250 or so who dropped.

The three who were killed were all from the 2nd Parachute Battalion:

Private D. Reid
Private L. Shelley
Lieutenant P. Street

It now seemed that a move overseas was on the horizon but only a few people knew exactly where. A useful clue to the fact that the Brigade might be going on operations soon was when the units were brought up as close to war establishment as possible. This meant in certain instances taking men and equipment from other elements of the newly-formed 1st Airborne Division.

John Bellamy again:

> Towards the end of October 1942, it was known that 16 PFA would soon be proceeding overseas. One night, just before their departure, a medical officer and two senior NCOs went out for a drink or two in Salisbury. Regretfully they got rather too 'oiled' and in a dispute that erupted in a fish and chip shop, they ended up putting the cash register in the deep fat fryer. As Jack said, this may have been forgiven as high spirits in the paratroopers were often looked on as inevitable, but unfortunately the officer was overheard by an intelligence or security man to comment that his unit was soon going overseas. I believe this all happened around 10.00 p.m. in Salisbury and somehow or other they made it back to Bulford and slept it off.
>
> But unbeknown to this gang of three things moved quickly that night, the breach of security must have been reported and the War Office, who were often thought to be incapable of swift action, moved into top gear. That particular night I had been acting as the duty clerk and as usual when on such duty, I slept in the office. Around 7.00 o'clock, as I was folding up my blankets just before going off duty, I had to take an incoming phone call. A voice on the other end of the line stated: 'This is the War Office, Department AMD6, Captain Blank RAMC is hereby posted to Fort Augustus Inverness, and will today proceed by the 10.45 a.m. train from Salisbury. Rail Warrant to be issued, motor transport to Salisbury Station is authorised.'
>
> The voice then asked for my name rank and number as indication that the message had been duly received and would be acted upon. It was. Few in our unit even witnessed the departure of the officer concerned, for he went so swiftly. The NCOs concerned got off with a reprimand, and were required to reimburse the owner of the fish shop for the damage they had caused. However it was a lesson to

us all that we shouldn't go around speaking about military matters as the walls in this case did have ears just as the posters said.

The following are a few words about the training carried out by the 2nd Parachute Battalion during the middle part of 1942. There were a lot of inter-company exercises, interspersed with exercises against the Home Guard and long route marches. Examples of these marches are the 80 miles covered by A Company in three days, and the 113 miles in four days by the Mortar and Signal Platoons. Perhaps the record should go to A Company, who covered 54 miles in 24 hours. A number of parachuting exercises were carried out with a variety of aircraft, including the Wellington. The culmination of this training was Exercise Dryshod, which was carried out in southern Scotland.

In April 1942, Brigadier Gale was moved to another airborne job and Lieutenant Colonel Flavell was promoted to take command of the brigade. In his place Major G. Gofton-Salmond took over as CO.

In mid-July 1942 the Battalion undertook a large-scale field exercise covering field firing, battle skills at section, platoon and company level. Towards the end of September 1942 the Battalion began to sort itself out for what proved out to be operations in North Africa until, on the 29th October 1942, the 2nd Battalion entrained for the port of Greenock in Scotland. A final complication for the unit was the fact that once on board the CO, Lieutenant Colonel Gofton-Salmond, was found to be unfit for overseas service and was disembarked before leaving territorial waters. Major J. Frost, who by now had become the 2 i/c, was promoted to become their third commanding officer.

For the medics of 16 PFA the warning order 'to mobilise for service overseas by October 6, 00.01 hours' was received at 18.00 on 24th September under War Office Urgent Memorandum 79/Mob/5554/12 (AG5 Mob). Over the next few days medical and kit inspections were carried out and deficiency reports for personal and medical equipment were filled in, submitted and for the most part fulfilled, so that the unit was up to its full scale issue.

At the end of October 1942 most of the units of the 1st Parachute Brigade were heading north from the Salisbury Plain area in trains for Scotland. A few people had been left behind and we will look at what happened to them shortly.

For the men of 16 PFA the first party, consisting of Major Whatley, Lieutenant (QM) Anderson, Lieutenant Wright and Lieutenant Rob and 37 ORs, left Bulford at 10.20 on the 29th October. The remainder, consisting of Colonel MacEwan, Captain Young, Lieutenant McGavin and Lieutenant Longland again with 37 ORs, left at 19.50 on the same day. By around 12.00 the next day they had all arrived at Greenock and were taken out to the waiting troop transports.

Shortly before sailing the senior officers were given 'sealed orders', with the instructions they could be opened at sea. For the men however, there were more serious matters to worry about as Gower Davies, a member of the 2nd Parachute Battalion recalls:

> I was one of the surprised men who embarked on the troopship at Greenock in October 1942 for what we later found out to be North Africa. In the Parachute Regiment and not flying out! The ship was so crowded that the only place I could find to sleep was in an air conditioning plant. During the second day out I was put

on latrine door duty by the CSM, [although] my Platoon Sergeant ordered me to get on parade. In vain did I tell him of my previous order and next day found me on Company orders and serving seven days in the cells. Did I worry? Meals in comfort, a bed to sleep in, none of the chaos below, even escorted walks around the deck watching the boys doing their PT. One of the best weeks I had spent in the Army.

The men of the 1st Parachute Brigade were accommodated in two ships – the SS *Arundel Castle* and the SS *Strathmore.* The ships sailed on 1st November 1942 and once at sea, the senior officers were given instructions to open their sealed orders.

For the CO of the 1st Parachute Battalion, Lieutenant Colonel Hill, these revealed that his unit was to seize El Aouina airfield at Tunis. If the enemy got there first, he was to capture the aerodrome at Setif. Maps, aerial photographs and a model of the area accompanied his orders. Whilst sailing to North Africa detailed planning was carried out. This was somewhat difficult as they had been told they would be jumping from Dakotas, of which no one in the Battalion had ever jumped from before. However, like many operations before and since, whilst they were still at sea, news was received that the Germans had occupied El Aouina.

The following are the entries from the war diary of 16 PFA (HQ A and No 2 Section) for the journey to North Africa:

Greenock, 1st November – Colonel MacEwan was appointed OC troops on board ship. 2130 Ship sailed. Skin inspection.

At sea, 2nd November – First aid discussion held before boat drill in the morning. Colonel Lewis gave the men a German lecture. 1650 Air raid alarm given but no raiders sighted.

At sea, 3rd November – Training consisted of PT, German and compass work.

At sea, 4th November – 1130 The officers informed of the ships destination, probable date of arrival and the intention of the force. Colonel MacEwan gave a lecture on 'Direction Finding in the Desert' to all ranks. Pay parade.

At sea, 5th November – Brigade Operational Instructions 1,2 and 3 received together with relevant books and pamphlets. Training – PT and German.

At sea, 6th November – Major General Cole DSO lectured all officers on 'Hearings and Claims', this was followed by a short talk on officers pay.

At sea 7th November – Officers attended a lecture by Father Gaffney CF on 'customs in Algeria'. Training – PT, German and first aid.

At sea 8th November – Voluntary church parade, all denominations, held in the morning.

At sea 9th November – Pay Parade. All ranks given 2 mepacrine tablets. Training – PT, German and current affairs talk on 'Algeria'.

At sea 10th November – Training – PT, German and water duties.

At sea 11th November – Colonel MacEwan and Captain Young attended a Brigade Conference. Standing Orders (North Africa) 1st Parachute Brigade issued.

Captain Young attended a conference on billeting. All ranks given 2 mepacrine tablets.

At sea 12th November – 0730 Arrived in the Bay of Algiers and docked at 1230. No disembarkation.

Algiers 13th November – 0815 Disembarked. No 2 Section and Surgical Team proceeded with 2nd Battalion to Maison Carrée. HQ A joined up with HQ B commanded by Major Wheatley and moved into Rouiba.

Here is a comment from George Thompson, one of the early volunteers:

I joined the 3rd Parachute Battalion in March 1942, having completed my parachute course in late February. On arrival at their base at Bulford I found that apart from the Medical Officer, Captain Rutherford, there were only 6 other medics there. At the time the Battalion seemed well under strength and although we had been told we would be going to act as 'company medics', we spent a lot of time in the Medical Inspection room. This meant we seemed to have a lot spare time on our hands. I made use of this time by keeping myself fit. Most afternoons I went cross-country running in all sorts of weathers. I also became the automatic choice as centre-half for the Battalion football team, I also was in the rugby and 440 yards relay team.

In due course the Battalion was made up to strength and some medics were posted in from 16 Parachute Field Ambulance to enable 4 medics to be allocated to each of the companies. This was normally a Corporal and 3 Privates. The first company I went to was A Company. A lot of the training consisted of route marches with nights spent out under the stars. At the end of each day, it was my job to look after any medical problems before sorting myself out. Usually the problems revolved around the feet. I don't know how some men marched with some of the really bad blisters I saw. My usual treatment, and it seemed to work, was to open the blister up and pour iodine into it. I usually had the patient either held down and biting onto something before the moment of truth!

Similar treatment has been carried out in more recent times on the feet of men suffering usually during P Company (Pre-Parachute Selection) where bad blisters have been injected with tincture benzyl benzoate compound. This was nearly always guaranteed to get a crowd of interested spectators, especially those in the know. Perhaps the best way of explaining the effects of such treatment is to say that you are given a feather duster as it'll give you something to do while you are 'up on the ceiling' screaming the place down! George also commented that during these early days he made a habit of keeping close to Bren gunners in order to help with their heavier load. He also said those guys would also let him fire when using live ammunition.

Perhaps to end this chapter it might be appropriate to take a small step back and look at the general situation in North Africa in 1942. For much of the year the fighting had been carried out between the British 8th Army and the Deutsche Afrika Korps and the Italians. The fighting had to a large extent been concentrated in the eastern end of the Middle East in Libya and Egypt. It is probably fair to say that the fighting had ebbed and flowed until the Afrika Korps under the command of Rommel seemed to have made a massive breakthrough in the summer of 1942and pushed the 8th Army back to the area of a small railway station called El Alamein, about 50 miles from Alexandria. Without going into too much detail here, the 8th Army got a new commander, General Montgomery, who managed to galvanise them into an effective defensive and fighting force. He also spent a lot of time reorganising and retraining the 8th Army. On 31st

August 1942, Rommel struck the El Alamein line, and was repulsed with heavy artillery fire. Both sides now prepared for the Second Battle of El Alamein.

This battle perhaps is one of the most decisive of the war, a major struggle which was meticulously planned and executed.

The start of the Allied attack on Rommel was codenamed Operation Lightfoot and took place on 24th October 1942. There was a reason for this. A diversionary attack in the south was meant to take in 50% of Rommel's forces. The main attack in the north was to last – according to Montgomery – just one night. The infantry had to attack first. Many of the anti-tank mines would not be tripped by soldiers running over them – they were too light (hence the code-name). As the infantry attacked, engineers had to clear a path for the tanks coming up in the rear. Each stretch of land cleared of mines was to be 24 feet wide – just enough to get a tank through in single file. The engineers had to clear a five mile section through the 'Devil's Garden'. It was an awesome task and one that essentially failed. 'Monty' had a simple message for his troops on the eve of the battle: "All that is necessary is that each and every officer and man should enter this battle with the determination to see it through, to fight and kill, and finally to win. If we do this, there can be only one result – together, we will hit the enemy for six out of Africa."

The attack on Rommel's lines started with over 800 artillery guns firing at the German lines. Legend has it that the noise was so great that the ears of the gunners bled. As the shells pounded the German lines, the infantry attacked. The engineers set about clearing mines. Their task was very dangerous as one mine was inter-connected with others via wires and if one mine was set off, many others could be. The stretch of cleared land for the tanks proved to be Montgomery's Achilles heel. Just one non-moving tank could hold up all the tanks that were behind it. The ensuing traffic jams made the tanks easy targets for the German gunners using the feared 8.8cm anti-aircraft/anti-tank gun. The plan to get the tanks through in one night failed. The infantry had also not got as far as Montgomery had planned. They had to dig in.

The second night of the attack was also unsuccessful. 'Monty' blamed his chief of tanks, Lumsden. He was given a simple ultimatum – move forward – or be replaced by someone more energetic. But the rate of attrition of the Allied forces was taking its toll. Operation Lightfoot was called off and Montgomery, not Lumsden, withdrew his tanks. When he received the news, Churchill was furious, as he believed that Montgomery was letting victory go.

However, Rommel and the Afrika Korps had also been suffering. The Germans only had 300 tanks left to the Allies 900+. 'Monty' next planned to make a move to the Mediterranean. Australian units attacked the Germans by the Mediterranean and Rommel had to move his tanks north to cover this. The Australians took many casualties but their attack was to change the course of the battle.

Rommel became convinced that the main thrust of Montgomery's attack would be near the Mediterranean and he moved a large amount of his Afrika Korps there. The Australians fought with ferocity – even Rommel commented on the 'rivers of blood' in the region. However, the Australians had given Montgomery room to manoeuvre.

Montgomery launched Operation Supercharge. This was a British and New Zealand infantry attack made south of where the Australians were fighting. Rommel was taken by surprise. 123 tanks of the 9th Armoured Brigade attacked the German lines. But a sandstorm once again saved Rommel. Many of the tanks got lost and they were easy for the German '88 gunners to pick off. 75% of the 9th Brigade was lost. But the overwhelming number of Allied tanks meant that more arrived to help out and it was these tanks that tipped the balance. Rommel put tank against tank – but his men were hopelessly outnumbered.

By 2nd November 1942 Rommel knew that he was beaten. Hitler ordered the Afrika Korps to fight to the last but Rommel refused to carry out this order. On 4th November, Rommel started his retreat. 25,000 Germans and Italians had been killed or wounded in the battle and 13,000 Allied troops in the 8th Army. It was the start of a long retreat that eventually ended in Berlin.

Meanwhile plans had been generated to land in the western part of North Africa in Morocco and Algeria with the intention of getting as far as Tunisia. Hopefully here there would be a link-up with Montgomery's troops advancing from Libya and Egypt.

Operation Torch was the codename for the invasion of North Africa. Churchill and his military advisers wanted to remove the Vichy French authorities from the territories they controlled on the North African coast before they fell into German hands. Torch was an American led operation under Eisenhower with substantial UK support.

The Allies decided to occupy Vichy French-controlled North Africa, thus denying the territory to the Axis forces. Churchill and his Combined Operations planners were closely involved with the Americans in working out the details of Operation Torch. There were many differences of opinion about timing, landing locations and the perceived reaction of the Vichy French forces to American as opposed to British forces. Churchill, however, accepted that Torch was an American-run project and he telegraphed President Roosevelt, "In the whole of Torch, military and political, I certainly consider myself your lieutenant, asking only to put my viewpoint plainly before you."

On 1st November 1942, the Naval Commander-in-Chief of the Allied Expeditionary Force, Admiral Sir Andrew Cunningham, reached the fortress of Gibraltar in the cruiser *Scylla*. Fours days later, Cunningham was joined by his Supreme Commander, General Dwight D. Eisenhower, who had flown from England in a B-17 bomber through fog and rain. The Expeditionary Force Headquarters, complete with a joint Navy/Air Force operations room, were located in the old tunnels built into the Rock itself. They were airless, dank and dripping but completely immune to any bombardment. Only three days remained until the Allies launched the largest combined amphibious operation in the history of the warfare. Eisenhower considered the operation to be "an undertaking of a quite desperate nature".

Eisenhower himself had never before commanded a major operation of war and was about to receive his baptism of fire. Apart from all the usual operational hazards there were other considerations for him to deal with. Would the Vichy French, whose territories the Allied force would invade, co-operate or resist? … and what of neutral Spain immediately north of Gibraltar? If it sided with Germany it could unleash its fury against the exposed airstrip and crowded anchorage at Gibraltar. These were major uncertainties but Eisenhower drew strength from the unflaggingly optimistic Naval C-in-C, Cunningham.

Throughout the first three years of the war Britain learned many painful lessons about amphibious landings, notably from Dieppe. The plan for the invasion of North Africa identified the first three assault locations as Philippeville and Bone, Casablanca, and Oran and Algiers. However, limited resources and the Americans inability to supply sufficient ships for the landings, threatened to restrict the assault to Philippeville and Bone in the east of Algeria. Washington however took the view that the landings in Morocco should go ahead at the cost of all others, except Oran. This effectively removed the option of capturing Tunis with the aim of denying it to the Axis forces. Tunis was vital in restricting the Axis supply lines. On 5th September 1942 the final compromise was reached after much negotiation for three landings at Casablanca, Algiers and Oran.

The landing forces were divided into:

- Western Assault Force: Major-General George S. Patton, 35,000 American troops. Objective: Casablanca in French Morocco.
- Central Task Force: Major-General Lloyd R. Fredendall, 18,500 American troops building up to 39,000. Objective: Oran.
- Eastern Task Force: Lieutenant-General K.A.N. Anderson, 20,000 troops in the first wave, half American and half British. Objective: Algiers.

All these commanders reported directly to Eisenhower.

To ensure the ships arrived on time in the assembly area at Gibraltar Admiral Ramsay, the author of the plan, issued Ton 2, which detailed the routing and scheduling of convoys, escort and task forces outwards from Britain and the forward assembly area on the Bay of Algiers, with carefully calculated tables of convoy routes complete with lettered routing positions.

The first convoys left the Clyde on 2nd October. The first troop convoy left on 22nd October with others following on 26th October and 1st November. The last convoy was due in Gibraltar on the 4th November. The covering warships left their respective bases between the 20th and 30th October. The concern over U-boat attacks didn't materialise since their command in Germany failed to realise the significance of the convoys despite spotting two leaving their bases. At this critical time in the Mediterranean U-Boats were engaging a convoy *en route* from Sierra Leone to Britain so they too missed the naval build-up.

As some 340 ships converged on Gibraltar the Allies had one last vain attempt to persuade the Vichy French to join them or at least not interfere with the landings. On the 5th November the whole operation hung in the balance as the entire force passed through the Straits of Gibraltar in just 33 hours. This involved the smaller vessels diverting to Gibraltar and refuelling, which demanded a flexible and fast refuelling programme.

On 7th November RAF reconnaissance patrols commenced along a line between the east coast of Spain and the Bonifacio Strait (between Sardinia and Corsica) in order to detect any threatening moves by the Italian fleet, and north and west of Dakar in French West Africa to give early warning of any northward move towards Admiral Hewitt's task force by French warships. All the while Coastal Command aircraft were flying anti-U-boat operations and reconnaissance sorties over Italian and French naval bases.

The Torch landings were opposed by Vichy French forces numbering 120,000 in French North Africa. They were mostly native rank and file with French officers supported by 500 aircraft and a sizeable Naval fleet at Toulon. Their army and air force both suffered from obsolete equipment but the Navy posed a great threat in the collective mind of the Allied commanders. Its firepower could wreak havoc on any landing it chose to oppose. The Italian fleet also presented a threat but it suffered from low morale, irresolute leadership and a lack of fuel oil. Finally there was the Luftwaffe's presence in Italy and North Africa, which had the potential to inflict serious damage. Up to the 7th

November the German Naval High Command still believed the Torch armada was a Malta-bound convoy.

The Allied convoys came together at prearranged locations guided by infra-red signal beams from Royal Navy submarines.

At Algiers, the Navy put ashore the American 34th Infantry Division under Major-General Charles W. Ryder, one brigade of the British 78th Infantry Division, and No 1 and 6 Commandos. A second brigade of 78th Division acted as a floating reserve. The landing operations were directed from the headquarters ship *Bulolo*. The invasion plan was staged as two landings (A and B) west of Algiers, and one (C) to the east.

In the last hour of 7th November, the landing forces were launched from their mother ships, in a moderate swell, a new moon and a westward current of about 4 knots. There were three sectors:

The A sector landing went according to plan, with 7,230 soldiers of the British 11th Infantry Brigade (78th Division) and a reconnaissance squadron. There was no French resistance.

The B sector landing consisted of Regimental Combat Teams of the American 34th Infantry Division and the British No 1 and No 6 Commandos, 5,420 strong in all, landing on five separate beaches. Some ships were pushed out of position by a force 3 breeze resulting in modification to the disembarkation procedure. Some landings went in on the wrong beaches but there were no repercussions since there was no French resistance; in fact the French commander openly welcomed the invading forces.

C sector fared the worst. There was fog over the beaches as 6,000 soldiers of the 39th Regimental Combat Team of the 34th Infantry Division and five troops of Commandos landed. Thankfully there was no resistance apart from a few rounds fired from a coastal defence battery, which was quickly silenced by the Commandos.

The only fighting took place within the port of Algiers itself, when two destroyers attempted to put ashore a party of American infantry to prevent the French from scuttling ships and sabotaging the dock installations. Heavy shells badly damaged one destroyer but the second got through and disembarked her landing party. This destroyer was pounded severely by coastal defence batteries and field artillery for four hours before she was compelled to put to sea, leaving 250 Americans on shore. She was sunk the next day under tow. From daylight on the 8th November the four carriers provided air cover over the invasion area while reinforcements swelled the lodgements. The spearheads quickly thrust inland despite resistance by a handful of forts and coastal defence batteries. At 1100 RAF Hurricanes from Gibraltar flew into Maison Blanche airfield after its capture by the Americans. In the afternoon of the 8th General Ryder agreed a local cease-fire with General Juin, who represented the absent Admiral Darlan, who was in Algiers visiting his sick son.

The eastern sector was secured by the end of the day just as German bombers arrived to attack the shipping off the coast.

The Oran landings were directed by Commodore T.H. Troubridge, RN, Major-General Lloyd R. Fredenhall and Major-General James Doolittle (Commanding the Allied Western Air Command) on the Largs. The landings were supported by a battleship, three carriers, an anti-aircraft ship and nine destroyers acting as a covering force in the event of Italian Navy interference.

In the early hours of 8th November the weather at Oran was calm with good visibility. However, the westerly winds were having a disconcerting effect on the landings.

X Sector, some 30 miles west of Oran, was delayed by a French convoy getting in the way of the minesweepers clearing the path for the landing forces of Task Force Green comprising 2,250 soldiers, plus tanks and trucks of the American 1st Armored Division with a navy escort. The landings began half an hour late because of the French convoy and went in at 0130. The unexpected shallowness of the beaches resulted in damage to ten of the thirteen assault wave landing craft, which left only three operational. Through the same 50-yard wide stretch of sandy cove over 3,000 soldiers came through over the next three days along with 458 tanks and trucks.

Y Sector was 20 miles closer to Oran. 5,262 soldiers of the 26th Regimental Combat Team of the American 1st Infantry Division were put ashore by landing craft in the bay of Les Abdalouses. Delays were experienced caused by problems with the disembarkation ladders on the *Monarch of Bermuda* and a sandbank, which damaged the landing craft rudders and propellers as they bludgeoned their way through it. A northerly swell caused grief as many craft broached on top of the bar. Most of these delays could have been avoided if Headquarters had allowed beach reconnaissance parties instead of submarine periscope observations.

East of Oran was Z Sector. The landings here comprised 10,472 soldiers of the 1st US Ranger Battalion, the 16th and 18th Regimental Combat Teams of the 1st Infantry Division and the Western Column of Combat Command B of the 1st Armoured Division. The assault wave went ashore at 0016 from 68 landing craft on beaches Green, White and Red south of Arzeu, a little port beneath a rocky headland and overlooked by the Fort de le Pointe.

Here, as at Algiers, the landings were bloodily repulsed in the centre when HMS *Walney* and *Heartland*, flying under dual flags, attempted to land US Rangers in the harbour at Algiers. They broke through the harbour boom at 0310, but the *Walney* was reduced to a flaming hulk by a French sloop and crossfire from other vessels. She later sank. *Heartland* was shattered at point-blank range by a French destroyer, after which three French destroyers put to sea in an attempt to engage the powerful covering force near the landings. Two of them quickly succumbed to the accurate fire of HMS *Aurora*. The sloop responsible for the sinking of HMS *Walney* attacked the shipping off Y Sector but was sunk by HMS *Brilliant*. The remaining destroyer ventured out the following day with a second destroyer and were both driven ashore after being engaged by the *Aurora* and *Jamaica*.

Throughout the 9th November the French and Allied forces lobbed fire between the taskforce and the coast while French troops stoutly defended the approaches to Oran. Aircraft from HMS *Furious*, consisting of Seafires, Albacores and Sea Hurricanes, attacked two airfields, destroying 70 aircraft. At noon that day Task Force Red from the Z sector beaches took Tafaraoui and 28 British and American Spitfires flew in shortly afterwards. The French Air Force attacked the last four aircraft with Dewoitine DW 250 fighters, shooting down one Spitfire for the loss of three aircraft. It was not until 1600 that the armour of Task Force Green from X Sector beaches fought through to take the second airfield at La Senia. Meanwhile, the American 1st Infantry was slowed by tough resistance at St Cloud on the road from Arzeu to Oran. It took a bombardment of the coastal batteries by *Rodney*, *Aurora* and *Jamaica* to bring about the final surrender of Oran to the Allies.

The other landings on the coast of Morocco were complicated by heavy Atlantic swells and fierce but short-lived fighting against the French Navy and Army. Casablanca fell early on 11th November. It is important to note that because of the lack of a headquarters ship at Casablanca, General Patton was helplessly carried away because the warship he was on was needed to repel a French naval attack just as he was about to go ashore.

It was against this backdrop that the men of the 1st Parachute Brigade arrived in the early part of November 1942.

We will leave the final words in this chapter to one of the members of the 1st Parachute Battalion on the *Arundel Castle*, Private Thomas Davies:

> On a bleak November day in 1942 we left Clydeside on board the *Arundel Castle*, a liner of some 22,000 tons, for what was to us then an unknown destination. There was much speculation as to where we were bound in many sections of the troops on board; many wild rumours went about, always coming from a good source. The places mentioned covered practically half the globe but it was not until we were well out on the high seas that we were told officially that we were heading for Algiers and that the invasion of North Africa was about to begin. There was great excitement aboard and spirits ran high at the prospect of the adventure in store for us.
>
> The voyage took about ten days, escorted by battleships, destroyers and cruisers. The huge convoy had to make a wide detour to keep clear of the Bay of Biscay and the U-boat menace, so much so that we edged fairly close to the coast of America. Many aboard experienced the dreadful effects of seasickness for a spell as the crossing became more tempestuous.
>
> Bill Wilson, with whom I had struck up a friendship, and I, along with a few others, including 'Big Frank' Garlick and Joe Waterhouse, Cockneys from Mill Hill and Bethnal Green respectively, were detailed for a working party on board ship, passing a lot of the time keeping the galley supplied with vegetables, etc. Joe, who had been employed at Covent Garden before being called up for service and had spent a couple of years humping bananas about, stuck his thumbs in, hitching up his trousers in a theatrical manner said, "Now mates, I'll take charge here. This is right in my department". Needless to say, nobody agreed with him.
>
> 'Big Frank', as he was affectionately called, was an ex-Grenadier Guardsman. In his early parachute training days, he had the misfortune of having his harness caught up in the rear of the aircraft just as he jumped. He was just hanging there on the end of the strap while the pilot circled a few times in an effort to shake him free but to no avail. Eventually it was decided to land with Frank hanging below. The parachute, which of course had not pulled open, acted as a shock absorber to cushion the occasional bump as the aircraft came to a halt on the runway. Luckily he was not seriously hurt, but suffered a nasty shake-up with severe shock and a few bruises which needed attention.
>
> Boxing tournaments and concerts were organised on-board ship with quite a lot of the leisure time spent playing 'Tombola' (bingo). Then, there were the regular daily sessions of life-jacket drill and periods of physical training on the deck for

the troops. At night, we would be aft and lean against the railings, staring into the ocean. I was fascinated by the trail of phosphorescence left in the wake of the ship. Rocket flares were let off from time to time and when we first saw them we thought we were being attacked, but later learned, much to our relief, that they merely signalled a change of direction by the convoy.

Those continuous days at sea, seeing nothing but the sheer expanse of water day after day made me realise just how small and insignificant is man in comparison with the vastness of the world. When passing through the fifteen-miles-wide Straits of Gibraltar, which separates Africa from Europe, Corporal Silbury, an ex-Grenadier Guard who consequently kept up a constant banter with 'Big Frank' referring to him as "You Big Ape", cried out, pointing in the general direction of the Rock, "Hey Frank, we're not far away from your mates now", referring, of course, to the Barbary Apes. Frank, good humouredly, joined in the joke, and adopted a gorilla stance, arms swinging at his sides, and showed his amazing set of white teeth as he roared with laughter.

The previous night we had been talking about Gibraltar and how the Barbary Apes had been brought over to the Rock by the Moroccans during their long occupation many centuries ago. I tried to visualise the huge, formidable mass of grey rock which reached a height of 1,400 feet and was a huge mountain of limestone rising out of the Mediterranean. Through the ages, it has been the keystone to many spectacular and historic events. We heard later that General Eisenhower had directed operations for the North African landings, in which we were involved, from a command post in a bastion tunnelled into the Rock.

We disembarked at Algiers in bright sunlight, which brought to life the romantic picture I had envisaged of this North African port, with its cool, white-domed buildings and clear blue sky. The scene was like an illustration of a biblical scene. We were destined for Maison Blanche Aerodrome, a few kilometres outside Algiers. We marched through the streets of the city to the seemingly indifferent looks of the local inhabitants. My eyes burned with sweat as we tramped mile after mile in dazzling sunshine until we arrived eventually at the aerodrome, weary and exhausted, thankful for the cool of the evening which was descending upon us as the sun set.

Immobilised German aircraft of various types and sizes were strewn about the airfield, one or two of them up-ended, others sagging in the middle like pregnant ducks, victims of hand grenades planted in their belly by the withdrawing German forces.

4

Bone, October-November 1942

Not all the men of the 1st Parachute Brigade left for North Africa by sea and it was felt that it would be good to quickly get an airborne capability in-theatre. The quickest way to get a force there was obviously to fly them out. The problem with this was one that had raised its ugly head before, and that was the aircraft. Even with American help ther were nowhere near enough aircraft to transport a complete battalion, never mind the whole brigade. It was therefore decided that a small headquarter element and two rifle companies of the 3rd Parachute Battalion, C Troop of the 1st Parachute Squadron RE and No 3 Section and a Field Surgical Team of 16 Parachute Field Ambulance RAMC would go by air.

It seems appropriate to relate a few salient points about the command structure faced by the fledgling 1st Parachute Brigade and how difficult this was going to prove in an operational environment.

The Supreme Allied Commander General Eisenhower had allocated the 1st Parachute Brigade to the British 1st Army under the command of General Sir Kenneth Anderson for specific operations, although he had retained the right to use them as strategic troops on any part of the front as he felt fit. So from the outset the brigade commander, Brigadier Flavell, had to deal with HQ 1st Army for all matters relating to operations, planning, administration and possible movements. Meanwhile, the Divisional Commander Major-General Browning, together with his HQ, advised and assisted where necessary but concentrated on getting the brigade ready for war. In spite of repeated requests by Major-General Browning for the appointment of a 'senior airborne advisor' to fight the corner for the 1st Parachute Brigade at 1st Army HQ, or at any other senior HQ which might command the brigade, this request was refused by the War Office. The result both during planning in England and during actual operations in North Africa was that the brigade commander was available neither to plan at a high level nor command his brigade to the proper extent. Put simply, he could not be in two places at the same time.

In October 1942 the 3rd Battalion group was now commanded by Lieutenant Colonel R.G. Pine-Coffin, who had replaced Lieutenant Colonel R. Webb in October 1942. Webb had also replaced the first commanding officer, Lieutenant Colonel G. Lathbury, who had also moved on to pastures new. Lathbury is probably best known for his time as commander of the 1st Parachute Brigade in Sicily and Holland later in the war.

It is probably fair to say that Lieutenant Colonel Pine-Coffin had a difficult job when he took over command in mid-October 1942. Amongst other duties, he had been previously been 2 i/c of the 2nd Parachute Battalion. He obviously did not have a lot of time to get to know his battalion as there was talk of operations in the air, and within three weeks they were actually operational. What time there was available was naturally spent on operational preparations, and these of course were done at the double. It is also worth adding that Pine-Coffin probably also did not have the luxury of putting into place the changes and adjustments that a new CO wants to make.

Things cannot have been helped by the many 'ifs' and 'buts' in those plans that did appear. If the French offered resistance to the landings then there would have to be a minor campaign to overcome them before Operation Torch could really start. Secondly, they might not oppose the landings and things might go ahead according to the plan or in a best case scenario actually come over to the Allied side. Until troops were actually on the ground it was difficult to decide which was going to happen.

As stated before, the Americans had offered Dakotas to take those men selected to go to North Africa and also to remain in-theatre as their means of getting to war. Many men had not jumped from a Dakota before and so the 3rd Battalion was given priority in training. Fuselage mock-ups were constructed in barracks at Bulford and exit drills devised and practised.

Only around half of the 3rd Battalion out of the whole Brigade was able to fly to North Africa. Following paper loading trials it was decided that two rifle companies, one spare platoon, a small HQ party and some supporting engineers and medics could go by air. For the sappers and medics it was probably an easy decision as to who to send, as they were already used to supporting a battalion and so their normal supporting elements were sent. For the medics this was No 3 Section of 16 PFA (OC Captain J. Keesey) and for the sappers C Troop under the command of Captain A. Hewitt and Lieutenant T. Livesey.

The problem then became one for the 3rd Battalion as to who should go by air and who would go by sea. The question of the spare platoon was decided by Pine-Coffin, who ordered that the Mortar Platoon would go by air (it was felt that their 3 inch mortars would be useful whatever the nature of fighting). With regard to which two of the three rifle companies were to go was less clear-cut. It is recorded that Pine-Coffin did not really know which of them was the most efficient, nor the abilities of the three company commanders. So, in the end, the decision was made in the orderly room, where the three company commanders solemnly cut a pack of cards and decided their fate this way. The two lucky winners were Major Dobie (OC B Company) and Major Hall (C Company). The unlucky loser was Major Terrell and his A Company, who were now destined to go by sea.

Pine-Coffin at the same time was occupying himself with working out various plans of action for whatever task he might have to perform in North Africa. Obviously secrecy was paramount, but it was impossible to conceal the whole truth from the men. It was fairly clear that the 3rd Battalion at least was up to something, as every bit of kit was carefully checked, deficiencies made up and Fairbairn Sykes fighting knives issued. It was noticed that not everyone was getting this special treatment in the 3rd Battalion, nor the other two battalions in the brigade. It seemed this was a bigger operation than the one company Bruneval affair and excitement was on the increase.

All the plans were just about complete when the Dakotas arrived in England and their commander, Colonel Dorset, visited 1st Parachute Brigade HQ to discuss forthcoming missions. Previous discussions had led the paratroopers to believe that each Dakota would be able to carry a payload of 5,000 lbs. However, it soon became clear that due to the installation of extra petrol tanks in the aircraft the load was down to

3,000 lbs. So a quick rethink was called for and plans adjusted in line with the new load restrictions.

On 5th November 1942, as the war diary of the 3rd Battalion puts it, A Group consisting of Force HQ, B and C Companies and attached troops moved to Hurn aerodrome, where they arrived at 13.30 hours. The remainder of the unit,, known as B Group, moved a few days later, as the following entries in the war diary show:

> 8th November 1942 – B Group (Sea Party) i.e. Battalion less A Group, ordered to proceed in two ships, destination Algiers. R Company entrained for Liverpool for ship P19. 1 Officer and 50 ORs entrained for Avonmouth for ship P22 and embarked the same day.
>
> 9th November 1942 – B Group (less above details) i.e. A and HQ Companies entrained for Avonmouth for ship P22 and embarked the same day.
>
> These ships did not leave Avonmouth until the 13th (P22) and 14th April (P19) and proceeded in a convoy to North Africa.

An interesting little aside comes from the OC of the 3rd Battalion advance party:

> In early November 1942, I left Bulford with an advance party to an aerodrome from which a parachute force was to leave England. Security in barracks had been strict, and only a few privileged knew of our ultimate destination. Moreover, the name of the aerodrome for our departure was withheld from us. But we all knew that we would leave in C47s, Dakotas, and so it was possible for the uninformed to

A picture taken by an unknown member of the Brigade on 10th November 1942. It is captioned "convoy just after passing through Gibraltar". (Airborne Assault Duxford)

draw a circle on a map, and by its circumference learn the points such aircraft could reach without refuelling.

As only the privileged few were supposed to know the name of the airfield from which we were to depart, my first job, as leader of the advance party, was to collect a sealed envelope from the Adjutant in the Orderly Room. This was done with due ceremony and a couple of salutes. Inside the usual buff-coloured envelope, I was told, was the name of the aerodrome to which I was to lead my small band of heroes. Having returned to my truck, I opened the envelope (I can hardly say with bated breath) and read 'Hurn'. Apart from telling my driver to move off, I gave no instructions and yet he drove me and led the convoy to Hurn. The 'secret' information so carefully guarded and handed over with such ceremony to me, was obviously common knowledge. Determined to play this game a little more, I asked the driver if he knew the route he should take beyond Hurn. He gave me a knowing smile as he informed me that he had no petrol to go beyond Hurn and took us all into the aerodrome. It seemed to me that, somewhere, someone ought to revise the rules relating to the practice of security methods. It also came to my thoughts that I had a knowledgeable, diplomatic and secretive driver.

For the next few days after their arrival at Hurn the weather conspired against the 3rd Battalion Group and they were fogbound. It was felt they needed to leave England at the latest on 9th November. On this day, after having been shrouded in fog for all this time, the weather forecasters gave an optimistic report to Pine-Coffin, stating that it would be possible to say during the early afternoon whether the fog would clear or get thicker, that if it got thicker at Hurn it would also get thicker at most places in England, but that there was just a chance that it might remain clear in the extreme west of England.

The decision, when it came, was that the fog was going to get thicker and that it would be impossible to take off from Hurn that night. There was now nothing for it but to move the troops down to west Cornwall – and to get them there with the utmost speed. What happened next must hold some sort of informal World War Two record for quick administration. The 3rd Battalion Group and some of their kit was driven to Bournemouth Station in RAF lorries, issued with an individual ration bag, embarked on a special train and moved almost non-stop to Newquay, where further RAF trucks were waiting to take them to RAF St Eval. It is reported that on arrival at Newquay these RAF drivers broke all records getting to the airfield, and it was just after 2300 when the first trucks arrived there. All of the Dakotas were already there except for two, who had suffered from engine trouble and had been unable to take off. This called for some further last minute adjustment because the missing aircraft had in theory been taking some key personnel and so some people were moved to alternative aircraft. The fact that their kit was in the main part left at Hurn was of no consequence. It was hoped, of course, that the two aircraft would catch up soon. After a quick hot meal at St Eval the first Dakota took off at 2330 heading for Gibraltar.

The aircraft were due to take off at five minute intervals and fly on a course which took them far out to the west to a point in the Atlantic, before heading towards Gibraltar. This was intended to get the aircraft as far away as possible from any German fighter interference from the west coast of France. Any navigational problems had been overcome with help from the RAF, who had provided, at fairly short notice, a navigator for each Dakota.

The first aircraft arrived at Gibraltar around 0730 on the morning of 10th November and during the next hour or so 29 out of the 31 Dakotas that took off from England arrived. Luckily, apart from these two losses (described below), some normal air turbulence was all the danger that the rest had faced. Upon arrival the men were taken for a welcome meal in RAF messes.

After breakfast Lieutenant Colonel Pine-Coffin and an attached Staff Officer, Major R. des Voeux, visited the local HQ to get the latest information. Prior to leaving England the plan was that they would carry out one of two operations:

(i) In the event of French opposition they were to capture an airfield, Djidjelli, in conjunction with a seaborne assault by the 36th Infantry Brigade.

(ii) In the event of French co-operation with the seaborne landings, they were to land on the airfield at Bizerta and hold until relieved.

Once at the local HQ they got the good news that it now seemed unlikely the battalion group would have to carry out either of these operations and that in spite of expecting to sort the kit and loads out in North Africa, they were now expected to land 'combat ready' at Maison Blanche for an immediate airborne operation. In vain the two officers argued their corner that this was a bit impracticable but they got no joy and returned to the airfield.

This reorganization, which may have sounded so simple to the officers at HQ in Gibraltar, was, in reality, a bit of a nightmare to put into practice. The aircraft had been dispersed all over the airfield, there was very little transport available for moving the equipment around and many of the pilots, believing they had been stood down, had locked up their aircraft and gone off to see the bright lights of Gibraltar. So these men would have to be found before any transfers could begin and there was still the question of the aircraft which had failed to arrive. The question of the payloads of the aircraft over which so much trouble had been taken back in England now had to be completely readjusted and under completely different circumstances which were far from ideal. Even though it sounds a comparatively simple operation to load up the 27 aircraft left, it actually involved the complete repacking of every container so they could be stowed in bomb racks instead of being carried as baggage inside the aircraft. Also, the sticks had to be readjusted to take into account missing men. In theory, it should have been possible to put all the balance of kit into the remaining aircraft without exceeding the permissible payload, but, in practice, this was not possible as it was found that there was far more kit to be loaded than those aircraft could carry. The work took so long that it continued after dark with the aid of searchlights, Gibraltar at that time not having to carry out air raid precautions and impose a blackout. Eventually the job was finished and the first aircraft took off for Maison Blanche at around 0430 on the morning of 11th November followed by the other 26 at around five minute intervals.

Here are a few words from Lieutenant D. Bentham of B Company about the flight to and time spent at Gibraltar:

> At midnight on a dark November night I took off from an aerodrome in southern England headed for North Africa via Gibraltar. The novelty of gazing at the sea lit by a dim moon soon wore off, and the majority of the men on my aircraft fell asleep.

> We were quite comfortable despite the parachutes, Mae Wests and other pieces of equipment. When I awoke we were well past Lisbon and quite soon the Rock loomed into sight. My aircraft circled round about 6 times and we were bumped about a great deal. The runway looked too small for our heavily laden transport, but we soon taxied in after a good landing. We were given a good breakfast at the barracks and bought cigarettes at 100 for 2/6 and delicacies that we hadn't seen for a long time like oranges and bananas. In the evening I had dinner at the Rock Hotel with David Dobie and Giles Bromley-Martin. That evening we again took off for our destination Maison Blanche aerodrome, just outside Algiers. For a long time we flew low over the sea, then suddenly we saw below us vineyards.

This shorter flight was not without its problems, one of the Dakotas crashed into the sea shortly after take off and caught fire as it struck the water. Lieutenant Bentham again:

> At Maison Blanche we found out that Tiny Crichton, second in command of the company had been killed when his aircraft crashed into the sea taking off at Gibraltar. This was a blow as Tiny was popular with all of us.

Aerial photograph of Bone airfield, taken just before the 3rd Parachute Battalion jumped into it in November 1942. (Airborne Assault Duxford)

A container is packed with guns and ammunition and other equipment prior to an operation. (Imperial War Museum)

Captain J.L. Crichton is now buried at Gibraltar (North) Cemetery grave 2E10. Two other 3rd Battalion men also buried here are Private G. Farrell (although his date of death is given as 9th November 1942) 2E8, and Private H. Refford 2E9.

For the flight to Maison Blanche the American pilots had been warned not to fly over Algiers harbour but one, either by accident or design, did so, and was fired at for his sins. This fire wounded one paratrooper in the arm and also damaged the undercarriage of the aircraft, but this was not apparent until it came in to land at Maison Blanche. The flak damage sustained caused it to crash, which injured another paratrooper aboard. However, by about 0900 on the morning of 11th November the last aircraft had landed and it was now possible for Pine-Coffin to take stock of his position. Of the 33 Dakotas originally loaded in England, two still had to make their way out to North Africa, one had crashed at Gibraltar and one at Maison Blanche, leaving 29 for the forthcoming operation.

Soon after arrival Lieutenant Colonel Pine-Coffin and Major des Voeux set off to try and find General Anderson and get his definite orders. They discovered that he had set up his HQ on a ship in the harbour and on arrival were taken to his quarters and given their operational orders. Neither of the previously advised schemes were going to take place, instead General Anderson advised that he wanted an airfield at Bone seized. He pointed out on a map that as Bone lay about halfway between Algiers and Tunis it would be a great advantage to the 1st Army if they got it before the Germans. He also added that he thought the Germans would find it equally useful if they got there first. It was known the Germans had parachute troops in North Africa and they might be planning an airborne operation there also. He emphasised he only wanted the 3rd Battalion Group to hold the airfield for a short time. He was going to send No 6 Commando by sea to take over defence of the area – in fact, they were boarding landing craft as they were speaking. It was decided that as the American pilots were complete novices in dropping paratroopers and locating drop zones, a night drop was out of the question so take off would be in the early hours of the 12th, at such a time that would get the leading aircraft at Bone for 0830.

Pine-Coffin is said to have commented that it was good to get some definite orders at last. It was hoped the airfield at Bone would be relatively easy for the American pilots to find, being situated about five miles south-east of the harbour. It was felt that if the airfield was deserted then the best plan would be to drop there, but if it appeared that the German paratroopers had got there first, this would be impracticable. There would have to be two alternative drop zones and the final decision could only be made at the last minute. This would complicate things from the airmens' point of view and the CO of the Transport Group, Colonel Dorset, would need to be involved.

An airborne officer checking the apparatus which holds the containers on the aircraft. After release the containers fall away and the 'static line' which is attached to the aircraft assists in the deployment of the parachute. (Imperial War Museum)

Dorset was then consulted and he agreed that it was essential to have some alternative drop zones. He saw no real problem in the unavoidable last minute decision, as he said he intended leading the formation himself. He felt it would be better not to mention to many others the alternatives so as not to cause too much confusion. He said he would tell the pilots to follow him and drop their loads when he did.

The various other administrative details were thrashed out and in the early afternoon the men were briefed.

The plan was as follows... Take off time would be at 0600 on the 12th and the aircraft would fly in line astern, keeping close to the coast line until they came to the harbour at Bone. Here the leading aircraft, hopefully still piloted by Colonel Dorset, would turn south-east towards the airfield and prepare to drop its loads on the airfield itself. All pilots would give the order 'Stand By' to their parachutists when they turned south-eastwards over the harbour, but they would all hang back as much as they could and keep their eye on the leading aircraft. Colonel Dorset intended to fly over the airfield at a low altitude and to size up the situation as he did so. If the Germans were there he would probably be able to spot them and, in any case, they would probably fire at him. If he decided that the airfield was not occupied by the enemy he would circle and drop his parachutists right on it and the other aircraft would come in and do the same. But if he was fired on, or he decided that the Germans were there, he would turn inland and drop his parachutists about one mile inland from the aerodrome. There was no difficulty about selecting a suitable place for dropping as the whole country was flat and free from obstacles and if the party were put down at a point not closer than a mile from the airfield they should get time to form up before they were attacked. Once formed up they could set about capturing the airfield using a normal ground attack.

The possibility of a simultaneous parachute descent by both the British and Germans on the same airfield was one that could not be ignored. However, whilst it might have provided a small amount of excitement in the air and on the ground, it was an eventuality that little planning could be done for. During the briefing it is reported that much use was made of a RAF model of the airfield at Bone based on aerial photographs. Every man was given a chance to study it and to see where he might land and where it was intended to set up the HQ. By 1630 the briefing had been completed and the aircraft had been loaded so there was nothing further to do except rest and wait for take off. There was one final matter to attend to and that was the briefing for the American pilots, with Lieutenant Colonel Pine-Coffin in attendance. Just before the appointed start time it was felt a German aircraft was flying around Maison Blanche. In spite of this the briefing went ahead, even though the hut chosen by Colonel Dorset was far from being properly blacked out. Worse to some observers a distance away, it seemed the pilots were not that punctual as every few seconds a shaft of light seemed to blaze out as the door was opened to admit another late arrival. Fortunately the German aircraft did not seem to be carrying any bombs. Perhaps for Pine-Coffin worse news was to come, as it seemed that the Americans had very little idea of what was expected of them in the dropping of parachutists. It appears most of them were under the impression that provided they reached the rough area of the drop zone, the paratroopers would choose their own moment to jump. They did not understand the significance to the British of the red and green lights. This point and a great number of others were explained to them by Pine-Coffin. It is reported that he then spent a restless night hoping that the points he had tried to put across would be remembered by them in the heat of battle next morning.

Take-off the following morning was achieved without incident and the force flew almost in line astern along the coastline. The first real incident of note occurred at about 0730 when the 'Stand To' order was given as the formation swung inland. It was commented later by Pine-Coffin that he felt this was a bit strange as it was about 45 minutes too early. The No 1's of each stick strained their eyes as they stood in the door for a sight of the aerodrome at Bone. No signs of any aerodrome could be seen and soon the order to 'Stand Down' was given. It appeared that Colonel Dorset had mistaken the harbour of Bougie for that of Bone. As noted later, it was a good job there wasn't an aerodrome in the same relative position as that at Bone as the 3rd Battalion Group would undoubtedly have landed there.

It was almost exactly 0830 when the order to 'Stand To' was given again. This time it was the real thing and the outline of an aerodrome could be seen by those standing in the doors. Various extra items of equipment were being carried that day, which included powerful wireless sets for communication with Algiers and charging engines and petrol to keep them going. These had been packed in what seemed like large laundry baskets. Each aircraft carried two of these with its own parachute attached. When the green light came on it was necessary to push the two laundry baskets out first followed by the stick as rapidly as possible. The rest of the equipment carried under the wings would hopefully be released at about the same time.

Fortunately the drop was accurate and the whole group came down on or close to the aerodrome. However, it was not like a 'training jump' in England. Most men found they had a much heavier landing than they had become accustomed to. This was put down to one of two reasons, firstly the atmosphere in Algeria, which was said to be thinner than that in England, and secondly the fact that most men were carrying far heavier loads than they ever had before. Whatever the reason (probably the latter), thirteen parachuting injuries were sustained. Only one of these was fatal, with the majority of them being broken bones. The one fatal casualty was Sergeant J. Godfrey. who now lies in Bone CWGC Cemetery grave 5B2. It is recorded in the 1st Parachute Squadron RE war diary that their landing injuries were one broken fibula and one case of concussion.

The only opposition was provided by the local Arabs, who set about robbing the party of its equipment before it could be collected in from where it had landed. As one officer later said "The descent from heaven of pure parachute silk by the hundred and containers of valuable equipment was a stronger temptation than the Arabs could resist and they descended on them like locusts and managed to get away with a great deal before the situation could be got under control."

Lieutenant D. Bentham:

> At dawn the following morning we took off for Bone – what would it be like? We had heard stories that the Germans were already there, a grim and disturbing thought. We kept a sharp look out for enemy aircraft, but fortunately saw none. Red light on! I stood in the door and prepared to jump. I saw an airfield. Green on! Out I went closely followed by the others. I looked about when my parachute had opened but could see no sign of Hitler's robots. I had a hard landing but picked myself up and met Giles and walked to our rendezvous with him. We saw

a Senegalese soldier standing in a trench with a rifle in his hand but he just smiled and said "Bonjour" as we passed. At the RV we collected the Company and found that Sergeant Godfrey was dead – shot! He was a nice chap and a good soldier and our first casualty of the operation.

The local population treated us very well and I had more oranges than I could possibly eat. Eventually some Spitfires arrived, and the airfield and docks at Bone were attacked but at little cost to ourselves.

The following are a few comments from Captain Alan Bush about the flight to Bone and the first few minutes after landing:

Soon we were flying east in some sort of formation over the Mediterranean. As the sun rose I could see an armada of aircraft flying at different heights. Our escort weaved this way and that. It was consoling to notice that the ships I could see were sailing eastwards. Soon the warning order was signalled – surely much too early – but we had to hook up and the aircraft suddenly swung inland. As we swung out to sea for another hour's flying, I allowed myself a smug smile and a chuckle, and imagined what I would have said to the pilot had I been sufficiently mobile to stumble to the cockpit.

As we approached Bone harbour, I stood in the door and saw the hills inland towering above the starboard wing. Suddenly the aircraft was lifted and then thrown this way and that, for we had entered a heavy black rainstorm. Rain was slashing hard on the fuselage when on came the red light. As I looked at my stick, each one mouthed that he was ok, so I could concentrate on my immediate problems. Suddenly the green light; down go the switches to release the containers. I throw out my folding bicycle; I follow it immediately and stare at the indistinct ground below me; a tug on my shoulders, now the sky I see and aircraft spilling out their occupants.

When my parachute was fully open I was probably about 400 feet above the ground. Now I had to be quick to recognise what I could remember from the photos I had studied with such care the evening before. I had to pick out the hangar, the runway, the perimeter road and the several farm buildings. Perhaps I was sharper than usual for when standing at the door, I had glimpsed a column of troops moving on the road towards the airfield. I suppose it was apprehension which made me assume that they were wearing German helmets. It was not until after I had landed that I remembered that we could rely on Commando assistance from the sea and that that they were wearing American headgear, or something which looked extraordinarily like German tin hats, especially from the air.

Quickly everything focused and fitted into the memory left to me from what I had looked at some 12 hours before. I could see the runway but I would land a long way from that, the hangar I could not see unless it was nothing more than the two huts I could see, however, the perimeter road I could see clearly. Suddenly I saw something which I had not prepared for, I was drifting towards wire which could be telegraph or electric. For the next few seconds self-preservation was my sole consideration; I decided I needed two hands free, so there goes my Sten gun. So, with a bit a freedom I was able to lift my knees chin high and clear the wires,

> actually landing in a drainage ditch about four feet deep. Having got rid of my parachute I looked round for my stick and could see a few of them moving towards me, and that sight was consoling. Less consoling was the sight of a machine gun, some 50 yards away, manned by French colonial troops. It was a relief to see them pick up their heavy gun and stroll off in file towards the road. I could not believe they knew the nationality of their invaders. But what really mattered was that they were willing to leave the defence of the airfield to us.

One member of the RAMC attached to the 3rd Parachute Battalion was Private G. Thompson. He jumped with this unit in the attack on Bone airfield. As George recalls casualties were light with only one fatal casualty: shot accidentally by his own Sten gun. After the securing of Bone airfield the Battalion moved into the hills, the first stop being Beja, where they dug into rocky ground with great difficulty, and, as George remembers, disturbing a few snakes hibernating for the winter. As George said, it seemed to rain continuously and it was "bloody cold".

Another account of a rough landing comes from Private S. Chamberlain:

> Bone was without doubt, my worst drop ever, twists galore, no time to attempt to kick out my twists. Before I knew it Bone airfield came up to meet me and I had a really heavy landing and was temporarily winded, but eventually I felt a bit better and struggled to the RV.

The aerodrome itself seemed almost deserted and it was certainly not occupied by the Germans, or by anyone else for that matter. After Pine-Coffin made his dispositions accordingly and his men settling into defensive positions, they waited for the men of No 6 Commando to arrive. It was later discovered that they had only just beaten the Germans to it. Soon No 6 Commando arrived to bolster the defences and the two units settled down to defend the area. It can be said that the operation was, on the whole, successful and there can be no doubt that the arrival of British troops helped considerably to raise the morale of the local French population and to convince them that the Allied cause was the correct one to choose. In other ways it was also an example of using airborne forces and their mobility to forestall enemy intentions. Soon a squadron of Spitfires flew into the airfield to provide local air support. However, this did not stop the Germans launching several air raids on the area.

The 3rd Battalion war diary for the time records:

> 12th November 1942 0845 – A Group drop Maison Blanche aerodrome no opposition. Casualties 1 OR killed, 12 ORs injured. A Group came under command No 6 Commando.
> 13th November 1942 – enemy aircraft bombed Bone harbour.
> 14th November 1942 1045 – 2 German fighters machine-gunned Bone aerodrome.
> 15th November 1942 – enemy aircraft bomb Bone aerodrome, no casualties to A Group.
> 16th November 1942 – enemy aircraft machine gun Bone aerodrome. Three aircraft shot down by Spitfires.

17th November 1942 1200 onwards – enemy commence heavy bombing Bone aerodrome and harbour. A Group ordered to return to Algiers by train.
17th November 1942 2300 – A Group entrain at Bone station.
19th November 1942 – A Group arrive at Maison Blanche station and proceed to billets near aerodrome, personnel of two missing aircraft rejoin A Group.

To end this brief account of the Bone operation here are some comments from Captain Alan Bush about their time on the ground in and around the aerodrome:

> The stick assembled quickly and I retrieved my folding bicycle and all the containers except one, which unfortunately mainly contained the stick's rations for two or three days. That container, I learnt later, had fallen off from its bomb rack on take-off. I suppose my pilot would have returned my smug smile if we had ever met again to discuss the take-off! One thing I learnt, and it was a lesson I was to relearn soon, was that if you keep your eye on your rations in transit you won't lose them. We had hit the ground a considerable distance from the rest of the force, and to reach them I had to pass through farmhouses and their adjoining out buildings. Our progress, therefore, was tactical, and what we then described as evil-looking natives and the French military were kept covered by our weapons. Eventually I met up with my Company Commander, who immediately despatched me to contact the Commandos. I went on my folding bicycle and met them; the machine worked perfectly though laboriously. It was a good contact to make so soon after the drop, for, as they said, they had a lovely view of it, and gave me a general location of several containers which had left aircraft between Bone and the airfield. When I returned to HQ, I was informed that some of these contained wireless sets, medical supplies and some important supporting arms, and that it was vital to retrieve these. 'Go and get them' I was told. But how to bring these heavy brutes in without transport?
>
> Fortunately some French troops who had been defending the airfield were still assembling from its remoter parts to be transported to their barracks in town by truck. A truck and its driver were parked not far from our temporary HQ, and I had no trouble in commandeering this with its driver. The driver appeared delighted to join me in this part of my duties. His excitement certainly exceeded mine, and I suspect he regarded the new role he was playing as a welcome addition to whatever importance he had in his locality. After collecting several of the missing containers, I was overjoyed with my success until the driver made known to me, by signs more than language, that he was running out of petrol, and apparently it was only in Bone, at the barracks, that he could obtain more. To finish my job I needed petrol, and so I sat beside him in the truck, leaving the few men I had to guard the containers we had found. I suspected my reception would be at best lukewarm. What right had I to demand a few gallons of their precious 'essence'? I felt, however, I had a friend in the driver, who, I slowly realised, was a man of real character.
>
> The journey through the town was infrequently amusing but usually terrifying. My driver had not yet accustomed himself to his new importance, but was determined that all and sundry should be aware of it. He drove at frightening speed, blowing his horn incessantly and hurling abuse in what I suppose was Arabic at any human or animal who dared to cross his path. All conceded to him the right

of way; the alternative would have resulted in grave physical harm; the citizens took off like frightened birds. In no time we entered the gates of the barracks to be greeted by much commotion and excitement.

My driver went to organise petrol, leaving me on a barrack square, surrounded by soldiers of every rank. They examined me and each bit of my equipment with chattering curiosity. Luckily I had come by a couple of American grenades – pineapples – and I also carried a.45 revolver, so it was easy to give the impression that I was American without having to state the fact or deny it. I had an awareness of the unpopularity of the British to these people, who regarded Giraud as a national hero and de Gaulle as a traitor. Soon I was sitting at a table, brought out from the Guard Room, and was being offered wine. I tasted it and disliked it intensely, but for the sake of good manners, sipped at it, with gestures expressing enjoyment until the return of my driver. Then the mad race through the town was repeated as we went in search of the lost containers. The rest of this day I spent on this task, but it was boring for my driver, for his importance was being observed by but a few. Just before dusk we shook hands and went our ways, he the man with the triumph, and yet I felt I had not done too badly. Most of the equipment had been recovered, but most parachutes and bulk rations had been seized by the natives.

Our HQ was an uninhabited farm just off the perimeter road of the airfield. With us lived the Commando officers; it was our joint responsibility to hold the airfield until the infantry passed through us or until aircraft could operate from it with adequate ground protection. I suppose we stayed here for about a week, and certain events remain in my memory; a visit by an 'American Consul', though why he came I have no idea; a visit by Randolph Churchill, who was probably at that time a war correspondent. Also Ju 88s on recce flights, flying over the airfield at ground level at dawn, our fighters flying in to land at last light one evening, strafing and bombing by German aircraft with our fighters taking off for safety as they were being machine gunned from the air. But, sometimes, when it was the harbour or the town being attacked, we sat back and watched the spectacle.

The difficulties of supply for any advanced force were obvious to all when we witnessed the arrival of petrol for the fighter squadron on the airfield. It came in by air, carried in by our old friends, the Dakotas. A fleet of these escorted by Lightnings, arrived at dusk one evening. There was just sufficient light to get the transports down safely on what was little more than an airstrip. When it was the escort's turn to land it was dark. A small flare was placed at one end of the runway and a Dakota shone its lights down it from the other end. A very tricky job was accomplished without incident. The Spitfire pilots, our messing companions, watched the operation, and were unanimous in their opinion that they had witnesses some of the best piloting of fighter aircraft they had ever seen.

We ourselves admired also the British pilots. They served as if inspired by the memory of at least one of their former, famous commanders. By nightfall each day they were dead tired and would enter a very uncomfortable and untidy mess for a couple of glasses of rough wine before going to kip. Some things come to mind, the pilot who walked back to the airfield covered in burns after being shot down; the slaughter of 4 Me 109s who were caught napping in their over-confidence; a Spitfire flying too steadily behind a Ju 88 and being shot down by the rear gunner. Also, a

Heinkel with full bomb load crashing on the airfield. The work of that squadron, the devotion and modesty of its members will live long in the memory of those who saw it operate in difficult conditions. When we left Bone we were depressed to see so few of these men and their machines still in operation.

Once the infantry were through to us we were withdrawn to return to Algiers. We assumed we were to prepare for another parachuting operation. I was made responsible for assembling rations for the train journey. Why should an inexperienced and very ordinary officer be allocated that sort of Q job? Our Q staff were travelling by sea, and any 2 i/c of a company was given the Q jobs. At Bone I must have done my job well for somehow I secured double rations for the journey and without the slightest hint of foul play. The extra rations simply appeared. I did not return them. The surplus added a little to our daily ration for several days to come. The enemy gave us a splendid farewell. As we were about to board the train, several Junkers came in fast and low to bomb the railway station. But we were lively on our feet and escaped any serious personal damage; we needed little warning to move very fast.

5

Souk-el-Arba, November 1942

While the 3rd Battalion Group was cutting its teeth and taking part in the largest British parachute operation of the war so far the rest of the Brigade was catching up and arrived off the coast of Algeria on 12th November 1942.

The Brigade disembarked at Algiers and marched out of the town towards an airfield known as Maison Blanche. They were not destined to reach here the first night and as dusk was falling they were directed off the road into what seemed like a large park. The men were told to bivouac here for the night. One officer set up his *basha* and awoke next morning to find outside a large bunch of bananas. He was Captain V. Coxen, the 2 i/c of T Company of the 1st Parachute Battalion, and later commented,

> I saw over my head a huge bunch of bananas. I remember saying to myself this is not so bad. I can stand his sort of country. I think they were the only bunch of bananas that grew in North Africa. We had been billeted in the botanical gardens.

Men of the 1st Parachute Brigade marching away from the docks at Algiers, having just arrived on troopships from the UK on 21st November 1942. (Airborne Assault Duxford)

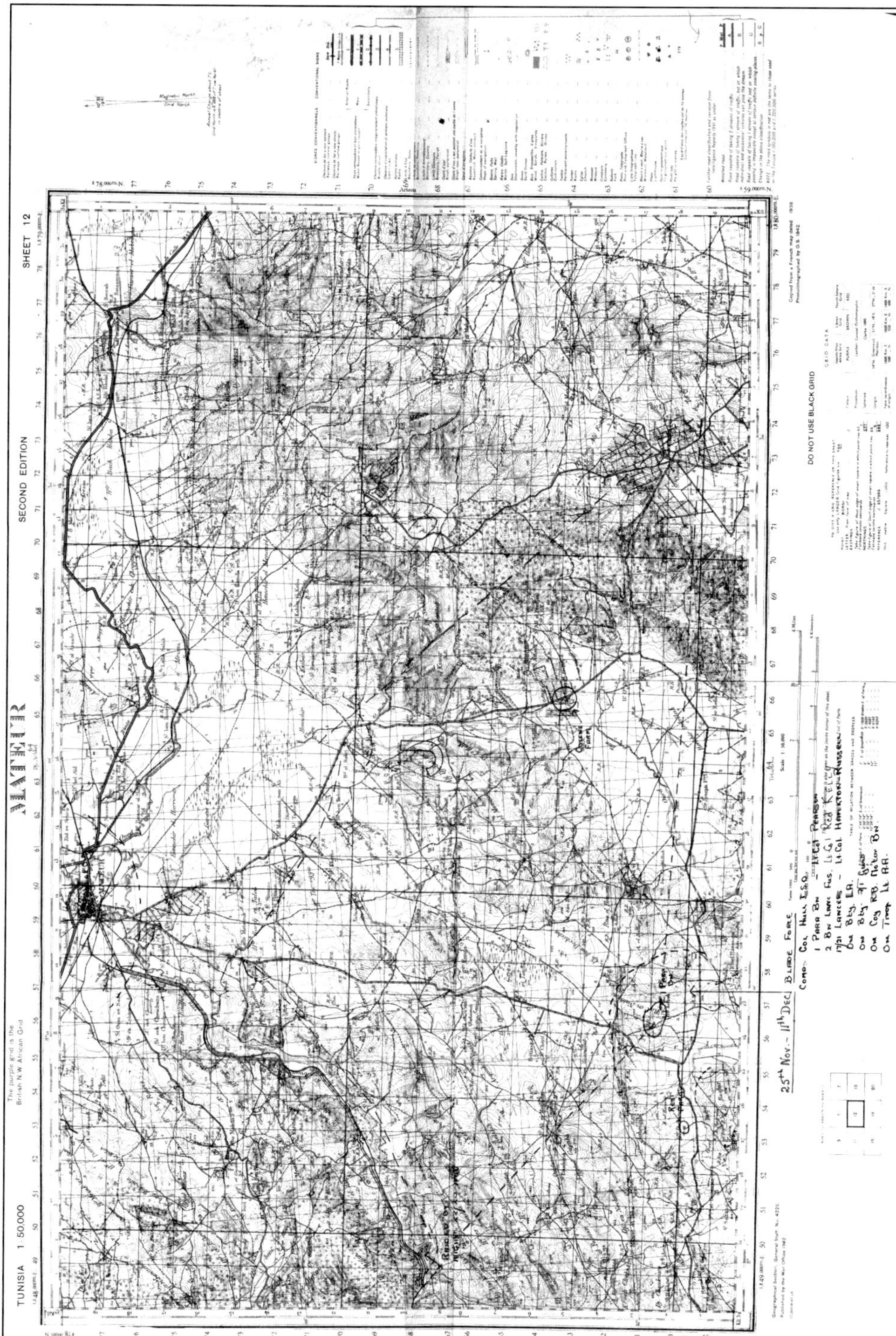

Map of the Mateur area used by Lieutenant Colonel A. Pearson in November 1942 including his handwritten notes (James Macrae)

There were several heavy rainstorms during the night and the following morning the 1st Battalion moved to Maison Blanche, where they were given a 48 hours warning order for an airborne operation. You may recall that their original objective during the sea transit had been El Aouina airfield near Tunis. This had been cancelled and they had been told to plan for an alternative airfield at Setif. Perhaps now poor prior planning and preparation with regard to this new arm came to the fore. The Brigade had no transport and was now expected to move itself and all its heavy equipment to the airfield at Maison Blanche about 12 miles away. Whilst this distance would not be a problem for the men with personal loads, to bring the heavy items on foot was somewhat impracticable. So they were given about 10 commandeered French trucks, minus drivers, trucks that had definitely seen better days! There was also a lack of labour at the port and so the Brigade was expected to unload the ships themselves.

The battalion 2 i/c Major A Pearson:

> On 12th November we landed at Algiers and I had to remain at the docks to supervise the unloading of stores and parachutes. The parachutes were in sealed waterproof containers, which was a good thing as a number fell into the dock and had to rescued by a diver at 500 francs a go. I thought this was a good bargain and money well spent, but unfortunately for me, Allied Forces HQ thought differently and refused to pay because I had no authority to employ a diver.

A wet or damp parachute is not good news and likely to lead to severe difficulties if used. To prevent this happening a small section of RAF personnel under the command of Flight Lieutenant Hare had travelled out with the Brigade to look after the parachutes. The parachutes themselves had travelled out from England packed in crates of 12, wrapped in greased paper lined with barrage balloon fabric.

Soon after arrival in Algeria news arrived of another proposed airborne operation. This time it had been decided to use the 1st Parachute Battalion, under the command of Lieutenant Colonel Hill. He was warned to prepare for an operation in 24 hours' time in the Beja area, about 50 miles west of Tunis. Lieutenant Colonel Hill:

> After arrival at Maison Blanche I was sent for and given my new orders by General Anderson. I thought he was probably a good general, but he was a crusty old boy who didn't know anything about parachute troops and didn't like what he had heard about them. I think he was pleased to get rid of us. He gave me very clear orders. The first one was to seize the key road junctions at Beja in Tunisia some 400 miles to the east of where the British Army was forming up near Algiers. The second was to harry the enemy wherever we could find them; and third, and most important of all, was to bring the French Army in on our side. We also had to see if Souk-el-Arba, which was about 20 miles from Beja, was suitable as an airlanding strip for fighter aircraft.

It was a very 'much come as you are party', aerial photographs of the proposed area of operations were non-existent and it is recorded that Colonel Hill used a quarter of an inch motoring map as the main planning tool. The 1st Parachute Battalion was to be accompanied by some medics and sappers, these being No 1 Section of 16 PFA under

Men of the 1st Parachute Battalion *en route* to Souk-el-Arba on 16th November 1942. Note that the man in the right foreground is wearing some sort of knee-pads. (Imperial War Museum)

the command of Lieutenant D. Wright. They were also supported by a surgical team, led by Lieutenant C. Rob. A Troop of the 1st Parachute Squadron RE, commanded by Captain P. Geary, were the integral sapper support to the 1st Parachute Battalion. By around 0500 on 15th November all the necessary packing and loading into the Dakotas had been completed at Maison Blanche. It is reported that not all the equipment had arrived at the airfield until about 1630 on the previous day and this then had to be sorted out and packed into containers.

The aircraft for this operation were again provided by 64th Troop Carrier Squadron (TCS) of the 51st US Troop Carrier Group (TCG) and numbered 32 under the command of Colonel Dorset. This was not enough aircraft to take the whole group and a company had to be left behind to hopefully follow on later. Those that did go took off at about 0730 on 15th November 1942. Colonel Hill:

> As we were taxiing out I looked out of the pilots window and was horrified to see about 20 soldiers, a parachute in one hand and a weapon in the other running after Dakotas. In many cases they successfully managed to stow away.

Due to the inexperience of the American pilots in dropping paratroopers, Hill had decided to ask Colonel Dorset if he could sit in the cockpit with him. When they decided they had located the best DZ in the vicinity of Souk-el-Arba, he would go back and hook

Men of the 1st Parachute Battalion emplaning at Maison Blanche for the drop at Souk-el-Arba. (Airborne Assault Duxford)

up and jump. This would be the signal for the rest of the Battalion, hopefully following in line astern also to jump.

Major Pearson:

> I was responsible for the packing and loading of containers on the aircraft. This was not completed till 0500 hours on the 15th. The commanding officer, James Hill, decided that we should not go on the first lift. This was disappointing but sensible. The Battalion took off and I went for a sleep. I was no sooner asleep when I was wakened to be told the Battalion was returning. Bad weather on the route had caused them to return.

Once on the ground, news of their return spread and Colonel Hill was instructed to report to General Anderson. He was furious at the unit's return and did little, if anything, to conceal his dislike of paratroopers in general. He instructed Hill that in the event of bad weather interfering again on the following day, he was to land as near to the enemy as possible. Hill decided that in this event his unit would drop on the sandy plains to the north of the road to Souk-el-Arba.

At 1100 the following morning the 1st Battalion Group took off again with much the same arrangements. Their role had been altered slightly, in that Hill's HQ was now to be set up in Beja and to send out patrols on an 'advance to contact' basis. This would hopefully secure the Souk-el-Khemis/Souk-el-Arba plain for use by the RAF. It was expected that once on the ground they would have to commandeer or capture transport. Just as on the Bone operation, Colonel Hill would have to choose a suitable DZ from the air. Once in the area Hill found what he was looking for and jumped out near Souk-el-

2.00 p.m. November 16th 1942, collecting arms and ammunition from containers after dropping. Getting ready to surround the town. (Airborne Assault Duxford)

A picture taken by an unknown member of the 1st Parachute Battalion on the way to Souk-el Arba, 16th November 1942. (Airborne Assault Duxford)

Arba. Again, luckily, there was no opposition on the ground from either the French or Germans. The drop was highly successful, with only one fatal landing casualty and five other casualties. The one fatality was Private W. Webster, who unfortunately drifted into some power cables and was killed. He is now buried at Medjez-el-Bab CWGC Cemetery grave 12B2. Again it was a race between the 1st Battalion men and the locals as to who would get to the containers first. It is reported that about 90% were successfully collected.

Major Pearson and a few others were left behind at Beja to act as a salvage party, it being stressed to them that the parachutes were vital and needed to be got back to Algiers as soon as possible. Meanwhile some local vehicles were commandeered to give some much-needed mobility; it is recorded that some of them used charcoal for fuel. Sergeant Eric Seal:

The station at Oued Zarga as it was in November 1942. (Airborne Assault Duxford)

For our move from Souk-el-Arba we were to use some old French producer-gas-burning charabancs, operating on charcoal. We hoped they would last the journey. In our company, we had two brothers, both sergeants, Ted and Tony Baxter. As we lined up for our move Tony put his Sten gun between his knees to adjust his pack, but it fell to the ground and discharged a number of rounds into the legs of the nearest soldiers. Not a great start.

L/Corporal Reg Curtis:

It was dark when we arrived just outside Beja. Getting out of the buses, the Battalion spread out, kipping down after posting sentries. The night was very cold, being spent among the rocks and sandy waste. When morning came I saw a vast area of wilderness stretching out around me. However, I was soon to get used to this over the coming months.

Whilst the majority of the Battalion was heading in their commandeered buses to Beja, Major Pearson was left behind with a small salvage party collecting and looking after the very valuable parachutes, although certain members of the 1st Battalion have recounted that some locals did manage to steal a few. On the following day Major Pearson and the others attended the funeral of Private Webster, he being accorded the appointment of chief mourner, which meant he ended up shaking the hands of about 500 people, as it seemed nearly all the population of Souk-el-Arba turned up for the funeral. After this he commandeered a railway engine and two cars, loaded the parachutes and

A picture of two of the Dakotas taking the 1st Parachute Battalion to Souk-el-Arba over the Mediterranean on 16th November 1942. (Imperial War Museum)

other stores that couldn't be fitted into the previous days convoy and caught up with the Battalion at Beja.

Lieutenant Colonel Hill:

> I left orders for the Battalion to stop at the top of a hill overlooking Beja and I went down into the town with Major des Voeux, our liaison officer, to interview General Barre, the French area commander. The French had a great inferiority about German armour and so I was cross-examined as to what weapons we had to deal with German tanks. I told him in the most glowing terms of the armoured divisions that were rushing to our aid and of our very latest, secret type of anti-tank mortars. I asked how many men he had holding the junctions. He told me had a regiment of 2,500 men. Quite obviously we could not take over in broad daylight and my small number of around 500 would be exposed.

The Germans had warned the French that severe action would be taken against them if the British were allowed to enter and occupy Beja. However, Hill had his orders and to convince the French that letting the paratroopers into Beja would not be a problem Hill used some underhand tactics. It was agreed that the 1st Parachute Battalion would take over from the two French battalions. To avoid exposing his lack of numbers, Hill agreed that he would take over at dusk on 17th November, and during the day Hill marched the Battalion through the town twice, once in helmets and once wearing berets, well spread out in order to disguise the actual numbers he had.

L/Corporal G. Stanners of No 1 Section 16 PFA, attached to the 1st Battalion, remembers being the trolley man on this occasion, pushing the barrow laden with medical supplies covered by a groundsheet on the first journey. The trolley was altered on the second trip by using a Thomas Splint to convert the trolley into the new airborne anti-tank weapon, or so the CO of the 1st Battalion told the local French Garrison Commander! The garrison school was requisitioned and converted into a makeshift twenty-bed hospital. Later the French Garrison's MO made arrangements for the use of the towns Civil Hospital and Lieutenants Rob and Wright and three orderlies set up shop leaving the rest at the 'Military Hospital'.

This bluff succeeded and the French let the British take over, but true to their word, when news got out the Germans sent bombers to attack Beja. This attack took place on 20th November, leaving a large number of wounded civilians. Lieutenant Rob performed over 150 operations with Lieutenant Wright acting as anaesthetist. Whilst working during this period a bomb fell outside the building wounding Lieutenant Rob. He suffered a fracture of the left tibia and kneecap. In spite of his injuries he carried on working and the next day, after operating on about another twenty casualties, donated a pint of his own blood as the supply of plasma was exhausted. For his efforts during this period Lieutenant Rob was awarded the Military Cross. It has been said that Lieutenant Rob's results as a surgeon were the best ever by a surgeon in a parachute unit. It may be that his prior experience as a surgeon at St. Thomas' Hospital in London during the Blitz gave him a head start in dealing with traumatic injuries.

The schoolhouse at Beja used as a makeshift hospital by 16 Parachute Field Ambulance in December 1942. (N. Cherry)

Battalion HQ was set up in a local abattoir and Lieutenant Clements was sent by train to Algiers with the recovered parachutes. Additionally it was learnt from the French that a patrol of German armoured vehicles used to visit the French Garrison at Sidi N'Sir station at about 1100 every day, have a smoke and then return back to Bizerta. After some negotiation the French agreed to let some British troops through their lines. As the unit war diary states, "Transport was to lift one company (S Company) to harass the enemy lines of communication running from Mateur to Sidi N'Sir. This company moved off at 1200 hours under Major Cleasby-Thompson to what proved to be the initial battle of the Tunisian campaign."

A brief account for now of what happened to S Company is as follows. The company moved out and spent the night a farmhouse near Sidi N'Sir. As previously advised the following morning the German patrol did appear and consisted of three armoured cars and three scout cars. The convoy was allowed to go past the ambush site with just a few shots fired at it, and reach the French post. Some minutes later, presumably having exchanged whatever was available, the convoy retraced its steps. In the interim anti-tank mines had been laid across the road, the first vehicle passing over without incident, but the second set one of them off. This was the signal to spring the ambush and close on the enemy. Some vehicles were destroyed at close quarters with grenades and several enemy killed. There were no fatal casualties in S Company.

Sergeant Eric Seal:

> On the morning of 17th my platoon and another, both of S Company, and a few sappers, together with a three-inch mortar team, embussed and headed for Sidi N'Sir, which I thought was the last French outpost before Tunis. Our orders were, I think, to take some German prisoners. When we arrived it appeared to be well

The railway station at Sidi N'Sir in a somewhat dilapidated condition. (James Macrae)

The area of the ambush site at Sidi N'Sir in November 1942. (James Macrae)

guarded by native troops led by French officers. We then pushed forward. I say pushed because of the three buses, two broke down, and we had to do a lot of pushing! After an uphill struggle we arrived at a farm, and after a cup of tea we rested.

In the early hours of the morning I woke to the sound of Sten gun fire, looked over a wall and there, about 150 yards away, on the Sidi N'Sir road, was a convoy of about six German armoured vehicles heading towards the French post. We let them pass. I think it was a good thing the buses had broken down because the farm we had stopped in was in an ideal position for an ambush. Our plan was for the sappers to string out their Hawkins grenades across the road; a number of men would go under a viaduct with Gammon bombs and we would hide among the rocks with Sergeant Tucker and his mortar. I thought Major Cleasby-Thompson was in rather a vulnerable spot behind a small haystack in the open ground.

It seemed rather a long nail-biting time for the return of the convoy, then suddenly they burst into view. The sappers were great; the Hawkins grenades were pulled across the road and one of the cars went up with a bang. The Germans tried to get out and were shot by the REs. All hell then was let loose as we opened up with Brens and rifles. The Gammon bombers now went forward and threw their bombs. The armoured cars seemed to be blowing up left, right and centre, but the last two proved to be very, very dangerous, especially the larger armoured one. It suddenly ventured onto the open ground which we had realised was our most vulnerable point and really opened up on us. Our area made it doubly dangerous with splinters of rock flying everywhere, one of which I got smack in the face. As it got closer towards us, Sergeant Tucker opened up with his mortar, which luckily bought it to a halt. After a short, but exciting battle, we finished up with three heavy armoured cars and two light scout cars out of action, one captured intact and a number of prisoners. We also captured, from these vehicles, the order of battle for the German forces in Tunis.

Meanwhile on the 18th November, after Colonel Hill had attended several conferences, it was learnt that the Germans were holding a line along a river bank to the east of Medjez-el-Bab with a force of around 300 men. It was apparent it was some sort of Mexican stand-off in this area, with the Germans making no attempt to cross the river and the French saying they would not open fire on the Germans unless fired upon by them. Fortunately reinforcements from the 1st Army turned up in the shape of a squadron of armoured vehicles from the Derbyshire Yeomanry under the command of a Major Inglefield and they were ordered forward to investigate the position east of Medjez. Later a platoon under the command of Lieutenant Wandless was also sent to the area. He was told that his job was to try and provoke the Germans into opening fire and so get the French to enter into a 'shooting war' proper.

Due to actions like this the Germans were dissuaded from advancing westwards through and past Medjez until the night of 19th /20th November by which time the paratroopers and newly Allied French troops and advance elements from the 1st Army had dug-in fairly strongly around Oued Zarga. This was situated on the main road between Beja and Medjez, roughly halfway between the two places. The 1st Parachute Battalion sent out many fighting patrols and reports from some of these are contained in appendices later. It was these patrols, however, that kept the Germans uncertain of the exact positions of the British and probably prevented any major advances by them. The main aim had, of course, to keep this plain clear for use as an air base and this was achieved by the paratroopers and later by Blade Force (of which they became a part) and the 78th Division, when they arrived.

Perhaps one of the more significant and sadder incidents that involved the 1st Battalion whilst they were in the Beja area occurred on the night of 23rd/24th November 1942. Early in the day a discharged French naval sailor provided information that an Italian force of about 300 men supported by about 20 tanks used to spend the night on a hill known as Gué Hill to the north east of Beja. He further stated that they did not normally put out much in the way of guards or patrols. Lieutenant Colonel Hill thought that they needed to be paid a visit and later the GOC of the 78th Division General Eveleigh gave permission for this 'raid' to be carried out. Hill's forces consisted of his unit less R Company and a detachment of Senegalese troops. At 1500 Hill held an O Group and Zero Hour was set for 0300 the following morning, with the Battalion leaving at 1800. Hill's plan called for two platoons to attack from the west (from T Company and a composite platoon made up of Battalion HQ personnel), another platoon from T Company to attack from the south. Two platoons from S Company together with the CO and his HQ to attack from the east. The remaining platoon of S Company was to move to the east of the hill and to attack some anti-aircraft guns which were reported to be on some high ground north-west of the main position. The accompanying mortars were to put down a barrage from Zero to Zero + 4 from a position by the bridge south of the river. The accompanying sappers from the 1st Parachute Squadron RE were to mine the road to the east of the position. The Senegalese were to assist by carrying up mortar bombs and then to go into reserve. The final element of the group consisted of No 1

Section of 16 PFA RAMC commanded by Lieutenant D. Wright. After receiving what treatment they could, any serious casualties would have to be got back to Beja where the Field Surgical Team was still positioned. The Battalion moved in single file guided by the French sailor, when they were about half a mile from the enemy position they split up into their relative assault groups and were all in position by about Z – 20.

The Adjutant of the 1st Battalion Captain M. Whitelock:

> That night, Battalion HQ, the Mortar Platoon, a party of sappers, two rifle companies and a contingent of Senegalese set out along the valley. In bright moonlight the mountains on either side seemed deserted, the only sound the barking of dogs. We crept along a rough path in single file. James Hill's and my batman acting as scouts, followed by James and I, the local informer and the remainder of the force. When we had gone about six miles we could see, in the moonlight, the hulls of the tanks. Leaving Alastair Pearson with the mortars and a company, James and I and the sappers crept on around the enemy. We tried to get the sappers to the rear of the position to mine the track thus hindering their retreat.

However, as the hill was approached by the Sappers one of the anti-tank mines exploded, which set off all the other mines killing the entire party. Obviously any element of surprise was now lost and enemy tracer flew through the darkness. What caused the first explosion will probably never be known but it set others off in sympathetic explosions. The 1st Parachute Squadron RE war diary records for 24th November 1942, "1st Parachute Battalion reported Captain P. Geary and 1 OR killed, also Lieutenants G. White and J. Holland with 15 ORs missing." No details of the action were given.

Gué Hill from the north-east showing the old road. (James Macrae)

Looking in an easterly direction from the summit of Gué Hill. (James Macrae)

From the CWGC records I have found the following 18 Royal Engineers who all have a date of death of 24th November 1942 and have no known grave and are therefore commemorated on the Medjez-el-Bab Memorial to the Missing:

Sapper A. Calcott
Sapper J. Elvidge
Captain P. Geary
L/Corporal E. Harris
L/Corporal F. Hill
Driver J. Hillings
Lieutenant J. Holland
L/Corporal F. Hornsby
L/Corporal N. Manning
Corporal R. Mercer
Sapper J. Mitchell
Sapper V. Mitchell
Sapper L. Moat
L/Sergeant W. Muir
Sapper J. Rickelton
L/Sergeant L. Sayer
Sapper F. Stanmore
Lieutenant G. White

Looking west from the base of Gué Hill showing the old and new roads. (James Macrae)

In spite of this setback the operation still had to continue and S and T Companies put in an assault on their nominated objectives. The hill was found to be held by a mixture of German and Italian troops. Lieutenant Colonel Hill saw that were there only three Italian light tanks on the hill and decided to take care of them himself accompanied by the Adjutant and a few soldiers.

Approaching the first tank he took out his service pistol and thrust it through an open port hole and fired a single shot in the first tank, the Italian crew inside immediately surrendered. He then went to the second tank and tapped on the closed turret with the same result... immediate surrender. Thinking he was on a roll, he approached the third tank expecting surrender, only to be faced with a German tank crew who emerged firing their personal weapons and throwing grenades. Hill dispensed with the crew fairly quickly, but before doing so received three gunshot wounds to the chest. His Adjutant, Captain Whitelock, received shrapnel wounds to his chest.

For this action Hill received his first Distinguished Service Order. His citation reads:

> For inspiring leadership and undaunted courage. This officer who led his Battalion after a flight of some 400 miles, and a parachute drop, displayed on every occasion conspicuous gallantry under heavy enemy fire. Leading his Battalion in raids against enemy AFVs he personally destroyed at least two and was mainly responsible for the successful results achieved. In a raid on an enemy post he led his Battalion forward under heavy machine gun fire and by his utter disregard of personal danger, and by his brilliant handling, was successful in entirely destroying the post and capturing a number of prisoners. This leadership and courage was an inspiration not only to his own troops but also to the French who recognised his gallantry by the award of

the *Legion d'Honneur*. On one occasion although severely wounded he continued to command his battalion until the successful completion of the operation.

Sergeant Eric Seal:

Our next attack at Gué was tough; a lot of killing went on and a lot of prisoners were taken. The adrenaline was going and I had to stop one of my chaps who was trying to bayonet a poor little Italian who wanted to surrender. We were then moved back along the railway line where we saw some tents. In case there were Germans I shouted', "Hande hoch!" but there was no reply so I ordered shots to be fired through the tents. Out came a few screaming Arabs who had been doing a bit of looting. During this period a number of wounded were being brought along the railway line, including the CO and the Adjutant. They looked rather a mess at this time and were unconscious. I then followed on helping to push along some of the lads who were wounded, and at Sidi N'Sir we got a welcome cup of coffee and some vinegar bread.

Lieutenant Wright, who had been collecting the Battalion's wounded at the RAP, took these two seriously wounded officers back to Beja. First they were evacuated on a captured Italian motor tricycle and travelled along a railway track. This was very rough going for about four miles until a set of bogey wheels was discovered. The stretchers were laid on this and pushed along by Lieutenant Wright, the CO's batman and about six RAMC personnel. Later still a donkey was found to pull the bogey until a station was reached and they were transferred to a car to move them quickly back to the hospital

The railway line near Gué Hill along which casualties were moved. (James Macrae)

where Lieutenant Rob performed emergency operations which saved the lives of these two officers.

Lieutenant Colonel Hill:

> Our immediate objective was a small hill called Gué. It was a moonlit night and you could see the stars. We were endeavouring to keep as quiet as possible, but every farmhouse we came to had a bloody dog that barked. However, we got to the foot of the hill undetected. I sent our excellent Royal Engineer troops, under Captain Geary, round to the back of the hill to mine the road leading to it, so if any armour tried to escape they would be blown up. As we got ready to attack three loud explosions shook the air. The sappers had been carrying their Hawkins anti-tank mines in sandbags ready to lay them. Somehow, one of them had accidentally exploded and set off the rest. I think they were all killed.
>
> The Germans opened up at once. Heavy machine gun fire was coming from a conical hill with a gradient of one in three. The assault went straight in and the two platoons swarmed the stone wall to finish off the enemy with bayonets. Sitting where I was I could see three tanks which were firing rather *ad lib* down the hill. I thought this was too good to be true, we must do something about it. So I got hold of two or three chaps and went up the side of the hill where we could see the first of these tanks which was blazing away. It was rather a small tank, but it was dug in. Most armoured vehicles have a little round hole which they can open up to peep through. I put my revolver into the hole and pulled the trigger and of course the bullet went whee-e-e-e all the round the inside of the turret. Up went the hatch of the tank and out came a chap shouting "Italiano, Italiano!" This seemed to good to be true. That was the first tank dealt with. We went up to the next tank. I put my revolver in and again the same thing – "Italiano, Italiano!" I guess I was now feeling very lucky. We went up to the third tank and tried the same thing again. Everything looked as if it was working all right, but instead of an Italian, out came a great big German. He was a much tougher chap. He came out with his hands up and I saw that he had a pistol in his right hand. As he jumped down, he opened fire at me. One bullet hit me in the middle of my chest and two others in the neck and arm and I went down.

Captain Miles Whitelock:

> As we neared the top of the hill, James (Hill) sent me to give a message to the company commander behind us. I rejoined James just as the fun started. He advanced on the first tank, pushed his pistol through a port in the side and fired, to the consternation of the crew, who promptly surrendered. He rapped with his stick on the turret of the second tank, whose crew also surrendered. As he rapped on the third tank, the occupants came out firing and throwing grenades. James was shot three times through the chest and a grenade exploded at my feet. Shrapnel went through my nose, into my head, arms and legs; we were both in a pretty poor way.
>
> James and I were carried down Gué Hill to the railway line. We were laid on a motorcycle and sidecar combination and pushed slowly down the line to Beja, the Senegalese doing most of the pushing. Halfway back at dawn, we were visited

by Messerschmitts and machine-gunned. Mercifully they missed. But I felt very isolated, the medical staff and the Senegalese wisely having dived for cover. At Beja we were operated on by a parachute surgical team, who saved our lives.

The rest of the Battalion's wounded were evacuated under arrangements made by Staff Sergeant Clegg. These arrangements started with a ten mile carry to reach transport, where they could then be transported to the hospital. Fortunately there were only thirteen casualties who required evacuation. Geoff Stanners remembers on one of these trips staggering with a casualty on a stretcher along with his mate Don Smith; they had started off in the dark and it was now becoming light when out of the gloom dived a Spitfire. Fortunately the men were carrying yellow Celanese recognition triangles and waved these. The pilot pulled out of his dive and waggled his wings and then circled the medics for about an hour providing cover, and then he disappeared, probably running low on fuel. Geoff remembers that about twenty minutes later another Spitfire appeared, and as he said "they gave us a great lift as it felt as if we were being helped". The casualty and medics safely reached the transport point.

The 1st Battalion's 2 i/c now took over command and tidied up the situation, all in all it was probably a score draw in modern day speak. A number of tanks had been destroyed and around 25 Germans and Italians were taken prisoner but around 10% casualties had been suffered. It is believed the 1st Parachute Battalion suffered six fatal casualties as a result of the attack on Gué Hill. These being as follows:

Private A. Cowley 24th November 1942 Medjez-el-Bab CWGC Cemetery 4B17
Private J. Higgins 24th November 1942 NKG Medjez-el-Bab Memorial to the Missing
Captain J. Stewart 24th November 1942 NKG Medjez-el-Bab Memorial to the Missing
Private R. Stirling 24th November 1942 Medjez-el-Bab CWGC Cemetery 4B19
Private D. Watton 24th November 1942 Medjez-el-Bab CWGC Cemetery 4D11
Sergeant A. Ellis 25th November 1942 Medjez-el-Bab CWGC Cemetery 5E18

Upon arrival back at Beja Pearson reported to Colonel Hull at Blade Force HQ. Major Cleasby-Thompson was appointed as the new 2 i/c and they got orders to protect the 17/21 Lancers' tank harbour on the Sidi N'Sir/Mateur road. As Pearson later commented he was advised that he was to move by day – the 26th – with air cover provided and be in position by sunset. The only air cover that arrived was German and caused several casualties on the way. Eight men, apparently all from S Company, were killed and they were as follows together with their burial or commemoration details:

Private T. Forkin Beja 1J5
L/Corporal E. Glyde Beja 1J6
Private G. Johnston Beja 1J4
L/Corporal R. Jones Beja 1K2

Private W. Painting Medjez-el-Bab Memorial to the Missing
Private S. Playfair Medjez-el-Bab Memorial to the Missing
Private M. Reid Medjez-el-Bab Memorial to the Missing
Private H. White Medjez-el-Bab Memorial to the Missing

An additional 12 men were wounded and they were taken by ambulance straight back to Beja. On arrival in their area the Battalion took up position at a place known as Kowshok Farm. Captain Coxen led a fighting patrol and scouted a farm, which afterwards became known as Coxen's Farm, about three miles from the Battalion position. He reported it was unoccupied except by animals which were all staggering around drunk. The farm had been attacked and the wine vats holed so that the place was swimming in red wine. Apparently there was a massive drunken bull, so he was persuaded to head in the direction of the enemy. Eventually it became a base for patrolling, activities which seemed to inflict quite a lot of casualties on the enemy.

On the 28th November the 2nd Battalion Lancashire Fusiliers arrived in the area and Pearson came to an agreement that they could work by day and the paratroopers by night.

The Battalion remained in this area until 11th December, when it was withdrawn to Souk-el-Khemis for a rest. No 1 Section 16 PFA and No 1 FST moved from Beja on 13 December to join them. Their facilities and accommodation were taken over by the remainder of 16 PFA.

Meanwhile, back in England, some first line reinforcements were on their way.

A sister ship of the *Strathmore*, the SS *Strathallan*, took reinforcements out to North Africa in early December 1942. Aboard was Vernon Minton:

Kowshok Farm as it is today; it was used as a battalion position in November 1942. (James Macrae)

I was a private in the 2nd Parachute Regiment when we boarded *Strathallan* at Greenock on the Firth of Clyde around 12th December 1942. My Regiment was billeted in the lower decks deep inside the troopship. We were told eventually that we were on our way to be reinforcements for the North African campaign. We heard this enormous explosion in the early hours of the morning. The ship gave a massive shudder as the torpedo struck. It took us a long time to reach the upper decks with the bottleneck of soldiers, all with one idea of getting out of the bowels of the stricken ship.

Once we reached the main deck an officer asked for volunteers to go back into the engine room to man the pumps. My mate and I stepped forward and did what you were never supposed to do, volunteer that is, and went below. Funnily enough his name escapes me after 58 years. We made our way below and passed members of *Strathallan's* crew who were on the way up. During all this upheaval a very human touch took place which would probably have met with disapproval from the authorities but nevertheless was greatly appreciated at the time. The crew had 'liberated' some drinks from the bar and offered us a nip of whisky. In the early hours of the morning onboard a sinking ship below decks it was just what the doctor ordered.

Operating the pumps was hot, exhausting, work. We took spells about having a rest and breather. During a break I took a walk, which was not easy because of the list to port. I found myself at an external cargo door with the sea inches below the line of door. While I was at these doors I spotted someone floating close by. He was only wearing a vest and must have stripped off his uniform. He was covered in oil. I managed to grab him but because of the oil I was unable to hang on to him.

Looking in a southerly direction from Kowshok Farm. (James Macrae)

I don't know to this day what happened to that man, whether he survived or not. I rejoined my mate at the pumps and stayed there for a considerable period until a crew member told us to get up on deck as there was nothing more to be done.

On deck I helped free the last of the rafts. A cruiser sailed slowly past *Strathallan* and allowed us to jump onboard. We were taken below to the locker where the anchor chains were stored. Not what you would call the best of accommodation but believe me it was more than welcome. We thought *Strathallan* was going to sink at anytime, which it did eventually. The cruiser turned around and began an anti-submarine sweep. They began dropping depth charges. The noise was horrendous. After every explosion the chains lifted off the deck and came down with an almighty bang. This, coupled with the sound of explosions, and with dark cramped conditions made it an altogether unpleasant experience … one I have never forgotten to this day.

Another comment comes from Dave Brooks:

In December 1942 about 200 of us left Hardwick, paratroopers maybe, but trained soldiers nevertheless, drawn from a number of infantry regiments from all over the place. We were under the command of Lieutenant Colonel Gofton-Salmond. By train to the Clyde, transferred by tender to the SS *Strathallan*, a P&O ex-passenger liner built in, I think, 1938, probably quite luxurious, but a different kettle of fish when carrying 5,000 troops. Soon we slipped down the Clyde, to take up station in what was a very large convoy. We were to take a wide sweep around Ireland in order to avoid U-boats.

For some days an uneventful voyage, almost monotonous. Then we met very heavy seas, must have been the Bay of Biscay, many of us became seasick. When you stood on the deck you were able to see the ships nearest you doing all sorts of crazy things. It was something of a relief to enter the Mediterranean and quite a novelty to see bright lights on Spanish shores.

A few days later, at around 0100 hours, there was a terrific roaring crash, the poor *Strathallan* seemed to be shivering and shaking for what seemed like minutes. We realised we had been torpedoed, it was pitch black but some emergency lights were found. I don't remember any panic, in fact I am sure the transition from living deck to boat stations was very orderly by all units who were aboard. Nevertheless I was very happy to see the sky when we emerged on to our boat deck.

By the time we got to our boat station, all the lifeboats were away, only those on one side could be used, as by now *Strathallan* was listing badly. I also had the thought that we were now completely alone, the rest of the convoy had kept going. Next thought was what do I do if I have to go in the drink. I didn't think much of those kapok Mae Wests, nor of the sea itself, although it looked calm enough. I saw wooden dining chairs in a nearby saloon and thought one of those would do, then I saw a large life belt hanging on the rail, so I commandeered it and agreed to share it with the man next to me.

Strangely nothing much happened in the night, we were still afloat and when dawn came, we were joined by an ocean-going tug and a couple of destroyers. Then more ships turned up and started to take people off, although I think it was the early afternoon before it was our turn. We boarded a destroyer which we later found out was HMS *Pathfinder*. We circled the *Strathallan* for a couple of hours, by now she was listing quite badly. Then we were relieved by another ship and headed for Oran which was in American hands.

Perhaps a more formal idea of the journey to North Africa comes from the war diary of 16 PFA RAMC for the second group of medics to go.

2nd November 1942 1100 – Visit of ADMS Airborne Division to inspect billets. Muster parade in full G1098 equipment.
5th November 1942 0815 – Captain Keesey and 11 ORs leave to join 3rd Battalion.
6th November 1942 0800 – Field exercise for all RAMC and RASC personnel. 1500 – Orders for reinforcements move received.
7th November 1942 2115 – Reinforcements A comprising Captain Ridler, Lieutenant Percival and 65 ORs parade in billets. 2300 – Entrain Bulford siding.
8th November 1942 0010 – Train departs Bulford siding. 0720 – Halt Nottingham for tea. 1530 – Embark P19, Liverpool dock. No casualties.
9th November 1942 0900 – P19 moves to berth at Mersey Quay. Men's mess deck changed.
11th November 1942 1200 – P19 proceeds to midstream and lies off Cammell Laird's yard Birkenhead.
12th November 1942 1200 – P19 leaves Liverpool.
13th November 1942 1000 – P19 anchors in Clyde off Dunoon and convoy assembles.
14th November 1942 1500 – P19 sails. Sea medium. Wind strong.
15th November 1942 – Weather fine. Course mainly west.
16th November 1942 – Weather fine. Course mainly west.
17th November 1942 – Wind freshens. Course mainly west. Training programme of lectures and PT. Lieutenant Percival lectures Airborne on tropical hygiene.
18th November 1942 – Sea medium. Action Stations at 1500. Unidentified aircraft seen. No action.
19th November 1942 – Sea high. Several birds sighted, probably from the Azores.
20th November 1942 – Escorts report two pings on asdic. Possibly submarines. No alarms however.
21st November 1942 – Escorts receive reinforcements. Some depth charging. No Action Stations. Pass through Straights at 1000.
22nd November 1942 – Stand To at dusk.
23rd November 1942 1100 – Anchor Algiers. 1900 – Stand To. Bomb exploded 150 yards off the port bow.
24th November 1942 0415 – Stand To. 0545 – Torpedoed by Heinkel 111. No 1 hold flooded. Casualties about 40. Five serious. No dead. Dock 1300 hours. 2000 Disembark and march with reinforcements to L'Ecole D'Equitation. Laager for the night.
25th November 1942 1100 – Captain Ridler and 40 ORs RASC march to rejoin HQ 16 PFA at Rouiba. Lieutenant Percival and 21 ORs RAMC march to Reinforcement Camp Fort de l'Eau. Baggage party 1 RASC, 1 ACC and 1 RAMC.
26th November 1942 1630 – Lieutenant Percival and RAMC rejoin Field Ambulance.

Private Thomas Davies recalls his first few days in North Africa after arriving at Maison Blanche and landing at Beja:

> We trudged slowly into the large hangar where we were to bed down for the night, appreciating the few hours' respite allowed us before taking off at first light the following morning as we slumped down on to the concrete floor. Joe Waterhouse let out a groan, "Dai, my feet feel as if they've been massaged with a couple of razor blades". I assured him that I had passed that stage hours ago and that my feet now felt as if they belonged to someone else, but before we could fall into a conversation about the anatomy of feet, Lieutenant Webster, the officer in charge of the mortar platoon, came dashing around with instructions for the job we had to do the next day.
>
> Meanwhile, there was plenty of activity at the aerodrome. Aircraft, mostly American Dakotas manned by their American crews, which were to take us on our mission in a few hours, were coming in to be serviced and refuelled.
>
> The 1st Parachute Battalion, under the command of Lieutenant Colonel Hill, was taken by the 64th Group of the American Air Force and dropped on a plain near the market town of Souk-el-Arba, deep in the south of Tunisia. Our stick landed close to some hayricks at the far end of some fields which made up the dropping zone. Here a couple of black African farm labourers were working, their polished ebony faces glistening in the sun. At the sight of us, they dropped their pitchforks in abject terror, jumped down from the bundles of hay on which they were working and ran across the fields, making for the village as fast as their legs would carry them. We must have looked pretty weird to them, dressed in camouflaged jumping smocks with camouflage nets spread over our jumping helmets, dropping practically on top of them from out of the sky.
>
> We soon got organised into our respective companies on the dropping zone. A couple of men had been severely injured and one had tragically fallen to his death with a long streamer of silk from his unopened parachute trailing uselessly behind him. These were the only casualties from what was otherwise a comparatively successful drop.
>
> As the battalion moved into Souk-el-Arba, we were met by a French Army commander and some of his men, who were obviously impressed and much heartened by our appearance and offered to join us. The assistance of a French intelligence officer, who could speak Arabic acting as an interpreter when Arabs were brought in for questioning, proved invaluable in gaining information on the whereabouts and movements of the German forces in the area. As we entered the village, a lone German bomber flew low over us, its black crosses clearly visible, probably returning safely to base from a bombing mission.
>
> Life in these remote parts, where even the wheel is not frequently used on these sparse mountainsides, is certainly no bed of roses. Their very meagre existence amounted to keeping a few chickens, possibly a goat and the benefit of the little food they could grow from the hard earth.
>
> On one occasion, an Arab was suspected of indicating the position of one of our companies to the enemy by marking the shape of an arrow pointing to the hillside they were occupying by ploughing or should I say scratching the ground

with a primitive implement. From the air a German reconnaissance plane would be able to see the arrow of freshly-tilled earth clearly pointing the way.

We were soon to lose the services of Lieutenant Colonel Hill who was badly wounded when he, together with his Captain Whitelock and two orderlies, attacked a couple of German tanks. After disposing of the first one with a Gammon bomb (so-called after Lieutenant Jock Gammon), the commander of the second tank raised his hands in surrender, but a few seconds later his machine gunner opened fire wounding both officers. The second tank was eventually knocked out. Lieutenant Colonel Hill was awarded the DSO for this action.

Major Pearson, previously a company commander, took over the command of the battalion. He was a heavily-built, dark-featured man, who hailed from Glasgow, a dour Scot, very curt and abrupt in speech and manner. He was not cut out for the parade ground type of soldier, a born active serviceman, who had the habit of dropping his head forward when he walked as if pondering over some problem. He was soon to earn great distinction in the field as a lieutenant colonel, gaining the DSO and the MC in a matter of a few weeks. Bill Wilson related with amusement how, when on guard duty one night in our position in the hills, a figure appeared out of the gloom and when challenged by Bill "Who goes there?" replied with a growl from the darkness "Your bloody C.O.! Who do you think it is?"

The nights in the hillsides of Tunisia were bitterly cold in contrast to the blazing sun of the day. Huddling together for warmth among the rocky slopes under the starry sky, awakening to the first light of day, gave us a great sense of communion which was a life apart from the peace and security we had experienced prior to the outbreak of war. This true spirit of comradeship, forged by the unnatural conditions of constant danger which became our life, each of us losing a little of himself, whatever walk of life he had come from in peace time, moulded the pattern of the soldier equipped to brave the elements of the heat and dust of the day and the cold bitter nights among those hills fighting for survival with the German army.

All we carried with us were our arms, ammunition and emergency rations as the main force of the 1st Army that would be coming by road from Algiers with supplies of food and blankets was not expected to reach us for some days.

Our objective was to move on to the heights overlooking Tunis plain and establish positions around the area of Medjez-el-Bab until the main forces of the 1st Army joined up with us. The problem with this was that the Germans had the same idea and sent an airborne force, possibly from Sicily, with the same purpose in mind. So, in the early days, a state of guerrilla warfare ensued with a series of bloody skirmishes going on all the time. Sleeping in old disused locals houses among the rocks and hedgerows, anywhere that offered cover of some kind, it was only to be expected that we did not smell too sweetly, caked with dust and stained with sweat, a few weeks' growth of beard on our faces, as washing facilities were pretty hard to come by. When we did come across the occasional stream or brook, we went wild with delight, stripping off and after a thoroughly good wash, meticulously going through the seams of our clothes in search of lice, as many of us were plagued by the discomfort of crabs and other skin pests.

Bill Wilson and I, always on the look-out for something to supplement our rations, picked and ate what resembled corn cobs from an allotment kept by the local Arabs, which gave us both a violent bout of dysentery, leaving us feeling very weak and washed-out. This was a lesson we learned the hard way and thereafter took great care with what we ate and drank, ensuring that we boiled every drop of water, often after having scooped tiny newts and minute insects out of the mess tin before making our tea, the water perhaps having been taken from a nearby stream. Without fail, the tea tasted like wine to us.

6

Oudna, November-December 1942

Whilst most of the 1st and 3rd Battalions had already taken part in an airborne operation the men who hadn't, particularly those of the 2nd Battalion, were looking on somewhat enviously. However, if they were aware of the political wrangling going on behind the scenes, they would probably have been glad not to have taken part in what from this distance in time appear to be some seriously flawed airborne operations.

On 17th November the commander of the 1st Parachute Brigade, Brigadier Flavell, was ordered by the commander of the 1st Army to send the remaining company of the 1st Parachute Battalion to drop in the area of Enfidaville in western Tunisia and 'harass' the main route from Tripoli to Tunis. Encouraging reports were given to Flavell that there were not a great many German troops in the area, and this company group would have to use guerrilla tactics and be self-sufficient for ten days. Fortunately Flavell managed to get those at HQ to see sense after he pointed out that one company would be entirely inadequate for such a task and the operation was cancelled the same day.

A hangar at Maison Blanche airfield near Algiers was badly damaged in an air raid in November 1942 whilst units of 1st Parachute Brigade were based there. This photo taken by Sergeant West on 21st November. (Imperial War Museum)

Inside of a hangar showing the devastation caused by the air raid. (Imperial War Museum)

The next day the 1st Parachute Brigade received orders to warn the 2nd Parachute Battalion for an operation in the areas of Sousse and Kairouan, with the intention of denying the port and airfield to the Germans. Again, due to a shortage of aircraft, it was intended to deliver the troops in two lifts on two days. Again they were to be self-sufficient for up to ten days. Late in the evening of the 18th the operation was postponed for 24 hours and Brigadier Flavell recommended that the size of the force was inadequate and should be enlarged. Another complication was that these locations were some distance from supporting British troops and the troops were only to be used in small pay packets. Fortunately, the staff saw sense and somehow managed to scrounge up some more aircraft. It was decided to send the 'spare' company from the 1st Battalion with the 2nd Battalion. Then just to keep up with the 'on the bus, off the bus' game, at 1430 on the 19th, the operation was postponed for at least three days. Also on this day, the 3rd Battalion group arrived back at Maison Blanche from Bone and one of their first jobs was to help with the repacking of the parachutes brought back.

Just to make things even more difficult, the Germans launched two moderately successful air raids on Maison Blanche on the nights of 20th/21st and 21st/22nd November. Whilst the number of casualties was relatively low, a fair number of containers were destroyed and several aircraft damaged.

On 22nd November the HQ 1st Army ordered that the 2nd and 3rd Parachute Battalions should be warned for an airborne operation on 25th November. Again the two American carrier groups (62nd and 64th) were available for the operation, but after a quick look at the numbers and loads, Brigadier Flavell warned General Anderson that both groups would be required by each unit if they were to drop in one lift at full strength. So again a rethink was called for and new orders issued, and on 27th

November it was 'requested' that just one battalion group be ready from dawn on 28th November for an unspecified operation. All of these false starts can hardly have been likely to instil confidence in those in the know or indeed the privates faced with growing uncertainty. Perhaps being fair, Brigadier Flavell selected the 2nd Parachute Battalion under the command of Lieutenant Colonel J. Frost. Regardless, later that day Flavell was advised by HQ 1st Army that this unit was to drop at a place called Pont du Fahs, where there was an enemy airfield, and to destroy any aircraft and stores there. They were then meant to move to two other airfields at Depienne and Oudna and perform the same task there. This 'raid' was timed to coincide with a general advance by the 1st Army from the area of Medjez-el-Bab and Mateur towards Tunis and Bizerta. Frost was advised that enemy opposition was expected to be slight. It was expected that Frost and his men would be on their own for up to five days before a join-up was achieved in the area of Tebourba. Again, it was vague how many aircraft might be available, but it was hoped around 40 would be provided. At 2230 on 27th November the operation was postponed until 29th November.

Then just to finally add to the dislocation of expectation in the 2nd Battalion, at 2300 on 28th November news filtered through that Pont du Fahs had been reached by elements of the 78th Division, Depienne airfield appeared to have been ploughed up and 56th Reconnaissance Regiment were operating west of a line Pont du Fahs/Oudna.

A picture of men jumping from a Dakota. Whilst taken on a training exercise in May 1943 it does give an idea of what it was like to 'exit an aircraft over Tunisia'. (Imperial War Museum)

After a polite enquiry as to whether it was still intended to drop at Pont du Fahs, the instruction came back that the unit should drop at Depienne and still head for Oudna. A new link-up point with the 1st Army was to be at St Cyprien.

Lieutenant Colonel Frost:

> After arrival in North Africa and spending some time at Maison Carrée, where we had an awkward time, waiting for some sort of role we saw the 1st and 3rd Battalions being used and it was my fear that we would only be used in an infantry role. Eventually it was thought we might drop part of the Battalion at Kairouan and the remainder at Sousse. I was sent on a recce of the area in a Bisley bomber and told to liaise with the Americans at a place called Tebessa. On my way back as we came into land, the Americans opened up with small arms and punctured our tyres so we had a most dicey landing and could not take off again. The only American officer I met had never heard of the 1st Parachute Brigade. Fortunately there was a Dakota there and I persuaded the pilot that I was needed to lead the attack next day that would bring an early finish to the fighting in North Africa. He obviously felt that he might get back to the USA faster if he took me back.
>
> When I got back I didn't have a chance to relate my adventure because I was told we were now going to drop on Enfidaville. I carried out a recce of that area the next day, only to be told that was off too!
>
> I was very relieved when they found us a task at last. I was briefed to take my Battalion to Pont du Fahs in Tunisia and destroy the enemy aircraft there; likewise on an airstrip at Depienne, twelve miles further on; repeat the dose at Oudna and finally link up with the 1st Army. We were to find our own transport if we could when we landed. On 29th November I went to the pilots' briefing and needless to say there were changes. Enemy aircraft had left both Pont du Fahs and Depienne so we were now to land at the latter and take up the remainder of our task.
>
> I had to choose a DZ at Depienne from the leading aircraft but fortunately there was a great big space nearby and we all came down there.

For this operation the 2nd Battalion was again reinforced by some sappers, this time B Troop from the 1st Parachute Squadron and No 2 Section from 16 PFA commanded by Lieutenant J. McGavin. 44 Dakotas from the 62nd and 64th Groups again had been nominated to act as the transport force and it is recorded that they started to take off with their loads at 1130 on 29th November. Heavy rain had unfortunately turned parts of the airfield into thick mud and some aircraft struggled to move through it, the last aircraft taking off at 1245 with one aircraft apparently getting stuck fast and unable to move.

The flight was relatively uneventful and not interfered with by any German aerial activity, although many men recall that the aircraft flew higher than normal because of the mountainous terrain and consequently it was very cold. The leading aircraft containing Lieutenant Colonel Frost arrived in the area of Depienne by around 1500 and he selected "a great big open space near there" and jumped out to be followed by the rest of his stick. The other aircraft seeing the lead aircraft despatching its human cargo switched on their green lights at what they thought was the appropriate moment and soon the 500 or so men were on the ground. Obviously this was not perhaps the

Sergeant D. Grieve's grave at Enfidaville CWGC Cemetery. (N. Cherry)

best method dropping a Battalion in a concentrated group and it is recorded that the area over which the 2nd Battalion landed was about 1½ miles by ½ mile. The rally was further complicated by the fact that a fairly large watercourse ran across the DZ. Frost did his best to rally the troops by standing on a small mound and blowing his hunting horn.

Perhaps it might be best to explain the use of this hunting horn, which he later used at Arnhem and even made it into the film *A Bridge Too Far*. A pre-war regular officer, Frost had been commissioned into the Cameronians (Scottish Rifles) in 1932, with whom he served in both England and Palestine. As a Captain, he was transferred to the Iraq Levies in 1938 and was still stationed in the Middle East when the Second World War began. His contract with the Levies expired in June 1940 and, eager to return home, he applied to return to the Cameronians, however this was refused on the grounds that his presence in Iraq was useful as he had knowledge of the area and could speak Arabic. Frost however persisted. One morning his Company Clerk, Mr Sethi, handed him a paper concerning the establishment of a parachute battalion. Frost told Sethi "What on Earth made you think that I would be interested in this? You don't suppose I would ever want to get involved in that sort of thing, do you?" Frost was eventually relieved of his post and returned to Britain to join the 10th Battalion of the Cameronians. As a parting gift he had been presented with an inscribed copper hunting horn, which he would later take into battle to use as a rallying call for his men. He hadn't been with the Cameronians for long before he received a request from the War Office for Captains willing to join the newly formed Special Air Service. Frost had little idea what the SAS was, but imagining it to be a variant of the Commandos, and having grown tired of mundane home duties, he applied without hesitation. His battalion commander politely suggested that Frost ought to keep his feet on the ground as "I can't imagine any sensible person choosing you to be a parachutist". Nevertheless, Frost passed the interview and was posted to the 2nd Battalion of the Parachute Regiment.

The copper horn with silver mouthpiece was inscribed "Capt JD Frost with best wishes from the Members of the Royal Exodus Hunt", and he described it as "one of the best presents I have ever had". Frost found it useful as a rallying call on the DZ. Four men from the 2nd Battalion have a date of death of the 29th November 1942 although it is not certain if all died as a result of the drop. One account gives just one fatal casualty on the drop. In any case these are the four men whose date of death is given as 29th November:

Sergeant D. Grieve MM Enfidaville CWGC Cemetery 2A2
Private E. Harrison NKG Medjez-el-Bab Memorial to the Missing
Private G. Jenkins NKG Medjez-el-Bab Memorial to the Missing
Sergeant A. Prentice Enfidaville CWGC Cemetery 6B22

Interestingly the war diary for the 1st Parachute Squadron RE records the following for the 30th November:

> B Troop and 2nd Battalion dropped on landing field unopposed. Sapper Craighan was killed owing to his parachute failing to open. Men and containers were widely dispersed. L/Corporal Simpkins and Sapper Wright were missing. It was learnt afterwards that their plane had failed to take off. All RE stores and packs of extra explosives were loaded onto mules, donkeys and carts.

According to the CWGC there was only one man named Craighan in their records for 1942, he is Sapper H. Craighan, whose date of death is given as 28th November 1942. Aged 21 and recorded as being a member of the 1st Parachute Squadron, he is now buried at Massicault CWGC Cemetery grave III H6.

There were also a number of the normal injuries suffered as a result of a parachute landing. Not all the containers were released from the Dakotas and in some cases their parachutes failed to open, with predictable results.

Here is an account of the drop and its aftermath from Corporal McConney:

> I was attached to the 2nd Parachute Battalion with six men for operational signal purposes for the Oudna operation. At approx 1500 I made my descent. I had several twists in my rigging lines and hit the earth spinning. I was conscious of pain in my right arm but was able to free myself and find the signals container. The MO gave me an injection of morphine in my right hand and told me to lie down for a few minutes until he was able to attend to me. Later on he put me under chloroform and put my shoulder back in place. I do not recollect anything further until I found myself, with other patients, at a school in Depienne.

One of the medics attached to the 2nd Battalion for the drop on Depienne was Private F. Cozens and he recalls that they were to drop fifty miles behind enemy lines. Frank was the last man in his stick and on the way struggling forward to the door ready

Prise de l'Eau near Oudna. (James Macrae)

to jump his static line became entangled round one of the seats so that he couldn't move. One of the crew of the aircraft saw his predicament and went back and freed his static line. Frank got to the door and jumped and remembers the crack of his chute opening and almost immediately afterwards hitting the deck. Blood was streaming from his nose and he recalls that he thought his right arm was broken. He released his harness and assessed the situation. It appeared that he had landed in a small hollow and hearing gunfire away to his right, he headed in that direction. After cresting the rise he could see figures about a mile away and started walking towards them. He suddenly noticed a man on a white horse riding towards him, Frank drew and cocked his pistol. The man stopped about 100 yards from him and he could now see that he was an Arab and Frank advanced with his pistol clearly visible and the Arab turned tail and rode away. Shortly after this he reached some 2nd Battalion positions. He found the MO, Lieutenant McGavin and reported his injuries, especially his right arm. Lieutenant McGavin had a quick look at his arm and with a pair of tweezers pulled out a long cactus needle which was stuck in Frank's arm. Frank said that he must have landed in a cactus bush but had no recollection of this at the time. Fully restored to health once the needle was out he set about getting a brew on as it appeared that there were no Germans in the immediate area. Shortly orders came through to get ready to move towards a place called Oudna where there was an airfield and railway station.

There was no enemy opposition, which was of course a bonus. As with the 3rd Battalion's drop at Bone, it was vital to make sure that the parachutes and containers were salvaged, in case they could be collected and used again. Whilst a salvage party set about this task, some patrols from B Company were sent out, while the remainder adopted defensive positions. A search for local transport produced a few mule carts. Meanwhile, local French people appeared to be friendly and helped with the casualties. They also advised that the Germans had pulled back to the north about three days previously.

During the late afternoon three armoured cars from the 56th Reconnaissance Regiment appeared on the road running north from Depienne and patrolled northwards

C Company of the 2nd Parachute Battalion was positioned near this hill in November 1942, which is located to the south-west of Prise de l'Eau. (James Macrae)

towards Cheylus. Apart from offering to report their arrival there was little material help they could offer and to many it must have felt they were being left out on a limb. As many men had had a strenuous time assembling after the scattered drop and carrying their parachute and containers over rough ground, Frost decided to let them have a bit of rest and aim to reach the area of Oudna soon after first light on the 30th November.

Once darkness had fallen, Lieutenant Colonel Frost decided it was time to move towards Oudna, most of the mortars being carried in the few carts, but the rest of the kit having to be man packed. As one participant from A Company said,

> We moved off towards a place called Oudna with us bringing up the rear. Our column contained a motley section of mules, horses and carts in order to carry ammunition and stores. This extraordinary group of men and animals was described by L/Corporal Berryman, an old Middlesex Regiment regular, as "looking like a fucking travelling circus rather than a parachute battalion". I have to admit he wasn't far wrong!

The way was led by C Company and a platoon under the command of Lieutenant Buchanan was left at Depienne to look after the stores salvaged, evacuate the wounded and try and sweep up any stragglers.

This march is remembered by those who took part as one of the worst they ever took part in. By about 0430 on the following morning, having covered about 12 miles over really rough and stony ground, Lieutenant Colonel Frost called a halt for a brief rest. Most people tried to sleep but without blankets or sleeping bags it was just too cold, and many were glad to be moving away just to try and keep warm. John Frost later recorded that he and the unit 2 i/c Major Teichman tried to sleep back to back covered with their maps trying to keep warm, with little success.

Private F. Cozens from 16 PFA recalls that the march that night will forever remain in his mind as it was bitterly cold and the route was through very inhospitable country.

Approximate location of Battalion HQ and the mortar position near Prise de l'Eau, November 1942. (James Macrae)

Early the next morning the airfield was sighted and the 2nd Battalion attacked it. A dressing station was set up in a farm and after a while casualties started to arrive, although they were very low in numbers. Frank remembers that he was at the farm and some of the section went in with the actual assault. Very few Germans were found on the airfield and after mopping up the medics regrouped at the farmhouse.

At 0600 the Battalion stood to but nothing untoward happened and around 0700 on 30th November orders were given to move towards Prise de l'Eau, B Company to move in bounds to here with the rest of the Battalion following on. Again it was quite rough country and it became clear that most men were too heavily loaded and progress was slow. However, by about 1100 the well at Prise de l'Eau had been reached and permission was given for a brew up, wash and to fill water bottles. From their lying up positions the airfield at Oudna could be seen and although there was one crashed aircraft there did not appear to be any other activity going on.

Orders were given soon after noon for A Company to advance by the most direct route and to make a recce of the airfield, and if practicable, to occupy it. The men set off at 1315 and by 1500 everyone was on the move towards Oudna.

Soon after 1430 A Company came under fire from what were German positions on a low ridge near St Bon Sakouma. Support was requested and B and C Companies went to their aid. Using some words from 1944 it appears the 2nd Battalion fought a "tidy little battle" and by 1530 the Germans had withdrawn to the north of the airfield, with elements of A Company on the ridge. Additionally a platoon under the command of Lieutenant Rendell had occupied Oudna railway station.

From these movements it was clear that the opposition was not now using Oudna as a landing ground. It seemed there were some tents on the open ground south of the railway which it was thought might contain equipment, but on investigation these were found to be hayricks. A distinct failure of the airborne Mark I eyeball!

Things now started to go wrong for the 2nd Battalion, some German tanks appeared from the west of the airfield and opened fire on the positions of C Company. Several

The view westwards from Oudna railway station. (James Macrae)

casualties were caused and Lieutenant K. Morrison was killed. He is now buried at Enfidaville CWGC Cemetery grave 6B21. Gammon bombs were thrown at one of the tanks without causing damage, although they did not attempt to approach the Battalion's positions they remained a threat whilst in the vicinity.

Shortly afterwards they were attacked by German Me 109s, although due to a wish to conserve ammunition Frost had given orders that generally aircraft were not to be attacked. Then later they were dive bombed by Stukas, but again casualties were light. Frost and his unit were now in a difficult position. His original orders had been to destroy aircraft at Oudna and there were none to be found. I would imagine he felt a bit isolated, no news had been received of an advance of the 1st Army and for entirely sensible reasons, he decided to cut his losses and move westwards to meet up with friendly forces. The first part of the plan was to withdraw at dusk to Prise de l'Eau, but again 'Murphy's Airborne Law' came into play and C Company became embroiled in a firefight with the Germans. However, after a while order was restored and most of the Battalion made it to the RV point. Frost decided to remain here overnight but again it was bitterly cold and everyone found it difficult, if not impossible, to get any real rest.

Lieutenant Dennis Rendell gives his recollections of the events at Oudna on this day. Dicky Ashford was his company commander.

> That afternoon Dicky Ashford gave out his orders, which boiled down to having a look at Oudna airfield and if possible occupying it. Anyway, we moved off with 2 Platoon on the left under Slapsey Brayley, No 1 Platoon, mine, on the right with Company HQ slightly to the rear and No 3 platoon in reserve at the rear. I ordered 1 Section on the right, 2 Section on the left with platoon HQ in the centre and 3 Section in reserve at the rear – all to keep well spread out in a kind of

Looking towards Mont du Siphon farm from the outskirts of Oudna. (James Macrae)

box formation and to head in the direction of Oudna station, plainly visible with white buildings. I recall the Company 2 i/c Captain Keith Mountford, saying at Ashford's orders group that the "British Army could not fight a war without a red-roofed house – without that they couldn't indicate any target, but here was Oudna station complete with a red-roofed reference point."

After about fifteen minutes the sound of machine gun fire, very fast and certainly not our Brens, was heard and we all instinctively fell to the ground in the prone position. I was desperately trying to remember the crack/thump of bullets taught to me at my Small Arms School Bisley course, but I simply couldn't and as a result had no idea where the fire was coming from or if it was directly pointed at us. After a few minutes I thought it reasonably safe to continue, so shouted the order to move on and this we did. No 2 Section, however, was too far left, and I had some difficulty in getting them back on line. There was still a good deal of noise, chiefly small arms fire with the occasional crump of a mortar bomb or shell. On the way 2 Section assaulted a small Arab dwelling which they thought might contain the enemy machine gun – it didn't.

We were still making reasonable progress towards the station, but I had lost sight and control of No 1 Section to the right. Sergeant Forsyth, my Platoon Sergeant, was making sure No 3 Section remained with us. As Platoon HQ approached this tiny station I was looking beyond for any aircraft posted on the strip – there were none. The station seemed unoccupied, so Sergeant Forsyth and my batman, Private Fletcher took up residence. I then realised that none of the sections had shown up, but then 2 Section turned up on the left and I called them over. I was delighted to have this additional strength and set about preparing defensive positions around the station buildings. Later some men of 3 Section arrived.

I was rather pleased with the little operation, despite the fact that we were a section and a half down. I think all of us had been very scared, but at least we got to the objective. As far as I knew, we hadn't killed any enemy or even seen them! We had certainly fired our weapons, but all at rather doubtful targets. I went out on to what was laughingly called an airstrip; there were no aircraft on it, but a few abandoned 50 gallon oil drums, which suggested some previous aircraft activity. Strangely, there were tyre tracks, but I assumed these had been made by vehicles and not taxiing aircraft. We were out of touch with Company HQ and there was no sign of 2 or 3 Platoons. The stationmaster was found in one of the buildings and he told me that enemy armour was in the vicinity. He was a French-speaking Arab who I sent packing, which on reflection wasn't a very clever thing to do.

While we were preparing possible tank ambush sites we heard the sinister sound of engines and there, to the left across the airstrip, were three or four tanks and an armoured car about half a mile away. The armoured car approached us, running parallel to the railway. Our only anti-tank weapon was the Gammon bomb and that was only good at very close range. I ordered everyone to take maximum cover and at the same time was trying to think what I must do if the bloody thing stopped close to us. If the occupants saw us they didn't react, but I suspect they did not even see us. It was huge, with eight wheels and festooned with wireless masts. I think it was a command car and soon it drove merrily on towards Tunis.

A 3 inch mortar crew in action somewhere in Tunisia. (Airborne Assault Duxford)

We now come to the morning of 1st December 1942. Lieutenant Colonel Frost received the really good news by wireless that the armoured attack on Tunis had been postponed. This now really put the 2nd Battalion Group in a difficult position. It was known there were a lot of German forces in the area, far more mobile than the paratroops and more heavily armed. Additionally they had Germans on three sides of them and the nearest British troops were at either Medjez-el-Bab or Tebourba, about 40 miles away. Frost decided to wait until noon and then to move into the hills from which they could move at night across the plains towards friendly troops. However, before this time, a patrol of about two tanks, two armoured cars and a few lorries towing artillery pieces were seen approaching from the north. They stopped about 1000 yards from the Battalion positions, with one armoured car going forward on its own. They surprised a small group of paratroopers filling water bottles and after a rather inconclusive skirmish, both sides scurried back. The Germans deployed their artillery and began shelling. Frost replied by bringing his mortars into action and the Germans withdrew a distance leaving approximately six killed behind.

Then at about 1100 more German forces appeared from the south, displaying yellow recognition triangles (used normally by the British). The men in this area thought they were friendly forces and an NCO was sent forward waving his own yellow triangle and was quickly taken prisoner. He was then made to walk in front of a German vehicle which moved up to a few 2nd Battalion positions and took several men prisoner. This unlucky NCO was then sent at the Germans' request to Battalion HQ to demand their surrender, but Frost would have none of it and sent forces in a flanking movement which caused the Germans to withdraw.

Colonel Frost:

> I was sure the enemy would come and find us, so I laid an ambush down by a well at the bottom of a hill. Unfortunately, the enemy arrived just as a party went down to fill their water bottles. However, it didn't turn out too badly and we fought a fairly successful little battle. I then received a report of armour coming up from the rear displaying yellow triangles, which were the 1st Army recognition signs. We all heaved a sigh of relief; we'd not been forgotten. Then John Ross, the C Company commander came to me with a grave face and said, "Don't be taken in by the yellow triangles, these are German tanks and we are completely surrounded". This was a terrible shock. I told him that we must get into a stronger position, from which it would be possible to move north the next night. Unfortunately in the move we had to leave our wounded behind with Doc McGavin. As we moved, the Germans shelled us, sending splinters from the rocks. One man I passed had his face almost sliced from his head which he held together with his hands. Among the casualties was a mule which scampered off towards the enemy with the Battalion's bagpipes.

So at about noon the 2nd Battalion began moving to new positions in the hills and the wounded were moved to a farm near Prise de l'Eau. It is one of the unwritten rules of being a medic that if wounded have to be left behind in close contact with the enemy, certain people will be volunteered to also remain. The 1st December 1942 was no exception to this rule and the Section Commander Lieutenant McGavin remained together with a few others. Just before nightfall two German tanks came within one hundred yards of

Private G. Cadden being interrogated after being taken prisoner on the Oudna operation. (Airborne Assault Duxford)

the farm. Lieutenant McGavin sent Private Jenkins down to them waving a white cloth to tell them that the farmhouse contained wounded. Later a German officer entered the farmhouse but in the interim the medics buried their weapons in the sand outside the farm. The next morning all able-bodied personnel were paraded and sent out to look for any wounded (British and German) who might be still lying on the battlefield. Personnel were sent in all directions. Frank Cozens walked to the top of a small hill and at the top encountered disaster. At the top of the hill lay about what he thought were around 30 dead paratroopers. Some of the dead had been severely disfigured in the fighting, but some of the paratroopers were just alive. Frank thinks this was the last position of the Battalion rearguard. The wounded were collected and taken back to the dressing station. Frank also remembers that the German dead had to be collected but the British dead were left on the battlefield. When it was clear that the battlefield had been cleared of all wounded and German dead the medical personnel and wounded were paraded outside the farmhouse and a German officer started shouting and gesturing with his hands. The German soldiers lined up in front of the British and Frank thought they were going to be shot. The German officer had a mouth full of gold teeth. All of a sudden a German staff car drove up and a higher ranking officer jumped out and in Frank's words "started ranting on and on at old Gold Teeth".

Some German tanks then appeared and the medics had to load the German dead on the front of the tanks. When they had done this they had to sit on the back of the tanks by the exhaust pipes. The tanks then drove towards Tunis and just outside here the British had to get off the transport. They were formed up in two ranks and were made to march into Tunis accompanied by German propaganda photographers. Private Cozens remembers that the road was in places lined with jeering Tunisians who threw rocks, stones, bottles, indeed anything they could get their hands on at the British, some even spat. After a while they were put on transport and taken back to the original start point and made to run the gauntlet again, so it appeared the Germans had taken more prisoners than they had actually done. From Tunis the medical personnel and wounded were flown by Italian aircraft first to Sicily and then to Naples airport. From there they were taken to a POW camp at Capua.

The following is taken from the war diary of 16 PFA and was included as an appendix to the entries for November 1942, being signed off by Major Wheatley.

> Maison Blanche 29th November.
> No 2 Section. Lieutenant J. McGavin RAMC and 16 ORs No 2 Section accompanied 2nd Parachute Battalion in a parachute operation on Depienne. Lieutenant Longland and 7 ORs either took off and then turned back (aircraft failure) or were unable to go owing to scarcity of aircraft.
>
> It is known that Lieutenant McGavin and his men spent two nights and the whole of one day collecting casualties caused by the Battalion encountering strong enemy tank forces. On the second night his ADS was established outside the perimeter of defence of the Battalion. As no member of No 2 Section returned they have been reported missing.
>
> The nominal roll of missing is as follows:
>
> Lieutenant J. McGavin 7365227 Private J. Bottoms, 73700846 Private L. Cole, 7370849 Private F. Cozens, 7396429 Private L. Evans, 7370690 Private J. Garner, 7520059 Private S. Harris, 7386004 Private R. Jenkins, 7261183 Private F. Jones, 7518016 Corporal H. Jones, 7395204 Private Jenkinson, 7347091 Private J. Lowther, 7374220 Private L. Marshall, 7373834 Private R. Moore, 7380431 F. Shelton, 7370839 Private A.Taylor, 7370842 Private M. Wellings.

Another with recollections of this time was Corporal McConney, a signaller attached to the 2nd Battalion. We had left him in the schoolhouse at Depienne with Lieutenant Buchanan and his batman:

> We started to make a meal and by the time we had cooked the food we heard the sound of tanks and armoured vehicles on the road leading north. In between each AFV were a number of motor cycle combinations. The three of us lay down in a ditch facing the road. The crews of the column seemed to be Italians. Shots came from the direction of Mr Buchanan and his batman so I opened fire with my Sten. The range was approximately 50 yards and I got off five magazines with good effect on the motorcyclists. Mr Buchanan gave a cry and rolled over on his back and his batman lay face down with arms outstretched. By this time the tanks had traversed their guns round and were ramming the building with fire. Seeing it was useless to continue firing, I crawled to the lavatory and put my Sten and three magazines on top of the wall to hopefully avoid detection and then hid behind the half-closed door. About 30 Italians entered the yard and were very excited when they saw that a meal had been in progress.

A heap of parachutes in one corner of the yard aroused suspicion and several shots were directed at them; then they lifted them up to see if anyone was hiding underneath, they then began a systematic search of the out houses. A few shots were fired and luckily none touched me. Three of them then walked in to the lavatory and were greatly alarmed at finding me. I was taken and put on top of an armoured vehicle. After three or four miles they stopped at a small wood and I was assisted off. One Italian was with me and the vehicle went back. I at once set about a plan of escape. They had failed to find my fighting knife, which was concealed in its pocket.

To the sentry I must have appeared a very poor spectacle, for he did not seem to worry a great deal about me.

I think he thought there was a chance of an attack by the Battalion. As dusk approached he seemed to get more nervous and whenever he turned his back I loosened my knife a little. As last I got it out and put it in my left hand trouser pocket. When he next presented his back to me I whipped out the knife and struck at his back under the left shoulder. He gave a cry and fell forward on his face. I must have lost my head, for I struck again and again at the inert form.

I decided then to go back to the school and try and collect my arms if they were still there. I got there at about nine o'clock, for I was sick several times. The village seemed devoid of troops so I made my way to the lavatory. I found my Sten and magazines still on top of the wall, but all the equipment in the schoolroom had gone except for two small tins of cheese. I listened outside the door of the house and could only hear the voices of the schoolmaster and his wife. They had been very good to us so I knocked on the door and asked if they knew where the nearest English soldiers were. They said they were at Pont du Fahs and gave me bread and water and told me to go as the Italians might return. I went and lay down in a ditch and started to eat and drink. I had nearly finished when I heard tanks entering the village. They went into the school and seemed to be using it as some sort of headquarters. I thought it was time to get out and started crawling along the ditch. At last I got clear of the village and made off in the direction of Pont du Fahs using the compass from my escape kit. After walking a few miles I felt very tired, so went to sleep in some hay. Next morning I set off again. I stopped at a French farm and they gave me sausage and eggs and then they told me that Pont du Fahs was in the hands of the enemy. This was rather a setback, however, I had heard that there were British troops near Medjez-el-Bab, so I changed my course for there. The going was very hard over those mountains and the sun was very hot. On the morning of the next day I did manage to make contact with British troops.

One of the wounded also present was Private G. Cadden:

A staff car drove up, a high-ranking German officer stepped out and walked over to the first Italian officer. From what was said we knew we were to be shot as agents and saboteurs, even though we were easily recognisable as regular soldiers because of our uniforms. We were lined up against a wall and a machine gun set up in front of us. We put on our berets, raised our fingers in V signs and took our leave of Lieutenant Buchanan. The German officer ordered the machine gunner to fire but he was reluctant to do so. At this moment an armoured car pulled by and down from it jumped *Oberstleutnant* Walter Koch, commander of the 5th German *Fallschirmjäger* Regiment. Sizing up the situation immediately, he strode over and kicked over the machine gun. After a heated debate between the two German officers, Koch turned to us and said, "You are paratroopers and you put up a brave fight. You are prisoners of war and will be treated as such".

Meanwhile back at the main group, as dusk was falling, Frost decided that he would split the unit into company-sized groups who would move independently and meet up the following morning hopefully somewhere near the Djebel el Mengoub. Frost estimated that so far his unit had suffered about 150 killed, wounded and missing since the start of the operation – about a third of his strength.

The journey up and down various hills was another tough one and these were interspersed with trudging across ploughed fields and two fairly deep rivers which needed to be crossed. However, this did give the opportunity to refill water bottles, although the water was only just about drinkable according to several men.

A halt was called at about 0100 on the morning of 2nd December and an opportunity for a rest was given for about 90 minutes. It was noticed during this halt that Major Teichman and Captain Short had joined the ranks of those missing. Soon after the march restarted, heavy rain added to the discomfort of everyone. By about 0600 they were somewhere near the Djebel el Mengoub and Frost decided to halt here until daylight, when the priorities would be water and information. Soon after daylight Lieutenant Charteris and a small party were sent out on a recce patrol. They were back within a short time and reported that a farm not far away was inhabited by friendly Arabs who were prepared to help. The remnants moved here and after putting out sentries everyone had an opportunity to wash and have some breakfast. The Arab owner informed them that Massicault was occupied by the enemy but that Furna was in Allied hands. Later news came that another party of British soldiers were in a farm a short distance away. This party turned out to be Major Ashford and his group from A Company, who joined the others at this farm, which Frost called el Fedja farm.

However, the locals had warned that the Germans actively patrolled the area and in the early afternoon this is precisely what happened. The Germans realised that British troops were in the area and started to deploy their troops at what they felt was a safe distance. Due to a shortage of ammunition Frost had ordered that no one was to fire unless the target was within 50 yards.

In spite of the fact that fire, mainly from mortars and machine guns, was directed towards the farm and its surroundings, most of it was inaccurate and apparently only one casualty was sustained. Later in the day, as dusk was falling, some Germans came closer but were killed by a combination of grenades and Sten fire. Frost gave orders that when he blew his hunting horn everyone was to leave their position and run past Battalion HQ in a south-easterly direction and rally on the slopes of the Djebel el Mengoub. After a few more probing attacks the signal was given to withdraw at about 1815. Obviously in the darkness command and control was difficult and when Frost called a halt on the slopes he now had only about 100 men with him. These were mainly from his HQ and A Company. It was felt the others had moved south of this group. Frost's first plan was to head north-west to hopefully join the main Tunis-Medjez road. However, when reaching a minor road at a place called Bou Khail, it was decided to head towards Medjez-el-Bab along this. Water bottles were again filled at a well that was found and at midnight an hour's rest was given.

It was now 3rd December and the march continued after this short rest. Some local inhabitants of a farm were roused and confirmed Frost's suspicions that enemy armour patrolled the area. However, there was a small bit of good news in that Captain Vernon and his party of sappers joined up with the Frost group. I can imagine any extra hands were most welcome. By around 0400 everyone was dead tired and on their chinstraps and so Frost decided to rest up at the next farm until dawn. This was soon reached and fortunately the inhabitants were friendly. The owner did warn Frost that he thought a local Arab who was known to be pro-German had left to inform them of the arrival of the Frost group. Frost thought it might be a good time to move towards some high ground near Ksar Tyr, which was thought might be held by British units. This was achieved and from here Medjez-el-Bab and the main road leading to it could be seen and so Frost decided to move across the open ground leading to it in a loose open formation. Sounds of fighting could be heard coming from the direction of Tebourba but the Frost group managed to reach some orchards near St Medien unscathed. Here a halt was called and those with any food left scraped together a meal. From this orchard enemy armoured cars could be seen heading away from St Medien.

After a while Frost and his group ventured towards the road and soon after reaching it an American armoured patrol could be seen approaching from the north, also heading for the road. A link-up with friendly forces had been achieved after a rather tortuous five days 'behind enemy lines'. The walking wounded, Frost and a few others were given a lift into Medjez-el-Bab on the back of the armoured cars and arrived at about 1600. The wounded were quickly taken to a dressing station and Frost sorted out facilities for his men and visited the HQ of the 78th Infantry Division. He did request that search parties be sent out to try and round up any stragglers from his unit. The last ones arrived in Medjez-el-Bab on 5th December. Frost had about 200 men left, with about 260 men either being killed, wounded or missing.

The official history of the Airborne Forces sums up the Oudna operation most aptly in my opinion:

> The operation suffered from a lack of information and from a lack of adequate arrangements for a link-up between the ground forces and too lightly armed and comparatively immobile airborne troops. A speedy link-up in all such cases is vital. The Battalion carried out its orders and its presence at Oudna must have had a considerable effect on German operations elsewhere, but the cost was high.

To try and make the numbers up Frost was offered 200 gunners from the Royal Artillery and he accepted these with open arms. Regretfully it is not recorded what these gunners felt, but it seems most opted to stay with the 2nd Battalion.

Present throughout the entire action was the RMO of the 2nd Battalion, Captain R. Gordon. He said that the drop at Depienne will forever remain imprinted on his brain: the extremely cold nights coupled with the sight that lightly armed paratroopers hate tanks. He said that he knew then they were in trouble. Captain Gordon also recalls the withdrawal as being a time when he had to give treatment and encouragement to the wounded. He also had to berate the survivors about not drinking the water. Nobody died of dehydration, so he had some effect although as he recalls it was extremely difficult to convince them not to drink polluted water. Captain Gordon's efforts did not go unnoticed, with the award of a bar to the Military Cross he had previously won in France in 1940. Part of his citation reads:

> This officer on several occasions went forward under heavy fire to tend the wounded. He continually displayed great gallantry and devotion to duty and did everything in his power to alleviate the suffering of the wounded. During the trip back to British lines this officer was unfailing in his attention to the wounded, injured and sick by encouraging the many men who would otherwise have fallen into enemy hands, unsuccessfully negotiating the long and hazardous journey.

When questioned about this, the reply was "People stuck with me as I was their hope."

Here is the conclusion of the account by Dennis Rendell, who we left at Oudna station on the afternoon of 30th November 1942:

> At dusk we saw large fires to the left. I wrongly assumed it might be Slapsey Brayley with 2 Platoon or even C Company, who had been on our left when we started out. When it was fully dark we moved towards the fires, only to be fired on by something much bigger than small arms; someone said they saw a tank and that may well be so – anyway it set off a firework display that both helped and hindered our ignominious withdrawal back towards the station. By now it was pitch-black

From Oudna looking in a southerly direction towards the hills from which 2nd Parachute Battalion advanced. (James Macrae)

and we bumped into a previously unseen French Police post. Very scary, but they were helpful and offered us shelter for the night. This I refused, because I had in mind the need to get close to the protection of the hills in order to return to our previous Battalion position at Prise de l'Eau. I had previously taken a back bearing from the station to where I thought we had come from, so I knew that if we went on that bearing we would end up somewhere near our original position. So off we set, but it soon became obvious to me that the men were done in and that rest was essential for all of us. In addition I did not wish to bump into any other posts, be they French, German or our own; we had had enough for one night. So we laagered up in the scrub where we were. It was devilishly cold and I doubt if any of us got much rest – our cotton smocks giving little or no warmth.

We set off again before dawn and made for the protection of the hills. At first light I felt I could see our old Prise de l'Eau position with various small figures moving around. These I prayed would be our own men and ordered my chaps to display prominently our yellow identification silks. Much to my relief the first recognisable chap was the tall elegant figure of 'Popoff' alias Peter Naoumoff from B Company who said "Where have you bloody heroes been?" There were more pertinent comments from his men. Without the glimmer of a smile, Private Fletcher replied "Tunis". I think each one of us was very chuffed and secretly a little proud to have received this ribald welcome.

Back within the heart of our own Battalion and Company we felt safe and secure and after a shave and clean-up felt 100 per cent better. Various other members of 2 and 3 Sections rejoined, so we were again about 25 strong. We were sent to extend the A Company positions to the left of the Prise de l'Eau well, with 1 Platoon furthest right. Enemy armour and tanks moved towards the well and attempted to come round behind us. We could clearly hear the revving of engines as they ascended the hill – I must add a most frightening sound – and from my forward slope position the first thing I saw was a swinging radio mast, then the turret and finally the whole vehicle painted a sand yellow colour with a large black cross on the turret. "If it comes closer we'll have a go with the Gammons" I said, but thankfully it turned off to the right along the line of the hill. Fortunately no tanks came near and later in the final act of this battle, some Me 109s attacked the enemy instead of us. Prior to this attack, Fletcher was very badly wounded by shellfire. We carried him down to Doc Gordon's RAP. I think he died later that night.

We moved out when darkness came, the signal being a call by the CO on his hunting horn. I was told we would make for Medjez-el-Bab, where 1st Army were said to be. This proved to be a march over appallingly tough hill country and later on flat sandy plough land. 1 Platoon was leading, with both the OC and myself using compasses. Sergeant Forsyth was a tower of strength by encouraging the exhausted men to make even greater efforts.

Just about dawn we came to a farm run by French settlers, where we watered from the farm well. Then what was left of the company was put in a large straw filled barn where we slept. We were informed by the French owners that a German motorcycle combination was coming up the farm road. Dicky Ashford ordered the men to hide under the straw, while he and I and some NCOs with cocked Stens waited. They spoke at length with the French farmers and left, apparently satisfied all was well. For our part we had no intention of letting them leave alive if they approached the barn. We later heard that the CO and the rest of the Battalion was at a nearby farm, so we set off to join them.

We, that is No 1 Platoon, were given the task of defending the northern part of the farm perimeter, which consisted of a big cactus hedge interspersed with stone walls enclosing an olive orchard. By this time I was greatly concerned about the shortage of ammunition; despite economy we had wasted a large number of rounds by firing at too great a range. I asked the Company 2 i/c Keith Mountford if he could arrange some resupply, but he said we were all in the same boat.

I was quietly answering a call of nature behind the hedge a short distance from my Platoon HQ and idly looking at the ridge about 300 yards away, when I noticed a couple of dots moving along the skyline. Someone was looking at me, or more likely the Battalion position. I quickly finished my toilet and rejoined my Platoon HQ, only to find Keith, who said we would pull out as soon as it was dark. I quickly explained what I had seen and together we studied the ridge through our glasses; by now there were several dots, easily identified as helmets – but who were they? Keith said hopefully "Maybe they are Yanks?" They were Germans all right and soon the mortars started, followed by machine guns. Before Keith left to return to Company HQ he once again made us smile and so helped to lessen the tension and fear. "You know, Dennis," he said, "you are probably unique – you must be one of the few British officers to be caught with his trousers down in the face of the enemy!" and left. Shortly after this we killed half a dozen Germans within 50 yards of our perimeter, but even then I had a job to stop the men firing. A little later we scuppered a more determined attack in the same way, but this time the effect was more deadly and the control much tighter. By now the light was beginning to fade and various farm buildings were on fire. Most of them had straw roofs. By dark the fires gave off a ghostly light which, combined with the smoke, made accurate shooting almost impossible. This was very worrying as we could hear Germans very close. Keith again arrived to tell me we were moving out and the signal would be from the CO sounding away on his horn. We were to withdraw through the farm and move south-eastwards. I walked along the cactus hedge with Keith towards Company HQ. We heard German voices on the other side; pistols would have been useless, and in any case it was nearly dark, so after a quick debate we decided to use our Mills grenades. In the approved fashion we hurled two grenades each over the hedge in the direction of the voices. They burst with satisfying crumps and this was followed by cries of pain. Keith and I got up from our prone positions. "Good evening to you, Mr Rendell," he said and disappeared. I returned to Platoon HQ and briefed the NCOs on the plan.

Soon after dark, mortar and machine gun fire increased, but the machine guns appeared to be firing on fixed lines over the farm and the mortar bombs seemed to be doing little damage. We heard the CO's horn and as I slowly crawled from Platoon HQ I heard the whine of mortar bombs falling very close. My sole recollection is of a ghastly smell of sulphur just like school chemistry experiments. At some time later I felt someone pulling my belt and it was light. A German soldier in what appeared to be a pair of overalls was trying to remove my pistol from its holster and I tried to help him. But I couldn't my hands were too cold and I was

> shivering. My right leg was wet and my large pocket para trousers were torn. The man pulled me to my feet and I was dumped gently but firmly into a motor cycle sidecar and taken to what I thought was a RAP. There was no noise and no firing. I was eventually joined by some members of B Company and some sappers. The Germans came out with the classic line, "For you the war is over". They were right for a time, anyway.

Another member of A Company under Major Ashford was Sergeant Johnstone who has vivid memories of the march back from Oudna and of his company commander:

> We found the going down the side of the precipitous hills very tough and when we got down on the plain it was no better. I do not exaggerate when I talk of the agony of stumbling in a vineyard. It was like marching over a coal heap. It became a supreme effort to climb over a low wall or slight bank such as divided the fields. I was so exhausted I was staggering and I remember the Major's voice behind me, just piercing the fog of exhaustion, urging me on with "keep it up lad, keep going". I must pay tribute to that gallant man for the way in which he encouraged and cajoled his utterly exhausted and almost demoralised remnant of a company. That night was the testing point of all of us. I think it taught us that while you are conscious you can keep going and things never seemed so bad again.

Soon after the operation, Major Ashford was recommended for, and awarded, a Military Cross. His citation reads:

A view from Oudna in a southerly direction - the 2nd Parachute Battalion came from the hills on the skyline. (James Macrae)

For conspicuous gallantry and devotion to duty. After a flight of over 450 miles and a parachute drop. On Monday 30th November 1942, Major Ashford was in command of a company which was ordered to attack and occupy the landing ground at Oudna (Map ref Tunis K 0636). The company came under heavy machine gun fire and mortar fire from enemy positions to the south of Oudna and was pinned to the ground. This officer by his leadership, courage and example succeeded in carrying through the attack and occupying the southern edge of the landing ground. In the subsequent operations on 1st and 2nd December, when the Battalion was surrounded and attacked by enemy armoured units and infantry, this officers conduct and leadership were of the highest order, and by his splendid example was in no small measure responsible for the return of that part of his Battalion which successfully regained the British Lines.

Award: Immediate award of the Military Cross.

Awarded MC 11th February 1943.

Private Dusty Miller remembers:

On Monday at about 1600 I was separated from the rest of the company and attached myself to the anti-tank section. We went forward with the main attack on the aerodrome and came under heavy shell and machine gun fire. About 1700 German aircraft strafed us on the edge of the hill between the farm that 8 Platoon from C Company had been told to occupy and the aerodrome.

Lieutenant Charteris ordered us to get back by sections into the hills, but in the withdrawal Private Frank Welsh and I were separated from the rest of the section. At this point we overtook Corporal Dennis from A Company on a mule – his leg had been broken by shrapnel. Darkness was descending, so we decided to head for the water hole and we met Private Keyes of C Company and Private Stevens of A Company. As the shelling was still going on we decided to get Corporal Dennis to some place further back where we could make him comfortable and try to contact the rest of the Battalion.

We utilised two pistol rods as splints and bound up Corporal Dennis's leg as best as we could with shell dressings. We then headed for the dropping zone to try and contact Lieutenant Buchanan. We arrived at a gully about 5 miles from the dropping zone at dawn on Tuesday. We rested here as Corporal Dennis was in great pain and we had something to eat.

Keyes and Stevens suggested that they try and get some water and find out any information they could about the ground between us and the DZ, while Private Welsh and myself looked after Corporal Dennis. They took with them three of the four water bottles and headed towards a farm between us and the DZ. They didn't return and we were left with one half full bottle of water. Soon after this we contacted an Arab who told us that there were some Germans tanks about a kilometre away with many English prisoners.

We decided to wait until darkness and head for the foothills and where we might be able to get some medical attention for Corporal Dennis. We made our way down to the road at dusk and hid in a hedge alongside the road, when we saw approaching from the direction of Zaghouan three motor cycles and an armoured car. The armoured car stopped about 300 yards away from us and the motor cycles came on very slowly. Private Welsh threw some Gammon bombs and I fired my Sten as fast as I could. The first motor cycle was blown up and the others withdrew perhaps thinking there were more of us than there actually was.

We hid in the hedge for a little while and then two shells whistled over our heads, so we decided to make a break for it and got Corporal Dennis onto the mule's back and headed off in a south westerly direction towards the foothills. We had no water left but did not want to risk going near any farms. At one point during the night we tried to relieve our thirst by licking split cactus leaves but this was not very satisfying.

Wednesday at 0400 we stopped to rest until daybreak in a dried up riverbed, the mule was very tired and Corporal Dennis was in much pain. As dawn broke we saw that there was a small amount of water in the riverbed. I tasted it and it was very salty, however, we made some tea thinking this might take away the bad taste. At daylight we saw a farm further up and to the right of the riverbed. We just had to get some water in spite of the possibility of there being Germans at the farm. Fortunately some passing Arabs led us to believe that the farm was owned by a Frenchman and that no Boche or Italians were in the vicinity, so we went and saw them. They gave us eggs, water, bread, butter and wine. We offered to pay him but he refused.

At about 1500 on Wednesday afternoon we set off for Pont du Fahs with the Arab who took us about 5 or 6 kilometres towards there and then pointed out the best route. We gave him 150 francs and then proceeded on our way arriving at Pont du Fahs at dusk. The Gendarmerie was the first place we stopped and after convincing the Gendarme on duty that we were English soldiers he took Private Welsh and myself in for some food, while he sent his son with the mule and Corporal Dennis to the local doctor. The Gendarme then took us into an air raid shelter to let us sleep on some straw on the floor which he gave us. We rested here for about an hour, he returned with two French soldiers who took us on a motor cycle combination to a bridge west of Pont du Fahs. From here we went into the town and found a hospital where we were checked over and also to see if Corporal Dennis was all right. There were several other members of the Battalion here also. The following afternoon CSM Sharp came along to collect several of us and we rejoined the much depleted Battalion.

Jimmy Sharp recounts his story of Oudna, which gained him a bar to his Military Medal won as a member of the BEF in France in 1940:

On Monday night after being separated from the Company I marched to the well where the Battalion had formed up for the attack. There I contacted some more of C Company under Sergeant Gibbons. As there was no one who knew what was happening we decided to wait in the hills till morning. About 0200 Tuesday we heard troops moving south in the hills, but as we did not know whether they were British or Germans we decided to move parallel with them. This we did till we struck a road at 0300 and found a red beret. We presumed that the troops moving on our right were Germans, so I swung off south-east and got in the hills. At about

0400 we turned south again and kept pushing on till 0500 when we rested in some scrub. At daylight we moved into a valley and made tea. At this point two shots were fired at us and thinking that they must have been snipers or Arabs working with the Germans we pushed on again.

At about 1100 (Tuesday) we contacted Arabs and when I questioned them they reported Germans practically all around. At about 1100 a battle started about 3 miles north-west of us. We tried to make out what was happening but could see nothing as most of the fire appeared to be heavy stuff. Later some Arabs came past and we were able to get some bread and water. All afternoon German fighter aircraft kept circling the hills and machine-gunning somewhere north of us. We rested near a farm for a few hours and from there headed across the fields going north-west. We lay in the cactus until about 0600 about 5 kilometres north west of Moghrane. I placed a sentry with binoculars to watch the main road and during the day we saw a few vehicles passing along the main road. At about 1100 a tank and an armoured car came from the direction of Zaghouan and went into Moghrane, they then went into the fields for the remainder of the day and it appeared as if they were covering the road. During the day an Arab came and said British and American tanks were in Moghrane and Zaghouan. I had a talk with Sergeant Gibbons and we decided to chance sending a message by the Arab to the tanks. We asked in the message for the person receiving it to send a message in reply but when the Arab came back and said he had delivered the message but did not bring a reply we got suspicious.

He said he was going to take us into the village of Moghrane to the tanks, he took us part of the way and then left us. At this point dogs were barking behind a ridge and presuming that the Arab had tricked us and that a German ambush was obviously laid for us if we headed for Moghrane I headed off north-west and then swung west, crossed the main Zaghouan-Tunis road and passed between Moghrane and Depienne.

At about 0330 (Thursday) we lay up at a French farm. In the morning the farmer informed us that the Germans were in Depienne and had captured the paratroopers there. He advised us to make for Pont du Fahs. We set off south-west parallel to the road Depienne-Pont du Fahs. Soon afterwards we saw a motor cycle patrol come along the road. Later when the road was clear we crossed it and headed up into the hills and eventually we came across an Arab who gave us water, wine and food. He then guided us to Pont du Fahs where we contacted some French troops and also found some more of our men. I set off from there with two armoured cars (5 men and myself) to report to the nearest harbour of armoured cars to try and arrange transport for the remainder of the men in Pont du Fahs. We bumped into some German tanks and had to run for it so what happened to the two armoured cars and the remainder of the paratroopers in Pont du Fahs I don't know. The last report we heard was that they were fighting and they may have got out by the south or west road.

The men with me were:

Sergeants Gibbons, Kennedy, Maguire, Webster, Coates and Bennett.

Privates Bennett, Bond, Erby, Fleming, Buchanan, Wilson, Wright, Flitcroft, Harkins, Baxter, Venters, Cooper, Griffiths, Steel, Maysmith and Batten. On

> Wednesday night Privates Batten and Maysmith dropped out and we did not know until morning that they were missing.

Les Shurmer gives a graphic insight into his feelings about life in North Africa in a letter home:

> We sailed into Algiers harbour on Thursday 12th November 1942. We weren't thrilled much by the place, the squalor and the smells were new to us and we hadn't learned to despise the Arabs as we do now. We were stationed about 9 miles from Algiers in an Arab school in a small town. There was lots of work to do. We emplaned at midday Sunday 29th November. Our job was to land on the airfield of Depienne (which is 25 miles due south of Tunis) capture it, march to the airfield at Oudna (8 miles south of Tunis), capture that and then meet some British tanks and attack Tunis. We had rations for 4 days and we thought we'd be coming back after that.
>
> The flight from Algiers to Depienne took us about three hours. It was picturesque flying over all these mountains and it was also pretty cold. I was attached to C Company. They were mainly Scots and a lot of them had been on the Bruneval raid, so considered themselves good. The piper had even brought his bagpipes with him. Four of his mates were carrying a pipe each and he had the bag. He was going to play them as we went into Tunis but alas, we did not get there. We jumped at about 1500 and once on the ground I fixed my Sten together and doubled for the wireless set which came down in a container. I had to cross a path across the field down which some Arabs were running. When I met up with them they asked all smiles, "Anglais parachutists?" I answered, "Oui." So there was vigorous handshaking all round and I thought to myself, "This is a jolly fine war." Midnight came and we moved off to find Jerry.
>
> We marched till 0500 over the roughest of country and very steep hills covering about eight miles, and then rested for an hour till daybreak. It was impossible to sleep because of the cold. Obviously we had no blankets, as a matter of fact we had no battledress blouse, only a shirt, pullover and camouflage canvas jackets. When daybreak came we started marching again, over the same type of country. So hard was the going that even the mules we got from the Arabs bent at the knees and couldn't keep it up. Soon we were able to see Tunis and the coast, so that, although tired, we were still in high spirits. It was decided that we would attack the airfield at 1300. Jerry had prepared a warm reception committee for us. Besides the ordinary defences, they turned out three tanks against us, which was the first time I saw men die, and the first I had bullets whistle about me. The shells they lobbed took a certain toll. We had no weapons to tackle the tanks, except bombs which we carried to throw at them. We gradually pushed on and captured our objective, the railway station on the other side of the airfield. It was then decided that as Jerry obviously wasn't using the airfield we'd pull back to the valley and wait for the 1st Army to catch us up. Jerry hadn't finished with us, for as we pulled out, four fighters came over, up went two white signal lights in our direction from Jerry's positions and down came the aircraft blazing away with their guns.

I was with Trevor Evans and we dug down for about twelve inches. Breakfast was a tin of cheese, half a bar of chocolate, six biscuits, six boiled sweets and tea. Trouble was, Jerry interrupted it. Tea was just on the boil when up bowled three tanks and started shelling us. Our mortars got onto them after a bit and they sheered off. Then three others turned up from the other direction and we thought at first they were Yankee for they flew our recognition signals. One of our sergeants went forward to them and they turned out to be Jerries. They sent him back with an ultimatum to surrender. Our obvious reply was to open up on them, so they just sheered off and started shelling us.

We moved off round the hill for about three miles. Our water bottles were filled from a very dirty trickle of water oozing out of the hillside. We carried sterilizing tablets, but to take a swig from the bottle meant getting a mouthful of dirt. I tried drinking it through a handkerchief, but the dirt clogged it up after a teaspoon of water or so. The only thing to try and do was to drink the water and spit out the dirt.

We marched and marched until we came to a river. What a glorious sight! We had been gasping for water and I had imagined I could see rivers in the moonlight all night. I filled my bottle and swigged it down. I couldn't taste it at first because I was so dry, but then I realised it was salty and had a horrible taste. Still, I refilled my bottle, filled my tin hat and poured it over my head. I felt fitter then. Still we kept marching, or rather stumbling along over rocks and dried up wadis.

At every halt we just dropped in our tracks and I poured a mouthful of salty water down my throat. Many a lad had to fall out on that march. Once we had a heavy shower of rain which was very refreshing for I sucked the water out of my jacket and that wasn't salty. Towards dawn we rested in some scrub while somewhere was found for us to harbour for the day. When daylight came we repaired to a farm about half a mile away. There was a well there with glorious water in it. Twice my mess tin was filled and emptied down my throat and I felt much better. While we were washing, an Me [109] flew over and spotted us and not before long a Jerry motor cycle combination was watching us from the distance. Then some armoured cars and lorried infantry began to move up to attack us. All the Arabs cleared out and we took up defensive positions, we seemed to be in rather a tight spot Two Spitfires (the first we had seen) flew over, but never came back. Early in the afternoon the attack came in from all directions. Machine guns opened up from the surrounding hills and they started mortaring. We just lay doggo for we had very little ammunition left, and the idea was to wait till they came in close. Jerry was puzzled by the quiet and kept his distance, but soon sent a section to find out what we were up to. The officer poked his head over the wall, was grabbed and dispatched (to hell) and half a dozen grenades went over the wall, which settled that little argument. The Jerry mortar fire now intensified and that is how I 'hurt my arm'. One bomb dropped about three yards from me and a piece of shrapnel went through my arm. The MO saw me and put a dressing on it and as the arm went stiff and wasn't much use, I was left to cover a hole in the farmhouse wall.

I later found out that a piece of shrapnel had gone through my Sten gun and it was useless. Soon after it began to get dark and so the CO said when he blew his horn, we would all stream past the farmhouse door, through the cactus and over

The hills around Sidi bou Hadjeba. (James Macrae)

the hill, tackling anything in our way. By this time the thatch was well alight from the tracer that Jerry had fired into it. So the horn was blown and out we came. As luck would have it, Jerry had left open the side we came out, for there was no-one there and we sat on the top of the hill watching him firing away at the empty farm which was now burning nicely.

We left him to it and trekked away over the hills. We walked all that night except for an hour before dawn. Then we started again at 0600 on Thursday morning, because we heard that British troops held a nearby village. We kept walking, dodging any place where Jerry might be and late in the afternoon met up with some Yank armoured cars. You should have heard the cheer that went up from us when they turned out to be Yanks. We were then six miles from Medjez-el-Bab, which was the first town held by Allied troops. We arrived there late in the evening hardly able to put one foot in front of the other.

It was reckoned that we had walked over 100 miles since we had jumped out of that plane on Sunday afternoon. 550 jumped, 140 of us crawled into Medjez-el-Bab, another 80 turned up in small parties from 12 to 20 men during the next week.

Perhaps the best way to end the story of the ill-fated Depienne drop is to use some words from Lieutenant Colonel Frost:

After I got to Medjez with some wounded my first thought was to try and arrange means to find the rest of my Battalion. We still hadn't managed to find B and C Companies. I met General Allfrey, the corps commander, and General Eveleigh of the 78th Division, who said there was nothing anyone could do until the morning when they'd send a force of Americans with us to scour the country. That night we put our heads down in readiness for the morning search, but in the early hours we were roused to hear that a German parachute battalion was about to attack and that we must defend what they thought would be the most likely dropping zone. That was the end of our attempt to pick up the rest of the battalion.

The Americans did go out with some lorries, but without us being with them there was no way they could find our men. Although already less one platoon, C Company had borne the brunt of the Battle of Sidi Bou Hadjeba and so, when they withdrew, there was not much more than a handful of them. B Company had gone further right than we did and had been completely surrounded on ground much less defensible than we had managed to find. So there was really nothing much else to be found of the Battalion and I had about 60 men. The only thing that the High Command could say to me was, "Well, you drew off a lot of the enemy troops and armour and made it much more possible for our people to hold on to Tebourba."

But that was hardly what we were in the business for, specially as we had no real anti-tank weapons. It really was a sad and sorry story. We were then ordered back after one night off-duty to man an airfield in front of Medjez. A flight of Spitfires arrived to exert air superiority and were promptly shot down the next day – it was absolutely crazy. We dug positions near the railway station at Medjez where we stayed about a week. We were in a pretty poor state by this time. We'd had to drink all sorts of filthy water on our way and this caused many stomach upsets. We'd only been issued with two 48 hour ration packs and had to find food wherever we could. Then we found a French Army depot near this railway station, so we made ourselves warm by wearing the baggy trousers of the Zouaves and the blue jackets of the Spahis, much to the annoyance of the High Command.

Elements of the 10th Panzer Division attacked the outskirts of Medjez just as we were handing over to the Coldstream Guards. We went to Souk-el-Arba to reform and I now had time to rest and think about the month we'd been in North Africa. I'd lost several good officers, among them my second-in-command, Philip Teichman, my adjutant, Jock Short, and my intelligence officer, the very fine Ewen Charteris, who had gone off from Cactus Farm to try to make contact and explain our desperate position. He'd done so well at Bruneval; I thought he had a charmed life. We had been completely isolated and given bogus objectives and there had not been the slightest attempt to support us. Just one RAF aircraft could have flown out to see where we were. I found it very difficult to be polite to those responsible when I met them.

It was perhaps the most disgracefully mounted operation of the whole war. There seemed to be rather a lack of sympathy for my Battalion and this hurt, especially as there was so little understanding from Brigade Headquarters. The only person with any sympathy at all was Alistair Pearson, who was enough of a soldier to realise what had happened. The chief engineer of the corps, who'd done a lot of soldering, was one of the few who was really appreciative and on looking back I think that getting the 2nd Battalion out of that pickle was possibly the best thing I ever did.

7

Christmas 1942 and a New Year

Just because the remnants of the 2nd Battalion had reached the relative safety of Allied lines, it didn't stop them being given the Army run-around. For around eight days after 5th December they were moved from pillar to post, as the following comments from a report by Lieutenant Colonel Frost depict:

> 5/12/1942
> At 08.00 hours the CRA 78th Division arrived with the following instructions:- It was proposed to use the landing ground at Medjez-el-Bab for fighter aircraft. This landing ground being in front of the forward defence lines was to be held as strongly as possible against all forms of enemy attack. I was to organise and coordinate a plan for defence. 150 men of the Hampshire Regiment came under command at 21.00 hours. 80 men of a field battery came under command at 23.00 hours. The Battalion was divided into two sections; A under Major Ashford called Ashforce. The remainder under Major Ross called Rossforce. 1 Officer and 75 men of the Hampshire's being attached to each. The men from the field battery being kept as force reserve.
>
> At 14.00 hours CSM Sharp and 19 men arrived having been separated from the Battalion since the action at Oudna, Defence Force HQ was set up in the Gendarmie. Captain Moore was appointed Adjutant. Two companies of French infantry were already in position near the landing ground. A company of light tanks were under command until 19.00 hours, also 4 machine guns from the same unit. 6 Bofors guns from 32 Light Anti-Aircraft Regiment and a section of 72 Anti-Tank Regiment were under command until dark when the guns had to be moved back to the other side of the river.
>
> 6/12/1942
> The night passed uneventfully; at 08.30 hours a Staff Officer arrived from Divisional HQ with fresh instructions. The RAF would not now use the landing ground and we were to move to an area near Medjez and be prepared to:-
> 1) Assist in the defence of Medjez.
> 2) Be prepared to counter-attack in the event of enemy penetration at Sloughia or the bridge at Dar el Gassi.
> 3) Be prepared to thicken up any weakness in the French defences.
>
> I decided to move to the area near Medjez railway station as the most likely threat would come from Tebourba. I allotted areas to Rossforce and the Hampshire Regiment who were now organised under their own officers. I organised Ashforce into a mobile column standing by at 10 minutes' notice. I managed to borrow three lorries from an anti-aircraft battery as transport and I moved a section consisting of 4 x 37mm American anti-tank guns into the same area. The American Field

Armour Battalion were contacted and agreed to provide some light tanks should the column be required to operate.

At 14.00 hours I made a recce with Major Ashford, Captain Mountford and the American anti-tank gun commander towards Tebourba. We went as far as 11th Infantry Brigade HQ, I met the Brigadier and told him of our role and plans. A tank battle was taking place on the other side of the river about 2 miles away, we watched this for some time, then as it seemed to be progressing satisfactorily, returned to the railway station.

At 17.00 hours I visited Divisional HQ and told them what I was doing. I was informed that I was now under the French Commander at Medjez; I returned to Medjez and visited French HQ. While there I learned that the Corps Commander had ordered mines to be laid at all approaches to the town. Captain Vernon RE was in charge. The mines were also laid during the night by parties from the Battalion, The Hampshire Regiment and local artillery formations.

7/12/1942
The day passed without incident. Rained heavily.

8/12/1942
I visited Divisional HQ in order to obtain some news of future moves and to try to speed up various administrative matters. In particular the supply of blankets or warmer clothing. I was informed that we would probably be moved back to Souk-el-Arba during the night. I returned but was later informed that the move was cancelled.

9/12/1942
Nothing to report.

10/12/1942
Received information that we should move in the near future. Probably the following day.

11/12/1942
Attended a conference at French HQ. The commander of 1st Guards Brigade was present and arranged to take over my positions during the day. In the early afternoon the enemy attacked Medjez with tanks and infantry. A few shells and mortar bombs fell near our positions but no damage was done. Later in the afternoon the enemy appeared to withdraw. By 17.00 hours the Coldstream Guards had taken over our positions and the Battalion was concentrated in the sheds near the station.

At 19.30 hours 7 TCVs arrived to lift the Battalion and at 20.10 hours the Battalion was on the move to Souk-el-Khemis. The move was without incident and we arrived in the billeting area at approx 07.00 hours 12/12/1942.

Whilst the 2nd Parachute Battalion was suffering from the ill-planned Depienne drop and its aftermath, on 2nd December orders were received that the 3rd Battalion was to move forward to Souk-el-Arba by air and take equipment with them for an airborne

Father B. Egan (Padre of the 1st Parachute Battalion) supporting Major Dugdale of the 17/21 Lancers, outside the hospital at Beja, December 1942. (N. Cherry)

operation. Again the poor understanding and co-operation between commands came to the fore, as when Brigadier Flavell consulted with Eastern Air Command, he was told that no airborne operations would be possible. Eastern Air Command stated that in their opinion ground conditions in the winter made it impossible for aircraft to take off from Souk-el-Arba! Then 1st Army got involved and came to the decision that the 1st Parachute Brigade would now be used as 'ordinary infantry'. The specialist items for airborne operations such as remained would be left behind at Maison Blanche with a small rear party to look after them and bring them forward should the need arise.

In the evening of 7th December Brigadier Flavell reported to the GOC V Corps who was in charge of the Souk-el-Khemis sector and was told to bring his Brigade up to the area. By around the 12th December the 1st and 2nd Battalions were concentrated here. The plan being that they would cover the Beja area from attack.

The entry in the 1st Battalion's war diary for this day paints a familiar picture:

> The Battalion arrived at rest area in Souk-el-Khemis. No arrangements had been made for our arrival and the 2nd Battalion were already in occupation of the farm allocated to us at J0327. The day was spent searching for accommodation. V Corps were contacted for supplies and proved very helpful especially the DAQMG.

It was also intended for V Corps to launch an attack in the direction of Tunis, but this was cancelled due to adverse weather conditions. In December 1942 Major-General Browning came out from England to visit his babies.

The following extracts from the 1st Battalion war diary may be of interest for December 1942:

13th December 1942. The day was spent getting the Battalion settled in. R Company was sent off to another farm, but found it full of Americans who would not move out. However, V Corps said they would deal with the matter.

14th December 1942. The Battalion began to re-equip. A bath was found on the way to Beja, it was an Arab one supplied by hot springs, but the Medical Officer thought Lysol would answer the question. [Author's note: Lysol was a popular brand of disinfectant in the 1930s and '40s which contained a cresol solution and killed bacteria.]

15th December 1942. Battalion continued to reorganise. Reinforcements are on their way. R Company moved to new billets.

16th December 1942. Battalion HQ was ordered to move into Souk-el-Khemis at very short notice, the farm was cleared by 1400 hours. The JAG's (Judge Advocate General) representative arrived to assist us to fix up various Courts Martial. NAAFI stores were brought from Bone by Lieutenant J Jessop.

18th December 1942. News has been received that we may have to move on Sunday. The CO saw Major Bull and remainder of T Company who are forward near Beja.

A sergeant uses a bottle to break up biscuits which were used as crumbs for fishcakes. Picture taken on 26th December 1942 in the Beja sector. (Imperial War Museum)

19th December 1942. Battalion still at rest. JAG arrived from Algiers to conduct four Courts Martial. Lieutenant Wandless (S Company) visited Bone.

20th December 1942. Battalion mail sent off from Souk-el-Arba with Christmas telegrams. Warning Order arrived to the effect that the Battalion will move off tomorrow. Major A Pearson appointed Lieutenant Colonel. Lieutenant O'Brien appointed Captain and Adjutant.

21st December 1942. Battalion moved to positions north of Beja. Battalion HQ established at Viaduct Farm together with 11th Brigade B Echelon. 195425. R Company in farm at 175475, S Company in haystacks 205432 and T Company in wog village 212482.

Major-General Browning arrived and told us we would be in for 'fun' soon. He met the Battalion as we were leaving Souk-el-Khemis. The remainder of T Company and some reinforcements were already in occupation and we were nearly up to strength.

22nd December 1942. Warning Order received for attack on Tebourba. Preparations made for move to lying up area in Medjez-el-Bab. Weather – raining hard.

Sergeant F. Tucker of the 1st Parachute Battalion cleaning his boots on Boxing Day 1942. (Imperial War Museum)

23rd December 1942. 2 i/c sent off to recce Battalion area. Heavy rain continues so operation cancelled. A small number of reinforcements arrived and were distributed to companies. Major-General Browning arrived and discussed our former activities with the CO. Heavy rain all day.

24th December 1942. 2 i/c returned with report of activities of 2nd Coldstream Guards. More rain. Battalion remains in present location. Rum ration issued to all ranks. Padre Egan held a Midnight Mass.

25th December 1942. A very wet Christmas Day. A few stores were obtained from the NAAFI at Souk-el-Arba and distributed to the companies. CO visited company locations. The Brigadier called to convey best wishes to the Battalion. Move Orders arrive ordering us to take over from 3rd Battalion in Hunts Gap area tomorrow. A small number of reinforcements arrive.

The war diary for the 1st Parachute Squadron RE relates:

Christmas Day. Lieutenant J. Brown and 22 ORs arrive from base. Celebrated with church service, plonk and beer, although C Troop had to re-lay minefields in Battalion area.

This war diary also relates that whilst re-laying this minefield one Sapper was killed in an accident whilst laying a 75 grenade. He was Sapper G. Hepple, who now lies at Medjez-el-Bab CWGC cemetery grave 5D9.

Men of the 1st Parachute Battalion sorting themselves out after a patrol on 26th December 1942. (Imperial War Museum)

Lieutenant Colonel Pearson has a slightly different view of his Battalion's activities in this period:

> The Battalion withdrew to Sidi N'Sir. We had been in action fighting continuously for 26 days and it was now time for a rest and to take a look at ourselves. Having survived 21 days as acting CO I was now entitled to become a temporary lieutenant colonel, so I got myself a couple of pips – the only advantage of rank is that it gives you more power to negotiate – instead of dealing with the monkey it is now the organ grinder.
>
> We moved to a rest area at Souk-el-Khemis where we battled for billets against all and sundry and being 1st Parachute Battalion I think we won in the end. Our doctor, Captain Haggie, organised wine from the nearest monastery and we got a substantial NAAFI ration of booze and cigarettes. A bathhouse was found which was enjoyed by all. Oeufs and oranges were plentiful and cheap thanks to the Controle Civile de Beja. We also received some pay. We reorganised and began to look less like tinkers and more like soldiers.
>
> We moved back to the Beja area on 21st December. Morale was extremely high and the Battalion was briefed for an attack on Longstop Hill, which to our relief was cancelled.
>
> The padre was promoted and to celebrate his advancement to major went into Beja, joined a queue for what he thought was a shop and found himself in the local brothel. Much to his irritation this bit of intelligence spread round the unit like wildfire.

Longstop Hill on the left hand side of the hills running across the middle of the picture. (Imperial War Museum)

This is a picture of the home of the CO of the 3rd Parachute Battalion, Lieutenant Colonel Pine-Coffin during the Christmas period 1942. He commented, "During December 1942 my Battalion was ordered to carry out an attack which seemed quite suicidal and which few would have survived. The more I planned it, the worse it seemed. About the 20th it began to pour with rain and it continued day and night till after Christmas. The attack was cancelled on the 24th. This photo shows my slit trench during this period; not very comfortable but I slept very contentedly in it on Christmas Eve nevertheless." (R. Pine-Coffin)

> Christmas Eve was a very cold night and our sand-fire was going down in the officers' mess. I decided to put some life into it with petrol. It exploded and I caught fire. By the time I was extinguished I found that some bugger had nicked my watch. Then on Christmas Day it was raining as usual – no presents except for the 2 i/c who discovered he had tapeworms. The post then arrived with a parcel for him with 300 green lanyards – it was just not his day. The padre visited the NAAFI and got half a bottle of beer per man to go with their roast pig and mutton.

An officer, Captain A. Bush from the 3rd Battalion, also has vivid memories of Christmas 1942:

> Just before Christmas Day the rain came. It fell in volumes which I had never seen equalled in the Lake District in my youth. Our individual holes soon collected water which we tried to bale out and drain off, but as fast as we got rid of the stuff,

> so it returned. At night we were cold, wet and miserable. A slush of ankle-deep mud made movement away from one's trench undesirable except for a change of company. By no means too soon the Company Commander wilted and ordered us to withdraw into various farm outbuildings. They were filthy hovels full of dung and infested with fleas, but we welcomed the inadequate shelter they offered. Roofs leaked but they resisted much of the rain. Moreover, we could now sleep close to another body and generate some warmth. I had a warm companion in Taffy who was big enough to play in the second row of the Welsh pack. Yet on Christmas Eve we were both depressed. Having talked as much as we could and laughed as much as we could at our exaggerated reminiscences, we discovered that we had no cigarettes or any tobacco between us. Searching through all my pockets, I came across my tobacco pouch which I had given up as lost. Behold, there were enough dry grains lying in the bottom of it to fill half a pipe each. We sat up in the darkness and relished our pipes silently. For a few minutes, indeed, it did seem like Christmas.

With all of this bad weather the High Command realised that any attacks by V Corps in the direction of Tunis would be extremely difficult and would have to be postponed till after the rainy season. So Brigadier Flavell suggested that the Brigade should be withdrawn from the forward areas to reorganise, assimilate all the new arrivals into the Battalions and perhaps also do some exercises with the American transport squadrons. This was supported by the GOC of 78th Division but V Corps felt unable to do so due to a shortage of infantry. Additionally it was felt that daylight parachute operations into enemy-held territory would be too costly given the relative inexperience of the American crews in night flying.

An interesting outcome of the bad weather around this time is contained in a few words from a conference held on 24th December. On this day Generals Eisenhower and Anderson visited the HQ of V Corps located at Souk-el-Khemis. The plan was that the two top commanders would discuss what Eisenhower called "our final and most ambitious attack" with Lieutenant-General Allfrey, the Corps Commander. It is noted that General Eisenhower had to travel by car as conditions were too bad to fly. The 1st Parachute Brigade had been tasked to take part in this offensive as follow-on troops behind the 1st Guards Brigade. Their objective was Longstop Hill and the paratroopers were meant to exploit forward once the Guardsmen had taken this hill. The conference took place in pouring rain and it is recorded that the three Generals braved the rain to go forward a bit to see some of the ground over which the men would have to advance. Whilst on this inspection Eisenhower noticed four soldiers trying to extricate a motor cycle from some glutinous mud which seemed to stretch as far as the eye could see in every direction. After a while the four men gave up with the motor cycle stuck fast. Eisenhower later commented, "It was this incident which as much as anything else convinced me of the hopelessness of an attack."

Longstop Hill was otherwise known as Djebel el Ahmera. The German Army, having recognised the strategic value of Djebels el Ahmera and Rhar, fortified them both. While the Allies recognised that the capture of the feature was essential before a drive to liberate Tunis could commence, it was not known that it consisted of twin peaks.

On the night of 22nd/23rd December 1942, the 2nd Battalion Coldstream Guards mounted an attack, capturing what was thought to be all of the massif, before being

Sweeping for mines at the side of the Medjez-el-Bab-Tebourba road. In the background is the Longstop ridge. (Imperial War Museum)

relieved by the 18th US Regimental Combat Team while heavy rain fell. The Germans counter-attacked, driving the Americans off Djebel el Ahmera. The next night the Guards successfully recaptured the hill only to find, when daylight came, that another summit, Djebel Rhar, remained to be assaulted. During the night the Guards once again attacked but, after capturing the second hill, were driven off by a furious counter-attack by the Germans on Christmas Day. Thereafter the massif was known by the Allies as 'Longstop Hill' and by the Germans as 'Der Weihnachten Hügel' ('Christmas Hill'). It is located north-east of Medjez-el-Bab on the road to Tebourba.

The 3rd Battalion spent the few days between Christmas and New Year in the area of Souk-el-Khemis and for several soldiers there were more urgent matters on their minds than festivities, as Captain Alan Bush recalls:

> It all started in early December when the Battalion was on a long train journey and we got stuck in an out of the way station for about a day. Some of the men slipped off to see what this little bit of civilisation could offer in the way of excitement. Most returned quietly and sensibly enough to cover their absence. But two became fighting drunk and violently resisted the modest escort which had been despatched to bring them back. Then a senseless mistake was made; the men chosen to contain the drunks physically were of the same platoon. Reluctantly they refused to obey the command. These men, all very good men, were later to be charged with the serious charge of mutiny. On the day before New Year's Eve I was told that the four 'mutineers' had asked for me to defend them at their court martial the next day. These were four good men who had been forced to face the problem of divided

loyalties on that long train journey. I was given less than 24 hours to prepare the defence. I was not a lawyer and I had no legal knowledge. But I had achieved a reputation as a miracle worker from a case in England when I had defended a soldier successfully. He had refused to jump at the last moment and was charged with refusal to obey the lawful command of a superior. As he was the last man of the stick to jump, I queried the accusation that he had disobeyed an order which could never have been given. It transpired that no specific order had been given to him and so he was acquitted. Justice rested very unfairly on a sheer technicality on which I had based my defence.

I believe that after that case the order to jump was given to each jumper before he emplaned. But the case I now found myself involved in offered no such technicality. It was with a feeling of incompetence and legal ignorance that I attended the court. Moreover, it was common knowledge that High Command was determined to have an example set in view of instances of bad discipline by Allied troops in rear areas. These four men, good men all, had the misfortune to be chosen as the example. They had been misled at the time of their indiscretion, they could face up to four years of imprisonment if found guilty. I had known that my task would be difficult; once in court I knew it was hopeless.

The case was apparently considered sufficiently important to demand the presence of a senior member of the JAG's department. He was a sort of umpire to see that fair play and justice were observed. A member of the same department was the prosecuting counsel, my opponent. The President of the Court, in my mind, a weak, idea-less, frightened man was entirely in the hands of the two legal experts. Before I was called upon to defend, I pleaded for help to the umpire. Could I apply for an adjournment as I had been given so little time to prepare the case for the defence? I received a sneering twist of the lips but no verbal answer. Over a brief sandwich lunch I again pleaded for his help. The answer was a similar sneer with the announcement that I was wasting my time as "we've got them". The four men were subsequently found guilty but had to await confirmation of their sentences; within a couple of days they were fighting in the line again; shortly afterwards the sentence was squashed. I learnt, rightly or wrongly that my umpire friend was soon given another job. In spite of him, justice prevailed!

I was very depressed when I returned to my billet, and in no mood to enjoy whatever New Year's Eve had in store. But soon I forgot my misery of feeling that I had been incompetent in my defence of the four good men. Perhaps it was the knowledge that a warning order had been received to move back into the line again and the four 'convicted' men would be with us.

The 1st Battalion spent the early part of January 1943 in the front line and on New Year's Day their war diary gives an insight into how difficult it must have been dealing with the locals:

January 1st. New Year greetings poured in from the Army Commander downwards. However the New Year did not start too well for everyone – Lieutenant Wandless returned from his patrol with an interesting story. Whilst on patrol he met an Arab – this Arab thought Lieutenant Wandless was a German and warned him of the Allied dispositions, he then explained how he had seen a standing patrol of the Lancs Fusiliers at El Djenaine 4265, attacked and destroyed by a German patrol. Lieutenant Wandless did not arrest the Arab as he thought he might be useful later.

The weather was still very bad, with heavy rain and roads and tracks being virtually impassable to wheeled vehicles. The 1st Battalion's war diary contains the following comments about the conditions:

> January 3rd (after taking over a position from the French in the Beja sector). The trouble is we are taking over an area which is manned by 900 Frenchmen with a Battalion of 400. The Battalion area stretches over ten miles. R Company established in same area as Forward HQ with T Company on the right and S Company on the left. Major Bull and T Company are in a very exposed position being on a very bare mountain and of course it is pouring with rain.
>
> January 4th. The weather turned finer but the ground was still rather impassable to wheeled vehicles. The CO and IO spent the morning walking round the Battalion area starting with an assault on T Company's mountain. The Company was drenched completely during the night and were rather the worse for wear. However, the change in the weather gave them the opportunity to dry out. They managed to acquire two mules from the French, but so much water was coming down the mountain that even the mules were immobilised – the men had to manhandle all stores up to their positions.

Djebel Azzag or Green Hill. (Imperial War Museum)

Relief was on the horizon though as on 6th January a movement order arrived advising the 1st Battalion that they would be handing over to French troops during the night and them move to Souk-el-Khemis prior to returning to 'base'. For the 1st Battalion the 2 i/c Major Cleasby-Thompson was sent on ahead to arrange billets at Souk-el-Khemis and the unit's war diary records that "as usual the moment the movement order arrived the rain began to fall." The Battalion arrived at Souk-el-Khemis in the early hours.

But even out of the line some men of the 1st Battalion encountered problems. Private A. Brown was a 'new boy' and joined the 1st Battalion as a reinforcement just before Christmas 1942, being posted to R Company. Life in the field took a bit of getting used to and he recalls that the highlight of January 1943 for him was getting deloused. It was, to some extent, his own fault. He had never had lice before but one day he saw what he thought was a spare sleeping bag and bagged it. He commented,

> After only one night of sleeping in it I was itching all over and soon knew what lice were. At the time we were stationed in an abandoned mine in the hills and there appeared to be no immediate possibility of action, so I was allowed to go to the nearest field hospital which also had a delousing unit. I got there and my uniform was 'cooked' and I was deloused with the usual paraffin treatment but the 'cooking' process shrivelled up the chamois leather pockets of my paratrooper trousers and

3rd Battalion HQ in the area of Sedjenane, which had been set up in some empty Arab huts. As the CO commented, "This became known as the Woggery and provided fair comfort but a lot of fleas. It is the only time I have slept with chickens under my bed. The Arabs kept returning to try and sell us things. Here my Adjutant and Intelligence Sergeant are dealing with one of them." (R. Pine-Coffin)

From the British lines looking towards Djebel Azzag/Green Hill. (Imperial War Museum)

> I had to tear them out to be able to walk back. Perhaps this taught me to be more careful about picking up stray kit.

After spending a more comfortable Christmas than they would have got in the front line, the 3rd Battalion was warned to take part in an attack on a feature known as Djebel el Azzag, but more commonly known as Green Hill. This was situated close to the road between Sedjenane and Mateur. In fact Green Hill was one of a number of pieces of high ground which dominate this road. Green Hill was on the left of the road, Commando Hill and the smaller Bald Hill on the other. The paratroopers were given a support role to 36th Infantry Brigade, the intention being that Major Terrell's A Company would go in with the 5th Buffs on a night attack on the night of 4th/5th January 1943.

As the famous war correspondent Alan Moorehead wrote in his 1944 book *African Trilogy*,

> Sedjenane was a wayside railway town in the wet cork forests on the way to Mateur. Whoever held Mateur held Bizerta, and whoever held Green and Bald Hills outside Sedjenane held Mateur.

The fighting for Green Hill was intense and bitter. Initially some progress was made with a first ridge line being taken. But a second crest about a hundred yards away and higher was in enemy hands. The Germans had had plenty of time to construct defensive positions including concrete machine gun posts, lay plenty of barbed wire, mines and booby traps. A Company was stuck where they were under fire from what seemed like all sides and their position was not helped by the British artillery. They had called for artillery support and it is no surprise to learn that several shells landed uncomfortably close to the men of A Company. Several uncomfortable hours were spent here before orders were received to fall back.

Some hours later B Company under the command of Major D. Dobie had a go and were more successful, in that they took the second crest and were able to hold it for a short time. The Germans launched two counter-attacks, the first about 200 strong in almost a 'Great War' 'over the top' shoulder-to-shoulder extended line formation. It is said they were virtually wiped out. However, in so doing most of the ammunition B Company had with them was fired and the second German counter-attack forced them off the crest and back down the hill.

This is Lieutenant D. Bentham's account of his time at Green Hill:

> I stood at the bottom of Green Hill and listened to the CO while he explained our job and gave us the necessary information. It all seemed simple and I felt rather sorry for the Germans waiting at the top. We reckoned on a few machine guns in trenches and it seemed we should soon overpower these. At 11 o'clock we started up the hill and by 12.30 were waiting about 400 yards from the enemy, while the artillery put down a 30 minute barrage for us. When it lifted we got up and advanced. David told me to take my Platoon round the right flank, while the rest of the Company moved up on the left. As we moved forward I saw a German sentry moving up and down and resisted an impulse to have a pot shot, for surprise meant everything. We got nearer and suddenly three machine guns opened fire on us. Two of my section commanders were hit, one killed and the other very badly wounded. About six other men were also hit. We got down and due to the total lack of cover found that we were pinned down and thus unable to move. Sergeant MacDonald and I managed to crawl forward and lob a few grenades and managed to account for a few of the enemy, who, by now were working round my flank. I was feeling dazed as the result of a German grenade bursting near my feet and as more men were being hit, I decided to withdraw and join the rest of the Company. I therefore gave the necessary orders and when I had seen them go (on their stomachs) I withdrew myself. The fire had increased and Jerry was using his mortars also and my remaining men could not be found so I went round and found David. We took two enemy forts and they were of concrete construction with steel roofs. By now the casualties were fairly heavy and we discovered that there were still more of these bloody forts. Then Jerry counter-attacked with a fresh company. David gave the order to withdraw, an order we obeyed with heavy hearts. We collected ourselves at the bottom of the hill and reckoned up our losses. Many good chaps had gone including my batman. Jerry kept us his pressure and we were shelled and mortared all day. That evening an order came through for all troops to withdraw to a new line. We found out later that we had been fighting German parachute troops in superior numbers. After two days we were withdrawn and sent back to our base – there to re-equip and reinforce. The Company did well that night – for the majority their first baptism under fire, but none could forget Green Hill – or should I say Green Hell.

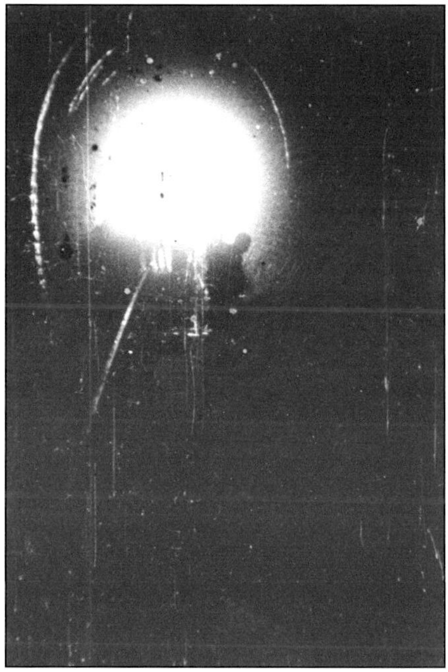

This shows an image of the railway tunnel in which the 3rd Parachute Battalion spent two days before the attack on Green Hill in January 1943. The trains were stopped from running but it was a lot colder here than expected and the wind seemed to whistle through the tunnel. (R. Pine-Coffin)

Private George Thompson was one of the medical orderlies attached to the 3rd Battalion:

> Our first Djebel attack was on Djebel Azzag, known as Green Hill, and we had spent a day and a night in a culvert facing the Djebel. It was like a scene from hell. There we were, encamped on concrete sidewalks with a stream flowing through the middle. The only light that we had was provided by the brew up fires, which made for a weird scene. Who could ever forget the voice of Hildyard-Todd echoing through the tunnel as he sang *Water Boy*, just as Paul Robeson had sang it [Sergeant Hildyard-Todd was killed at Arnhem in 1944]. We moved off at dawn preceded by an artillery barrage. On moving up the hill with a Platoon we eventually got to the top and I met Lieutenant Elton-Tuckett who said he wanted me to go with him and some other men across the top and recover two wounded men. I wasn't prepared to go only armed with a first aid haversack and so borrowed a Sten from one of the lads. We hadn't got very far before there were bullets swarming all around us. We went to earth and the man next to me, Private Wood, fell down beside me. He looked at me … as we were almost face to face and with an unspoken plea in his eyes … from his mouth emerged a balloon of bright red blood and I knew that a main artery had been severed. One of the men called out to me "Do something, Tommo", but I knew there was nothing that I could do for him and as we looked into each other's eyes I saw his life slowly ending. We did not find the wounded that

we had set out to rescue and Lieutenant Elton-Tuckett also died that day. He knew that he was destined to die in action as he told me that, with his favourite weapon, a German Luger, he would kill Germans until such time that they killed him. Such was his hatred of the enemy. We medics continued to patch up the wounded and evacuate them from the hill. Eventually the MO arrived at our position and thanked us four medics for our work and stated that he would see that we got official recognition for our work. Nothing ever transpired.

The 3rd Battalion's war diary reports the following:

1st January 0830 – CO leaves for HQ 36th Infantry Brigade at Sedjenane (map reference 3176 Tunisia 1/50,000 Sheet 11) to discuss role of Battalion in attack by that Brigade.

2nd January 1800 – Battalion leaves by TCVs. 36th Infantry Brigade operation order received.

3rd January 0330 – Battalion arrives at El Alouana station (map reference 3274 Tunisia 1/50,000 Sheet 11). 1100 – CO reports to Brigade Commander 36th Infantry Brigade. 1130 – CO visits positions to be taken over from 5th Buffs (map reference 3476 Tunisia 1/50,000 Sheet 11). 1545 – CO 5th Buffs gives orders for attack on Djebel el Azzag attended by CO and OC A Company. This Company placed under command 5th Buffs. 1800 – Orders received that attack planned night 3rd/4th postponed 24 hours owing to weather.

4th January 2000 – Battalion (less A and C Companies) takes over 5th Buffs position 3476 and C Company remains in defensive position El Alouana station. 2100 – A Company leaves lying-up area for the 5th Buffs assembly position.

5th January – 0730 OC A Company with 3 Platoon (Lieutenant Elton-Tuckett) ordered to investigate sniper fire. Met with machine gun fire. Found none of our own troops in area. 0900 – Messerschmitt 109 shot down. Pilot lands by parachute 1½ miles from 5 Platoon. Patrol sent out but finds pilot has escaped. 1030 – OC A Company ordered to take his whole Company and hold western end of Djebel el Azzag. 1115 – A Company complete occupation of western end of Djebel el Azzag. 1345 – Battalion (less two companies) ordered to move to 372771 to assist 5th Buffs carry their objective. 1530 – Battalion leaves position at J3247, C Company remains in defensive position El Alouana station. 1900 – CO gives orders for night attack on point 396. 2330 – B Company moves off for attack.

6th January 0030 – Artillery barrage for 30 minutes on point 396. 0110 – Enemy opens fire. 0145 – B Company assault point 396 from the north. Neutralised seven machine gun posts north of objective. Unable to make point 396. Lieutenant W. Blewitt killed. 0300 – Enemy counter-attacked. Attack driven off. 0330 – Enemy counter-attacked. 0345 – B Company forced to withdraw. 0715 – CO at request of CO 5th Buffs returns to Brigade HQ and reports on the situation on Djebel el Azzag to Brigadier 36th Infantry Brigade. 1030 – Lieutenant J. Elton-Tuckett killed. 1200 – Brigade Commander visits CO and CO 5th Buffs at 372771, plans formulated for Battalion withdrawal. Brigade Commander informs CO that Battalion will withdraw from 36th Infantry Brigade area on night 7th/8th and revert to command of 1st Parachute Brigade. 1400 – CO 5th Buffs issues orders for withdrawal to come into effect on receipt of orders from HQ 36th Infantry Brigade. Staff Captain 1st Parachute Brigade brings information that Battalion will proceed by road to Souk-el-Khemis on night 7th/8th thence by rail to Algiers area on the 9th.1815 – Withdrawal commences. Enemy launch attack on positions vacated by A Company.

7th January 0200 – Battalion arrives in lying up area El Alouana station. 2330 – Battalion leaves El Alouana station by TCVs.

8th January 0500 Battalion arrives at Souk-el-Khemis.

See Appendices XXIII, XXIV and XXV for more information on the time spent by the 3rd Battalion during this period. [Author's Note: I have a friend who was a member of B Company on Mount Longdon in June 1982 during the Falklands War and we have talked at length about the events there. He was most interested to read about the exploits of some of his predecessors and we were both struck how similar the two mountain battles were, it was almost as if the British Army had not learnt anything in nearly 40 years. Perhaps the most significant point is that the Toms of 3 Para in 1982 wouldn't take no for an answer and it is a good job there were not Germans at the top of Longdon.]

Captain A. Bush's recollections of Green Hill and the time afterwards:

Our splendid RASC drivers got us to our destination and soon the Company was in position near a railway station which had been reduced to rubble by enemy shell fire. Our immediate job was to give flank protection for a force, part of an infantry brigade, whose task was to capture Green Hill, one of the two hills which commanded the winding road towards Bizerta. Green Hill and the other known as Bald Hill, completely dominated the valley through which the road twisted and the enemy had fortified them strongly. We were expected to wait until Green Hill had been captured and then to help in the attack on Bald Hill. The attack looked unpleasant, for little cover seemed available to troops advancing up the hills.

The Company Commander set up his HQ in a culvert which ran under the railway line. Through it ran a fast-flowing stream which left enough room on one side for the construction of a kind of dog kennel made up of compo boxes. It was a beastly spot, for the wind whistled incessantly through the tunnel. We were without rations which lay in a ravine some miles back, but our misfortune did not disturb us; we had learnt from experience and now always carried something on our person, just in case.

The following morning the Brigade attack started, preceded by a heavy artillery bombardment. Two of our Companies were well forward, not committed as yet and waiting to carry out their role of mopping-up. The attack failed, and later I was to hear criticism of the troops who had not succeeded in their difficult task. I hated that sort of talk, probably because I could not conquer a fear that one day I would be a failure in similar circumstances. One Company was holding a forward area, another was preparing for a night assault; hardly the reserve or support role we had been grateful to have allotted to us originally.

In the afternoon, one devoted to rest, I lay on my back and watched a succession of dogfights between Spitfires and enemy fighters. We had greater numbers in the air and we cheered each success. I remember two enemy planes cornered by a dozen or so Spitfires at about a thousand feet. One German plane was hit in a matter of seconds; the pilot bailed out from his blazing machine. The pilot of the second plane, outnumbered and in desperate straits, turned into a vastly superior enemy, scattered the Spitfires and made good his escape at ground level. The other less fortunate pilot was drifting down to earth and we despatched a patrol to try and get him. His parachute was recovered but there was no sign of him. He was probably given secret refuge in the Arab village near his landing spot, for the locals were not always friendly towards us. We kept a careful watch on every egg-vendor, for they all had intimate local knowledge of the ground which lay between the enemy and ourselves, and as guides they were open to the highest bidder.

The night attack was initially a success, but, as usual, the enemy had an immediate counter-attack, meticulously prepared and rehearsed and the assaulting Company was too short of numbers to hang on. For the first time, we experienced the sight of enemy troops advancing towards us in close order, shoulder to shoulder, chanting and singing. We recognised and admired the thoroughness of the enemy's defensive positions. We could not hold out against such efficiency, and, eventually outnumbered as we were, we were withdrawn. I cannot remember how long we remained in that area; but I do recall three episodes concerning one of the characters of the Battalion – Sergeant White (Chalky of course).

He was an odd-shaped man, thick-legged and slightly bandy, only of medium height, but broad and muscular. He had a large head covered in black curly hair, a prominent Yorkshire jaw, an elongated nose over which his blue eyes focused with a pronounced squint. He spoke with much facility, seldom at a loss in his search for the right word. He was an excellent Sergeant, trained into the discipline of a regular soldier, self-cultured, his men admired him for his intelligence, knowledge and fairness but above all for his infectious sense of humour. He had the priceless gift of turning misery amongst his men into laughter and often because he could laugh at himself.

The rains had returned and we were trying to keep some of it off us by expert use of our gas-capes as we settled into our weapon pits. Chalky was lying silent in his trench over which he had fixed his gas-cape to form a roof. He was blissfully unaware that a large pool of water was collecting and straining to the limit the effectiveness of his contraption. Several of us collected to watch the inevitable collapse of his roof. When it did and amidst the laughter which followed, the good Sergeant scrambled to his feet, threw off his saturated clothes and holding his hands to high heaven, cried out:-

"Come wind, come rain, come hail, come snow; but
O Lord, please give us rain for our exquisite pleasure!"

One night, in the darkness and the miserable rain, Chalky's platoon were pulled out of their self-constructed comfort to march a few miles to give local protection to some American gunners who had arrived with their Long Toms without any infantry to protect the guns. There were few, if any, of the platoon who were not disgruntled and 'bolshy'. "Why can't the Yanks do the job properly themselves?" was one comment. Prior to moving off, Chalky went quietly down the line checking that each man had all his vital equipment. At the end of the line, he, of course, hit the fool. "Have you got everything?" "I haven't got my entrenching tool, Sergeant." "Entrenching tool, entrenching tool! You talk to me about your bloody entrenching tool, you who should have the blood of battle up your nostrils!"

And so, much reluctance and a lot of discomfort was forgotten as the platoon broke the dark silence with their raucous laughter. An hour or two later the wet and bad-tempered men arrived at the gun site to find their only cover was a very small out-building of a small farm. Half of the building was railed off to contain a few mature pigs wallowing in their filth which seeped under the rails to all corners. The stench was nauseating; the men's attitude bordering on rebellion. When Chalky returned from having posted and checked on his first guards, he found his men in a near state of mutiny. Immediately aware that he was dealing with a very disgruntled bunch of men, he acted in a way which surely deserves the highest military award, provided the pig can be considered to be the enemy in the face of whom the action takes place. With the words "If we have to live like pigs, we may as well live with pigs", he vaulted over the rails, fell flat on his back in inches of squelching filth, then, slithered to his feet, looking at his men, with the filthy mess dripping from all parts of his misshapen body. The roars of laughter persisted as he scrambled through the rails and moved to choose the filthiest corner for his own billet for the night. Bad tempers, reluctance and near-revolt disappeared in an instant. There was more laughter when he summoned the 'fool' and told him to clear up the more solid parts of the mess with his 'entrenching tool'.

Soon we were relieved and moved back out of the line to Souk-el-Khemis where we had left about a week before. From here we entrained for a return journey to Algiers, where, we were told, we would prepare for a parachute operation. We were lucky enough to gather in NAAFI rations just as we leaving. In spite of the first night it was comfortable and restful journey. Because of some scare we had to stand to until just before dawn, a boring and exasperating alternative to the comfort of our train seats; we had been promoted from mule trucks. The two or three days we were on the train we spent in reading, eating (mainly oranges); in the long evenings there was the whisky ration (not much) and the local wine we were able to purchase on the way (much more). I read a book called *Anna* and enjoyed it immensely, either because it was good by my modest standards or because it was the first book in English I had managed to get hold of since our departure from England.

One night, a night of many starts, stops and shunts, we invited the two train drivers in for a drink. They were an impressive pair, big build, dark with twinkling eyes. They loved our whisky and later on refused our offer of local wine. Our hospitality soon began to cause us some selfish concerns. Eventually when they left to take us on our journey, Peter, one of the subalterns, went with them and drove the monster for a time, thereby achieving one of his boyhood ambitions. This journey was a welcome contrast to those we had previously experienced. We had much more room to call our own and we could make frequent purchases at the stops – chickens, eggs, bread and wine. So it was with some sense of inward contentment that we reached Boufarik, a little town some 25 miles from Algiers From there we marched some six miles to our billeting area at St Charles. Here we found a mug of tea awaiting us; also it was here that our seaborne kit caught up with us. We unpacked it excitedly for most of us had forgotten what little gems we had stored away for ourselves.

So on the 7th and 8th January 1943 the reunited 1st and 3rd Battalions left by train for Algiers to apparently prepare for a parachute operation. It is probably clear to most readers by now that the troops were becoming a bit cynical at the amount of the 'on the bus, off the bus' moves that the 1st Parachute Brigade was suffering and this feeling comes through loud and clear in the following comment from the 1st Battalion's war diary:

> January 7th. The private train laid on for the Battalion arrived, first, second and third class cattle trucks. The Battalion spent the day loading, unloading, allotting and re-allotting the trucks. Special trucks for officers arrived later in the evening. By this time the CO and IO had selected a cattle truck divided in two by a partition as their travelling accommodation with rations in one half. Supplies were obtained from the NAAFI at Souk-el-Arba for the journey. All Battalion transport was handed over to 78th Division except captured transport which was sent off to Brigade to travel back to base in convoy.
>
> The Battalion entrained at 1730 hours. The REs and Field Ambulance arrived at 2300 hours. The train moved off at 0300 hours.
>
> January 8th. The journey continued in style, no washing or other convenience being available on the train. During last night the train arrived at the Algerian frontier and was split into two halves, both halves however rejoining at Duvivier.
>
> The train was a glorious sight having cooking tins and pots suspended all over it. Cooking was done in fits and starts. When the train stopped men were out like a flash and fires were got going and so we continued the pilgrimage.
>
> January 9th. The train moved along in its stately progress with hordes of Arabs chasing after it. The CO and 2 i/c awoke to find the door of their compartment missing. This is still an unexplained mystery. Our engine is replaced by an electric one. This enabled us to move along somewhat faster although it ended our source of shaving water, which the old engine provided each morning. A certain amount of difficulty arose over estimation of time judging. With the old engine one could stroll after it when it had started and catch it up with ease, but this new electric one moved off rather more rapidly – several people nearly got left behind at the first two or three halts.
>
> January 10th. The train journey continues as much appreciated rest; we arrived at Boufarik during the night and as the whole train was asleep Major Ince and Captain Whitelock had some little difficulty when they met the train on its arrival. However it was decided that we would stay on board and then march off to our billet area.

Others had more pressing problems on this train journey, as Sergeant Jack Bellamy of 16 PFA recalls:

> The journey was undertaken in cattle trucks well known to Tommies in the Great War with the words 'Hommes 40, Chevaux 8' painted on the side. Well, we had no horses, and only about 20 of us for what I seem to recall was about a five-day journey. We soon improvised hammocks from our blankets and straps from our webbing. We had been living off canned field rations for some time, a box that

contained enough food for 10 men for 1 day. The tea provided was a powder, a mix of tea, milk and sugar, that with the addition of hot water produced a pale brownish grey liquid that was in theory tea. Obtaining hot water when travelling in cattle trucks can be a bit of a problem, but initially we solved this by putting a wire handle on to one of the large tins of army biscuits that came with the ration packs. Some of the tea mix would be put in the tin and at one of the many halts one of us would rush along to the locomotive and get the driver to have some hot water from a pipe that protruded from just below the boiler by the cab. There would be a mighty swoosh and steam and boiling water would pour into the tin, and someone would return triumphantly bearing a brew of tea. This procedure was happily repeated for 1 or 2 days, until one day we forgot to put the tea mixture in the tin, and someone came back with a tin full of hot water that looked the same colour as our usual tea. It was rust and we realised that much of the brown colour of the tea over the past few days had been due to the rust rather than to its tea content! Needless to say other brewing methods had to be devised, and they quickly were.

Now the two Battalions were in Algiers news came out about the proposed parachute operation. Allied Force HQ had decided to place the 1st Parachute Brigade (just the 1st and 3rd Battalions and supporting troops at this time) under the command of the US II Corps for operations in the area of Gabes and Sfax. It was the intention to either cut or harry the German lines of communication between Tunis and their troops in Libya. Over the next week or so up to the 18th January various ideas and schemes were discussed and then Allied Force HQ decided that the 1st Parachute Brigade would not be required for this airborne operation, which in fact never took place.

Meanwhile, the 2nd Battalion was still up the front in the Beja area. On the 8th January Major Rothery joined the unit and took command of B Company; this was the same day that they were told that the rest of the Brigade was returning to Algiers. This must not have gone down too well with the old sweats in the Battalion, especially after their trying time at Oudna and then finding out that they were being sent to the 'Beja Left Sector' on the following day.

The Battalion war diary records the following:

9th January 1943 The Battalion is now under command Beja Left Sector.
1600 A Company moves into area J 2946.
1600 Mortar Platoon moves into area J 2945.
1800 Advanced Battalion HQ and Brigade Signals Link move into area J 2745.
1800 B Company, C Company, HQ Company and Battalion Rear HQ begins to move into Beja. Rear Party started to move to forward area.

On 11th January detachments from B and C Companies relieved A Company in the front line. It was a relatively quiet time for those at the front with the weather hindering a lot of activity. It was almost as though both sides had adopted a defensive mentality. Spirits in the higher elements of the Battalion were no doubt raised when on the 14th January five officers either were posted in or rejoined from hospital or detached duty. The main reinforcement, however, came in the shape of 198 men who came out from England. On the following day medals were presented to several individuals in

Lieutenant-General Anderson presenting Lieutenant Colonel J. Frost with his DSO for the Oudna operation on 15th January 1943. (Imperial War Museum)

the Battalions for actions on the Oudna operation. They were presented by Lieutenant-General Anderson, the GOC of 1st Army. He presented the Distinguished Service Order to Lieutenant Colonel Frost and Major Ross. Major Ashford and Lieutenant Brayley received the Military Cross and Privates Welsh and Miller the Military Medal.

The same day the reinforcements were allocated to their new units and the 2nd Battalion moved to the area of a small village called Monchar about 6 miles east of Beja. The war diary gives accurate locations of the positions as follows:

> 16th January. Companies moved into their battle positions. Locations Sheet 18 Tunisia 1:50,000 A Company to J 3441. B Company to area 3440. C Company to area 3438. HQ Company and Battalion HQ to area 3240. Battalion HQ and HQ Company were billeted in two farm houses about 500 yards apart. Bivouacs were issued to A, B and C Companies as shelters in their battle positions.

In spite of it being a relatively quiet time the 2nd Battalion were still looked on being general 'dogsbodies' for everyone else and Lieutenant Brayley's Platoon on 17th January was detached to the Sidi N'Sir area to assist the 1st East Surreys with patrolling. These detached duties also held dangers. When he returned on the 20th Brayley reported that whilst out on patrol contact was made with the enemy. They spotted an enemy column consisting of one small car, five motorcycle combinations and four trucks carrying troops. One of the trucks was also towing an anti-tank gun. In the ensuing firefight one

P34 was knocked out killing the crew and four others. This patrol had been carried out in conjunction with a Platoon from the East Surreys and they claimed to have killed six enemy, making a total of twelve. The 2nd Battalion reported three men missing, while the East Surreys got off lightly with four wounded and one man missing. As I have been unable to trace any fatal casualties for the 2nd Battalion during this period I have to assume they were taken prisoner.

When back with the unit Lieutenant Brayley was again sent out on a patrol on the 22nd and again made contact with the enemy. An attack was made against a small number of enemy in an observation post which was recorded as being on point 323, map reference 477607 from Sheet 11 of the Tunisian series. Two enemy were killed for no losses and copies of a propaganda leaflet called *Afrika Post* left behind.

Defensive work continued, with men putting up barbed wire and apparently laying anti-tank mines in front of their positions, with the odd offensive patrol thrown in. On the 27th January 1943 at 1000 a strong patrol of two Platoons from B Company was sent out to investigate supposed enemy positions in the area of J 5357 which was around the Djebel si Meftah. This patrol was led by Lieutenant D. Crawley and he was supposed to meet the Company Commander (Major Rothery) at a pre-arranged RV at 1500. This failed to happen and Lieutenant Crawley reported back that no contact had been made with the enemy and also there had been no sign of Major Rothery and the two others he had taken with him on his patrol. However, a report was received that three British paratroopers had made contact with a French Army patrol. Later Major Rothery, his CSM and batman made it safely back. The Battalion war diary records that "He had had many and varied adventures on a mule and with the French patrol at one instance he with his batman and CSM had fought a spirited engagement with our Allies but at last managed to extricate himself and his small force from a precarious position and make his way back to our lines." What happened to the mule is regretfully unrecorded.

As we come to the end of January and the beginning of February the men of the 2nd Battalion would probably have been glad to hear that it was intended to bring them back under the command of the 1st Parachute Brigade. This actually happened on the 8th February but there was still time for them to be messed about by other formations.

The war diary paints an interesting picture:

> 30th January. B Company patrol to Beida Valley (J 4452) to investigate the circumstances of a number of Arabs whose activities had aroused suspicion during a previous patrol. An Arab farm was searched and a length of webbing with two buckles thought to be off a British parachute were discovered. Also a few rounds of Italian ammunition. Two Arabs were removed for interrogation by the FSP (Field Security Police) but the Battalion left the area before the results of the interrogation were known.
>
> 31st January. A Company moved to area J 5924, Djebel Djaffa and reconnaissance was carried out with the view to moving the entire Battalion into that area.
>
> 1st February. The Battalion was warned for move to area of Djebel Djaffa (5825 Tunisia 1:200,000 Sheet 5). A Company were already in position on the feature and reconnaissance was carried out for the remainder of the Battalion.

Three officers of the 2nd Parachute Battalion - left to right are Captain R. Stark, Lieutenant J. Brayley and Major R. Ashford. This photo was taken in the Beja area days before Major Ashford was killed. (Airborne Assault Duxford)

2nd February. The move to Djebel Djaffa was cancelled. Battalion handed over to 4th Yorks and Lancashire Regiment (46th Division) and moved to positions west of Medjez-el-Bab, still under command of 11th Infantry Brigade.

3rd February. Orders received to be prepared to move to Robaa under command 36th Infantry Brigade. Battalion embussed and started to move off. An A Company position on Djebel Djaffa was attacked by an enemy patrol as the Company was preparing to move off; enemy casualties unknown. Own casualties 1 killed 1 missing.

4th February. O Groups moved forward to reconnoitre positions for the Battalion in area crossroads O 7669. The reconnaissance was carried out in three carriers, one of these hit a mine, blowing up and killing Major R. Ashford and Captain M. Moore, Sergeant Fisher of A Company and driver were injured. Major Lane assumed command of A Company. The Battalion moved into the above area and took up positions on the high ground north west of the crossroads.

5th February. Enemy shelled Battalion positions. Sergeant Maguire C Company killed and 1 OR wounded. Supply route from B Echelon to the Battalion had been mined by the French. It was necessary to bring the supplies across country by mule train. One mule was killed and the muleteer seriously injured as a result of the mule stepping on a mine.

Battalion less A Company moved to thickly wooded country south of Djebel Bargou O 7368. A Company moved to positions astride the Pont du Fahs road due north of crossroads O7069 Djebel el Glib.

> 7th February. 6th Royal West Kents relieved this Battalion. The Battalion marched to embussing point, road junction O 6881 arriving at 2300.
>
> 8th February. Battalion embussed and moved via Siliana and Gafour to area O 6390 (Tunisia 1:200,00 Sheet 8) into positions previously occupied by the French. As the result of this move the Battalion came under command of 1st Parachute Brigade for the first time since early January.

Lieutenant Colonel Frost later had some harsher things to say about how his Battalion was treated during this time:

> The Corps Commander still seemed to think we were expendable because at very short notice we were sent down to a crossroads on the extreme right flank of the British Army. We couldn't get there normally because all the routes had been mined so we had an awful move over the hills, which meant we couldn't bring any heavy equipment. On the way I reported to Brigadier Howlett, who told us to hold a crossroads in the Ousseltia valley. It was considered vitally important that we hold it and that we must be prepared to accept heavy casualties. I said "Oh, what does the enemy consist of?" He said, "Well, we know that there are 100 tanks." So I said, "I have no anti-tank guns, can you let us have some tanks?" He said, "I can let you have six light tanks from the cavalry." "Thank you, Sir, that's a great help." Then he said, "Well, they are of course no use against German tanks." So I said, "What about enemy infantry?" He replied, "It seems there are about ten Battalions up the road." I left shaking my head.
>
> The next day I made a recce with three Bren carriers. As we approached our assembly point I noticed the road had been recently disturbed. I immediately shouted to the two Bren carriers behind, but it was too late. There was a tremendous explosion and one vehicle turned over catapulting out its occupants. It was tragic. Dinty Moore, my Battalion HQ commander and Dick Ashford, the A Company commander, were killed and all the rest were very badly injured. Both the officers were great characters and would be sadly missed. Needless to say the 100 tanks and the 10 Battalions went somewhere else.

Both of these officers are now buried in Enfidaville CWGC Cemetery graves 1A1 and 1A2.

In the meantime the 1st and 3rd Battalions had returned to the Algiers area during the early part of January 1943. The 3rd Battalion left Souk-el-Khemis on 8th January by train and on the 11th arrived at Boufarik and from there marched to their billets. On the 19th January 94 reinforcements joined the Battalion and on the following day five officer reinforcements arrived. The previously mentioned parachute operation had now been cancelled and at 2000 on 22nd January 1943 the 3rd Battalion was warned they were at six hours readiness to move by rail back to the front. On the 23rd Lieutenant Colonel Pine-Coffin attended a conference at HQ 1st Parachute Brigade regarding this movement back to the front. Then on the 24th at 1500 the Battalion left St Charles by TCVs headed for the port at Algiers. In spite of what they had previously been told, the paratroopers were going to war by sea. At 1630 on the 24th they embarked on the *Queen Emma* which sailed at 0300 the following morning disembarking at 1700 at Bone. After

Major R. Ashford's grave at Enfidaville CWGC Cemetery. (N. Cherry)

Captain M. Moore's grave at Enfidaville CWGC Cemetery. (N. Cherry)

a bit more of the Army run around including brief stops at Ghardimaou and El Arousa, by the 28th January the 3rd Battalion was back in the front line relieving the 10th Rifle Brigade in this area. The war diary records that patrols were sent out on the last three nights of the month with apparently little incident except on 30th January when "1 Sergeant and 1 Private from C Company failed to return." I believe these two casualties were Sergeant W. Higson and L/Corporal J. Deasy, although their date of death is given by the CWGC as 29th January 1943. Both of their bodies were recovered later and are buried side by side in Medjez-el-Bab CWGC cemetery graves 14B15 and 14B16.

The 3rd Battalion's war diary ends for the month with their strength:

Officers	19
Other Ranks	586
Attached Officers	2

The following comments are taken from the 1st Battalion's war diary, whilst they were billeted in a farm:

> January 14th. Rumours reached the Battalion that there might be some operation in the near future. Spirits were revived although the operation was not due for another week. The Battalion is rather hungry as we are now on bulk fresh rations and many memories hang over Type A Compo and thoughts of dough.
>
> The farm is a paradise for oranges and tangerines and these being obtainable from the farmer at the price of 5 Francs for 25 or 1 cigarette for an armful from the wog guard.
>
> January 15th. Operation order for an airlanding operation arrived. Loading tables require a certain amount of juggling about. Conferences take place every half hour.

January 16th. Everyone worked frantically on re-equipping and reorganising and in the meantime trying to guess at our destination. Douglas aircraft were put at our disposal if required for practice at unloading. We are due to take nearly every piece of equipment with us and all personnel including fitters, carpenters etc. Several innocent soldiers were turned into fitters, joiners and sanitary men.

January 18th. Lieutenant Colonel Hill left for England. Companies began zeroing rifles – this business involved a long and very hot march.

January 19th. The operation is off. Loading tables are therefore filed in case an airlanding operation should come off one day.

January 20th. The following immediate awards were announced:

Distinguished Service Order:

Lieutenant Colonel S. Hill MC

Military Cross:

Lieutenant P. Mellor
Lieutenant S. Wandless
Captain M. Haggie
Lieutenant T. Robb

Military Medal:

L/Corporal Morgan
L/Corporal Wright
Private Meadows
Private Bainbridge
Private Ryan

January 22nd. An order arrived putting the Battalion at 2 hours' notice to move. Training programmes were put away again and the Battalion sprang to feverish life. No details were available and therefore no-one knew whether to prepare for airlanding or parachuting operation. Needless to say the order arrived in the evening – the night was a busy one.

January 23rd. The CO had to go to Brigade for a conference, he returned with a few details of the move. The entire Battalion was going to move and only a very small rear party was to remain behind.

In the evening a movement order arrived ordering the Battalion to move at 0900 hours. TCVs were to arrive at Boufarik at 0815 hours and the IO was detailed to meet them and lead them up to the Company areas. We were to move by road to Algiers and there embark for an unknown destination. Some enthusiasts imagined we were returning to the UK.

January 24th. Loading started early, in fact the QM and OC HQ Company were up all night. The IO met the transport and the Battalion moved off without a hitch. We arrived at the docks at Algiers at about 1100 hours and fell out on the dockside to await embarkation. In the evening after boarding the Officers were introduced to Sir John Dill, the Colonel of the Regiment, who called to see us as he happened to be in Algiers and heard where we were.

January 25th. We set sail at 0300 hours and awoke in the morning to a very excellent breakfast with white bread. We were on our way to Bone, where we docked at 1745 hours in the rain. No arrangements had been made for our reception and we marched from the docks to the civil hospital carrying full packs – a distance

> of about two miles – to find our 2 i/c fighting with Brigade and the 3rd Battalion for the doubtful pleasure of the limited accommodation. There was no light and therefore it was impossible to knock up a meal and we dossed down in our wet clothes.
>
> Details of the move by sea:
> 1st Parachute Brigade will move from Algiers to Bone on 24th January 1943.
> Ships will be employed as under: -
> *Queen Emma*
> *Wilton*
> *Princess Beatrix*
> *Wheatland*
> 80 tons stores and ammunition will accompany. 40 tons will be available for loading at 0900 hours, the remainder by 1200 hours and will be loaded to *Queen Emma* and *Princess Beatrix* in equal proportions. 1st Parachute Brigade will provide a loading party of 1 Officer and 30 ORs per ship to accompany first loads.
> Baggage will be limited to what Officers and men can carry.
> Nominal rolls in triplicate by ships, by units will handed over to ESO on embarkation.
> Compo rations to cover the voyage will be available for loading by 0900 hours.

More observant readers may recall the names *Queen Emma* and *Princess Beatrix* from the book *Striking Back* as they were mentioned in there during their involvement in a raid on the Lofoten Islands.

Perhaps the underlying theme of all of this is how shabbily treated the units of the 1st Parachute Brigade were during their time in North Africa. I suppose with the benefit of hindsight we can say the Staff work was poor at best.

You may recall a mention of Lieutenant Colonel Hill returning to the unit after he discharged himself from hospital after being wounded on Gué Hill, and this led to some debate amongst the 1st Battalion, as Lieutenant Colonel Pearson later recounted:

> When we arrived at Boufarik a half-colonel came up to me and said "I've just come to take over command." I told him to get lost. I was the CO till somebody senior to me told me otherwise or until I got it in writing. He went off in a huff.
>
> James Hill appeared back from hospital so there were now three lieutenant colonels all hoping to command the Battalion. A book was opened: I was 10-1 on, James Hill evens and Gofton-Salmond 5-1 against. Doc Haggie sorted it all out by declaring Gofton-Salmond medically unfit and James Hill was sent back to hospital from which he had unofficially discharged himself. This left some officers poorer and others richer, but I was back in the chair I'd never really left.

In the coming days certain units of the 1st Parachute Brigade were going to face some savage fighting for a rocky Tunisian mountain. In fact, several members of the Brigade who were present both here and at Arnhem say that the fighting for the Djebel Mansour was the toughest combat they saw in the Second World War.

8

Djebel Mansour and Djebel Alliliga, February 1943

Towards the end of January 1943 the Allies in North Africa were slowly gaining the upper hand, although in Tunisia a mountain range south of Tunis was felt to be a major obstacle to advancing across the Tunisian plains. This range of mountains was known as the Kabylie Mountains and the Germans had turned a lot of them into hilltop strongholds. One of the major obstacles appeared to be the triple peak of a hill known as Djebel Mansour. On one side, this overlooked a deep valley about half a mile broad, whilst on the other side it overlooked the main road to Tunis. All along this right flank it seemed a German build-up was threatened the advancing Allied forces and the high command felt they needed to do something to relieve this pressure. It was decided to attack and hopefully seize Djebel Mansour in the expectation that this would force the Germans to move troops from other sectors to the area and so allow an easier advance on a so-called 'broad front'. Once Djebel Mansour had been taken the advance would continue along a ridge to take the Djebel Alliliga.

It will probably come as no surprise to learn that the long-suffering 1st Parachute Brigade was specially selected to undertake this mission. Both the 1st and 3rd Battalions

Looking from Djebel Mansour towards Djebel Alliliga. (James Macrae)

were warned to take part in the attack, which was intended to take place on the night of 2nd/3rd February. To assist them they were allocated a company of the French Foreign Legion (it is said a number of them were German) and also the 3rd Battalion of the Grenadier Guards, who would be used to consolidate the positions once they had been captured.

A 'tom's' eye view comes from Reg Curtis. Although, in my opinion, there may be a few inaccuracies in his distances, it still makes interesting reading:

> Jerry had decided to make a concentrated effort in the Bou Arada area to shift British and American forces there. We travelled by boat from Algiers to Bone and from there to Bou Arada by trucks. Now, in this area of Bou Arada, the enemy were trying to bottle us up in a pincer movement, thrusting from a place called Goubellat, 12 miles to the north. Also from Sloughia 14 miles away to the north west, then at El Arousa, 10 miles away in the west. They were also pushing hard at Kasserine, where the Americans were 110 miles away in the south. These enemy forces consisted of the 5th German Parachute Regiment under Colonel Koch, a parachute engineer battalion under Major Witzig, the 10th Panzer Division, Tiger tanks and anti-aircraft guns from the 20th Flak Division. The enemy was getting desperate, what with Montgomery chasing Rommel. General von Arnim was trying hard to force a wedge in this area. It was felt important to hold this area and indeed expand it and the 1st Parachute Brigade had been chosen to come here. Bou Arada lies 40 miles south-west from Tunis, with a range of hills halfway. 15 miles south-east of Bou Arada is Pont du Fahs. Between these two towns is a hill called Djebel Mansour, the commanding height on the Pont du Fahs/Tunis road. This hill was known as Hill 648 and it was about 2000 feet above sea level, five miles round the base and with an easiest climbing angle of 45 degrees. This hill was occupied by numerous crack German troops we were told. Our job was to take Hill 648 at all costs.

The following is taken from the 1st Battalion's war diary:

> January 29th. Battalion moved to take over from 10th Rifle Brigade at Toutla square 6599. Battalion HQ occupying the farm and the Companies taking up positions on Toutla and M'Salla. The area was full of troops including some medium guns. Battalion took over at 2000 and 10th Rifle Brigade moved out but left their A Echelon behind.
>
> January 30th. Brigade Commander arrived during the morning and ordered the IO to recce for an attack on Djebel Mansour (Tunis sheet 41 7092). The CO and IO paid a visit to the French Foreign Legion, from whose area it was intended to operate, where they became acquainted with a Captain Faveau – an exceedingly nice fellow and very capable. The CO decided to send a fighting patrol of two platoons under Captain Coxen to carry out this recce. Captain Faveau promised to provide a capable guide to lead the party to the foot of Djebel Mansour. The attack was scheduled to arrive at its objective just before dawn but moved off from Battalion HQ to lie up with the French at 1645.

Major V. Coxen:

> It was decided that I should lead a patrolling force out on 31st January to see how heavily Djebel Mansour was held. Captain Faveau, who commanded a detachment of the French Foreign Legion, gave me one of his officers who had patrolled the area as a guide. This officer showed us to the bottom of this very deep wadi and then left. We crossed this difficult area and eventually got onto the smoother, but steeper ground on the far side of the wadi. We found out later that had we gone farther to the left we would have run into the enemy's defensive positions all the way down the side of the hill. It is possible that they thought the approach from the side we had come from was too steep for anyone to attempt. The fact that we didn't hit it was to prove a little costly the next day.
>
> When we got up near the top the scrub became slightly more open and with the moonlight you could see how far you could go. The hill was slightly convex and therefore the top always appeared to be 20 or 30 yards in front of you, so there was no great field of fire. As we had not come across any barbed wire and I wanted to be fairly close when we did, I moved up to be with the leading section. When we were almost to the top, I was challenged by a German sentry. He was not satisfied with my answer and threw a grenade, which bounced and exploded between myself and my batman. We were both hit; I had bits of grenade in my back and he had it in one arm, but it was not enough to incommode us. I began firing at the general position of the sentry to try and keep his head down, while the section was fanning out and going in. We overran the position completely and took about 14 prisoners. We started to consolidate the position but it was starting to get light by that time.
>
> I sent Lieutenant Norton along the ridge to have a look at the defences, with instructions not to go further than the dip, if he met any resistance. Fire started to come not only from the other high point on Mansour, but from Alliliga, which was quite strongly held. I had overrun, probably, the first two platoons of a company position. The rest of the ground was strongly held beyond and it was not a place I could see that we could have held during the day because Alliliga, which was about 500 to 700 yards away, commanded all the approaches. Frankly the only thing we could do was get the hell out of there. There was a fair amount of cover going down the slope but once we got into the wadi we were in range of their mortars and there was no place to hide. But we got supporting artillery fire from French 75mm guns and smoke, which enabled us to work our way back relatively unscathed.

Now that a successful reconnaissance had been carried out, in the afternoon of the 31st January the Brigade Commander arrived and complicated matters slightly by ordering that a "recce be made about 12 miles south of their current location against a possible German thrust up the road." Lieutenant Colonel Pearson sent his 2 i/c, Adjutant and the OC of T Company on this task. As the reader might imagine by now, nothing further was ever said about this attack and later the 1st Battalion was ordered to seize and hold Djebel Mansour on the night of 1st/2nd February.

Regretfully Lieutenant Norton was badly wounded in the thigh on the patrol and the only immediate medical assistance was provided by an attached RAMC soldier – Corporal Moffat. Pearson asked Corporal Moffat what they should do with him. Moffat said "Sir, if we try and get him back it's going to take the best part of four to five hours before we can get him to a doctor. After that its going to be another eight hours before he gets to a casualty clearing station and he'll undoubtedly die." Pearson asked him the best solution and Moffat replied "Well Sir, you know who's up there, they'll probably come down and collect him." Pearson then said "How do we tell them?" Moffat then said "He is capable of firing a Verey pistol." Pearson went and broke the news to Lieutenant Norton, who accepted it very well. Lieutenant Norton was told to wait five minutes while the raiding party withdrew before firing a flare. Pearson left a sergeant and one other soldier overlooking the position just in case the Germans did not come down. Shortly a German patrol came down and removed Lieutenant Norton. It would seem that Lieutenant Norton survived the war albeit with some time spent as a prisoner of war.

Sergeant E. Seal:

> I was on the recce patrol with Captain Coxen. After climbing for what seemed like ages we reached the enemy defensive positions and the battle began. I don't know who exactly took the prisoners, but Captain Coxen finally gave orders to withdraw. I did not rush my lads too much, trying to appear unconcerned, because by now the area was like a disturbed hornet's nest with Spandaus [machine-guns] and rifles blazing away. He shouted "Get a bloody move on, Sergeant Seal!" orders are orders, so we got a bloody move on! As we approached the deep wadi which led back towards our lines I could swear we were running through streams of bullets kicking the sand up as we ran. It appeared that the Germans taken prisoner were from the same area as some of the Saxon and Bavarian legionnaires.

Looking south-west along the Mansour ridge. (James Macrae)

Pearson's plan called for two of the rifle companies, R and T, to attack the Djebel Mansour feature crossing the start line at 0500 on 3rd February. After reaching the top of the Mansour they were to swing right along the ridgeline and take Djebel Alliliga. The third rifle company, S, would follow on behind and consolidate on the top of Djebel Mansour. The French Foreign Legion troops would assist by creating a diversion aimed at occupying in the first instance the defenders of Djebel Alliliga.

The initial positions of the 1st Battalion would be occupied by the 3rd Grenadier Guards in the expectation that after the positions were taken they would relieve the paratroopers on top of the two hills. Also providing support were some sappers from the 1st Parachute Squadron RE under the command of Lieutenant P. Stainforth, artillery support came from 17th Field Regiment RA and medical cover came from 16 PFA.

The medical cover was planned to be provided by No 1 Section, now commanded by Captain D. Wright. The CO, Lieutenant Colonel MacEwan, decided to carry out a reconnaissance of the proposed route for casualty evacuation. The route was found to be impossible for ambulances to travel very far until Djebel Alliliga was captured, and even then the roads would be difficult and dangerous. The ground was either very rugged and mountainous, or flat stretches were exposed to enemy fire or, worse still, rough ground with plenty of boulders and scrub chest high and thorny, making the going dangerous and arduous for stretcher-bearers. Captain Wright was advised of the CO's reconnaissance and told that until the success signal was fired from Djebel Alliliga casualties could not be evacuated to Ambulance Exchange Points (AXP), which were to be set up on the main evacuation route. An AXP is set up when the distance between a RAP and a MDS is quite a way and the casualty's condition can deteriorate on the journey. There would normally be two sets of transport, one moving between the RAP

Either shell holes or shell scrapes on the slopes of Djebel Mansour. (James Macrae)

and the AXP and the other from there to the MDS. One of the field ambulance sections would be sent to man an AXP so that a casualty's condition can be checked during the journey, any further treatments given and, if necessary, the priority for evacuation changed. Colonel MacEwan realised that if all casualties were to be removed within a reasonable time of being wounded, the whole unit's strength would need to be deployed. He therefore sent No 4 Section under the command of Captain Percival to Djebel Mansour, while the remainder of the unit moved up to the AXP.

The 1st Battalion's war diary contains the following comment for 1st and 2nd February:

> The attack on Mansour was put off until the following night and so the IO was sent to liaise with the French together with Major Robertson of 17 Field RA; friendly relations were established and a respect for the 2nd Company 1st Battalion Etrangers developed. They were now being equipped with American Springfield rifles. 3rd Battalion moved to the position further south and were guided there by the Adjutant.
>
> Early in the morning (2nd February) the IO was sent to tie up details with the French and the Battalion moved by marked route to lying up area at S'Arifa (6595). The Battalion then rested during the day and moved up by night.

To try and assist the Battalion to find the start line for the assault in the dark, Captain Coxen was sent out beforehand to lay white tapes. He later commented,

> I took our Frank 'Panzer' Manser and the Provost Section and got up there and laid the tape to the start line. We arrived more quickly than the first time and had about an hour to wait before the Battalion came. I spread my people out a little in the hope of spotting patrols. While I was doing this one of my men was coughing a great deal. I put my hand over his mouth, gave him a boiled sweet and told him that if he coughed again I would beat him on his head with my pistol.

As the men of the 1st Battalion started to struggle up the steep hillside it started to rain. Fortunately R and T Companies were able to follow the white tape and made it safely to the start line in good order. S Company following on behind were not so fortunate as they made a navigational error, probably as a result of the white tape being cut and sections of it being removed by a German patrol. Consequently, as Captain Coxen had commented earlier, they veered to the left and ran into German positions and machine guns firing on fixed lines. More on this later.

The other two companies had better luck and they managed to get very close to the German defences before they were spotted. They closed in and there was hand-to-hand fighting, with much use of the bayonet. In the first few hours the men of the 1st Battalion were able to secure the summit of Djebel Mansour and Djebel Alliliga. Casualties amongst R and T had been relatively low but then 'Murphy's Law' started to come into play and several misfortunes occurred. As previously stated, S Company had been confused by the lack of white tape and had veered off the best line and walked into a minefield. They also came under fire from machine guns and it was around this time that one of the characters of the 1st Battalion was killed. He was Lieutenant P. Mellor, who had already lost one eye and normally wore a patch over it. He had probably stood on a mine as it was reported that he lost a leg and was additionally wounded by machine gun fire. He was last seen alive crawling towards a machine gun post firing his pistol. It is also reported that when his body was subsequently recovered he had suffered 17 bullet wounds. However, his body or grave was subsequently lost and he is commemorated on the Medjez-el-Bab Memorial to the Missing. Philip Mellor was 40 years old at the time of his death, so was certainly one of the older paratrooper volunteers and casualties. In spite of these difficulties S Company forced their way past these defences and got to the top of Djebel Mansour while R and T pushed along the ridge towards Djebel Alliliga.

Additionally, a mule train bringing forward ammunition to the bottom of Djebel Mansour was seen by the German defenders and came under long-range machine gun fire. The handlers, all local Arabs, decided this was too much for them and quickly took flight. However, the 2 i/c and a French officer who were both 'horseborne' managed to grab a couple of mules each and bring the badly needed resupply into the Battalion area.

Although somewhat battered S Company did make it to the top of Djebel Mansour and did their best to consolidate here. However, the Germans, fully realising the importance of the two positions, quickly launched a counter-attack on the Alliliga feature and forced the men of R and T Companies back. Lieutenant Colonel Pearson decided for the time being to concentrate on holding Djebel Mansour, with the hope that the Grenadier Guards might later be able to take Djebel Alliliga. Meanwhile some of the attached French Foreign Legion were ordered to take over a neighbouring position known as point 646 to cover the left flank of the 1st Battalion. Throughout this first day the paratroopers were under heavy artillery and mortar fire and it is reported that around 105 wounded men had to be evacuated. You may recall that the Mansour was overlooked on the right by the Alliliga and Pearson was probably pleased to hear during the early afternoon of the 3rd that the Guards were going to make an attack on Djebel Alliliga on the next day.

However before describing that here are a couple of comments about the early part of the action. First, Captain V. Coxen:

> R and T Companies followed the tape, came up and were put on their start line with a difficult but straight climb. However, S Company lost the tape and didn't turn up at the start line. Unfortunately they had slipped too far to the left and had encountered enemy defensive positions near the foot of the hill. They ran into intense machine gun fire and mines and took quite a lot of casualties, but fought their way past the defences and up and took their objective. But people like Philip Mellor were killed, a splendid chap. He'd already lost one eye and now he had his leg blown off, but he was last seen sitting up, one eye, one leg off, still shooting at the Germans. When we recovered his body he had 17 bullets in him. S Company's move to the left was a very costly error.
>
> The rest of the battle went on throughout the day and R and T Companies took the other hill and S Company stayed on Mansour. It was hoped that the French Foreign Legion and the Guards would have been able to come through and consolidate on Alliliga as well, but the amount of fire brought down on them prevented this. The main advantage the Germans had was the terrain. Behind hills with razor-like tops they were able to bring up reserves to counter-attack. Firing

ordinary field guns or 25 pounders, you couldn't get the crest clearance in to hit the area where the reserves were. The enemy on the forward slopes you could deal with, but you could not stop the build-up of the forces behind, because you couldn't hit them. What we really needed was howitzers or mortar fire, but we were seriously lacking them. Peter Cleasby-Thompson brought up a column of mules loaded with mortars but regretfully it got scattered and only a few loads got through. During the battle, which took place all the next day and night, we ran out of ammunition and even to take a casualty back was a four-hour hump.

Sergeant Eric Seal:

In the main battle for Djebel Mansour, S Company suffered very heavy casualties, including Lieutenant Mellor who was killed attacking a machine gun post, which was typical of the man; thus died an irreplaceable soldier. After the enemy had been killed or driven off the high ground we consolidated our position. We certainly spent a night filled with bullet and bombs and our battle cry "Waho Mohammed". A few of us went down with Captain Coxen to check on the enemy ambush area where S Company had been and to bury our dead. Until then I did not really realise what damage German Spandaus could do. There were bodies everywhere, some with arms and hands cut off, still holding weapons.

At 0630 on the morning of the 4th February Pearson sent his IO, Lieutenant Perrin-Brown, to get in contact with the Guards, but as someone aptly put it the only contact he made was with the Germans. Later a company of Guards was found some way down the hill having tried and failed to take it. In the afternoon, as the Adjutant reported,

At 1430 a heavy concentration of high explosive was put down by our guns on Djebel Alliliga preparatory to the Guards assault. The enemy replied to this by heavy shell and mortar fire on our positions. Twelve Stukas came over and dive-bombed the valley behind our positions – presumably expecting to catch reinforcements. No casualties were caused. At 1530 the shelling on Djebel Alliliga lifted and a concentration of smoke was put down under cover of which the Guards attacked.

Contact with them was immediately lost, as wireless communication broke down. We did not know whether the attack had been successful or not; at any rate it had not dislodged the machine gun on the eastern side of Djebel Alliliga, nor had the Guards occupied the feature nearest to us. During the remainder of the day our position was made most uncomfortable by this gun which overlooked us, and repeated messages were sent to the Guards via Brigade to ask them to deal with this side of Djebel Alliliga, but to no avail.

At about 2300 that night there was some firing east of Djebel Mansour and the IO was sent to contact the French to find out what it was about. The French did not know.

At dawn on 5th February heavy firing broke out from the French positions and it was soon obvious that the enemy were counter-attacking. Within half an hour the enemy were in possession of the French positions overlooking our own. Captain Faveau and his lieutenant had been hit and removed back to the aid post.

After the fighting was over officers of the 1st Airborne Division were taken on a 'battlefield tour' of relevant scenes of action. This picture shows a group looking at Djebel Mansour (far left on the skyline). (Imperial War Museum)

The Company had been left in the hands of the sergeant major, who ordered fixed bayonets and charged the enemy but could not retake the position. After some time it was found that the French had been driven off the hill altogether and what remained of them had withdrawn. It was now obvious that unless reinforcements arrived to drive the enemy off this high ground the 1st Battalion could not hold their position. There was no possibility of this and the CO therefore decided to hold on as long as possible. Shelling and mortaring of our positions then began, and so heavy was it that casualties began to mount up. By 0915 our own mortars were out of ammunition and the enemy had placed his mortars down the valley to the south of Djebel Mansour.

The FOO tried to get artillery fire to bear on them, but, owing to the height of Mansour and the steepness of the valley to the south, the guns could not reach the targets. A message at 1000 established the fact that S Company was completely out of ammunition but were remaining in their positions brandishing grenades. R and T Companies had about 100 rounds between them, the greater portion belonging to T Company. Major Conron had been killed and no other officers were left in R Company when they had run out of ammunition altogether. At this point the CO wirelesses for permission to withdraw, but no authority was forthcoming, so a message was sent to the companies to stay in their positions at whatever the cost. At 1030 the mortar fire and shelling ceased and it became obvious that the enemy was closing in. Some 40 yards from our positions the enemy went to ground and opened fire whilst S and R Companies sat hugging their grenades and shouting to

> the enemy to come within range. 15 minutes passed and the CO again applied for permission to withdraw. He was told to wait 5 minutes for an answer, but replied that unless the answer came within 2 minutes it would be too late. Permission was then given to withdraw.
>
> Lieutenant Jessop was despatched to tell S Company to withdraw, bringing their mortars. Major Bull led T Company out and the IO got R Company on their way.
>
> The enemy were within 40 yards of the crest and so it was not many seconds before a hail of fire began following the Battalion down the hill. Orders had been issued to reform at its foot where the gully, down which it was retreating, turned right.
>
> As the Companies reformed the Adjutant sent them off to make their way back to the French lines. By this time shells and mortar bombs were falling in the gully [and] casualties were being evacuated by every means available – carriers, mules and stretchers. One or two tanks laid a smoke screen across the very open ground in front of the French positions and so the Battalion struggled back under continuous fire.

It is reported that for their time on and around Djebel Mansour the 1st Battalion suffered 13 Officers killed and wounded and 169 Other Ranks killed, wounded and missing.

As far as I am aware the following were those killed in action from the 1st Battalion:

3rd February 1943
- Private H. Bainbridge MM
- Sergeant G. Campion
- Private C. Child
- Sergeant H. Dawany
- Corporal W. Engeldow
- Private R. Hodgkinson
- Sergeant L. Jenkinson
- Private A. Kinseley
- Private K. Lane
- Private W. Latham
- Private P. Locke
- Private F. Mallinder
- Lieutenant P. Mellor MC
- Corporal A. Severn
- Sergeant S. Wood

3rd February to 5th February 1943
- Private P. Colechin

4th February 1943
- Private H. Slack

5th February 1943
- Private R. Brant
- Corporal R. Cable

Corporal J. Campion
Major J. Conron
Private J. Coy
Private J. Dempsey
Private P. Dolan
Private H. Dorsay
L/Corporal H. Fisher
Private F. Holroyd
Private J. Howes Medjez-el-Bab CWGC Cemetery 6A35
Private T. Hughes
Private T. Hunter
Private G. Hurst Medjez-el-Bab CWGC Cemetery 10F20
Private N. Kenyon
Lieutenant J. Lloyd Medjez-el-Bab CWGC Cemetery 10H2
L/Corporal T. Miller
Private S. Mitchell
Private E. Parker
Private F. Samborne Medjez-el-Bab CWGC Cemetery 10H1
Private C. Shorter Massicault CWGC Cemetery 1D2
L/Corporal A. Tanner Medjez-el-Bab CWGC Cemetery 6A1
Private E. Thompson

Medjez-el-Bab CWGC Cemetery and Memorial to the Missing. Many men of the 1st Parachute Brigade are either buried or commemorated here. (N. Cherry)

Sergeant R. Thornton
Private W. Waters
L/Corporal T. Woodruff
Corporal D. Worrod

Unless otherwise stated all of these casualties have no known grave and are commemorated on the Medjez-el-Bab Memorial to the Missing. The thing that instantly strikes me is that the majority have no known grave and perhaps due to the arduous conditions for moving casualties, the majority were not collected; if given a burial by the Germans their graves were subsequently lost. The dead totalled 44, which was about 10% of the Battalion.

There was one fatal casualty from 16 PFA:

5th February 1943
Private W. Riddle

He also has no known grave and is commemorated on the Medjez-el-Bab Memorial to the Missing.

L/Corporal Stanners of No 1 Section 16 PFA remembers the battle for Djebel Mansour as being the worst battle of the war for him; he recalls the long approach march across very rough terrain, no roads and thorn bushes up to chest height which made the carrying of stretchers very difficult. Geoff remembers the ground sloping down about

No 1 Section of 16 Parachute Field Ambulance in January 1943. Captain D. Wright is second from left in the back row. Geoff Stanners is third from right also in the back row. Jimmy Riddle, the first airborne medic to die in action, is second from the left in the row second from the back. (N. Cherry)

500 feet into a wadi before rising steeply up about 2000 feet, this was Djebel Mansour. It was also on this approach march that one of the members of No 1 Section was killed – Jimmy Riddle – from blast injuries caused by a mortar bomb that landed between him and Lance Corporal Stanners. Stanners was slightly wounded – flesh was stripped off his cheek but he sprinkled on some sulphadimidine powder (used to treat infections) and carried on.

Also present among the medics at Djebel Mansour was Staff Sergeant E. Pruden. He remembers that British troops were withdrawing from another hill in the near vicinity of Djebel Mansour and he was called on to lead a section onto the hill to collect wounded. They climbed through the descending troops to collect the wounded men from the top of the hill. Eddie remembers that the Germans were mortaring the retreating men, but the medics collected the wounded and descended the slope intact. For this action Corporal G. McKenzie was awarded the Military Medal and Staff Sergeant E. Pruden a mention in despatches.

The following are the entries from the war diary of 16 PFA for this period:

> 2nd February 1943. Orders received to move – unit packed up – orders to move cancelled. CO was informed that 1st Battalion The Parachute Regiment was attacking Djebel Mansour feature this night. Battalion already had No 1 Section under Captain D. Wright attached. Strength of No 1 Section – 1 Officer and 19 ORs including S/Sergeant Clegg and Corporal Hatcher. CO made reconnaissance of area.
>
> 3rd February 1943. 0500 Attack on Djebel Mansour started. No 1 Section went into action with very light equipment. Captain Cassidy RAMC of Brigade HQ set up car post. Carry from top of hill to car post took 10 hours. Evacuation took place from car post at 667952 to ADS of 165 Field Ambulance at Djelida Station. Shuttle service of ambulances worked between ADS and car post.
>
> Time of this run approx 1 hour each way. Casualties were evacuated from Djelida to MDS 165 Field Ambulance at Gafour by ambulance train – time approx 35 minutes. 1st Battalion took Djebel Mansour and Djebel Alliliga but had to withdraw from Alliliga in the morning.
>
> Stretcher-bearers of No 1 Section became very tired with the long carry. CO returned to unit HQ in the afternoon and ordered No 4 Section under Captain Percival with 17 ORs to proceed to the action. They arrived at the top of Mansour about dusk and immediately proceeded to evacuate casualties.
>
> 4th February 1943. CO decided that more stretcher-bearers were required and Lieutenant Anderson and 13 ORs proceeded to the car collecting post. Lieutenant Anderson took over this point and Captain Cassidy moved forward with some of these fresh stretcher-bearers to bring in casualties. CO and Major Wheatley visited Brigade in the morning and were given orders to move the HQ of the Field Ambulance to farm at 536934. CO proceeded to Mansour. Message sent to RSM to move unit. Major MDS at Gafour. HQ had moved to new location by dusk.
>
> On Mansour CO established intermediate car post and placed Captain Percival in charge of it in the main ravine and another one behind it (car post A) at point 680942 under Captain Wright. Carries were now made from the hill to ravine post. Guards carriers were used between ravine and car post B. Light ambulances could

now reach car post B along the road newly made up and they took cases back to Lieutenant Anderson's car post.

Stretcher-bearers and both forward posts were under continuous mortar and shell fire and were dive bombed. All casualties were evacuated from the hill by nightfall and CO withdrew to ravine post.

5th February 1943. As no message had come through to unit HQ Major Wheatley proceeded on motor cycle to Lieutenant Anderson's car post and he established himself there as wounded were coming in, some not having been seen by an MO. In the meantime the CO had sent a message back that every available man was to come forward – 13 ORs arrived about noon including No 1 Surgical Team, clerks, dental Corporal and 4 RASC. The Surgical Team took over the car post and the others went forward to replace the stretcher-bearers. Casualties came in steadily and the post was kept clear by pushing light casualties on to passing cars and lorries when no ambulances were available.

On the hill itself with every available stretcher-bearer used all casualties were cleared by 0800, but the 1st Battalion then suffered further casualties and a party of 20 stretcher-bearers under Captain Cassidy proceeded up the hill, although orders for the evacuation of Mansour were given when they were halfway up the hill. They evacuated every casualty and were given protection by a small party of infantry.

The CO organised a party to search all the ravines and intermediate ground and they evacuated all casualties before dark.

By this time the 1st Battalion and the Grenadier Guards had been relieved by the A&SH and were embussing in the region of the first car post. The Field Ambulance with the exception of Major Wheatley, Lieutenant Anderson and 10 ORs who remained at the car post overnight returned to camp.

Casualties evacuated by the unit during the action:

1st Battalion, The Parachute Regiment	129
Grenadier Guards	45
Argyll and Sutherland Highlanders	3
16 Para Fd Amb	1
RASC	2
French	9
German	1
Total	190

Unit casualties 1 OR killed, 1 OR wounded and evacuated and 2 ORs wounded but remained with unit.

Here a few personal accounts to end with.
Thomas Davies recalls his memories of the fighting on Djebel Mansour:

Prominent hills and mountains of North Africa were called Djebel. One such mountain was Djebel Mansour, which stands out for me among all others. It was here that some of the most bitter fighting we had experienced took place. Djebel Mansour was in the hands of the German Army, who were well dug-in when we attacked. After many hours of attack and counter-attack, we eventually forced our way up the mountain, crawling and scrambling up different paths under pretty intense fire, the bullets bursting on the rocks about us, throwing up little fountains of earth and stones. The deadly rat-tat of machine gun fire and rifle-shot reports sounded like whiplash. My breath rasped as I took in great painful gulps of air as we finally reached the summit, driving the enemy down the slopes at the far end of the mountain into the valley below. Realising that it was just a matter of time before the Jerries would put in a counter-attack, we lost no time in trying to establish our positions firmly on the mountain, whilst attending as best we could to the casualties we had sustained. The bodies of a considerable number of Germans who would take no further interest in the war lay strewn around, some caught in the oddest poses. One victim, probably a sniper, whose helmet had dropped off revealing a shock of blonde hair, was wedged in the fork of a small tree, his eyes staring wild and unseeing into space. He was suspended like a huge rag doll whose seams had come apart spewing mangled flesh through his tattered uniform, most likely the result of the cruel blast of a three inch mortar shell.

Not many hours later, we were on the receiving end of an attack by the deadly Stuka bombers. I cannot imagine anything more demoralising to bleeding, weary troops. There is nothing one can do but hold tight and watch them plunge down from above like huge birds screaming their way earthwards, able to pull out of their dive only after they had jettisoned their bombs. The whole mountainside trembled with the impact of the exploding bombs, as earth, stones and shrubs were thrown into the air, half-burying us as debris beat a tattoo on our tin helmets. After this 'softening up' process, their ground troops started moving in with a counter-attack, throwing everything they had into the onslaught on our positions in the fight to regain the ground they had lost. Our number one gunner, Jock Miller, a Scottish lad, fell backwards into the mortar pit, shot clean through the head. He died in our arms not able to say a word, just a faint rattle coming from his throat as his colour changed from a deep tan to a greyish-white in a matter of seconds.

We were taking quite a hammering all round at this stage and getting desperately short of ammunition. Apparently the mules that were being used for transporting the ammunition up the mountain to us had stampeded in terror at the sight and sound of the shells landing close by. Their drivers, tall, lean Senegalese Africans, who were serving with the French North African forces being unable to check them.

Our position now became pretty hopeless, the Germans relentlessly fighting their way up the slopes and steadily closing in to gain a firm footing once again on the mountaintop. The order to fix bayonets was passed around and we expected at any moment to hear the command to charge, which would start the shouts of "Waho Mohammed", the battle cry adopted by the parachute troops which was to strike terror and dismay into the hearts of the enemy long before the campaign was over. The idea of the call came from the lads imitating the Arabs, who used to shout "Waho Mohammed" to their donkeys when urging their animals into action.

However, instead of the order to charge being given, we were ordered to withdraw. It was hard having to leave behind many of the more seriously wounded but we had some consolation reasoning that they stood a better chance of survival if they were taken prisoner as they were in dire need of medical attention. They would get this from the Germans who were likely to send them to Tunis, which was only thirty or forty kilometres away, for hospital treatment.

We half-carried, half-dragged as many of the wounded that we could manage through the undergrowth, forcing our way into the bushes as a thunderstorm of gunfire bellowed among the hills. We groped our way down rocky slopes, some of the wounded bleeding profusely, screaming out in pain when perhaps an arm or a leg would catch in undergrowth or a rock. It was not easy to distinguish the wounded from the rest of us as we were all covered in blood; a gory sight, stinking of the sweat and dust of the past few days. We were assisted off Djebel Mansour by a contingent of the French Foreign Legion who set up a rearguard action, enabling the remnants of the battalion to be guided through a wide gully at the foot of the mountain. We shouldered our way through this ravine to the accompaniment of falling mortar bombs and eventually arrived very slowly indeed, with the shambling gait of thoroughly exhausted men, at a large olive grove.

After a while, we ceased to hear even the remotest echo of the battle. Licking our wounds, we took toll of the casualties which were considerable, about three quarters of the Battalion having been either killed or wounded.

Signalman A. Brown:

At 0830 4th February I left Brigade HQ for the 1st Battalion forward position with Signalman Seviour. We went by lorry to the 1st Battalion Command Post and from there to the wadi at the foot of Djebel Mansour by carrier. The journey on foot up to the 1st Battalion position was rather awkward because of the bushes also the wireless set hampered us quite a bit, we took over three hours to do this journey. I arrived at 1st Battalion HQ at 1400, the only activity then being our artillery shelling Alliliga prior to the Guards attacking it. I put up the set and got R5 communication to the control set. 1st Battalion Command Post set then went off the air and so they moved to a new location which then worked. At 1500 the Guards attacked Alliliga, encountering as far as I could see very little opposition. The enemy then began to mortar all three features of Djebel Mansour. At approx 1600 1st Battalion Command Post set came on the air again and obtained R5 to Brigade and my own set. Major Ince (OC HQ Company) then spoke to Major Cleasby-Thompson asking for SAA and mortar HE bombs. At 1630 Colonel Pearson returned. By 1900 enemy mortar fire had ceased. Having only one bank of batteries I decided to switch off the set to preserve them as I did not expect further supplies of batteries till morning. Seviour and I then tried to get some sleep.

The enemy shelled us lightly with mortars from 0500 till 0530 and then at 0600 he must have begun his attack on the French positions as the mortar fire became heavier and machine gun fire began. By 0930 the mortar and machine gun fire was intense and coming from both flanks. Apparently the French on our left had had to evacuate and reports from T Company proved this true. An enemy machine gun post was firing at us from our right. The Guards were informed but failed to stop it. At 1000 Colonel Pearson informed Major Cleasby-Thompson of the situation and asked for reinforcements and ammunition. By 1045 the CO thought we might have to evacuate but he did not want to do this because of exposing the Guards left flank and his plan was to get round behind and support them if evacuation became necessary. At 1100 Brigadier Flavell spoke to Colonel Pearson, had the situation explained to him and he said he would see what could be done. I asked the CO if I should burn my cipher W/T diagram and diary. He said yes. At 1200 Colonel Pearson spoke to the Brigade Major, Major Yeldham and asked for a reply within two minutes. The reply was that we should evacuate our positions. The Companies in W/T communication with Battalion HQ were informed by that means, the others verbally. Signalman Seviour and I smashed the wireless equipment, the set being put off frequency first. The CO put two shots in the set. Seviour and I then followed him out of the trench and down the hill. After 50 yards or so I lost Seviour as I stopped and tried to put on my equipment but as I was being fired on I was unable to do so and left it behind. About halfway down the hill I saw Colonel Pearson directing his men to the rendezvous, he seemed to be unhurt. I arrived at the rendezvous but could not see Seviour. We moved off by Company's along the wadi at the foot of Djebel Mansour. I went with HQ Company. The wadi was very muddy and we became spread out and I lost the main party and with a few others made my way to the hill on the opposite side of the valley. Our artillery put up a smoke screen which seemed to help us a great deal in our getting away safely. When we reached the other side of the hill we met two French Officers who told us the way to go.

At 1600 I arrived at the 1st Battalion Command Post where I had some very welcome refreshment and also I was relieved to discover Signalman Seviour had arrived there safely too. After a while it was decided Seviour and I would go back to Brigade HQ and we were taken there by Lieutenant Lyske and we arrived there at 2100.

Private A. Brown describes his experiences after being wounded on the Djebel:

We were in the process of collecting rocks to make cover when I received a sledgehammer blow in the left hip and knew I had been hit. I rolled over and undid my trousers and saw a jagged bleeding hole from my hip to my groin and poking out of my abdomen a bullet, which I took out and still have to this day. I applied my shell dressing to the wound, which it just covered, and then buttoned up my trousers to hopefully apply some pressure on my wound. The next thing I did was to take out the two hand grenades in my lower pocket of my jumping jacket, which were both fused. One was ok but the other had absorbed the shock of the bullet which had ended up in my abdomen and a piece of the grenade about 1½ inches square had broken off showing the explosive inside. This I then threw down the mountain away from our side. My left leg seemed incapable of movement and I lay where I was. I do remember looking at my watch and it was 0830. Even though I had been wounded several hours after we started the advance it seemed like minutes. From then on, probably due to shock, my mind seemed to float in the clouds and I remember little. I lay on the mountain all day and that night a patrol passed me but I made no sound as they smelt like Germans. The sun rising the following morning gave me some welcome warmth after the cold of the night and I lit a cigarette. As I drew my right hand away from my face while holding the fag I received two bullets in my upper right arm. About two hours later a party of stretcher-bearers arrived and placing me on a stretcher they carried me shoulder-high down a long gulley, it seemed that mortar bombs followed us all the way but none of us were hit.

First I was taken to our Battalion MO (Captain Haggie), a marvellous man; he examined me as if it were a bedside visit from his practice at home. I can hear him now as he said his diagnosis and wrote it on my field medical card, "Out all night, some rigidity of stomach etc etc" and all this while our artillery flung shells over with abandon. From him I was taken down the mountainside in a Guards Bren gun carrier, a journey that was not without its moments of anxiety when the ground became almost too steep for the carrier. At the dressing station my card was looked at and a cursory glance made at my wounds. My recollection is rather vague at this point but I do remember asking if I might urinate and was given a bottle to do so. This entailed moving my legs apart to place the bottle between them. I recall that I filled it up and then half filled it again, the bottle being emptied somewhere. I had managed somehow to get my bad leg off the stretcher but could not get it back on again and had to ask a medic to put it back for me. I was taken from this dressing station to a hospital and I didn't rejoin the Battalion for a couple of months.

It would be appropriate to close this chapter by letting Lieutenant Colonel Pearson have the closing words:

I was ordered to take and hold Djebel Mansour. With Chris Perrin-Brown I visited Captain Faveau of the French Foreign Legion. A fine man. He promised to provide a guide and assistance with a fighting patrol. Vic Coxen was in charge of the patrol, but I went along because I wanted to see the best place for the start line and also work out the enemy's fixed lines of fire. It was a long walk and we had to climb down and up this bloody great dry wadi about 30 feet deep. The Germans were very good at firing on fixed lines at night, but you could get underneath if you were careful. The patrol was a success and we captured three Germans from their Mountain Division who occupied Djebel Mansour, although we had to leave Lieutenant Norton on the hillside, as he would have died if we had brought him back. We left him a flare gun to hopefully attract German attention and they would treat him.

We finally agreed on a plan of attack with the French. Two thousand yards of white tape normally used for marking minefields was used to mark the route to the start line. I had a theory that if we were going to get lost then let us all get lost together. The Captain with his French guides would run out the tape and we would all walk along it till we reached the start line. Even with this elementary precaution S Company got lost. We crossed the start line at 0500 and began to climb the Djebel through the scrub. It was a hard climb of 500 yards, being machine gunned and mortared the whole way. We reached our first objective according to plan just before first light. The Germans withdrew and brought down a devastating mortar concentration on our positions and followed this by an immediate counter-attack, which we managed to defeat. S Company arrived having suffered heavy casualties on the way from a German machine gun. So Djebel Mansour was captured and we then tried to get on to Djebel Alliliga but we had too few men to exploit the situation. I decided to consolidate on the centre of the position. An urgent message was sent for the Guards to come and assist as promised. The day was spent digging in and evacuating the wounded. Some 105 casualties were evacuated and 35 PoWs. We had captured a German medical orderly who told us they had picked up Lieutenant Norton and while he was in a bad way they had got him to hospital and he was certain he would survive, minus a leg (which he did).

Major Cleasby-Thompson arrived with a mule train bringing rations and ammunition and also the good news that the Guards Brigade were mounting a large-scale attack through Alliliga to the Pont du Fahs road. During the night Captain Faveau's Company arrived and were put on the left flank. A Company from the Guards also arrived and their commander, Major Tufnell, said he was in reserve and was to move onto Alliliga as soon as it was taken.

I sent the IO, Perrin-Brown, at first light to see what was happening on El Alliliga. The Guards reserves had moved during the night – where to nobody knew. Perrin-Brown returned in a filthy temper saying that the Guards had not attacked and the only contact he had made was with an enemy machine gun.

The Guards were found later, down at the bottom of the hill. They'd not been told to attack. I then learned that they were to attack later that afternoon. To cover this we laid down smoke. Their attack did not dislodge the machine gun on the eastern side of El Alliliga because that continued to give us difficulties. I sent a number of calls to the Guards Brigade, but to no avail. At dawn the French were overrun by a German counter-attack and their positions occupied. It was no mean feat by the Germans as the French had fought well. All their officers became casualties and their sergeant major led an unsuccessful counter-attack with fixed bayonets.

By now we were in big trouble; we needed urgent reinforcements as we'd suffered a lot of casualties and our mortars had run out of ammunition. But I decided to hang on as long as possible. At 1000 S Company were completely out of ammunition but brandishing grenades. R and T Companies had about 100 rounds between them. Major Conron had been killed and no officers were left in R Company.

I tried to get permission to withdraw at 1010 hours, but they wouldn't give it. At 1030 the German mortars stopped which meant they were going to close in any minute. At 1045 I asked again for permission to withdraw as the enemy were about 40 yards away. S and R Companies were calling for the Germans to come closer so they could throw their grenades at them. But I was told to hang on for five minutes and I'd get an answer. I told them that if I hung on for two more minutes there would be no one here to take their bloody answer. I got permission and told the Companies to withdraw, leaving the seriously wounded behind.

It was difficult to get the lightly wounded down. We carried them on mules and stretchers – but we were under fire. But once the Germans realised we were withdrawing they lifted their fire. They were very good like that – very professional. We'd worked hard and were desperately tired, but morale was good. We had heavy losses – 35 dead, 132 wounded and 16 missing – nearly 50% of our strength and we were back where we started.

The brooding mass of Djebel Mansour in 2010. (N. Cherry)

To this day I have never been able to discover the importance of Djebel Mansour or El Alliliga. For the overall battle all we did was to occupy about a regiment of a crack German division for about four days which may have helped the general situation, but I always ask myself, was it worth the cost?

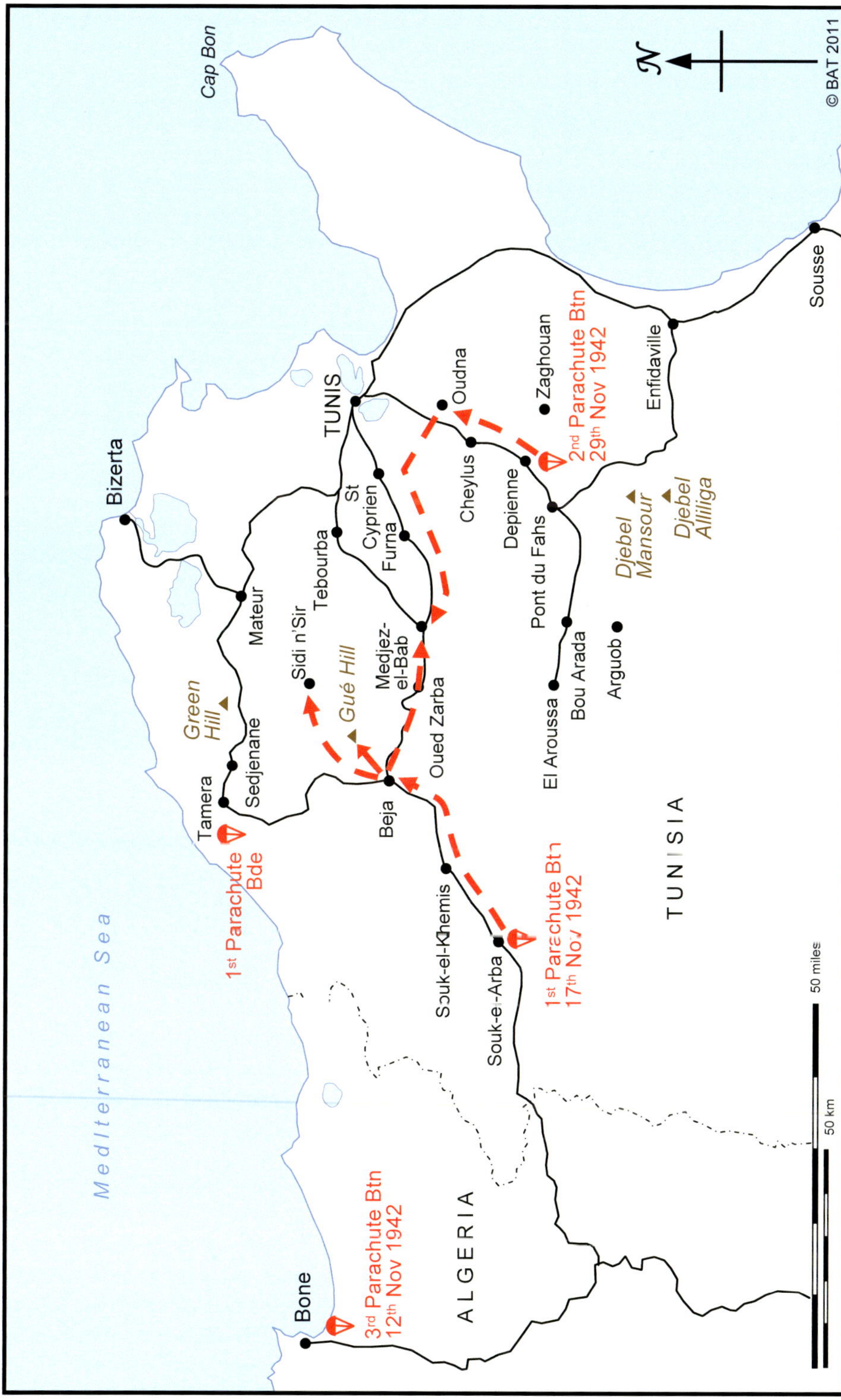

General Map of the Tunisian Theatre of Operations (based on author's map)

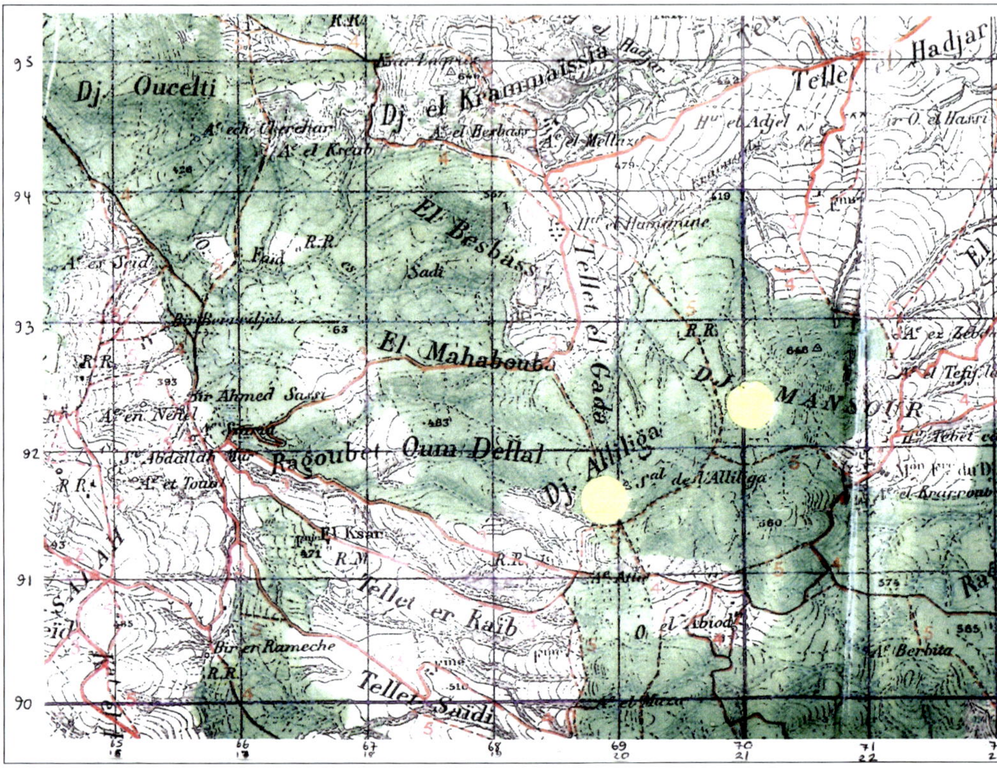

The Djebel Mansour area (courtesy of James Macrae)

Notes to accompany Map of the Mateur area on opposite page

Note 1: Raided by night 23/24 Nov 1942

This was the raid on Gué Hill (see Chapter 5) undertaken according to the 1st Battalion's war diary on the night of 23rd/24th November 1942. It was during this raid that the CO, Lieutenant Colonel Hill was wounded which led to Major Pearson assuming command. Pearson's original map was dated wrongly, showing 22/23 Nov (see the original on page 93).

Note 2: 1st Parachute Btn

This was the location to which the 1st Battalion moved after the raid on Gué Hill around 26th November 1942.

Note 3: Coxen's Farm

On 26th November 1942 Captain Coxen led a fighting patrol and recce'd a farm, which afterwards became known as Coxen's Farm, about three miles from the main Battalion position. He reported it was unoccupied except by animals, who were all staggering around drunk!

Note 4: Rest Farm

This is the location R Company moved to on 2nd December 1942.

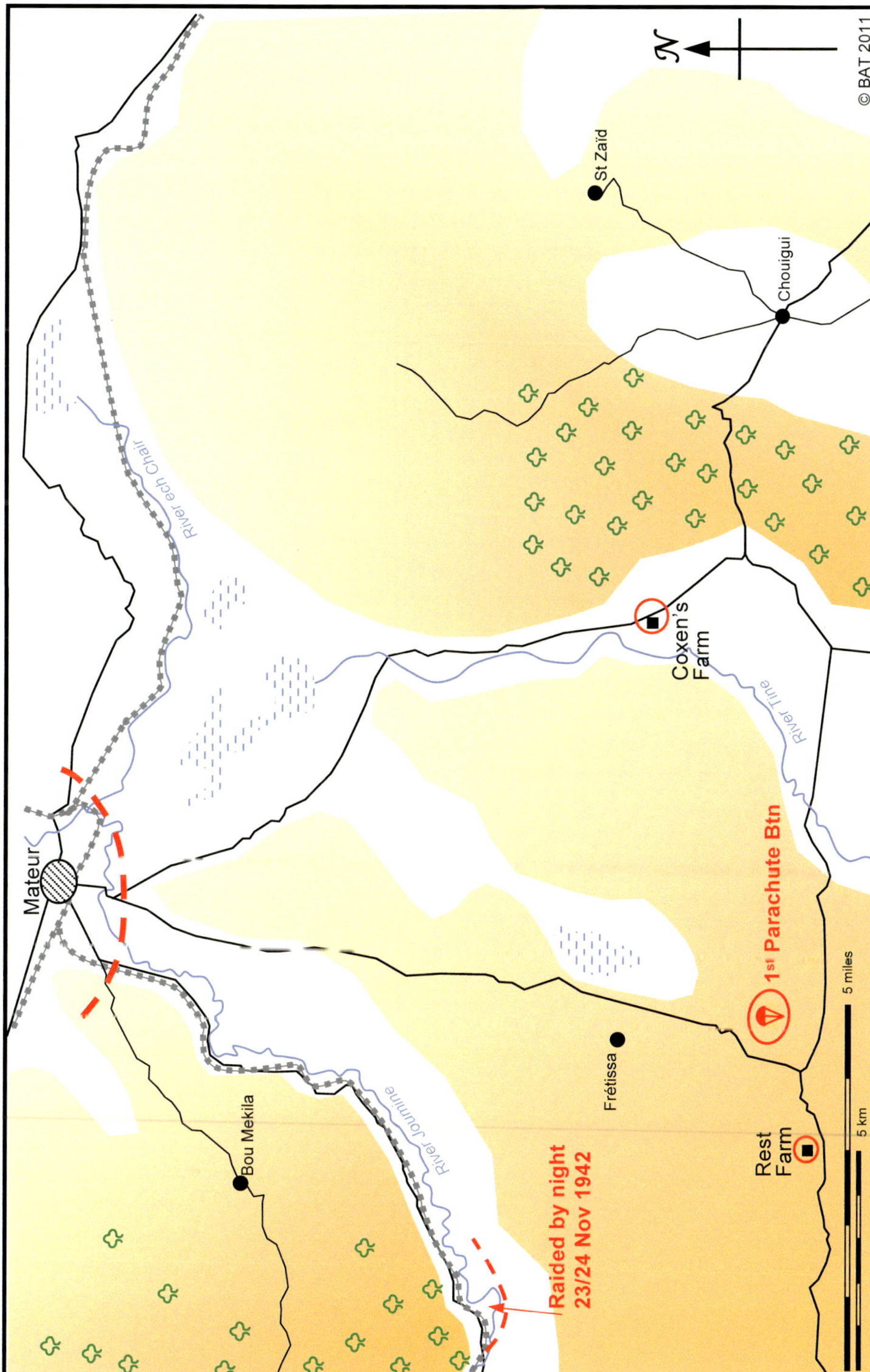

The Mateur area, based on a map marked up and used by Lieutenant Colonel A. Pearson in November 1942 (courtesy of James Macrae)

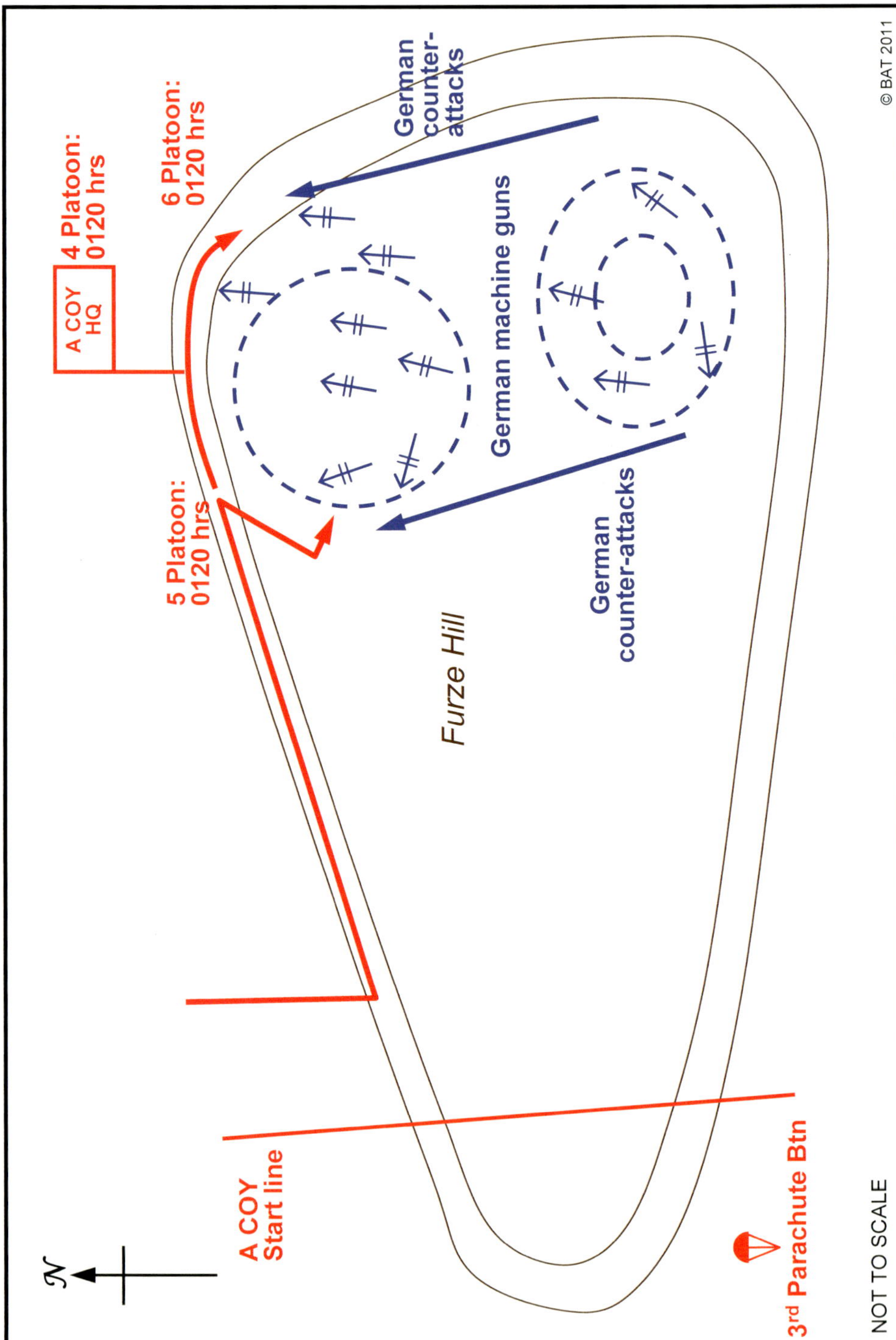

Green Hill, based on a sketch by Major D. Dobie (original in Airborne Assault Duxford)

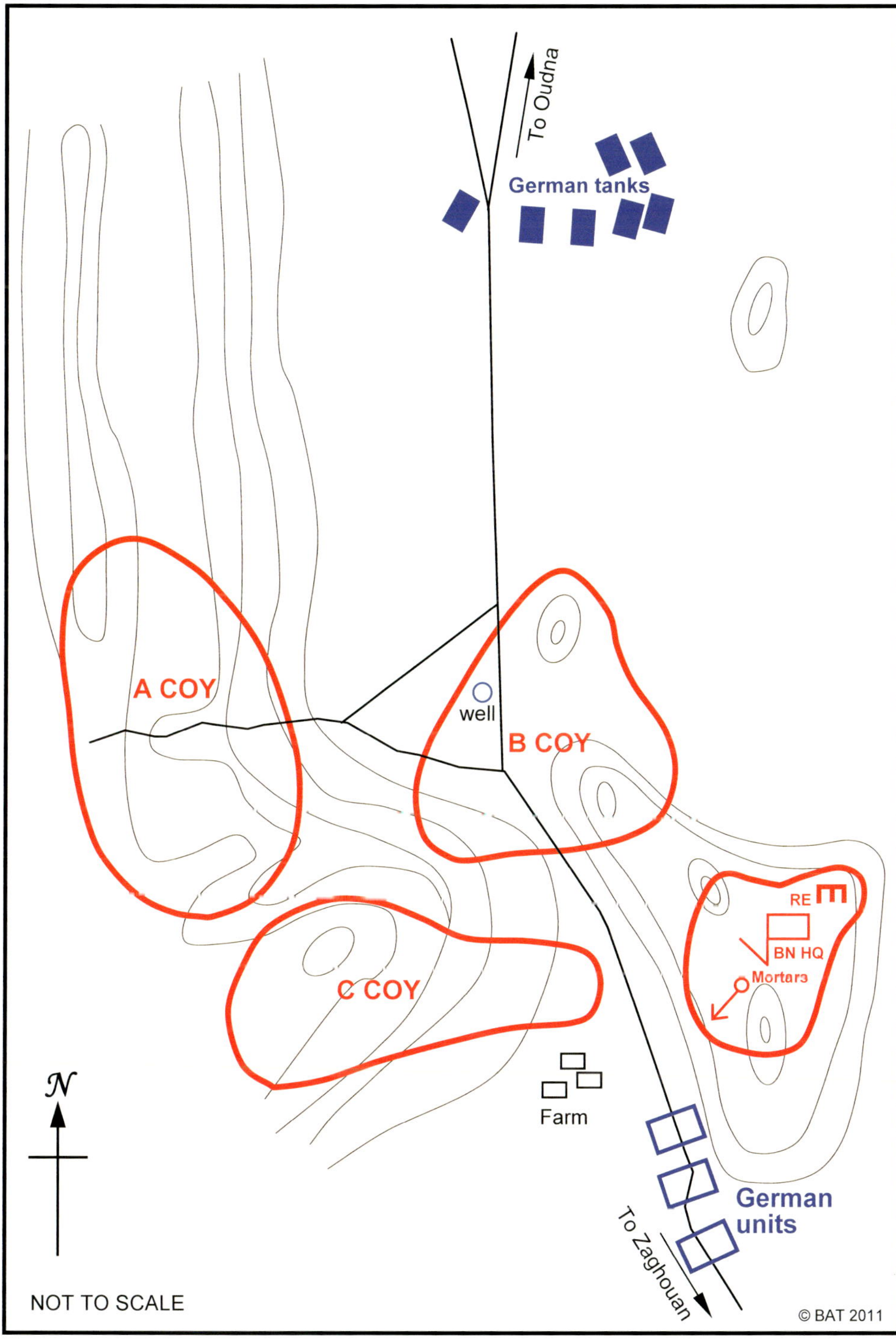

Prise de l'Eau. Based on a sketch drawn after the Oudna operation, and which originally appeared in the 2nd Parachute Battalion's post-action report (original in National Archives).

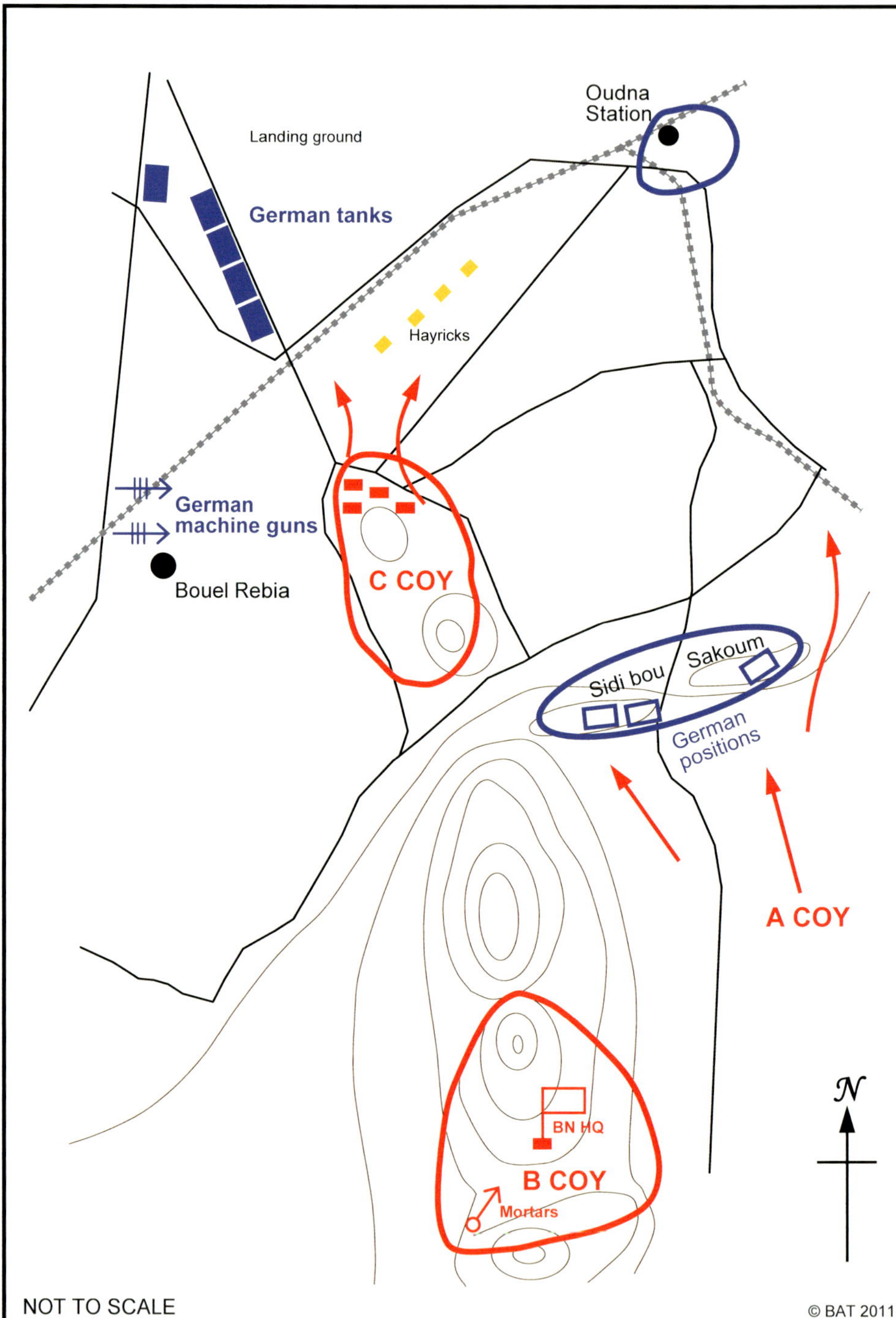

Oudna. Based on a sketch drawn after the Oudna operation, and which originally appeared in the 2nd Parachute Battalion's post-action report (original in National Archives).

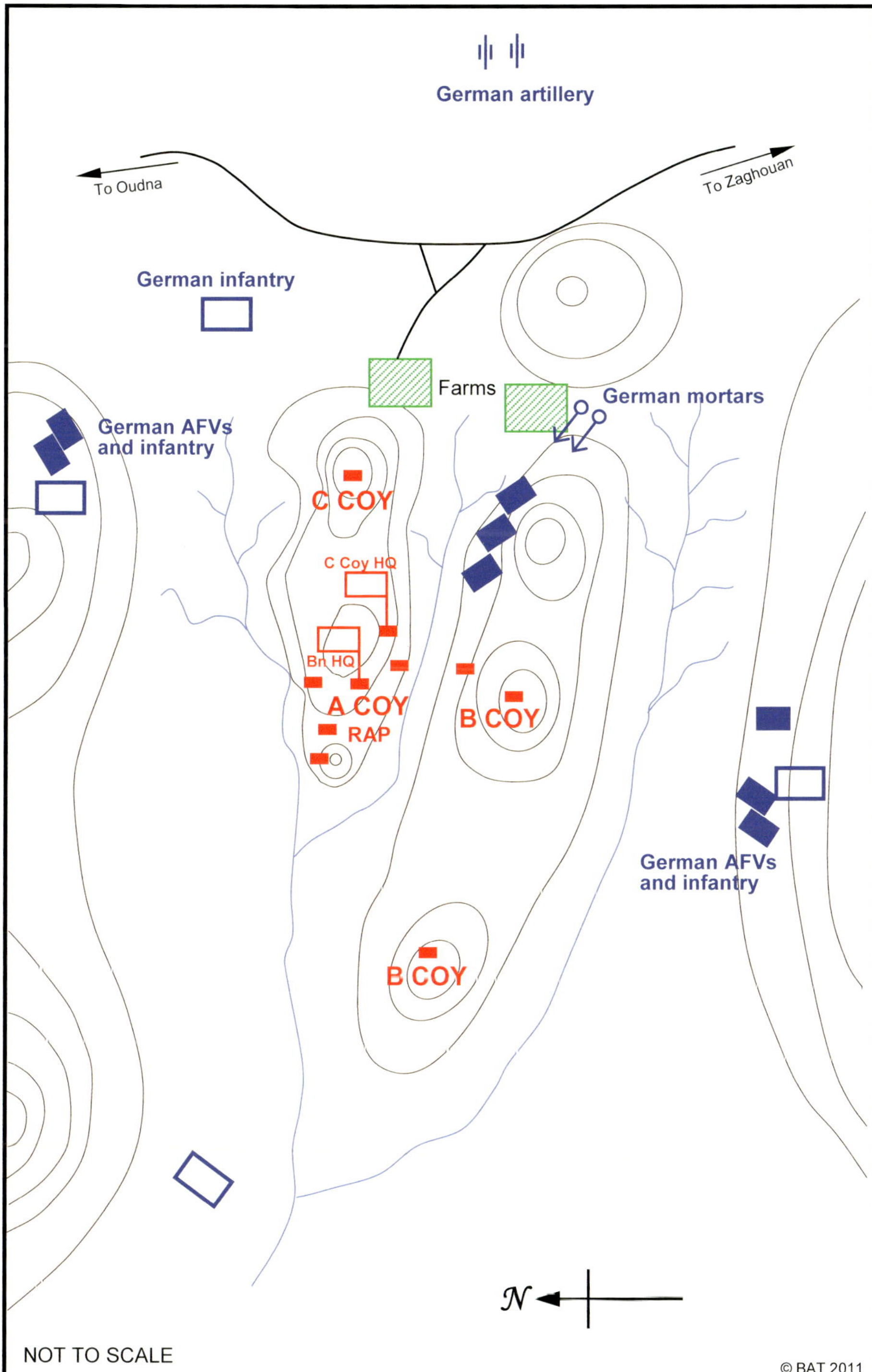

Djebel Sidi Bou Hadjeba. Based on a sketch drawn after the Oudna operation, and which originally appeared in the 2nd Parachute Battalion's post-action report (original in National Archives).

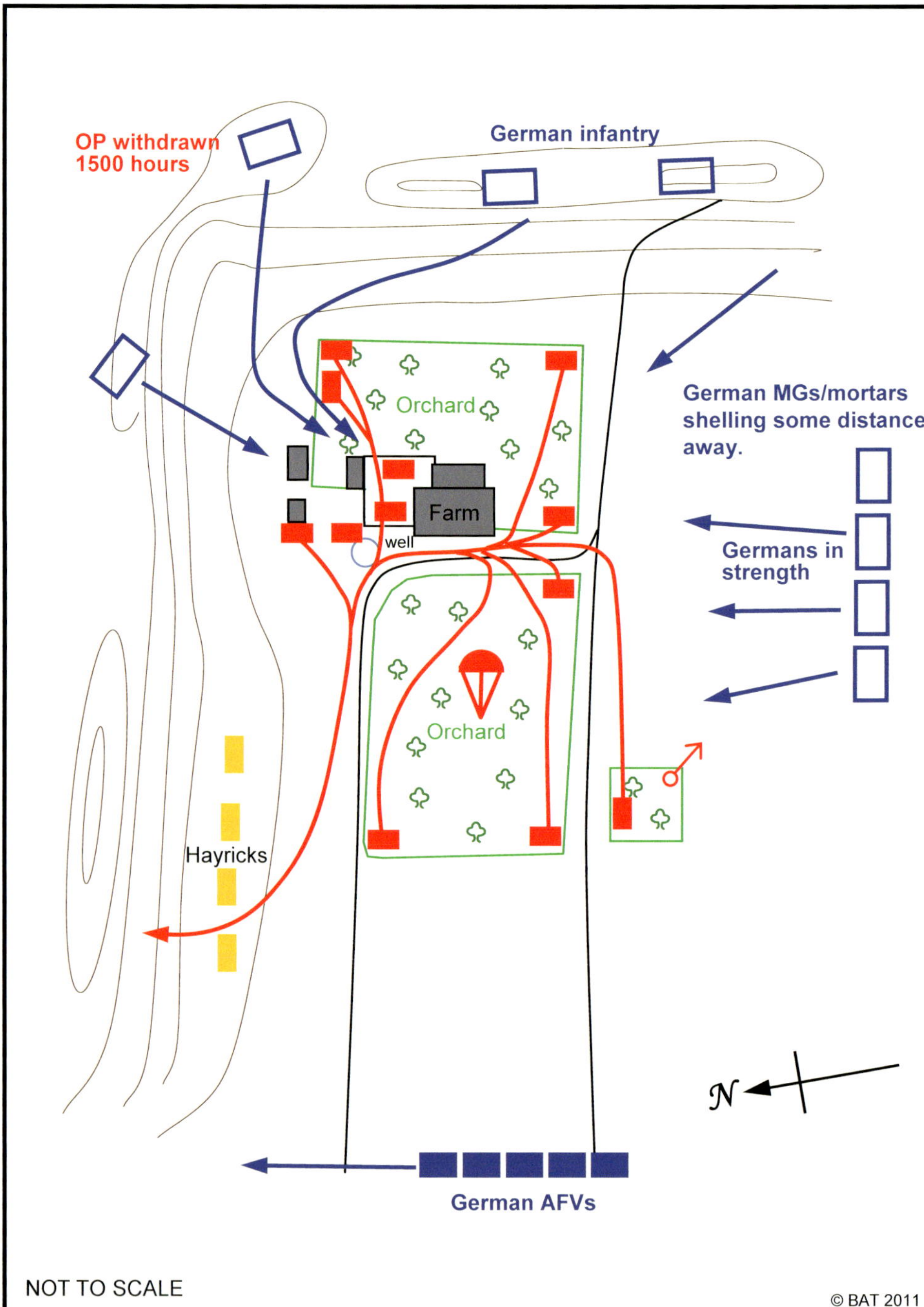

The retreat from El Fedja. Based on a sketch drawn after the Oudna operation, and which originally appeared in the 2nd Parachute Battalion's post-action report (original in National Archives).

9

Happy Valley, Argoub and Tamera, February 1943

By the beginning of February 1943 the three Battalions of the 1st Parachute Brigade were all, once again, under a unified command in the area of Bou Arada. Obviously the 1st Battalion had taken a bit of a stuffing on Djebel Mansour and was in need of some reorganisation, however it was soon a case of 'no rest for the wicked'. The 1st Battalion's war diary records that on 7th February they spent the day at a farm sorting out men and equipment. That evening Lieutenant Colonel Pearson dined at Brigade HQ and discussed the reorganisation of the officers and men in the Battalion. The war diary also records that of the 25 or so officers of the 1st Battalion who sailed to North Africa in November 1942 only seven were still present. On the following day they moved by route march to a new location, with the baggage and tents being moved by lorry. The Companies camped out in olive groves, whilst Battalion HQ was in a farm building, it is recorded that it was a "luxurious location but we are a sadly depleted gathering."

Reinforcements for the 1st Battalion arrived on 15th February in the shape of 9 officers and 144 ORs who came from Souk- el-Arba. They are recorded as coming from the 5th Camerons and the 6th Royal Welch Fusiliers. These are the names used in the Battalion war diary, although, in fact, they came from the 5th and 6th Parachute Battalions who had been formed with a nucleus of men from these units. Also arriving were about 10 old sweats who had been wounded in previous engagements and managed to get themselves back in the airborne fold. The arrival of these men was a double-edged sword as what the 1st Parachute Brigade gave with one hand they got some back with the other. On the same day as the reinforcements arrived, Brigadier Flavell came to choose some men for the HQ Defence Platoon.

Meanwhile, the 3rd Battalion took up positions near a place known as Argoub, which became known as 'Happy Valley' as it was a lot quieter than areas the paratroopers had previously served in. However, as the Brigade had an aggressive patrolling policy the quiet period did not last for long.

One officer from the 3rd Battalion gives an insight into the policy that flowed down from Brigade HQ:

> A policy of intensive patrolling was decreed by Brigade. We were not in any way against this, provided essential principles were not ignored and they were. Orders were rushed, patrol commanders were not given sufficient time for recce and serious planning; they had scarcely enough time to show their men what they were about to set out to do. Moreover, the lack of precise orders left confusion in the patrol leader's mind. Was his patrol recce or fighting? Nothing was ever clear. A leader would be told to take ten men to the enemy lines, grab a prisoner but not to have any casualties. How could a commander be sure that he could obey both orders?

Thus a number of insipid patrols went out with priorities not clear. They usually returned with a casualty, no prisoner but with plenty of useful information. I hope that this was collated and used well to balance our infrequent yet irritating losses.

Soon it came to my turn to try my hand. It was the usual story. Orders were given to me some two hours before dusk. A force of ten, a prisoner please, no casualties please, create a diversion to an attack on heights on the right which was going in that night, be back by 0300. There should be cloudless skies, but the moon will be shining in all its glory by 0200. There was no time to rest, only time to pick the men, give orders about their dress, show them the route I intended to follow, pick out a few landmarks to help anyone to make a safe return should he become detached from the patrol.

At dusk we set off on a new route to the enemy lines, for the usual one had been used too much for my liking. We made our way down, up and across the numerous wadis, which in the darkness and their unusual close proximity, took on a strangeness which created confusion and doubt in my mind as to my exact location at any moment. Several times, I stopped and the patrol looked back to examine the skyline of our positions. It was a strange experience to look at them as if we were the enemy. Eventually we were lying silently some twenty feet below and some twenty yards away from a narrow road which ran in front of the enemy's positions. Assuming that the enemy would use the road now and again, probably by a defensive patrol, I decided to prepare an ambush; a prisoner taken so easily would spare us a lot of trouble and we would be home safe and sound, hopefully in no time at all. I despatched half my force across the road to a position on my left where the deeper darkness suggested a ditch of some cover. Before they had crossed the five yards or so, machine gun fire swept down the road from my right. The enemy were gracious enough to use tracer bullets, for their use told me that the gun was firing on a fixed line. A few moments later mortar bombs exploded on the road and in the lower ground where I was lying with the other half of my patrol. This was very disquieting, for obviously the enemy knew where I was, but I could not pinpoint him. The only way to work out where the gun was to make some noise on the road as this would bring bursts of fire from it. There was no point in risking our lives by using the road, so a few of us dug out small rocks and threw them onto the hard white surface. This action brought several bursts of tracer down the road, [and] I was able to convince myself that the gun was positioned on or near a small pimple on my right. Then during a lull in the firing we rushed over the road to join the rest of the patrol. My plan was now to move further away and to settle down to a period of silent inactivity, hoping to give the enemy the impression that we had given up and gone home.

After a while I led the patrol up the sloping hill, which, I hoped, would eventually take me to a point behind the enemy machine gun position. This would I felt provide me with the prisoner so ardently desired by Brigade. We had to be very cautious and crawled a long way silently and slowly. Suddenly I saw the machine gun team outlined against a star lit sky. I realised that we had penetrated into an enemy defensive position, for the sort of skyline I saw could only be seen from inside it. But before I could whisper orders for a final assault, a second gun opened up with violent bursts from behind us, throwing lines of tracer amongst us, fortunately no one was hit. This was a shock; we had avoided all skylines, but I had not realised that just as the gun crew were obvious to me, so we could be skylined to other defensive positions built in-depth on a reverse slope.

The machine gun behind us was doing us no harm, but it had destroyed my plan. Another was necessary and that took little thought – if we turned our backs on the first gun, we would not be skylined if we attacked the second. Word was passed from one man to the next somehow and I hoped everyone got the change of plan. At that moment a frantic working of the moving parts of a gun and a series of guttural oaths told me that our desired prize had a stoppage. I felt this was the moment; we could be in amongst them when their attention was on the gun and not on the likely arrival of enemy intruders. We had only just started our rush when a third gun opened up, firing across the ground between us and our objective. The rush turned into a scramble for cover in the uneven ground. The stoppage was rectified and we suddenly found ourselves in the middle of a triangle, at each corner was an enemy machine gun. Even so, we were in a relatively safe spot provided we remained out of sight. I felt the danger did not lie with the guns but from their infantry emerging from trenches who might be on us before we really knew it. To my right I observed a small bowl in the ground, but large enough to contain us all; it seemed a good place to reorganise as there was cover surrounding most of it. We scrambled here but soon afterwards enemy incendiaries hit the cover, which blazed alight, revealing all of us I feel to the enemy. We moved out of our cover with astonishing and self-preserving speed; no need for orders in such circumstances. A narrow path, clearly defined under the clear sky, twisted away from the blazing undergrowth. To cross this into infrequent and dwarfish cover was the only sensible route to take unless we were to give the enemy a prisoner or two, and one of the objects of the patrol was not to present them with such a gift. Each member of the patrol chose this area as the first step in his retreat and so it was possible to retain control of my small force. Had I been a braver man, or perhaps had I been given a simple, straightforward object for my journey, it is possible I might have returned to base with a frightened prisoner. "No casualties please" is an order which offers an excuse for almost any action which takes you out of the danger area. A commander, under whom I was to serve for a short time in the future, would have dismissed from his mind the orders he had received and decided to "do it alone"; but I was not of his quality.

No longer were the guns firing on fixed lines for we had moved outside the beastly triangle. As we moved we were visible and movement had to be short and sharp, followed by a period of lying doggo. I found it possible to get orders through to most of the patrol – everyone would withdraw to the depression from which we had originally crossed the road. Each man must have known that if he continued in the direction in which we were facing, he must hit the road and once there it would be simple to find the wadi which had led us to the enemy lines. My own retreat was accomplished in a series of bounds, moving fast in a semi-upright position, then crawling as fast as my equipment allowed and then lying as if dead. Because of the burning scrub I felt I was carrying out these manoeuvres in daylight. But the greatest danger to my personal safety was not the enemy but from one of my soldiers. He persisted in following and imitating my actions. He was seconds late in completing his movements and thus when he hid himself beside me, he could have highlighted my spot to the enemy. Either he had admiration for me or was certain I had a charmed life. I suspect the latter. However, we got away with it and eventually reached the depression.

There I found I was short of a sergeant and two men. I was not unduly concerned, for the sergeant was able and reliable and provided they had not been hit he would see them back safely. The moon had now risen and the whole countryside was bathed in a brightness which made another attempt to get a prisoner impossible. After some consideration I decided it was time to go back to our lines. My decision was hastened by the arrival of mortar bombs in our location; our presence was still known. Fortunately several of the bombs were duds. So I led the bulk of the patrol back to what I believed to be the comfort and safety of our lines. We all felt it consoling to be trudging to the crest, clearly outlined in the moonlight, for this was our temporary home.

It had been arranged for my patrol to return through a certain area which was commanded by a platoon commander who was an amateur explosive expert. I had made certain that the path we would take on our return would be free of his beastly booby traps. As we climbed up the slope, now casual and pretty noisy, I was amazed at the lack of a welcome. There was a deadly silence apart from our footsteps, which resounded from the rock into the moonlit air. Suddenly I came upon strange and unknown faces which doubted my identity. "What is the pass word?" I was asked. I had no idea, but after some debate we were allowed through and learnt that our unit had moved out during our patrol but no-one seemed to know where. There was obviously no-one to receive my report and so there could hardly be any hurry for it. Fortunately the missing men turned up and as it was only a couple of hours before dawn, I thought it would be a good idea to try and get some sleep. As I dozed off, I wondered how Brigade would receive my report; no prisoners, no casualties, possibly a diversion to the attack. Was there another object possibly to the patrol – to hide the fact that another unit had moved in as my own battalion had moved out? But where had they gone? It was not the last time in the war that I had a strange feeling that I had been forgotten.

At first light I sauntered down to the slope to where Battalion HQ had been. Dried sweat and the unwashed skin of my face gave me a feeling of drowsiness in spite of the fresh biting air of dawn. There I found a tank squadron; fortunately they were the Lothians, some of whom I knew. I was able to beg some hot water and a fried breakfast. Later, they let me borrow a scout car to assist in moving my men. But I was in no hurry for this, I wanted to let them sleep. So I spent the time drawing sketch maps in detail of what I had learnt of the enemy positions. I felt I had to do it before I forgot vital details. I was conceited enough to think what I drew and what I described would be of real value to any attacking force. Before noon a truck arrived to take us back to our unit, we had not been forgotten after all. It had orders for me to call in at Brigade HQ. On the way I told the driver to stop where a fresh, fast-flowing stream ran parallel to the track. I sat on the bank, taking in the warm sun and dangled my feet in the cool, rushing water. Eventually I had an unwelcome lunch at Brigade; it would have been a good deal more pleasant

Digging a command post for the 3rd Parachute Battalion HQ. In the foreground is Captain J. Moore, the Adjutant. Note the two pockets on the rear of the trousers, which were large enough to hold a field dressing each. (R. Pine-Coffin)

if I had brought a German along with me. Thoroughly dispirited, I was relieved to rejoin my unit in the afternoon.

Another view of these patrols in the so-called quiet sector of 'Happy Valley' comes from Lieutenant D. Bentham of B Company of the 3rd Battalion:

> Tom Gotto was sent out one night on his first patrol. He only covered 500 yards having crawled all the way. David [Major Dobie, his OC] was annoyed. He was sent out two nights later and his men came back at 0200 and said he had stepped on a mine and had sent them back as he was dying. Giles [Bromley-Martin] immediately went out with a stretcher party but could not find him in the dark. David took out another party in daylight and although the Germans were only about 1,000 yards away they did not shoot. They found Tom very badly wounded and brought him in. He was conscious when he reached our lines, looked up at David and said "Did I make up for it, Sir?" Poor Tom died in the ambulance, a loss felt by all. What he must have suffered that night by himself no one will ever know. [Tom Gotto now lies in Medjez-el-Bab CWGC cemetery grave 10F15.]

Private R. Priestly had originally volunteered to try and be a glider pilot but had failed to meet the required standard in an algebra exam and so was offered the opportunity to train as a paratrooper, which he accepted. Passing through Hardwick Hall and Ringway he joined the 2nd Battalion in late 1942 and was one of the many reinforcements sent out to the 1st Parachute Brigade. He arrived with the Battalion just before Christmas 1942. He recalls a later incident:

> If my memory serves me right we then moved to Happy Valley. Here I had the time of my life – we were billeted close to some Foreign Legion troops. I well remember riding their Colonel's beautiful white horse and him threatening what he would do to me if anything happened to the horse. Needless to say I'm still alive and kicking. I seem to recall that we were short of numbers and our section had about five men instead of the normal ten, and so we had to do four hours on guard instead of the more normal two. In the early hours of one morning I was struggling to stay awake and I was staring at this bush so hard that I was convinced it was moving and so I opened fire and the whole Battalion stood to until dawn. I was not that popular that day.

On 9th February 1943, at 1400, the 3rd Battalion began to move to the area of Argoub, south of Bou Arada and west of Djebel Mansour. It was still a relatively quiet area, although soon after arrival they were dive-bombed by Stukas, and later on the 21st the Battalion HQ was shelled and took 5 direct hits with one man wounded. After this the Battalion HQ moved to a new location at 703978 on Sheet 41 of the Tunisian series. It was a time of patrolling by both sides, with B Company being attacked on the night of 22nd February and two prisoners being taken. It was also a change in some of the senior commanders, with Major J. Hall being posted to the 1st Battalion. Captain A. Bush took over command of C Company (he had been the 2 i/c) with Lieutenant A. Waddy taking over this role. Students of the Arnhem battle will recognise these names, as in 1944 Major Bush was 2 i/c of the 3rd Battalion and Lieutenant Waddy was then a Major and OC of B Company. This area was overlooked by the enemy, although at first it was a mixture of Italians and Austrians, who did not seem too anxious to do anything hostile, the 1st Battalion being positioned to the left of the 3rd Battalion. For a couple of weeks it was a quiet time. However, the odd incident did occur, as Lieutenant G. Street recalled:

> I went forward in the half-light of dawn to visit my advanced posts and I heard movement in the thick scrub which covered the hillside. I called out to these men in the scrub to keep quiet since the enemy were close by. I was challenged and so I shouted out again something like "Don't make such a bloody row there may be Germans about." I then felt the barrel of a sub-machine-gun in my ribs and a German ordered me in fairly good English to walk in front of them towards the Battalion HQ. I thought that they wanted to attack it and as I had no intention of taking them there I led them to the nearest strongpoint, they soon opened fire but I was not hit and took cover in a small dip. The German who seemed to be in charge of the patrol was also here, I said to him, "Look out, there are grenades being thrown at us." He turned his head and so I hit him, quickly took what I could off him and made it back to our lines.

Captain Alan Bush – a picture taken when he was second-in-command of C Company. (R. Pine-Coffin)

For this and other actions Lieutenant Street was awarded a Military Cross. Captain A. Bush recalls:

We were ordered to move further to the right and settled into a position, leaving a gap between ourselves and our immediate neighbours, who, I was told, were French troops. I think they were just under a mile away. It was an awkward area to defend for the gaps between our Companies and our flank support were wide. I was particularly concerned about the undefended expanse on our right. There was not even a single strand of wire to protect it, moreover, most of that area was hidden to us by heavy, though patchy undergrowth. My Company Commander, who did a splendid job in positioning the Company, did not share my concerns about the right flank and laughed off my worries when I spoke to him. He had placed two Platoons forward of Company HQ on the forward face of two spurs which overhung the plains between us and the enemy. From their positions they could stop any enemy advance up the obvious routes they would take in any attack. Such positions, on the front of the cliff and visible to the enemy across the plain in day time, were prepared by night with a thoroughness which was later on to prove worthwhile. The third Platoon was kept well back, behind HQ in the hope that it could cope with any enemy who swept round our flanks.

The creation of our forward defences was hard going, for the slopes were rocky and work on them could only take place at night. The workers were withdrawn at dawn, having done their best to hide from the enemy the little they had accomplished during the night. To hurry things along a group of sappers joined us with a drill. Positions on the rock face would be created overnight. The machine made a horrendous noise which echoed across the hillsides, but made little impression on the ground. In spite of this, reasonable defences were hacked out of the unyielding ground. A few men were put into these positions at dawn to be relieved at dusk; their 12-hour job was simply to observe and report and it was a long, boring job. They were relieved before dusk by a full compliment whose job was to guard the position during the night.

Apart from the exposed right flank, I worried about other matters, which brought little concern to my commander's face when I discussed them with him. There was the problem of communication; the 3-inch mortar, our immediate artillery, could not be sited without more communication if it was to be effective and not a danger to our own troops in the forward positions. The 38 wireless sets, after the bashing they had taken, were unreliable and we had no telephones. Our forward positions could only be reached by runner, the mortar OP was completely out of touch with the tube. Reluctantly my OC asked for telephones and eventually got them and so we laid lines.

The weather was unkind and in spite of my previous experience, I made an elementary error in my camp. The OC and I shared a trench to start with, but I sited it too near the trunk of a tree. Rain followed the natural line of the tree and soon we had to enjoy a trench which was seldom without several inches of water in the bottom.

Soon after this we split up and I moved to my own home. I created a small fireplace in my trench where I heated water for my morning shave. One morning I found it impossible to create a lather from the water I had heated. By constant rubbing with the brush my cheeks had turned an unusual pink and were sore. I cursed the French shaving stick I was using and as I dipped my brush into the heated water, it burst into flames. There had been petrol in the mess tin as well as water! I went berserk trying to keep the flames away from my few possessions. I'd taken the trouble to try and set an example to the men and my efforts had left me with a sore and raw face with singed eyebrows and a good laugh to all those near me.

We started to patrol again, but now, it seemed, more sensibly. The patrol commander was given a precise task and this "new" policy gave us more confidence. When the moon shone brilliantly in clear skies, little or nothing was asked of us. At other times patrols were mainly for reconnaissance purposes. The information gleaned of enemy defences and dispositions were pretty accurate as we learnt from maps captured by the enemy when they attacked. One unique patrol I remember. One man somehow got permission to go out on his own. He stayed all day sufficiently near the enemy to observe what went on in the 'dead ground' behind the German lines. He returned with all sorts of useful information and sufficiently accurate to give the gunners a very effective shoot at breakfast time which we hoped killed a lot of the enemy.

It was around this time that a more extraordinary and bewildering command reached down as low as us. Cap comforters which if folded correctly gave a pleasant and soothing form of headgear, were forbidden to be worn in daylight. A lot of my chaps had lost their berets and to ask them to wear their parachute helmets for about 12 hours a day was I felt unreasonable. We were all very angry at this stupidity, for that is what it seemed to us. Perhaps there was an explanation; perhaps in our widely dispersed defensive locality where penetration by the enemy was a constant threat, the use of such headgear could mislead our own troops as to the identity of the troops they saw. We were in any case given no explanation for the order. Once again our sense of irritation was the reluctance of higher command simply to say why.

However, I was soon to forget this nonsense. First there was an expected visit by the CO, he wore a worried face and his arrival prefaced what was to be a long and painful interview with John, my OC, who, at the end of it all, took me into his confidence to tell me that he had been ordered to leave the Battalion to take over a Company in one of the other units. "I don't loose rank, but it is humiliating to be told I have to leave the officers and men I know when they are about to face an enemy attack."

It was a sad sight to watch him walk out through trenches occupied by angry and sympathetic soldiers. His batman asked if he could go with him; I was very glad of that and I could see John was lifted slightly by his loyalty. It was 24th February 1943 when I became a Major; on 24th February 1942 I had been promoted Captain. I suppose it should have been a proud day for me; it wasn't, I felt very sad and gutless.

A typical sleeping place for a member of the 3rd Parachute Battalion in February 1943. This day was one when they were attacked by the Germans, and captured and killed around 300 of the enemy. (R. Pine-Coffin)

> As it turned out I now had two days of feverish work to change the former plan of defence to mine. More telephones and wire were come by; communication inside the Company was improved and a direct line with a Company on my left was established; although it was unreliable, it did work when it was required some time later. After a few practice shoots which took place when the enemy were making a hideous noise as they shelled the French on our right, I was satisfied that our mortars could do their job. The reserve platoon I moved out to the right, where, lying below the crest, they discovered a superb skyline shoot; moreover I felt they were in a better position to perform a counter-attack. The forward platoons were given alternative positions back on the slope from the cliff face, from which they could fight in daylight should their exposed position become untenable.

Meanwhile, whilst all of these preparations were taking place, on the other side of the hill the enemy had decided to attack. It was a 'three-nation assault' with the previously mentioned Italians and Austrians being reinforced and stiffened by some German troops. The main point of the attack was directed towards the positions of the 3rd Battalion and it came in the morning of 26th February 1943. The Germans and their allies had made good use of the wooded country to infiltrate fairly close to the 3rd Battalion positions before launching a full-scale attack. It is reported that A and B Companies were involved in savage hand-to-hand fighting for about an hour and the area was a "mass of individuals trying to kill each other." Gradually the men of the 3rd Battalion got the upper hand and the enemy troops withdrew down the hill until taking what they thought was refuge in a wadi. However, this had been pre-registered as a target for the supporting guns and mortar tubes. It is said that in just under two hours around 3,000 rounds were fired into the wadi. The troops sheltering here were not helped by the fact that the machine guns of the 3rd Battalion could also fire into this area. It is recorded 'it was a pleasing sight to see scores of Germans jumping out of the wadi to avoid the shelling and jumping back to get away from the machine gun fire. It was, as we might say, a 'no-win position' – around 400 casualties were sustained by the Axis troops and around 200 surrendered. It is further recorded that when some of the prisoners were searched they were found to have pamphlets giving detailed instructions as to the best methods of fighting and defeating 'the Red Devils'.

The 2nd Battalion was also present in the area and on the night of 25th/26th February a strong patrol from A Company was sent out to attack enemy machine gun positions with the added provision that they were to bring back some prisoners (if possible, of course). This patrol came back with 7 Italian prisoners comprising one officer, 1 sergeant and 5 other ranks. On the following day, whilst the main spearhead of the attack was being directed at the 3rd Battalion, the 2nd also came under attack at about 0930. The main brunt was borne by B and C Companies. B Company was forced to give up the forward OPs and most of their easterly Platoon positions in the face of a severe attack. About a company of Germans moved round the left flank of C Company in the area of the Djebel Salah and the Djebel Gaalil but strayed into an area pre-registered by the supporting 25 pounders and were forced to take cover. Around the same time the mortars supporting C Company also fired on about two platoons'-worth of Germans, stopping their forward movement. Reserves under command of Lieutenant Colonel Frost in the shape of some French Colonial troops (Spahis) were moved forward and positioned on the extreme left flank of the Battalion positions. This virtually stopped any chance of C Company being outflanked. For a while there was a Mexican stand-off and it seemed the Germans, having considered their options, withdrew to fight another day. It is said the 2nd Battalion inflicted about 150 casualties at a cost of one man killed and two wounded.

Lieutenant Colonel Frost:

> On 8th February 1943 we returned to the fold of the 1st Parachute Brigade south of Bou Arada, which was lovely country and soon became known as 'Happy Valley'. Here we took it fairly leisurely; I had three Companies stretched over three miles and only sporadic shelling interrupted our peace. Then on 26th February we heard intensive gunfire and found out that the 3rd Battalion was being hard pressed. A few hours later our own forward positions came under fire and a large number of enemy infantry could be seen advancing. However, I knew for the first time in North Africa that we had plenty of ammunition, a defensive fire plan worked out, wireless communication between Companies and that my men were well fed and fit.
>
> The enemy initially came up against C Company, failed there and began to work their way round the flanks. Our artillery was brought in and pinned them down. I then moved the Spahis forward on foot, which made certain our left flank was secure throughout the battle. The enemy's next push was from high ground against B Company. Although we were well spread out the gaps were covered by mortar and machine guns so the enemy could be dealt with. Towards the end of the day the French anti-tank gunners, tired of waiting for enemy tanks, opened up on the enemy infantry. The French Observation Officer, who was standing on a hill, had no communication with his Battery other than a megaphone through which he would shout orders and corrections. Two Squadrons of the *Chasseurs d'Afrique* on our right had been particularly good when patrolling so I thought as the enemy could not withdraw because of our machine guns nor come forward, I would use them in a combined strong right hook that night. But to my amazement their commander said he couldn't move without higher French authority. As a result I gave Captain Ronnie Stark a couple of Platoons and told him to go out straight through A Company, sweep across our front and them come in through C Company. Off he went and we heard his progress through the night as he moved across No Man's Land, making full use of grenades and Stens. He came back at dawn, with a large grin on his face with 78 Italian prisoners.
>
> Elsewhere of course the 3rd Battalion were having a hell of a fight and in places had almost broken through. Brigade had little knowledge of what we'd been doing and after the battle even said, "What! Were you fighting as well?" That's exactly what we were doing, performing a model defensive infantry battle where the fighting is being done by mortars and machine guns and where in some cases the infantry don't use their weapons unless they are actually being assaulted. In our previous battles our losses had been grievous; now we'd lost only one killed and two wounded, whereas the enemy, mainly Italian and Austrian, had lost about 150 killed and wounded.

The 1st Battalion was also involved and when the enemy's artillery barrage on their positions became intense, Lieutenant Colonel Pearson ordered a withdrawal from their forward positions to alternative ones dug in a reverse slope location. The 1st Battalion had had ample time to cleverly construct barbed wire defences which funnelled the Germans into killing zones and they suffered heavy casualties and withdrew without really threatening the 1st Battalion's positions.

Sergeant Eric Seal of 5 Platoon S Company 1st Parachute Battalion:

> S Company was in a mobile company role for Argoub and we were sent to assist the 3rd Battalion who had come under fairly heavy attack. We were given orders to attack a German-held farm called Frenchman's Farm. We moved down the wadis towards the farm and attacked. After quite a heated little battle we captured it and took some prisoners. We also recaptured a British 2 pounder anti-tank gun and an American jeep.

It is perhaps fair to say that this was the first time that all the units of the 1st Parachute Brigade had been in action in the same area. It had only taken nearly four months for this to happen. The other units of the Brigade, the 1st Parachute Squadron RE and 16 PFA RAMC, also got involved at Argoub.

At this time the 1st Parachute Squadron was split amongst the three Battalions of the Brigade, A Troop with the 1st Battalion, B with the 2nd and C with the 3rd.

Due to the situation with the 3rd Battalion the sappers attached to the 1st Battalion were sent over during the course of the day as reinforcements. The post-action report from A Troop is included as Appendix XXXII in this book.

Major A. Bush OC C Company 3rd Parachute Battalion:

> We guessed something was in the wind when a few patrols hit our forward defences. Also the French on our right were being regularly shelled, we were spared that, but we surmised that it was a bluff to hide the main point of the attack.
>
> The attack came at first light, just as my forward platoons were withdrawing from their fully manned night positions. They left in small groups, gradually leaving the trenches virtually unoccupied except for the daylight troops. Although some of my men were static, just as many were on their way back to their daytime rest area, when the attack came in. There was confusion. Tracer bullets were flying over my HQ; the noise of rounds being fired by the enemy told me that they were close; there was no reply on the field telephone to my forward positions. It was a menacing situation as I could identify figures as Germans in the half-light less than 50 yards away and once through us they had a clear run to Battalion HQ. For some time from then on I had to behave more like a Section Commander than the Company Commander. But eventually matters eased and I could order the reserves to clear one crest. Also I was able to make contact with a breathless Platoon Commander on the telephone. I seem to recall the conversation went as follows:
>
> "Where the hell have you been?"
>
> "I was captured, just escaped and am now back in my trench."
>
> "You took a long time about it."

"Yes, you have to be patient to wait for the chance to kick a man in the balls when he is holding a pistol to your head."

"I don't believe a word of it. Take over the reserve platoon when they reach you. Keep me informed, but cut out the silly stories until we are out of the battle."

At dusk he returned, with a German blanket wrapped round his shoulders and carrying a German helmet. Later I questioned him. What he had told me was the truth. For this action, mainly, but for others as well, he was awarded the Military Cross.

By about noon the enemy had given up and were willing to retreat. Then another company moved through our positions to mop-up. A considerable number of prisoners were taken and a hundred or so of the enemy reported dead. In my Company I had one man killed and a few wounded, only one severely.

Towards nightfall we were employed in the handling of prisoners and sorting out of captured material. Such a tedious job went on until the next morning for disconsolate lost souls would emerge from the undergrowth to give themselves up. Many it seemed had been wounded in Russia and sent to North Africa to recuperate and felt they had suffered enough. Others on the other hand were arrogant and insolent.

One other incident I do remember was when my friend the Medical Officer (Captain J. Rutherford) visited us at some point during the day. A soldier was lying near my HQ with a nasty ankle wound which prevented him walking. When he saw the injury, the doctor's eyes brightened with the glint of opportunity; he saw a chance to practise his surgeon's skills. Seldom did he experience a heaven-sent opportunity for normally such casualties were sent down the line after his initial examination. When he produced his satchel a piece of gleaming steel and made ready to boil a tin of water, I found other things to do away from that spot.

Lieutenant D. Bentham of the 3rd Battalion:

At Argoub we started off with patrols – nearly everyone went and we lost some good NCOs and men whilst we were here. We overlooked the Pont du Fahs valley and the Germans seemed to switch their positions about. We found out that the Germans had a supply point in a farmhouse about a mile behind their forward positions and a plan was worked out to attack and destroy it – my Platoon was given the job. I was told to go out on a recce patrol with a sergeant and two men and find a way through Jerry lines. The night came with bright moonlight and with the country in front of me seemingly bare of trees and cover but orders were orders. We set out at 2330 feeling none too happy about it. We were crossing what seemed to be a ploughed field when suddenly a voice shouted out "Halte! Wer da?" It seemed to be only 25 yards away or so. We all dropped on our faces and the challenge was repeated twice. None of us made a sound, then about three machine guns fired in our direction. We got up and ran back to a dip in the ground. My sergeant was hit in the leg and how I escaped unscathed I'm not really sure. We managed to get the wounded man back, stopping every so often to check we were not being followed. Three nights later a German patrol hit my Platoon area, almost reaching my HQ before they were seen. I was out of my dugout in a flash and started throwing grenades.

Captain G. Bromley-Martin's grave at Medjez-el-Bab CWGC Cemetery. (N. Cherry)

Sergeant MacDonald slipped round the back and took Alf Guthrie's Section round behind them and caused havoc. We killed three and took two prisoners. I had positioned a listening post of a L/Corporal and three men at the bottom of the hill and I could not understand how they had got past unnoticed.

Six days later I was awakened at dawn to hear firing and dashed outside. Alf Guthrie was there and shouted "It's ok, Sir, just another patrol" and without awaiting orders dashed down the hill with another man to try and get a prisoner. Poor Guthrie, as he realised too late that it was a big German attack on the whole front and ran into about 20 of them, but bravely kept going and was shot and killed. I realised now by the amount of firing that the whole Battalion was being attacked and I was facing a Company attack. They were coming from the same way as the patrol. They had overrun my listening post consisting of one man on duty while the other three slept. We found them dead afterwards, three of them with their blankets still wrapped round them. I shot two of the enemy trying to cut the wire near my HQ and then we started once again. I decided to visit my Sections and ran from one to another with a German machine gun following me all the way – he was either a bad shot or very nervous. When I got back to my HQ I received the most awful shock – there was Giles (Bromley-Martin) lying outside dead. He was my best friend I had in the Battalion and the sniper that got him nearly got me.

After three hours of fierce fighting we got the upper hand and finally counter-attacked and drove them off. The Company killed 50, wounded 90 and took 120 prisoners. Our casualties were 2 Officers and 9 Other Ranks. Leslie Wilson was the other officer killed leading a counter-attack. It took us two days to bury the dead.

For once it can be said that 'Murphy's Law' was on the side of the 1st Parachute Brigade in February 1943, and soon afterwards they were relieved by American troops and sent off to yet another sector.

10

Tamera, March 1943

The month of March 1943 turned out to be one of the busiest for the units of the 1st Parachute Brigade in North Africa. Around the 5th March American troops relieved the paratroopers in the Bou Arada area. If the men thought they were going to get a bit of a rest period they were wrong. After spending time on the southern front they were now moved to the northern or left flank. It seemed the Axis offensives had failed all along the line except in the north, where they had concentrated a division against a weakened brigade with a view to cutting through the coastal road and so hopefully achieving an 'Axis Dunkirk'. In keeping with General Anderson's policy of using the 1st Parachute Brigade as his fire brigade he sent them north at short notice to the Tamera area.

As one commentator put it, "The Germans were hemmed in on the coastal plains around Tunis by the steel ring of the massive Allied forces; frantically, they sought a way out. General von Arnim thought he had found an escape route along a coast road which ran from Tamera to Algiers."

In any case it was still rough country and there were plenty of hills and prickly cactus bushes to contend with. Additionally there were a lot of cork woods in the area which obviously gave a certain amount of cover for infiltrating troops. However, as the reader may suspect by now, not everything would go to plan. The 2nd Battalion was given another small job to do before going to Tamera. They were moved to 'Chemical Corner' near Beja, where they arrived at 2200 on 5th March. Immediately on arrival they received orders to prepare to attack suspected enemy positions on the Djebel Zebi. At 0330 on 6th March the 2nd Battalion was in position at the foot of this hill and by 0530 A and B Companies had reached the top without meeting any enemy. HQ 46th Division then ordered the unit to clear a feature known as Kef Ouiba. Again this was found to be unoccupied. Third time lucky, 46th Division propelled the 2nd Battalion towards the Djebel Kermote, known locally as Spion Kop. This was a very large feature, strongly defended and they were promised the whole Divisional artillery in support. C Company went forward to draw the enemy fire and so reveal their positions for a softening-up barrage. Regretfully no fire support came and as this feature was found to be occupied so it probably best to let Lieutenant Colonel Frost give his summing up of the situation:

> Our next move was to 139th Infantry Brigade where I was briefed by a Brigadier Howlett. He looked at me sadly and told me that he had a very unpleasant job for me. I had to clear some Germans off some positions with the support of another Battalion. However, Divisional HQ stopped the other unit on their way to me, without even asking the Corps Commander, to clear some other Germans off a hill called Spion Kop. I wasn't at all happy about this, but was assured that the Divisional artillery would support us. We got up to the hill facing Spion Kop relatively easily

> and then we started going down towards Spion Kop. The Germans exposed their positions because we drew their fire. I called on the Divisional gunners, but we never got a single round of support from them and the troops and tanks on our left withdrew. I was so angry I called the whole thing off and went back somewhat angry to Divisional HQ. I found the GSO and said, "We were promised the whole of your Divisional artillery but we haven't had a single round." He said that the situation had changed since the promise was made. I was glad to be told we were going to join the rest of the Brigade.

At this time there were two Brigadiers in the Brigade, Brigadier Flavell was visited by Brigadier E. Down, who had arrived from England on a visit. Brigadier Down had been CO of the 1st Parachute Battalion in 1941. He was now in command of the 2nd Parachute Brigade, who would eventually be moving out to North Africa.

The 2nd Battalion travelled north to join the rest of the Brigade so that by the 7th March 1943 they were positioned as follows:

- 1st Battalion in the area of Tamera with Battalion HQ at 113758 on Tunisian map Sheet 10.
- 2nd Battalion with HQ in the village of Sidi Mohammed Belkassim and the companies south of the Djebel Abiod-Mateur road.
- 3rd Battalion around a mine at grid reference 095744.

Private Arthur Letchford of the 2nd Battalion relates his experiences on a night patrol:

The viaduct south of Tamera station. (James Macrae)

Djebel Abiod. (Imperial War Museum)

We were to take up defensive positions on the south side of Bou Arada, Dickie Spender our platoon officer was given the task of carrying out reconnaissance patrols close to the enemy lines. He decided to set up a listening post some distance into No-Man's-Land aiming to achieve more information of enemy movements. Brother Phil and I were the first detail of this mission, which was to be carried out at 2100 that night. Our Platoon Sergeant led the way.

After we had stealthily gone a distance of several hundred yards, he quietly indicated that we were now in an ideal spot for a listening post, Phil and myself made a brief survey of this hollow partly taken up with grass and scrub.

The three of us clambered into the hollow and agreed it was a suitable place. Our Sergeant reiterated to keep our ears open for sounds of vehicles i.e. tanks, trucks or anything on wheels, and eyes open for enemy patrols that were known to frequent this area. Then he wished us good luck and said that he would return soon after dawn. He then climbed out and left Phil and me to settle down to begin our vigil of listening and eyeing through the darkness whilst our bodies wrestled with the night's chilly air.

Our issued watch was ticking its way towards 0200 when Phil nudged me abruptly and whispered, "We've got company." I looked to the left of Phil's side and saw many pairs of staring eyes that were bright luminous green and brown. More eyes gathered around us as they closed nearer to our hideout. We decided to confront them by moving and waving our arms, they just stood still and stared back at us. It as a bit unnerving as we didn't know a lot about the wildlife in Tunisia and all you can see of an unknown animal is its eyes.

> However, after some thought, we settled for them being African jackals or wild cats and thought we ought to try and get rid of them. So we carried out our own little bombardment of stones and off they scattered taking those bloody piercing eyes with them. Gratefully more time ticked on, bringing it close to 0300. We continued our vigil and looked to the approaching dawn and thoughts of some hot food and drink on our return. These thoughts were disrupted suddenly by slight sounds. We slowly brought our rifles to the aim, uncocked the safety catches and waited, but not for long. An enemy patrol cautiously strode past within a few feet of us, the thought coming to my mind that if one of them lost his footing he would land right on top of us. However, they continued on their way when seemingly from out of nowhere a missile landed on Phil's helmet with a loud clonk, bounced off and then rolled to a stop a few inches from my face.
>
> I picked up the missile as the patrol was moving out of sight, which turned out to be a tin of Maconochie stew. Phil eyed it then whispered, "F**king cheek, throw it back at the b*****ds." Not wishing to comply I tossed the can into the clearing above us. Soon dawn was breaking and in the growing light we noticed a number of tin cans at the bottom of our hollow. Maybe our listening post was a food source for the local wildlife, but certainly a rubbish pit for our counterparts.
>
> The voice of our Sergeant broke the silence as he called out "Letchfords," then asked if there was anything to report. We were not really sure on how to give him a run-down on what had happened, we started to give the details, but he cut in to say, "Never mind, give it when we get back." He then gave us the good news that he had been informed of a possible minefield in the area and told us to keep behind him, which we did on the way back.

Warrant Officer M. Forsyth has vivid memories of Cork Wood; he had been one of the early volunteers, had been on the Bruneval raid and was now a CSM.

> We arrived during the night to take over from a battalion up in the wooded hillside. We couldn't find them and ended up shouting for them. Soon a voice replied, "We're over here. Sorry, we thought you were the Germans." The OC went absolutely bananas at this and shouted for this rabble to clear off. We were then ordered to spread out in a circle formation. In the morning just before dawn the Germans attacked and got the surprise of their lives. They didn't expect to find paratroopers waiting for them. In spite of this we had several hours' tough fighting. At one point one of the junior officers ran past Company HQ so fast he nearly burnt us. The OC told me to go forward to see if I could find out what had happened. The Platoon seemed to be at the point of wavering and so I shouted at them "The bastards are more frightened of you than you are of them." This seemed to do the trick and they put up a spirited show. I was always a bit outspoken and I think I said this officer ought to be in front of a court-martial. I think he was moved to one of the other Battalions, if he had been a soldier his feet wouldn't have touched the ground. It was I think a combination of this and the fact that a new OC didn't really like me that led shortly after Cork Wood to me being RTU'd.

On 7th March 1943 the two Brigadiers, Flavell and Down, visited the positions and it was a quiet day – the lull before the storm. On the following morning, around 0630, a strong German attack was launched against the 1st and 2nd Battalions. The first report came in from S Company of the 1st Battalion, who had seen a number of troops in a railway cutting and asked Battalion HQ if they knew of any friendly patrols expected in that area. The answer was negative and soon S Company reported back that they had identified the troops as enemy and they were advancing towards their positions using the road as their axis of advance. This force was estimated at about two companies strong but was now heading towards the location of R Company. The OC of S Company, Major Lloyd-Jones, ordered his men not to open fire until the enemy were a lot closer and then take them under enfilade fire. He also contacted the Battalion mortars to be ready to open fire and also warned the supporting gunners that they would be needed soon. Around 0730 the order was given to open fire; it was one of the rare occasions in North Africa when it was a full-scale supporting arms battle. The war diary records, "Battle began. Artillery, mortars and machine guns opened up with devastating effect when the enemy was within 300 yards of our position. The enemy was pinned down in some dead ground just in front of R Company and in the railway cutting." Around 15 minutes later Major Lloyd-Jones asked for and got permission to send out a fighting patrol of one Platoon to clear this dead ground. No 5 Platoon commanded by Lieutenant Cairns was sent out on this and returned shortly afterwards with around 40 prisoners. Other moves were also afoot, T Company were moved up to a position close behind Colonel Pearson's command post and Lieutenant Mayhew with his 7 Platoon was ordered to occupy Djebel bel Harch.

However, in spite of this initial setback the Germans were not going to lie down quietly. Around 0800 they concentrated their fire on the positions of S Company and

Looking down on the Cork Wood area from Djebel bel Harch. (James Macrae)

Colonel Pearson came forward to assess the situation, deciding to send T Company out on a sweep to clear the enemy in front of R Company, whilst 6 Platoon from S Company were sent out to clear the right flank of the Battalion.

It took around 45 minutes for T Company to make it up to the CP and their OC, Major Hall, was ordered to first concentrate his men in the wood immediately behind S Company and then to move forward via the gully to a large wood in front of the position and then return by the road through R Company's positions. This sweep was to be supported by artillery fire on the wood and suspected enemy OPs. It was also around this time that Brigadier Down pitched up at Pearson's CP as he had heard that a battle was imminent. This patrol was successfully carried out, albeit with several casualties, mainly caused by artillery fire, and returned with around 100 German prisoners, 3 light artillery pieces and other items of equipment. There was now a bit of a lull, perhaps while both sides licked their wounds. However, around 1400, the Germans made another effort against S Company and Major Lloyd-Jones asked for two companies to come and support him. All he got promised was the movement of the reserve platoon from R Company to a position to support him on his right flank. T Company was also moved up to the edge of the wood to be ready for a counter-attack.

About an hour later a report came into Pearson's CP that S Company were holding the attack but they had suffered casualties. Lieutenant Colonel Pearson did send a situation report to Brigade HQ and also asked for some reinforcements, as there had also been heavy casualties in T Company. A message came back from the Brigade Major that the Brigade Defence Platoon would be there within the hour.

At 1635 a message came in from S Company that they were still in position but had been completely overrun from their right flank and were still being heavily shelled and

Tamera railway station. (James Macrae)

The railway line at Tamera heading towards Sedjenane. (James Macrae)

mortared. This report described the situation as "critical". Then 10 minutes later a further report came in that said they had been completely overrun (again!) and Major Lloyd-Jones and Lieutenant Cairns wounded. Lieutenant Sinclair and Lieutenant Norton (who had stayed with the S Company mortar detachment) had been killed.

Lieutenant Colonel Pearson ordered a counter-attack to be carried out by T Company, which was successful, although again, at a cost. The 2 i/c of T Company, Captain Stevenson, was killed in this attack. Major Hall reported that he was occupying the hill but was thin on the ground. Then to add to the discomfort for the 1st Battalion some enemy aircraft strafed the position. By now the Brigade Defence Platoon had arrived, and, together with several men who had returned to the unit after discharge from hospital, was sent to the assistance of Major Hall together with most of the Anti-Tank Platoon.

This was about the end of the excitement for the 8th March. The unit's war diary states:

> 1800 – The situation was under control and a report to this effect was sent to Brigade HQ. The Battalion was reorganised and disposed as follows: R Company no change, T Company and Brigade Defence Platoon in S Company's positions; S Company and Anti-Tank Platoon in wood south of CP.

Lieutenant Colonel Alistair Pearson, the CO of the 1st Parachute Battalion. It is recorded that this picture was taken during the fierce fighting in the Tamera valley in March 1943. (R. Pine-Coffin)

2000 – Major Bull returned from leave and was sent to command T Company in place of Major Hall who was sent to S Company. It has been a hot sunny day and the Battalion was glad when evening came.

Lieutenant Colonel Pearson:

Our next big task was Tamera. We got there in the evening of 6th March, took over from a Guards Battalion and lay in the bushes in the rain all night. We knew where the Germans were but we did not know their strengths. Fortunately they had no idea how weak or spread out we were. We didn't really dig in but each company took up an area. Vic Coxen took the front company and remained in one place while the others were prepared to move. We were all within shouting distance of each other. The first attack came down the road at 0730. It was about two companies strong. They hadn't expected anything other than Vic Coxen's company and they didn't spot the other two. We let the enemy advance to within 300 yards of our main position where they were enfiladed by S Company, commanded by a wild Welshman, Major Taffy Lloyd-Jones. We then brought down artillery and mortar fire and the enemy were pinned down in some dead ground and 40 prisoners were captured. The main attack was on S Company. I ordered T Company to make a sweep to clear up the front. While this was going on Brigadier Down who was determined to see the fight arrived at the command post.

I was sitting there in this hole in the ground and I wanted to get a written message to Vic Coxen. I was busy, so without looking up I shouted for a runner. "Take this to the OC R Company – urgent", and thrust it into a hand. When I looked up Brigadier Down or "Charlie Orange" as he was affectionately called, was streaking across the country clutching my message. I thought I might have to do a bit of explaining if he got killed! But he got through. The troops loved it and it was a great morale booster to see a bareheaded brigadier acting as a runner.

That afternoon battle commenced again with an attack on S Company and Taffy Lloyd-Jones called for reinforcements. I ordered R Company to move to the right of S Company. Two hours later S Company reported that they had been completely overrun. I had anticipated this and moved T Company in ready for a counter-attack. They retook the position but not without heavy casualties. By 1800 the situation was under control and so ended a day of very hard fighting where the Battalion came out on top, but with the loss of four officers.

Major V. Coxen:

We moved up to Tamera and took up positions on the Sedjenane road which the Guards had vacated. We had not been there long when S Company reported that the Germans were advancing down the road. We just waited and waited until the first company came over the rise and down towards us and as their second company had just got over the top of the rise, we opened fire. I couldn't fire at the second company from my position but S Company under Taffy Lloyd-Jones, could and did. The gunners and mortars opened up as well. Within a short time we had the situation under control and had over 100 prisoners, who were marched off with about a dozen or so chaps to guard them.

Two hours later a second attack came in and engaged S Company. Taffy asked for reinforcements and so a reserve platoon from R Company was sent. T Company were ordered up, ready to counter-attack when the opportunity came. S Company were still in position but had suffered a lot of casualties including Taffy. Alistair ordered T Company in and the position was restored – but it had been a very costly six-hour battle with four officers killed and many wounded. I spoke to Taffy, who had been shot in the chest and asked him what had happened. He said, "It was old 55 (55 Jones was his batman, he himself was 78 Jones), I was just about to shoot at this chap and he told me not to because he was one of ours! But he was a German para in an identical smock, so he shot me!" I said, "You're lucky because a couple of inches higher and he'd have got you through the heart!" He replied wryly, "No, a couple of inches the other way and he'd have missed!"

It is common practice when soldiers have the same surname to use some of the numbers at the end of the Army number to differentiate between individuals, so you may have, for example, 36 Smith and 84 Smith.

Sergeant Eric Seal:

Picture of men of S Company of the 1st Parachute Battalion after having been taken prisoner on 8th March 1943 in the Tamera valley. (Airborne Assault Duxford)

In early March we were transported north in lorries that were full of fumes, so by the time we got to Tamera we were as sick as dogs. Little did I realise as we sat in those trucks that within a couple of weeks most of my platoon would be dead, wounded or prisoners.

My platoon, 5 Platoon S Company, was on the point jutting out from the high ground which was later known as Shell Shock Ridge. At about 0700 on 8th March we saw German patrols coming down the road from Sedjenane, followed by hundreds of Germans with machine guns and light artillery. It was what was to be, for me, one of the hardest days of almost continual fighting I engaged in. I was manning one of the Spandaus we had on loan from the Germans. During the next half an hour the Germans were pushing us very hard and we were getting short of ammunition, so I borrowed a Thompson sub-machine-gun from the FOO. Our Vickers machine gun had been completely put out of action and shells were falling thick and fast. We had killed and wounded on the forward slopes, but it was difficult for the medics to get to them because there were snipers picking off anyone who approached. My relatively new platoon commander, Lieutenant Sinclair, and I stood side-by-side firing pistols at almost point-blank range. Then Mr Sinclair fell shot in the chest. I lifted his head, but he was dead. Most of my men by this time

> were either killed, wounded or captured. I moved over to the edge of the wood to report the death of Mr Sinclair and I was given orders to get my men back. I told what few men were left to withdraw. We moved off quickly, with the German fire cutting the branches around our heads.

After having looked at the actions of the 1st Battalion it would be good to look at the position facing the 2nd Battalion, who also came under attack on this day.

Again, soon after 0600 enemy troops were seen to be heading towards the 2nd Battalion positions, which were to the right of the 1st Battalion's. It was an attack directed towards the entire frontage of the Battalion. At one point it appeared that A Company was surrounded, as the Germans were infiltrating round the left flank. Fortunately, reserves, in the shape of A Company from the 3rd Battalion, arrived and two of their platoons carried out a successful counter-attack which cleared the Germans away from positions close to the left hand platoon of A Company (of the 2nd Battalion). Sporadic fighting went on all day and in the early evening the Germans still had some machine guns in position in a gully on some low-lying ground in front of the 2nd Battalion positions. Although a patrol was sent out to try and dislodge them they were unsuccessful, although they did return with two captured machine guns. The Battalion war diary records that,

> ...the support given by the 70th Field Regiment Royal Artillery was of the greatest assistance in breaking up enemy concentrations and blunting the edge of the attack. Captain Radcliffe was killed early in the battle and Lieutenant Willcock slightly wounded. Seven ORs were killed and 35 wounded. Enemy casualties not known but thought to be considerably higher than ours. This was confirmed by prisoners subsequently captured.

Lieutenant Colonel J. Frost:

> The day before we arrived the Germans had sent a strong patrol onto a hill in a cork wood, held by the Lincolnshire Regiment and had taken several prisoners. I was told to take over during the night, because it was likely the Germans would attack in the morning. Sure enough, as we arrived at dawn on 8th March, the Germans attacked. They had been told they were going to meet the Lincolns on top of the hill and when they found Paras they were rather upset!
>
> It couldn't be helped but I'd got my HQ in a position from where I couldn't see very much. News coming back from the companies was sparse, but it nearly all concerned their lack of ammunition. At 1000 Johnny Lane, commanding A Company, got through to tell me that he was surrounded – but he was confident. Willoughby Radcliffe, the Adjutant, frustrated at having to remain below at HQ, decided to organise a mule train, loaded with ammunition for A Company. As he was climbing up he was killed by one of the enemy parties who had got between HQ and A Company. Fearing further infiltration between ourselves and the 1st Battalion, the Brigadier called for A Company of the 3rd Battalion to link up with part of our C Company. This was a highly successful counter-attack and they captured over 60 prisoners. However, the enemy had not finished, as just as before

This photo is captioned by Pine-Coffin, "Private Ewen, my batman, off to collect my water and breakfast. The thing under his arm is a rubber basin, which I took off a German and found very good. It would fold up and go in a pocket but was as big as any ordinary wash basin. The Germans seemed to be well ahead of us in this sort of thing." (R. Pine-Coffin)

dark a flight of Stukas dived on A Company and dropped their bombs among them. This brought our casualties up to 8 killed and 35 wounded.

Private Priestly recalled an incident in Cork Wood:

...we arrived at Cork Wood and if I recall correctly it proved to be one of one of the most savage encounters of all my Army days. We had just about dug ourselves in when the Germans attacked. I well remember Frank Lyoness stopping a particularly troublesome German machine gunner with the Boys anti-tank rifle. He said as he was firing it "I'll get the bastard somehow". I was then sent to help with the mule section; what an experience this was. Close by where we loaded the mules up with hot food and tea there was a gunner position and it seemed every time we would take this up to the boys in the front line they opened fire. The mules usually went crazy with hot tea pouring over them. I do remember one particular incident when we were told we needed to go to A Company, although it seemed the Germans knew the route we would take and shelled us fairly regularly. So on this night when A Company called for an urgent ammo resupply and so Kenny Kenyon and myself after a drink of rum set off in the darkness. We were really lucky that night as we lost our way and it was only when a German patrol crossed our path did we

Lieutenant Colonel Pine-Coffin's batman, Private Ewen, emerging from a slit trench in March 1943. He commented that they now had experience in making themselves comfortable, and the trench incorporated a ration box shelf on the left. (R. Pine-Coffin)

> realise we'd gone too far and turned down the hill. We spent the rest of the night blundering around Cork Wood and didn't make it to the A Company positions until well after dawn and the remarks we got were delightful.

Although the 3rd Battalion area came under shell fire they had a relatively easier time than their sister Battalions, as the Germans did not approach any of their positions until about 1100. This is when C Company reported that enemy patrols were approaching their position. Then at 1120 Brigade HQ ordered a counter-attack to try and alleviate pressure on one of the 2nd Battalion companies which was in difficulties. Then C Company reported that their right-hand platoon was being heavily engaged. Lieutenant Colonel Pine-Coffin asked Brigade HQ if he could be relieved from this counter-attack role in the light of his own commitments. This request was refused and a compromise was agreed, that only two platoons from C Company would launch the counter-attack in the 2nd Battalion area. Additionally, just before midday, B Company sent out a fighting patrol of around 20 to check whether the Germans had infiltrated between their position and their French neighbours.

C Company saw three Churchill tanks coming up the road towards their location and these were commandeered to give supporting fire to the counter-attack. C Company went through some hard fighting on this day and suffered five dead and seven wounded amongst the ten fatal casualties. The rest of the day was fairly quiet for the 3rd Battalion.

The following day the 9th was a relatively quiet day for the 2nd and 3rd Battalions, the first mentioned spending the day digging in and consolidating their positions. They were sporadically shelled and mortared throughout the day suffering one man killed and nine wounded. The 3rd Battalion loaned out two platoons from A Company to the 1st Battalion to hold part of the line while they carried out what was recorded as a "demonstration with tanks".

If there was a job to be done it was normally given to the 1st Battalion, and today was no exception. Early in the morning of the 9th, around 0330, Brigade asked Lieutenant Colonel Pearson if six Churchill tanks would be of any use to make a recce down the Sedjenane road. He replied that it was not feasible to use them as they would be limited to staying on the road, however, he could make use of them to strengthen his positions. So the tanks did come up to the positions of the 1st Battalion, although at a later conference it was decided to send the tanks down the road supported by a creeping barrage from the gunners. Zero hour was to be 1215, the attack lasted about 45 minutes and was supported by R Company. The mixed force advanced until they reached some enemy positions which were attacked and 16 enemy taken prisoner. On the other side of the coin British casualties were 2 tanks knocked out, 3 killed and 5 wounded.

On the following morning the day began with a heavy mortar barrage on the long-suffering 1st and 2nd Battalions' positions followed up by an infantry attack. Officer casualties had been heavy in the 1st Battalion and to try and make good some of the losses, Captain Stark and Lieutenant Dunkell from the 2nd Battalion and Lieutenant Fleming from the 1st Parachute Squadron RE were temporarily loaned to them. In the morning C Company of the 3rd Battalion under the command of Major Bush arrived to give additional support to the 1st Battalion.

It appears that T Company of the 1st Battalion was taking the brunt of the attack and the losses, and some relief was promised, in the shape of B Company of the 3rd Battalion, as soon as they had been relieved by the 2/5th Leicesters. In spite of these reinforcements and promises Lieutenant Colonel Pearson was still wary of the position he was in. He was perhaps slightly concerned about his situation as earlier in the day the Germans had got to within about 50 yards of Battalion HQ. He later commented, "We had a bit of a shock when the enemy got within 50 yards of the Battalion HQ. Jock Clements initiated a counter-attack with about 30 men, cooks and clerks. They all went at them screaming like banshees."

The 2nd Battalion war diary recorded the following for this day:

> Throughout the morning our positions were subject to a heavy concentration of shells and mortar bombs. A further attack appeared imminent, enemy concentrations reported, they developed rapidly into an attack directed mainly against our left front and the 1st Battalion on our left. Again determined efforts were made to infiltrate through our positions. Little progress was made and the main attacks were strongly repulsed. Our casualties were 1 Officer Major Rothery, 6 ORs killed and 26 ORs wounded; it was difficult to estimate enemy casualties but they were fairly certain to have been heavier than our own.

The Brigade HQ was now coming into its own and actually being able to operate as a 'proper' HQ. Around 1100 on the morning of 11th March, after the Brigade Major

Field grave of Captain J. Cassidy RAMC RMO 1st Parachute Brigade HQ (N. Cherry)

had visited the 1st Parachute Battalion, it was becoming clear that the Germans were beginning to occupy the feature of the Djebel bel Harch in some strength and if the 1st Parachute Brigade's position was not to be untenable it was felt essential that a fresh unit, fairly strong, would have to be placed on this feature. It was believed the Germans had already established OPs there and were using these to bring down fairly accurate shellfire on the Brigade positions and also the gun line. Whilst such a unit was identified, C Company from the 3rd Battalion was temporarily placed under the command of the 1st Battalion for this purpose. During the morning the Brigade positions came under aerial attack and more casualties were suffered. The Brigade HQ position was in an exposed position and started to come under heavy shellfire and a decision was taken to move it to a new location further back. A recce for a new position was undertaken by Captain O'Brien around 1130.

Things appeared to be leading up to a heavy German attack and around 1200 Brigadier Flavell decided that he needed to make a personal visit to Divisional HQ to underline the seriousness of the position. Soon after his departure the Signals Section were ordered to move their set to a safer location, which was accomplished under heavy shellfire. However, it was during this barrage that the RMO for the 1st Parachute Brigade, Captain J. Cassidy, and Private F. Francis of the Parachute Regiment, were both killed. In the early afternoon both the 1st and 2nd Battalions reported that they were being attacked on all fronts and on the 2nd Battalion front the Germans were infiltrating round their left flank. The 1st Battalion seemed to be holding its own, although Lieutenant Colonel Pearson reported back that owing to the large number of

The caption from Lieutenant Colonel Pine-Coffin reads "An engineer effort near Djebel Abiod." (R. Pine-Coffin)

casualties he had suffered he did not expect to be able to hold out against another strong attack without reinforcements.

Meanwhile Brigadier Flavell was able to convince the Divisional commander of the situation and he had been placed in command of the entire left hand sector with the 139th Infantry Brigade now under his command. A decision was also taken to send a Company from the 3rd Battalion to each of the 1st and 2nd Battalions and the 1st Parachute Squadron RE sent a further troop to the 2nd Battalion. Reinforcements also came in the shape of the 2/5th Leicesters to occupy the 3rd Battalions positions and a Company from the 16th Durham Light Infantry to occupy a feature known as the Pimple, between the positions of the 2nd Battalion and the 6th Lincolns.

By the end of this day although no ground had been given up the Germans were still established on the left flank of the 2nd Parachute Battalion. Brigadier Flavell pointed out to the Divisional commander the dangers of the position and informed him that unless more troops were provided a general withdrawal to the Djebel Abiod position would become necessary and that the present positions of the 1st Parachute Brigade were untenable.

To assist this unpromising position a troop of tanks from C Squadron of the North Irish Horse were sent up around 0800 on 11th March to attempt to clear the enemy from the left flank of the 2nd Parachute Battalion. By the end of the day this had been achieved. It was a relatively quiet day for the 1st Battalion, still supported by B Company of the 3rd Battalion, in that they were attacked around 1000 and again at 1600 but both attacks were beaten off.

Perhaps the statement 'relatively quiet day' is an understatement, as may be judged from some comments from the Battalion war diary:

Field graves of four men from the 3rd Parachute Battalion killed in the Tamera area. The crosses were made by the Battalion carpenter out of scrap wood and replaced the originals which can be seen at the rear. They were made from ration boxes. (R. Pine-Coffin)

1000 – Small arms fire opened up on CP from close-quarters on the right flank. The Boche had penetrated right onto our flank and was within 50 yards of Battalion HQ when he opened fire. A Platoon from the 3rd Battalion who were guarding this flank were taken completely by surprise and withdrew back onto the CP somewhat out of hand, the CO ordered them back. The Anti-Tank Platoon was immediately thrown in to counter this attack together with the Intelligence Section and the Signal Platoon.
1600 – Major Dobie reported an enemy patrol had reached the dead ground immediately forward and below his positions. He said they had a mortar and were bombarding his positions. S Company now under Captain Stark was ordered to send a patrol round the front of the positions and contact a patrol sent by Major Dobie. The enemy beat a hasty retreat and only a few casualties were inflicted upon them.
1800 – Further movement was reported in front of our positions and a patrol was sent out to investigate – a German doctor was found working with medical orderlies, they were allowed to continue their work.

Sergeant J. Johnstone recalls his experiences with the 2nd Battalion at Cork Wood:

After a journey on some old trucks at about 0200 or 0300 we halted in a wooded valley and were told to dismount as quietly as possible as the enemy were close by. We were then led off the road, up into the trees. Laden as we were full kit, the going soon became tough and when we halted in a small flat clearing, presumably close to the positions we were going to, we dumped large packs and bedding rolls by sections, in neat lines and retaining only battle gear, moved on.

Shortly after, my section, guided by a Lincolns corporal, was shown to a shallow wadi-like depression on a steepish slope. There were no dig positions and when I asked for any information, such as the whereabouts of the enemy, he gave a thin tired smile and said that this was where they had finished up the day before and that was about all he knew. The enemy were somewhere out there and he gave a vague wave down the slope. Sensing his anxiety to quit the place, I signified my acceptance of this meagre information, whereupon he disappeared rapidly into the darkness.

When daylight came I was distinctly uncomfortable at our position in a shallow depression not more than four feet deep at the most, about six or seven feet wide across the slope and slightly longer down. About a hundred yards to our immediate front the ground rose again in a considerable hill, higher than the one that rose behind us and similarly covered in brush and small trees. To the right the valley opened out into a wider flat area on which we later observed Arab mud huts. We were on a forward slope with little cover and little clear fields of fire, while an advancing enemy would have abundant cover from view.

My immediate tactical response was limited to disposing the section in all-round defence and just as I was doing so the platoon sergeant, Pete Heyhow scrambled into the hollow. He made no comment about our position though he assumed that the enemy were somewhere on the slope facing us, for after scanning the view intently for a minute or so, he said suddenly "Isn't that a radio aerial?"

He was pointing over to the right and at a distance of about five hundred yards in an area of scrub and small trees, I did think I could distinguish a radio antenna, but it was difficult to be sure. There seemed to be no sign of movement here. However, there is little doubt that Pete's aerial was real enough, for he had no sooner returned to where I presumed platoon HQ was, than the early morning quiet was pierced by the vicious chatter of a Spandau. The fire did not seem to be directed at us, but I was acutely aware of our exposure on the forward slope. I did not have long to ponder on things for I heard Pete Heyhow shouting for our Bren. My section by now consisted only of the Bren pair and two riflemen, so I shouted for them to follow me and we all scrambled off in the direction of Pete's voice.

We had not gone far when we were fired on and one of my lads shouted out; "Johnno, Johnno, help me! I'm hit." The voice was coming from some bushes several yards away. I asked where he had been hit and he said in the legs. I then did the correct military thing, which has always troubled me. I shouted, "I've got to get this gun over. You'll have to crawl." I continued the wild scramble along the hillside, leaving him in lonely terror. Before we got there I suddenly got fed up with the attentions of his machine gunner and pausing in the shadow of a small tree, I saw what I thought was his muzzle smoke in the brush on the other side of the valley and at a lower level than we were. Young Stewart who had been carrying the Bren had flopped down beside me and I told him to pass the Bren over to me. Resting the Bren in a low fork of the tree, I took careful aim where I had seen the smoke and loosed off a couple of bursts. What the results were I never knew but it gave me some satisfaction.

We made it to platoon HQ but then had to crawl up the hill, expecting to be the target for a bullet at any moment. Eventually we were off the forward slope and among the flimsy cork oaks on top of the hill where we found the rest of the company crouching in scattered makeshift positions. There did not seem to be many of us. My section now consisted of myself, Stewart with the Bren and his number two who had a Sten. I can't recall there being many other members of our platoon here either. So we settled down with the Bren alongside members of another platoon – Lieutenant Timothy's, I believe. Before long we noticed enemy filtering down in single file on the opposite hillside. At one point when they were about level with us there was a wide gap in the bushes and so with some satisfaction we all opened up when ordered and stopped their progress by that route. Shortly afterwards as if in reply, there was a small explosion quite close and young Stewart was holding up with puzzled dismay, a rather bloody hand.

Probably to cover up my own alarm at this near miss, I fussed over him like an old hen with a new chick, escorting him to the aid post. It was really the first time I'd seen one at close hand and here were the victims of bullet, bomb and shell, grey-faced and dull-eyed, lying and sitting on the red earth under spindly cork oaks. I still have a vivid picture of a young boy who I had put to bed on Hogmanay, as he sat propped against a tree with a shattered leg stiffly in front of him with a bulbous dressing below the knee, in the centre of which a great crimson rosette was spreading. After I had handed Stewart over and wished him good luck I returned and told the last man left in my section to attach himself to one of the others as I'd been told to go to Company HQ. Some time later Lieutenant Timothy came over and asked if young Jackson belonged to any of us. This was the big lad who had been hit as we moved across the slope and I realised with a start that I had clean forgotten him. I said he was in my section and the officer said he was in a lot of pain and did anyone have any morphine. I offered mine and also asked if I could go along, but wasn't allowed to, much to my regret. However, a bit later there was a call for volunteers to go out and get some wounded and I went along. On the way down the hill we passed a spot where one section had been trapped without cover, as we had. A survivor told me later that several men had been hit in the first bursts of fire and most had been able to get to safety, but one man, although not seriously hurt had refused to move. We could see him, his face to the sky in the awful inertness of death. He had either been caught again by mortar fire or bled slowly to death. Several times that day I went past this spot.

A bit further down the hill we came upon a wounded man, he was in no real immediate danger, though he had a shattered leg. The officer said he would have to wait for the medics to come and get him. The lad looked rather scared and so I said I would wait with him, perhaps to make up for leaving Jacko. I gave the lad a cigarette and tried my best to keep his spirits up. He mumbled something about his mother and I told him he had a Blighty one and would soon be seeing her. After a time some medics came with a stretcher and it seemed a bloody long carry up the hill.

It was after this that Pete Heyhow suddenly stood up and said; "Well, I'm going down for my kit. Anyone coming?" I was not very keen to quit the deceptively comforting cover of the flimsy oaks and venture down into that sinister valley again, but seeing that three or four others were willing to give it a go I also went. Our platoon's gear was still standing in three neat rows where we had left them, much to my amazement. I remember being childishly tickled to recover my big pack containing amongst other things various souvenirs I had collected and several packs of cigarettes. Little did I know then that I would lose the lot the very next day. I also recovered my bivvy which, though we could not pitch it, proved useful that night when it rained heavily and Pete and I crawled thankfully between the folds. In the morning the rain-soaked red earth and the puddles shone blood-red.

It was now March 9th and I think the Battalion war diary says; "A quiet day spent digging and generally strengthening positions." It was for me, as I spent a good while and considerable exertion in excavating a long coffin-like slit trench about eighteen inches deep which might I hoped might give me some protection. During my digging I remember taking time off to shout irritably at a very young and somewhat feckless private from the latest batch of reinforcements, who was working like a beaver right out in the open in front of me. I said if he continued to expose himself to the enemy quite so blatantly, he was likely to get their attention.

Not long after this, I was in my funk hole when I heard the Company commander discussing some activity around the Arab mud huts in the valley. He asked for someone to tell a Bren gunner who was located some thirty to forty yards in front of us to keep an eye on that area. I volunteered to go and getting out of my hole I started heading to him. I had only covered a few yards, when I felt a great clout to the point of my jaw and sank to my knees like a knocked-out boxer. Then I saw blood streaming down the front of my smock. I lurched to my feet and

Another panoramic view of Tamera, Nefza and Cork Wood
from Djebel bel Harch. (James Macrae)

An idea of the hostile terrain on the slopes of Djebel bel Harch. (James Macrae)

> staggered back to the HQ where I muttered thickly but dramatically, "The bastards have got me."
>
> The company medic appeared and strapped a shell dressing around my jaw, but then I became aware of the frantic cries of the youngster I had warned. It seems he caught more of the mortar bomb than me and I told the medic to leave me.
>
> Having had this dressing applied, it seemed to staunch the blood flow and the medic disappeared. I never saw that stricken lad again, leaving me to be helped off the hill down to the dressing station in the valley. I remember being slightly surprised and pleased by the eagerness of another of the new intake, a fresh faced lad with flaming ginger hair, who quickly volunteered to take me down. This was the last I saw of the Battalion for several weeks.

Things quietened down (of a sort) for the Brigade, as on 12th March the Corps Commander, Lieutenant-General C. Allfrey, visited the area and agreed that in spite of the lack of troops in the area and indeed the Brigade, the feature known as Djebel bel Harch had to be taken if the Brigade was to remain where it was. At least Allfrey recognised that this was probably 'a bridge too far' for the men of the 1st Parachute Brigade and so decided that someone else would have to do it. This task fell to the 5th Sherwood Foresters. At 2000 a conference was held at the 1st Battalion, attended by Pearson, Pine-Coffin and the COs of the 70th Field Regiment RA and the 5th Sherwood Foresters. At this conference it was decided that one company from the 3rd Battalion would secure Commando Hill at first light with a guide to be provided by the 1st Battalion. The Foresters would then move forward and occupy Djebel bel Harch. They would be assisted by two platoons under the command of Major Bush to attack the northern end of the Djebel and from there assist the Foresters.

Captain A. Percival of 16 Parachute Field Ambulance at Nefza railway station in 1943. (Airborne Assault Duxford)

Around 0730 on the 13th Major Terrell's A Company went forward and by 0830 a message came back to the 1st Battalion HQ that they had reached the top but had been forced back by a counter-attack and were awaiting the arrival of their supporting mortars before having another go. Major Terrell did advise heavy casualties. The Foresters meanwhile were awaiting a success signal before starting their operation. Regretfully Major Terrell's force was unable to achieve its objective and so the Foresters would have to go and take it. The fighting continued sporadically all day but they were unable to secure Commando Hill, and at around 2000 straggled back. Meanwhile, the long-suffering 1st Battalion had been told they would be coming out of the line that night and their positions would be taken over by the 3rd Battalion, and this happened after dark.

It was a relatively quiet time over the next few days for most of the Brigade, the 3rd Battalion being relieved on 16th by the Sherwood Foresters and moving back to a rest area in a cork factory near Tabarka. The 1st Battalion received reinforcements on the 14th March in the shape of 96 men mainly from the 2nd Parachute Brigade, but also some men who had been wounded but now recovered. On the 16th a further 340 men arrived.

However, things were not so easy for the men of the 2nd Battalion. On the 12th they were given a Company from the Durham Light Infantry who were positioned on the right of the Battalion positions. On the next day they came under occasional mortar fire although only two casualties were suffered. The 14th was more eventful. B and C Companies came under heavy mortar and machine gun fire and they suffered three wounded. On the 15th A Company were again mortared causing two fatal casualties and six wounded. Some shells also landed in the vicinity of Battalion HQ and Lieutenant Colonel Frost was hit by shrapnel in the leg but not seriously.

By the 17th March the Germans were pressing on other forces around the 2nd Battalion and forced them to give ground and so men from the 1st Battalion were moved forward from their rest area to act as flank guard.

The 18th March was again one of those days when the Brigade got the 'Army run-around'. The Germans were making a determined effort to break through and seize the vital Tunisian coastal road. The 2nd Battalion received orders that they were to remain where they were until new dispositions had been taken up on some high ground centred around the Djebel Abiod. Once this was done the 2nd Battalion was to withdraw to some new positions at a location known as 'The Pimples'. 7 Platoon from C Company was nominated as the rearguard supported by three Churchill tanks from the North Irish Horse. The codeword for the withdrawal to start was 'Pimple' which arrived at 0900 and the Battalion began to thin out. The attached sappers blew up the road and left as many booby-traps as possible in the time allowed. The RV point was at the viaduct. After assembling at the viaduct it was decided the best route back would be along the river to a junction and then onto the Pimples. The road was not really a viable option as it was under observation from Germans on high ground. No sooner had the withdrawal started than they were spotted and shells began to fall in the area of the river. However, using cover afforded by the riverbank the group made it with only slight losses. The war diary relates the following

> The going was very hard and it was necessary at times to wade chest high in the water to avoid exposure. The Battalion again came under heavy fire and some casualties were suffered. At about 1500 the stream junction was reached and the withdrawal continued down the railway line to Nefza station without interference. Battalion HQ contacted B and C Companies and told them to take up positions

The feature known as Bowler Hat, for obvious reasons. (James Macrae)

Self-portrait of Lieutenant Colonel Pine-Coffin. His caption reads "Taken at arm's length with my minox. Taken in the Tamera valley on our way to Sedjenane. In the middle I got toothache and am off to the ADS where they pulled it for me." (R. Pine-Coffin)

> on the forward hill with A Company holding the rear Pimples with Battalion HQ on the wooded Pimple. Casualties during withdrawal were 2 killed, 11 wounded and 5 missing.

The results of these 'minor moves' was that the Axis forces were now able to control the important road junction near Djebel Abiod and this meant that Allied troops were somewhat isolated. The paratroopers' view of things was probably not improved by the fact that the Pimples were not nice places to be. It was virtually impossible to dig down into what seemed like solid rock and the slopes were quite steep to climb. The largest of the hills, which was called Bowler Hat (Sidi Bou Delaa), was overlooked on two sides by enemy positions and, probably worse still, was on the enemy side of the Oued el Medene river. It seemed that holding this was the key position and no offensive could really begin until it had been taken. At first Bowler Hat was held by the 2/5th Leicesters and a strong German attack pushed them off the heights. The 3rd Battalion was ordered to try and retake it on the following night – 21st/22nd March. It was a two-company attack – A and C taking part. Details of this attack are sketchy but it can be said that the attack failed, one message getting back reporting that nearly all the ammunition carried by the men had been used up and Major Bush, as OC on the spot, had given the order to fall back.

Four men from the 3rd Battalion have dates of death around this time and so I must assume they were probably killed in this abortive attack:

21st March
    Corporal A. Stewart Tabarka Ras Rajel CWGC Cemetery 4A3
21st/22nd March
    Private S. Sadler Tabarka Ras Rajel CWGC Cemetery 4E11
22nd March
    Private J. Pollitt Tabarka Ras Rajel CWGC Cemetery 4A4
    Private F. Walker Tabarka Ras Rajel CWGC Cemetery 3B6

Given the vital nature of this position it is probably no surprise as to who was called up to try and take Bowler Hat – the long-suffering 1st Battalion. However, Lieutenant Colonel Pearson had been given some warning that he might have to do this and had spent some time planning his operation. This included a temporary bridge over the Oued el Medene built by the 1st Parachute Squadron RE and a massive amount of artillery support. Again it was not a 'come as you are party' but an all-singing, all-dancing all arms affair. The attack was brilliantly successful at small cost. The paratroopers had probably been helped by the fact that there had been a handover of troops on Bowler Hat that night.

It is reported that Pearson led his men forward in the dark with as least noise as possible round the back of the hill and swooped on the German defenders as most of them slept. Apparently only around 15 rounds of ammunition were fired, they did not suffer a single casualty and took 40 men prisoner. Pearson had made a deal with the Corps Commander that whilst he would take the position he wouldn't hold it due to his lack of numbers and so once it was taken the 3rd Battalion moved up to relieve them.

After assembling at Nefza railway station, R and T Companies swung left and crossed the river by the newly constructed pontoon bridge whilst HQ and S Companies used the railway bridge. They crossed without incident but as soon as they were across a box barrage was fired by the Germans in the area of the railway bridge. R Company then climbed up the saddle of Bowler Hat from west to east and then down the north side. They were followed by two Platoons from T Company with the remaining Platoon going round the right flank. S Company were on the left flank and according to the war diary "took up a position near the woggeries 058689." R Company cleared their objectives without much difficulty and captured two machine guns in the process. They then moved forward towards the higher ground at 064696 before withdrawing back into a reserve position at 064684, leaving one Platoon from T Company on the feature. The other two Platoons of T Company were positioned on the right flank in the 'woggery'. As the positions were consolidated Major Cleasby-Thompson led up a mule train with additional ammunition and defence stores. As stated before the 1st Battalion was only in position briefly before the 3rd Battalion took over and went for, in my opinion, a well-deserved rest.

Lieutenant Colonel Pearson:

> At the bottom of the hill I met the CO of the 3rd Battalion, Pine-Coffin. He said, "Alistair, you must be mad to try to take that hill." I said, "Not half as mad as you, because you've got to hold it." Three-quarters of the way up the hill it was just beginning to get light when we found slit trenches with men in, still asleep – no sentries posted. We captured the feature and took a lot of prisoners by 0300. After

that we had three glorious days off in a farm where we could have a bath and catch up on some sleep and lie in the sun.

Sergeant Jack Bellamy of 16 PFA recalls his time in the Tamera valley:

Our Field Ambulance was set up in the Tamera valley and it was extremely close to the fighting and many of the minor wounded paratroopers joked that our forward orderlies and stretcher-bearers had been so near that "they caught me as I fell". Certainly casualties were quickly brought down the steep sides of the valley to where our Advanced Dressing Station hid beneath the cork oak trees close to the riverbed that ran down towards the plain behind us. Here they received immediate attention by one of our surgical teams before being evacuated quickly to the Field Ambulance that was serving the Division. It seemed to work out better for the PFA to operate totally as a forward unit, providing the stretcher-bearers and the immediately urgent treatment while the larger non-PFA remained a little further back and provided the on-going care and more involved surgery required before evacuation could be arranged to a Casualty Clearing Station or General Hospital.

At times our Dressing Station came under fire, although it must be said that the German aircraft always seemed to respect the red crosses displayed on the ambulances. On one occasion German mortar fire was harrying some of our troops quite close to us and mortar bombs landed in our immediate vicinity. Colonel MacEwan ordered us to move the wounded then in our care, to the shelter offered by banks of the dry gravelly bed of the river some 30 yards away. Typical of the man he was, he set an example by seizing one handle of a stretcher and others of us grabbed hold too and set off. We were crouching and involuntary ducking at the "crump, crump" of exploding mortar shells on the roadside by the Dressing Station. "It's all right! It's all right! No danger. Nothing to worry about", our gallant Colonel encouraged us – then stood spellbound like the rest of us, as a large mortar fragment scythed its way between the three or four stretcher parties, its path traced by the slow toppling of the stems of the huge onion like plants sliced off in its deadly path. The Colonel did have the grace to say, quite quietly, "H'm, not so all right after all. Let's get this man down into the riverbed."

At quieter times we would conceal an ambulance under one of the nearby trees and as minor wounded came in, treat them and despatch the ambulance when it had a load. One day, one patient had waited in the ambulance under the tree for some considerable time, he wasn't seriously wounded so we waited for further casualties to justify the trip. None came. It was very quiet and Sergeant Weatherby went to see if this patient would like a cup of tea whilst he was waiting. The answer came back as yes and so he went to get one for him. As he walked towards the tent which served as the cook house, he gave a cough and fell to the ground. We ran across and as we picked him up he coughed again and a bullet, which we could see through his open necked shirt lodged in his chest muscles, popped out. We assumed he had been hit by a spent bullet from the fighting in the hillside above, slapped a dressing on the wound, gave him a sedative and packed him off in the ambulance alongside the other wounded man. It was about an 8 mile journey back to the MDS, by which time it was painfully obvious that we had misdiagnosed his wound, for when his shirt was removed it was found that the bullet had not been spent at all, but had struck him in the back and passed through his chest and had stopped just as it was exiting through his chest muscle. He was treated accordingly and again sedated for the rail journey back to the hospital at Phillipville. Afterwards he told me he remembered little or nothing of the journey apart from some pain and indeed his first clear memory was waking up in hospital. His confusion was compounded by the man in the next bed looking at him and saying: "Hey! Where's my cup of tea?" It was the same man who had waited so long in the ambulance a few days ago.

By the end of March 1943 the two Allied Armies in North Africa, the 1st and 8th, were close to achieving a link-up and so trapping the Axis forces. To make matters worse for them Hitler had decided that the troops in North Africa should fight to the last round and the last man. In northern Tunisia it had been decided that the hoped-for final offensive would soon take place and the 1st Parachute Brigade had been specially selected to have a major role in this. Once again their task was centred around the Tamera area and the northern coastal road. In fact, Brigadier Flavell had been ordered to clear this main road, and as well as his own troops he was given the entire artillery resources of the 46th Division and some French colonial troops (*Goumiers*) from Morocco. Supporting them also in a subsidiary attack on their right flank was the 139th Brigade.

The plan formulated was that the 1st and 2nd Battalions would attack frontally, passing on either side of the 3rd Battalion who would be holding the Bowler Hat position, while the *Goumiers* moved round the left flank. It is worth adding here that both of the attacking Battalions were still somewhat understrength. H Hour for the attack was 2200 on the 27th March and it went in under an impressive artillery barrage, probably the best one that had been laid on for the 1st Parachute Brigade to date. The 1st Battalion had a fairly uneventful time attacking a unit of Italians who virtually surrendered *en masse*.

The 2nd Battalion, on the other hand, did not have such an easy time of it, B Company in particular having to move through an undetected minefield, which caused a number of casualties. This caused a delay, and by dawn on the 28th the 2nd Battalion was positioned on a false crest short of the summit of their first objective. Information was difficult to come by as their main set for communication had been damaged by an exploding mine and all messages had to be relayed through the 3rd Battalion.

By 0930 the 2nd Battalion reported back that they had now taken their first objective, had taken around 25 prisoners and were being held up by three enemy machine guns firing from around 072712. Then at 1015 the 1st Battalion reported they had reached 2470671 after fairly heavy fighting and were pushing on. The 2nd Battalion meanwhile were being strongly counter-attacked and reported that the situation was close to critical. At 1125 Lieutenant Colonel Frost asked for reinforcements as he had suffered fairly heavy casualties, and Brigadier Flavell placed A and B Companies of the 3rd Battalion under his command. It was a period of very confused fighting but gradually the paratroopers got the upper hand and there is a comment in the Brigade war diary for 1845 which underlines this – "2nd Battalion reported their strength now only about a company strong. Enemy opposition weakening and they intended pushing on to second objective during the night."

Towards the end of the day Brigade HQ started to get a grip on the situation after the Brigade Major had spoken to the Divisional Commander by telephone, and so at 2300 the situation and orders for the following day were as follows:

> Brigade Major pointed out that unless the road could be opened, for MT at any rate, as far as the viaduct, it would make the supply problem on the following day almost impossible, because the mules were dead-beat and some had been lost. He also pointed out that organised resistance on the Parachute Brigade front appeared to have ceased and suggested that if we were allowed to secure the Sidi Mohd bel Kassem (1073) and the high ground opposite to the west of the road, this might achieve the double purpose of opening the road for our supplies and assisting the attack on the right flank. The Divisional Commander agreed to this.

The following orders were then issued:

> At first light 29th March, 2nd Battalion to push on to second objective and push out patrols across the road to the east. 1st Battalion to secure Sidi Mohd bel Kassem and the Goums to occupy the high ground 0873 0973.

It is recorded that 658 PoWs passed through the Brigade cage on this day, of whom 550 were Italians.

The 29th was basically a mopping up and advancing day for the Battalions, but the sappers had more to do. All units achieved their third objectives on this day, but the road from Djebel Abiod up to the viaduct had been heavily mined and a bridge also blown up. The mines were cleared during the day and a temporary bridge constructed and by 1800 the road was passable by motor vehicles, which eased the supply situation.

Sergeant E. Seal:

> On 27th March we moved forward once more to the front; we were to start the attack towards Sedjenane with the 2nd Battalion and the Goums. We were to capture the wooded country to the left of Bowler Hat, the same ground we had covered in our withdrawal from Tamera. The first objective was a French farm. Ninety guns laid down a barrage. We came under fire, but by early morning our Company had pushed forward and taken the Italian and German positions.
>
> We now moved forward to attack the high wooded area which was one of our main objectives; the 2nd Battalion in the meantime had been having a rough time and some of our troops were sent over there to assist. It was a very bad area to attack – high rocky ground and very heavily wooded. A number of our men were killed on the approach but we gradually pushed the enemy back and managed to establish ourselves on the outer perimeter of the wood. A lot of the troops here were German and well dug-in. We were moving from tree to tree. Sammy Steadman was shot through the arm and one officer was killed. Ted Baxter poked his head out from behind his tree and shouted, "Be careful Eric, there's a sniper over there!" and bang, he fell dead. Ted had been shot through the eye. Ted had had a brother Tony in the Battalion and he had been killed a few days earlier. It was all very sad.

Lieutenant Colonel J. Frost:

At precisely ten o'clock on the night of 27th March the divisional artillery opened up. We had never heard an artillery barrage of such intensity before and we felt urged onwards in a strange and mystic way. It was a beautiful warm night and the night and the noise of the shells above us was orchestral in its infinite variation. My two forward companies went up unopposed. I followed behind with a small party laying the tape and following the shells burst to keep our bearings. Ahead of us we could hear the companies fighting. The enemy's reaction to the end of artillery fire was to fire a series of light signals. Every time one went up we froze as the glare lit up our surroundings. As it faded we went forward. Somehow we found ourselves on a plateau in the middle of an enemy defensive position. Around us we could hear German voices. One of them blundered into our group and was seized by Sergeant Cloves, the signal sergeant. We were only a party of ten and not equipped for this situation, so I called up C Company to deal with it. In the meantime as we slithered down the hill, Sergeant Cloves was twisting the chap's arm and he was making rather a lot of fuss I said, "Put that man down will you, Sergeant." He came back with, "Oh, I can't do that sir, I have never had one before!" C Company came up and cleared the situation.

I got the impression that the plateau we were on was very near the top and therefore would make a good firebase. The ground fell away on three sides and it now seemed that the crest of the hill, our first objective, was straight ahead and not very far. I decided that we'd attack as a Battalion at first light. As soon as it came it was plain that we were still a long way from the top. I had been taken in by a false crest and had failed dismally to take our first objective. Thank God this depressing moment was lightened by us finding, as we moved forward, that despite all the shelling of the previous night, many of the Germans were fast asleep in their trenches – these were not the brightest of men. A Company remained now to hold a firm base, while C Company, under John Ross, and B Company pushed forward. For a time they made good progress, but C Company came up against heavy machine gun fire. The enemy then counter-attacked. Closely packed groups of well-drilled men advanced through the trees firing from the hip as they came down. At one point they almost enveloped C Company's right flank. Dick Spender charged to push them back and although he killed four of the enemy, this fine and much-loved poet was shot down. John Ross had little option but to pull pack to the ridge, with heavy casualties. The situation was now critical. I informed Brigade who told me, "Hang on at all costs; things are rosy elsewhere." To support this message Brigade sent David Dobie with B Company of the 3rd Battalion to our aid. As he arrived Witzig's men moved in closer. I ordered fixed bayonets and we were to charge on the signal of my hunting horn. Somehow the fixing of bayonets always strikes a remarkable note among soldiers and morale reaches a peak. With the usual black humour some comedian was handing out grenades in a box, calling out like an usherette, "Cigarettes, chocolate, ice cream;" all this while shells were passing overhead.

Our own guns now got their range and our mortars caught the Germans as they closed in on us. This was greeted with shouts of "Waho Mohammed!" by everyone. But the enemy kept up a fierce volume of fire, of which A Company bore the brunt. So I brought a gunner OP to them, who was kept very busy. B Company was making excellent progress and had made contact with part of the 1st Battalion near the top. They struck in on the right and rear of Witzig's men, which had an immediate effect on their counter-attack on us. Unfortunately the 1st Battalion were called upon to switch their axis just when there was an opportunity to overwhelm Witzig. The remnants of B Company, now on their own, called for artillery support and although this was forthcoming, many of the shells fell among them and the casualties sustained left them too dazed and weak to do more. But Witzig's men had had enough as well and pulled back up the hill.

It was tempting to chase them but we now desperately needed to reorganise. We had a number of prisoners, and wounded from both sides who needed attention. I was delighted to see Mickey Wardle carried off by four Germans, for he had seemed so depressed before this battle. I felt now he was safe. Sadly, I was to learn later that he and the four Germans were all killed when a shell landed on them while they were sheltering.

The remnants of B Company came back to the main Battalion position. At this time we could muster no more than 160 men. Our patrols had found that although the enemy's counter-attack had failed they were still firmly holding positions further up the hill. To attack with the present strength in daylight would have cost us dearly. Fortunately the Brigadier realised this, and sent us a company from the 3rd Battalion. Out of what we now had I formed one rifle company and called it No 1 Company, and put John Ross in command. The two companies of the 3rd Battalion became Nos 2 and 3. As we moved forward it was pouring with rain and pitch black. The enemy let loose a considerable weight of fire and with this and the extremely difficult climb I was beginning to be concerned. But I need not have worried because the Germans had used the barrage to cover their withdrawal. Apart from several soldiers from the Tunisian Regiment and others who had lost their way, we met no opposition.

At 1145 on 29th March we arrived on our objective. The Battle for Tamera was over. We had been in action, as a Brigade, since 7th March. Throughout, nobody but the enemy knew we were fighting. Our presence in the forefront of the battle was not divulged and no reporters were allowed. We had had a very sticky and expensive battle and we had lost many friends, but now it all seemed so well worthwhile. It was time to relax.

Lieutenant Timothy recounted later in an interview how crude attempts were made to try and gain protection (of a sort) from German bullets by filling empty Benson and Hedges cigarette tins with whatever was felt to be bulletproof material. These were then placed in convenient pockets – whether these managed to actually deflect any bullets is regretfully not recorded but I am sure it did something for morale.

By now most units in the Brigade were well understrength and it was recognised that it was virtually impossible for them to take any further part in the campaign without a time out of the line reorganising and integrating reinforcements, which is precisely what happened, although it would take until mid-April for this to be actually carried out.

Sergeant Jack Bellamy of 16 PFA recalls an incident with a wounded German prisoner:

> One day some Germans prisoners were bought in with minor wounds for treatment. They were surly and barely spoke apart from giving their number, rank and name. Then one of them saw the parachute insignia on my arm and pointed at it – "Was ist das?" I spoke a bit of German and replied "Fallschirmjäger." "Ja?", he said with his face lighting up and then went on to tell me that he and his companions were from the Hermann Goering Parachute Regiment and we had a bit of a chat. However, it was common knowledge amongst our side that the German paratroopers had a pocket virtually hidden away which contained their fighting knife. This we all felt was a good one and much sought after as a souvenir. Later that day I went back in an ambulance to the other Field Ambulances MDS and in the reception tent there was a wounded German lying on a stretcher awaiting further treatment. He looked at me, saw my red beret and beckoned me across. I went over and bent down, not sure what he wanted and he fumbled with his hand somewhere near his knee and I jumped back hurriedly as he produced his fighting knife. But his intentions were kindly. His knife had been missed when he had been searched and now he told me if he was going to lose it, he would prefer to lose it to me rather than a hospital orderly miles from the front. He offered it to me handle first and I accepted it as gracefully as I could, for in a strange way I could feel and understand there was this link between us. We were both parachutists, both doing the same sort of thing – the only difference was that we served different masters.

11

The Airborne Medical Services

As we have already seen, the idea of sending medical units to war by parachute was totally new to the British Army in the early years of the war, as 16 PFA was only formed in 1942. In the early days it was all a matter of trial and error, and deciding what could to be taken given the limitations on weight and container space. It will be recalled that much time was spent in the UK on loading trials and exercises where much valuable knowledge was gained. This was really put to the fore in North Africa when a surgical team parachuted into Souk-el-Arba with the 1st Parachute Battalion and carried out operations saving many lives. The policy of taking the surgeon to the patient rather than the other way round was probably first used then. This policy has been developed even further in recent times, as my old friend Dr Steve Hughes (RMO 2 Para in the Falklands 1982) recently pointed out to me in that in Afghanistan there is virtually a mobile operating theatre in the back of a Chinook helicopter which means surgery can be carried out almost immediately the casualty is on board.

The majority of the developments and suggestions in the airborne medical services can be found in several reports written during 16's time in North Africa, a selection of which appear as appendices.

A document has recently been found in an archive which is headed 'Awards to 16 Parachute Field Ambulance 12th November 1942 to 12th November 1943'. This mentions many more people than my initial research for my book on the 1st Airborne Division, *Red Berets and Red Crosses,* found. I am more inclined to go with this latest list as a certain Stan Hope is down for a Mention, which backs up discussions with a relative, Chris Hollis. The family was always adamant that Stan *did* get the award but it was not mentioned in my first book, *Red Berets and Red Crosses*. Indeed, the same source had a document that stated that Stan had been recommended for a Military Medal but that it had been downgraded. The listing 'Awards to RAMC personnel 1st Parachute Brigade for the North African Campaign 1942-43' appears as Appendix XLVII in this book.

12

A summing up

By the middle of April 1943 the units of the 1st Parachute Brigade, much depleted in numbers, were amid a period of rest and reorganisation. Indeed, it is recorded that no company in any of the three parachute battalions numbered more than 60 men. There must have been very few men left standing who had come through the entire campaign unscathed. There was also perhaps a little resentment that after having fought in nearly every sector they were denied the privilege of being some of the first troops into the Tunisian capital,Tunis, which was entered on 7th May 1943.

The original commander of the Brigade when it arrived in North Africa, Brigadier Flavell, moved on to pastures new and on 28th April 1943 Brigadier G. Lathbury took over command.

The following is taken from Otway's book about the Airborne Forces and nicely sums up the fortunes and experiences of the 1st Parachute Brigade in North Africa:

> 1st Parachute Brigade (1st, 2nd and 3rd Battalions) had completed their three parachute operations and five months' operations as infantry with the 1st Army in North Africa. In the course of the campaign, the Brigade captured over 3,500 prisoners of war and must have caused over 5,000 additional enemy casualties. They had fought in every sector of the British front in Tunisia during the course of which they suffered 1,700 casualties. They had more battles than any other formation and in the Tamera valley, in the period 6th March to 14th April, did most of the fighting for the 46th Division. In fact, it may be safely said that the Brigade bore the brunt of the original operations of the 1st Army.
>
> It is not generally realised that during 1st Parachute Brigade's operations in North Africa they had to contend with frightful weather conditions in some of the grimmest and most forbidding country [sic.] in the world. Add these factors to a tenacious, brave and well-trained enemy and the distances involved and some measure of the great tasks which the Brigade accomplished can be realised.
>
> In addition, they had another problem to face. This was the unfriendliness and general unpleasantness of the Tunisian Arabs, who not only looted the wounded and dead, but also gave away information to the enemy on many occasions.

This general comment can be backed up with the comment written in the 2nd Parachute Battalion war diary for 22nd April 1943:

> Train arrives at Ghardimaou on the Algerian-Tunisian border and with its arrival the Tunisian story comes to an end. It had started nearly five months before when the Battalion had dropped on Depienne and since that date, with the exception of six days rest at Tabarka in mid-March the Battalion had never been out of the line. It had fought in almost every theatre of the central and northern Tunisian fighting.

> It had suffered heavily on several occasions and on like occasions had dealt heavily with its opponents. It had fought as infantry with none of the amenities such as carriers, transport and anti-tank guns which an infantry brigade expects. On occasions it had attacked with success but more often it had carried out a singularly aggressive form of defence often against heavy odds in the Tunisian mountains and for its labours had earned, with the 1st and 3rd Battalions, the name of 'The Red Devils' among the Germans. It came out of the line with a total strength of 14 officers and 346 ORs out of an establishment of 24 officers and 588 Ors, having already absorbed some 230 reinforcements in early January – a total casualty percentage of 80% of establishment.

This figure of 1,700 casualties is just about the normal strength of a parachute brigade and includes 518 men who paid the ultimate sacrifice in the fighting. However plans were made later to create a permanent reminder of their sacrifice.

So was the 1st Parachute Brigade's time in North Africa a success? This is a personal opinion but I feel I must give a mixed answer to this question. It certainly allowed the Brigade to carry out some Battalion-sized drops, but from the latter part of 1942 it is my view that they were treated very badly. The Oudna operation, in particular, was very badly thought out and planned and probably should not even have taken place and the 2nd Battalion took a stuffing as a result of these poor decisions.

Although they suffered 1,700 casualties it is said that they killed or wounded around 5,000 Axis soldiers and took 3,600 prisoners so purely in a numbers game it can be said their time in North Africa was a success.

It is also recorded that the Brigade was awarded the following decorations:

- 8 Distinguished Service Orders
- 15 Military Crosses
- 9 Distinguished Conduct Medals
- 22 Military Medals
- 3 *Croix de Guerre*

  and
- 1 *Légion d'honneur*

These numbers are taken from the book *The Red Beret* by H. Saunders and have been repeated since in several other publications but my research leads me to the conclusion that they are slightly inaccurate, as I hope the information in Appendix XLVIII shows. This can be summarized as follows:

- 9 Distinguished Service Orders and 1 Bar
- 1 Officer of the British Empire
- 24 Military Crosses and 1 Bar
- 5 Distinguished Conduct Medals
- 46 Military Medals and 1 Bar
- 32 Mentioned in Despatches
- 4 *Croix de Guerre*
- 1 Distinguished Service Cross
- 5 Silver Stars
- 1 Soldier's Medal

Major A. Bush summed up four main points from his time in North Africa:

(a) Hold vital positions with the minimum of numbers and counter-attack quickly with a mobile force, ready for and practised in the job.
(b) Never ignore the value of consistent camouflage. It will not deceive the enemy completely, but it may make him uneasy and frequently surprised. Many of the assault troops we faced had carried blanket rolls, as if they had been led to expect a simple move forward without any real fighting. Perhaps our camouflage discipline had been well worthwhile.
(c) Make sure your links in immediate communication are as reliable as you can make them. Perhaps I was lucky that nothing destroyed my links. I was able to move troops quickly and at least once on the request of another Company Commander.
(d) Cherish the value of your mortars and the support the artillery can give you. Use whatever charm you have to make the gunners feel they are part of your force, for then they may use their guns to assist you as if you were commanding a Division and not a mere Company.

It had been decided to construct a lasting reminder of the 1st Parachute Brigade in North Africa and the following is taken from a letter written by Brigadier G. Lathbury in November 1943:

> While the Brigade was at Sousse in August 1943 and still within reach of the Tunisian battlefields, it was decided to erect a War Memorial to the 49 Officers and 469 Other Ranks of the Brigade who lost their lives during the Tunisia Campaign, and to locate and erect crosses on all graves. We had started on this scheme when the Brigade moved to Italy in September and I left the Reverend R.T. Watkins to complete the work.
>
> **War Memorial**
>
> This has been constructed and erected by men of the 1st Parachute Squadron RE under Padre Watkins's supervision. Few of us have seen the Memorial but it has been photographed by the Army Film and Photo Section of Public Relations at Allied Forces HQ and I have ordered two of the prints be sent to you. I propose, also, that a photograph should be sent to the Next of Kin of those who lost their lives.
>
> The Memorial is of concrete construction with a cement screeding making a smooth finish, overall height being approximately 7' 6".
>
> It is a small obelisk of 5' 6" in height mounted on a pediment of three steps, the whole being in a gravelled 10' square, bounded by a small surround and being approached by a path with steps descending to it.
>
> On the forward side of the obelisk there are two plaques (inscriptions as below) surmounted by a small cross made of light oak, the lettering being cut and painted in white and lacquered for protection against the weather. Oak was used as bronze was unobtainable.
>
> The site of the Memorial is on the left-hand side of the road in Tamera valley, approaching Sedjenane and approximately opposite the former HQ of the 2nd Parachute Battalion and 100 yards below the ADS.

Wording on the plaques:

Bone
Souk-el-Arba
Depienne
Beja
Medjez-el-Bab
Djebel Mansour
Bou Arada
Tamera Valley
and
In Memory
of the Officers and Men
of the 1st Parachute Brigade
of the British Army
who gave their lives
for King and Country
November 1942-April 1943
erected by their comrades
September 1943

Graves

The locating and identifying of graves has proved difficult owing to the wild and thickly wooded country and to the fact that parts of the area are still mined and booby-trapped. In some cases, too, the Germans have buried our dead without identification. A number of parties were sent out to scour the country and included Royal Engineers with mine detectors. As a result, the large majority of the graves have been found and identified and each unit of the Brigade had erected its own crosses. We have worked in close touch with the Graves Commission who are in the process of collecting all the dead in two main cemeteries near Tabarka and Enfidaville.

Sadly, over the years this memorial fell into disrepair, probably due to a combination of the distance and that North Africa is an oft-overlooked part of the history of the Airborne Forces. The memorial plaque was rescued and now in located inside St George's Church in Tunis.

Another of the lasting legacies of the 1st Parachute Brigade's time in North Africa was that they got a nickname and a war cry, one of which lasts to this day, whilst the other seems to have fallen out of use soon after the end of the war in 1945. The nickname they gained was 'Red Devils' which, according to which person you speak to, either came from the colour of the berets worn or from the reddish hue to their mud-covered clothing and faces. The Germans certainly called the men of the Brigade 'Rote Teufels' and the accompanying image shows a copy of a signal received by the 1st Parachute Brigade confirming this.

The war cry that was adopted by the men of the 1st Parachute Brigade was 'Waho Mohammed' and in the immediate post-war period there was some debate about its

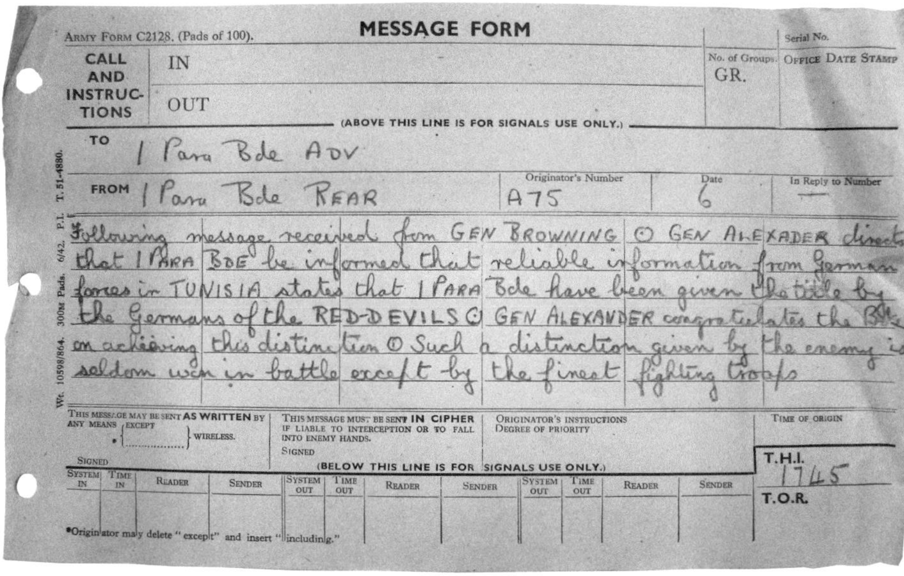

ARMY FORM C2128. (Pads of 100).

MESSAGE FORM

CALL AND INSTRUCTIONS: IN / OUT

No. of Groups: GR. | Serial No. | OFFICE DATE STAMP

(ABOVE THIS LINE IS FOR SIGNALS USE ONLY.)

TO: 1 Para Bde ADV

FROM: 1 Para Bde REAR | Originator's Number: A75 | Date: 6 | In Reply to Number: —

Following message received from GEN BROWNING ⊙ GEN ALEXADER direct that 1 PARA BDE be informed that reliable information from German forces in TUNISIA states that 1 PARA Bde have been given the title by the Germans of the RED-DEVILS ⊙ GEN ALEXANDER congratulates the Bde on achieving this distinction ⊙ Such a distinction given by the enemy is seldom won in battle except by the finest fighting troops

THIS MESSAGE MAY BE SENT AS WRITTEN BY ANY MEANS EXCEPT WIRELESS. | THIS MESSAGE MUST BE SENT IN CIPHER IF LIABLE TO INTERCEPTION OR TO FALL INTO ENEMY HANDS. SIGNED | ORIGINATOR'S INSTRUCTIONS DEGREE OF PRIORITY | TIME OF ORIGIN

SIGNED

(BELOW THIS LINE IS FOR SIGNALS USE ONLY.)

SYSTEM IN | TIME IN | READER | SENDER | SYSTEM OUT | TIME OUT | READER | SENDER | SYSTEM OUT | TIME OUT | READER | SENDER

T.H.I. 1745

T.O.R.

*Originator may delete "except" and insert "including."

The famous 'Red Devils' signal. (National Archives)

origins. Three possible explanations are presented here, although some sources state it was derived from the Muslim call to prayer.

The following is taken from an article in the January 1952 issue of *Pegasus – The Journal of the Parachute Regiment and Airborne Forces* – written by Lieutenant Colonel Pine-Coffin:

> It has been very interesting to read the many suggested explanations of this shout which was used as a battle cry by the original Red Devils in North Africa in 1942-43. I do not believe that it was really copied from the shouted prayers of the Arabs, although it would be pleasant to think that it originated in that way.
>
> The first time I heard it was on the day of the Battle of Djebel Mansour.
>
> A party of my Battalion, the 3rd, which was being held for possible use in the battle, was waiting near a stream when an Arab brought his cows there to water them. The following events caused this Arab to utter the cry for the benefit of one particular cow. As soon as the cows had started to drink, the troops nearby practised a cry which they had heard other Arab cow herders using and which was used for making them move faster – a shout of "Urrah" with much rolling of the 'r's'. The result was very effective and many of the better-disciplined cows immediately cut short their drinks and started moving off, to the delight of the parachutists and the annoyance of the Arab, who joined in with a series of "Woo's" and "Waho's" to stop them. The cows got a bit confused and did not know whether they were coming or going and most of them hung around for the situation to clarify. One of them, though, presumably named Mohammed, stuck firmly to the original order and continued to move away and even accelerated to repeated "Urrahs" until it was finally stopped by an agonised and loudly shouted "Waho Mohammed" from the Arab.

Three unknown airborne warriors who paid the ultimate price for the liberation of Tunisia. (N. Cherry)

> The cry was such a good one that the troops not only dropped their "Urrahs" in favour of it but continued to shout it themselves throughout the rest of the campaign and on all possible occasions. It became a very well-known cry in the 3rd Battalion from that day.
>
> The Battalion did not take part in the Battle of Djebel Mansour, but it fell to its lot to send companies to fight with the other two Battalions on many later occasions and naturally, these companies often used the cry in these battles. In this way it was passed on to the other two Battalions, who adopted it whole-heartedly.
>
> Its first use as a battle-cry was, I think, when a company of the 3rd Battalion (either Stephen Terrell's or David Dobie's) used it while helping the 2nd Battalion to beat off an attack during the first visit to the Tamera valley. To shout it really correctly, either for stopping cows or killing the enemy, the "Waho" part should be really dragged out as long as possible and the "Mohammed" clipped very short.

This article prompted a rapid response from G. Thompson, which was printed in the April 1952 edition. This gave an alternative viewpoint:

> As an ex-member of the 3rd Battalion I regret that I must have to correct Lieutenant Colonel Pine-Coffin on his article regarding Waho Mohammed. It will bring back memories of the early days of sojourn in North Africa and of the tiny village of St Charles which was our base then.
>
> Three companies were billeted at the farm there and on his farm worked a small black lad who answered to the name of Mohammed. Also employed there was a wog who appeared to spend much of his time searching and shouting for

> Mohammed. At numerous times throughout the day he could be heard calling "Waho Mohammed" and the cry was taken up by the chaps also. So was the battle cry born. It was first used as such by A Company, under the command of Major Terrell, at Bou Arada on the morning Jerry came to breakfast. At one point in the battle A Company were hard pressed and just when it seemed that the position would be overrun, there arose the cry "Waho Mohammed" and everyone appeared to go slightly mad. In no time at all, the hill crest was cleared and everything was under control. Soon the cry was adopted by the other Battalions.

A third view is that it came from shouted conversations and messages from one hilltop to another. Frank Nelson, who was a member of the 2nd Battalion, in the Machine Gun Platoon, commented:

> My gun and crew were situated at one time on a hill which overlooked a road junction. Not far from our position was an old shack occupied by several Arabs. Each morning the same old Arab would sit a short distance from the shack looking down onto the road in the valley. We used to keep an eye on this old bloke in case he might give our position away. After he had been sitting there for about 30 minutes a lone figure could be seen walking along the road in the valley. The old Arab cupped his hands round his mouth and in a high-pitched voice called out "Waho Mohammed". As the voice died away the Arab in the valley shouted back "Waho Said" and went on his way. He was the only person we saw walk along the road that day until he came back in the evening when the same shouts were

Paratroopers looking happy for the camera. The man second from the left appears to be wearing a captured German helmet. (Airborne Assault Duxford)

German prisoners looking even happier. Regretfully it is not known the area this was taken in. (Airborne Assault Duxford)

> exchanged. This procedure went on each day and soon the lads took these calls up and often during the day calls from the companies could be heard.

Now that the Brigade was out of the line and the fighting in North Africa was over thoughts turned to the next part of the campaign, which surely would be an invasion somewhere on the northern side of the Mediterranean, probably Italy. By now the 1st Parachute Brigade had been joined by the 2nd Parachute Brigade, 4th Parachute Brigade and the 1st Airlanding Brigade and the 1st Airborne Division came into being. The commander of the Division, Major-General G. Hopkinson, was determined that his men should be used in the forthcoming invasion although in a proper airborne role, but that is another story.

To end with here is a 'Tom's' eye view of the campaign:

> So ended five months hard slog for the 1st Parachute Brigade group who were originally trained as shock troops, but had to resort to the role of plain infantry. No disrespect whatsoever to the ordinary infantry man but a specialised and highly-trained shock force should be kept for shock attack only, not wasted on a long drawn-out defensive role. However, that's the way the wind blew for us and it was expensive, with approximately 2,000 casualties.

Appendix I

Composition of A Group, Bone, 12th November 1942

Table from 3rd Parachute Battalion war diary.

	Officers	ORs	Total
Two Company groups, each:	5	125	130
Btn Intelligence Section	-	2	2
Btn Medical Section	-	3	3
Btn Admin	-	6	6
Section 1st Parachute Sqn RE	1	9	10
Personnel 16 Para Field Ambulance	1	6	7
Btn Signals Section	-	6	6
Total	7	157	164
Force HQ			
CO	1	-	1
Adjutant/IO	1	-	1
Batmen	-	2	2
Clerk	-	1	1
J Section Div Signals	1	17	18
Btn Signals	-	6	6
Total	3	26	29
Attached			
Airborne Div HQ	1	-	1
Batman	-	1	1
Total	1	1	2
Total of Force	18	341	359

Appendix II

Points arising from interrogation of personnel of 3rd Battalion Parachute Regiment who crashed on their way to North Africa, November 1942

1. The plane was No 26, which took off from Hurn with No 19 twenty-four hours after the remainder, at about 2200 hours, 10th November 1942.
2. The wireless operator told one of the men that there was jamming and confusion on the air and that he finally received signals which were misleading, telling him to travel a certain number of miles on a certain bearing and he would make landfall.
3. When it was realised that it was impossible to make land the men were told to jettison some of their baggage and were offered the alternative of jumping or crashing with the aircraft. They chose the latter and later jettisoned their static chutes. A ship was sighted and the captain of the aircraft decided to come down near it. Everyone was quite calm and there was no panic. The pilot made a perfect landing although the port engine was torn away which probably caused the plane to float longer. This was about 1030 hours 11th November 1942.
4. The captain had not allowed the door to be jettisoned fearing that it would foul the tail plane. On landing the door was flung about inside the fuselage, fortunately missing the men but hitting and puncturing one of the rubber dinghies.
5. Everyone expected the aircraft to sink within a few seconds but it remained afloat for four or five minutes (?). In the rush the first dinghy cast off with only four men (instead of five) and the second got clear by passing under the tail of the aircraft which was rising and falling with the waves. One man put his hand out to ward off the tail as it came down and was cut on the hand. Six men were left on the aircraft but were taken off by the ship's boat.
6. The ship was a Spanish MV and was at first reluctant to pick up the men as they believed them to be Germans on manoeuvres. When they discovered they were British they were very cordial and the men received excellent treatment during their two and a half days stay on board. The captain was reported to be a Franco sympathiser but this did not prevent him making everything as comfortable as possible.
7. I asked what happened to the operational maps which were issued to the stick commanders at Hurn on the 8th November. Private Channon stated that he had cut them in half with his clasp knife and thrown them overboard. The same man stated that when the party had been on board for about half an hour he had thrown

the two dinghies overboard after puncturing them and also the Mae Wests. He noticed that one Mae West and all the rations out of the dinghies had been removed. He is certain that none of the British troops had them. All were positive that all equipment and documents went down with the plane.

8. Three of the men commented on the fact that escape money was issued only to the sergeants although all ranks were lectured on escaping at Hurn before the take off.
9. The party landed at Lisbon on Friday 13th November and were met by the British Consul who lodged them at the Hotel Europe. They spent eight days in Lisbon wandering about at large and reporting to HM Embassy daily. They left on Saturday 21st November and flew back to England being interrogated at Poole. All agreed that that they had not been questioned by anybody and that they had maintained strictest security. Their reluctance to say anything caused them some embarrassment at Waterloo station when the RPO (Regimental Pay Office) Corporal refused them any money to get to the Transit Centre at Marylebone, and they were obliged to beg off civilians.
10. L/Corporal Deasey commented on the universally pro-British attitude of the Portuguese and noticed that owing to the news of our successes in Africa the pound appreciated from 34 to 38 Escudos, during the week they spent in Lisbon.

Report by Captain de Silver, dated 26th November 1942.

Appendix III

Report by Sergeant Stevens of No 3 Section 16 PFA, 20th November 1942

Report by Sergeant Stevens of No 3 Section 16 PFA

Thursday 5th November 1942.
Left Bulford for Hurn aerodrome. Given hot meal, billets, bedding etc. and rested all afternoon.

Friday 6th November 1942.
Arrival of C47 Squadrons. Day spent on general duties – weapon cleaning, blackening brasses, shower-baths, pay parade etc.

Saturday 7th November 1942.
Containers loaded into planes for outward flight. This afternoon briefing took place. RAMC Section were divided into two sections and allocated to B and C Companies. We were informed at the briefing that our task would be to salvage parachute equipment from the DZ on landing. Further briefings were given by Captain Keesey to RAMC personnel of B Company and by Captain Rutherford to RAMC personnel of C Company.

Sunday 8th November 1942.
Whole force given further briefing this morning by Battalion Commander, who also informed us of the actual place to which we are to proceed and stressed the importance of attaining our objective. After the briefing, the force was addressed by Major-General Browning. Rest of day spent on checking containers as loaded into planes and checking jumping apparatus and emplaned for the outward flight.

Monday 9th November 1942.
At about 0100 hours the flight was postponed for reasons not given. The whole force went back to billets and paraded again at 1300 hours when we were taken by transport to Christchurch railway station and thence by special train to St Eval aerodrome in Cornwall. Arrived there at approx 2200 hours and given hot meal on arrival. Emplaned immediately afterwards.

Tuesday 10th November 1942.
The first aircraft took off at about 0100 hours. Captain Keesey and two PFA personnel in plane No 6. Rest of Field Ambulance Section split up into various other plane loads.

Outward flight uneventful. Landed at Gibraltar from 0800 hours onwards and taken to South Barracks where given hot meal and rations for the remainder of flight. Rest of day intended for resting but we were informed that a change of plan had been made and containers would have to be operationally packed straight away. All afternoon spent repacking containers on the aerodrome. Emplaned again at about midnight.

Wednesday 11th November 1942.
Took off for Maison Blanche from 0200 hours onwards. All planes containing Field Ambulance personnel arrived safely at Maison Blanche from 0730 hours with the exception of plane No 6 containing Captain J.H. Keesey and Privates Simpson and Hampshaw which was reported to have crashed on take-off at Gibraltar. No definite news of any survivors. Remainder of day at Maison Blanche spent repacking containers and bombing up. Captain Rutherford and Captain Keesey had agreed at Gibraltar that certain medical equipment could not be taken on the operation as our containers had been reduced from 5 to 3. The surplus medical equipment was left in the hangar at Maison Blanche with the remainder of the Battalion surplus equipment.

This evening Battalion Commander briefed Officers and NCOs for a new objective, our original objective (Djijelli) having already been taken by other forces. We were warned that enemy elements may be encountered at our new objective. Medical arrangements revised as follows:

Sergeant Stevens and Field Ambulance personnel to act as DZ Foraging Party with remainder of attached troops. Captain Rutherford and Battalion medical orderlies to treat and evacuate DZ casualties. No other casualties expected.

Thursday 12th November 1942.
Emplaned 0530 hours. Took off from approx 0600 hours with strong escort of Spitfires. Target located and dropping took place on Bone aerodrome at approx 0830 hours. No resistance encountered and aerodrome successfully occupied. About 12 DZ casualties were sustained including one fatality (Sergeant Godfrey 3rd Battalion), remainder of casualties treated at First Aid Post set up in aerodrome building and six of the more serious were later evacuated to the Civil Hospital at Bone. Field Ambulance Section spent remainder of day salvaging equipment from DZ.

Friday 13th November 1942.
Stand To 0400 hours but no enemy activity so far. Field Ambulance Section set up ADS near Force HQ (about 1/2 kilometre from actual aerodrome). Several minor casualties (accidental) treated there during the day. Two squadrons of Spitfires arrived at the aerodrome this evening.

Saturday 14th November 1942.
Aerodrome and surroundings machine-gunned by enemy fighters this morning and approx 6 slight casualties sustained. ADS moved from Force HQ to aerodrome

buildings. More casualties from machine-gunning sustained this afternoon including one serious evacuated to Bone Hospital.

Sunday 15th November 1942.
More bombing and machine gun attacks this morning, but no serious casualties sustained except for one British fighter pilot shot down in flames over the aerodrome, badly burned and injured, evacuated to Bone Hospital but died that same night. Two other casualties evacuated to Bone this afternoon.

Today one ward and the operating theatre of an empty French Military Hospital in Bone was opened by Lieutenant Tasker RAMC, RMO No 6 Commando. One 3rd Battalion orderly, 2 Field Ambulance orderlies and the majority of the Field Ambulance medical and surgical equipment were loaned for this purpose. This afternoon however, 3rd Battalion Group received instructions to move by rail and the medical personnel and equipment were taken from the Military Hospital to Bone railway station. Some items of equipment were left behind as the move was taking place at short notice and little time was available for checking.

Medical equipment loaded onto train with rest of Battalion stores this evening and troops entrained at about midnight.

Monday 16th November 1942.
Instructions for move cancelled this morning owing to insufficient reinforcements at the aerodrome. Personnel detrained, equipment off loaded and majority of medical and surgical equipment taken back to Lieutenant Tasker at Bone Military Hospital. Field Ambulance Section then proceeded back to original ADS position on the aerodrome. Much aerial activity but only few minor casualties.

Tuesday 17th November 1942.
Sharp bombing raid at breakfast, but no casualties, one enemy bomber shot down on the aerodrome but crew of four all killed. Bodies collected by medical personnel and sent to Bone for disposal. Another sharp bombing attack about midday – only two or three minor casualties. This afternoon 3rd Battalion Group again received instructions to move. ADS closed down at 1430 hours and Field Ambulance Section transported by lorry to Bone where the remainder of equipment was recollected from Military Hospital. On the authority of Captain Rutherford, RMO 3rd Battalion essential items of equipment was retained by Lieutenant Tasker including one stethoscope, two catheters, one kidney dish and certain expendable items i.e. plaster, drugs and dressings. 4 blankets had previously been lost during evacuation of casualties.

Medical equipment again loaded onto train together with rest of Battalion stores. Sharp dive bombing attack on Bone Docks adjoining railway station while wagons were being loaded at dusk, but no casualties sustained at railway station. First Aid Post set up on railway station manned until 2000 hours by Battalion medical orderlies and from then onwards by Field Ambulance personnel. All clear sounded at approx 1900 hours and troops were allowed into the town until 2200 hours. Personnel entrained at approx 2300 hours, Field Ambulance Section travelling with loading party in one of the luggage vans.

Wednesday 18th November 1942.
Started train journey back to Maison Blanche at approx 0430 hours. Halt for breakfast at approx 0900 hours, rations for the journey having previously been issued. Further long halt at midday at Duviviers. Train made very slow progress, halted again at dusk when several men including L/Corporal Brace of Field Ambulance Section were placed under arrest for stealing wine from station platform. Continued journey all night with frequent stops.

Thursday 19th November 1942.
Train arrived at Maison Blanche at approx 0930 hours. Personnel detrained and marched to billets in wine distillery approx 5 kilometres from Maison Blanche aerodrome in a westerly direction. Troops given hot meal, billets and spent afternoon cleaning up.

Captain Young contacted at Maison Blanche aerodrome this afternoon and instructions received from him to report back tomorrow morning.

Friday 20th November 1942.
Complete check made and inventory taken of all remaining medical equipment and submitted to Lieutenant QM Anderson at Maison Blanche aerodrome this morning.

Reported in to CO at 1400 hours.
Sergeant E Stevens
NCO i/c 3 Section
16 Parachute Field Ambulance
Rouiba 20th November 1942.

Appendix IV

1st Parachute Battalion – Report on Operations and Activities between 16th November 1942 and 11th December 1942

Monday 16th November 1942. The Battalion was briefed by the Commanding Officer, Lieutenant Colonel Hill MC on the night 15th/16th November. The Battalion was to take the aerodrome at Souk-el-Arba (Tunisia 1/50,000 Sheet 32 8611). It was not known whether the landing would be opposed by the French.

The Battalion marched off from the hangars at 1000 hours and was emplaned at 1030 hours. At 1100 hours the Battalion was airborne. The flight was uneventful, most of the journey being at sea level. No enemy aircraft were seen by the fighter escort.

At 1330 hours the Battalion dropped at Souk-el-Arba, two and a half hours after leaving Maison Blanche aerodrome, Algiers. Casualties on the DZ were one man killed and two injured [This first man killed was 2620089 Private W. Webster aged 36 now buried at 12B2 Medjez-el-Bab CWGC Cemetery]. The 22 set and several containers did not leave the aircraft. The Battalion formed up without incident. The CO and Adjutant were met by a French Officer who took them to a French HQ where transport was arranged to convey Major des Voeux, and escort to see General Barre and also to move the Battalion to Beja (Sheet 5 2037).

T Company and the Anti-Tank Sections were left on the DZ to salvage parachutes and equipment. Lieutenant Mackay RE remained to carry out a detailed recce of the landing ground. The entire party was under the command of the 2 i/c Major Pearson.

The French gave the Battalion a welcome and were friendly, courteous and helpful.

At 1700 hours the Battalion formed up to embus for Beja. Whilst doing this, a Sergeant (later killed in action) accidentally dropped his Sten gun which fired, wounding five men in S Company.

At 1730 hours the Battalion less the salvage party moved off, arriving about 2 miles out of Beja at 1930 hours, where it debussed. The CO and Adjutant went into the village to visit the French commander, Colonel Bergerou who advised them to remain in their present position for the night.

The Battalion spent a miserable night in the open. There was heavy rain and it was very cold. Meanwhile the salvage party cleared the DZ and arranged for its removal to base in the charge of Lieutenant Clements. The French arranged the funeral of our casualty to take place the following day.

Tuesday 17th November 1942. The CO went into Beja and interviewed Colonel Bergerou. One company was detailed to take over a sector of the French positions covering the town to the east.

Transport was provided to lift one company which was given a warning order at 1000 hours that it would leave during the afternoon to harass enemy lines of communication running south from Mateur (Sheet 2 5878) on the Mateur-Sidi N'Sir road (Sidi N'Sir Sheet 2 4159).

At 1200 hours this mobile column under command of Major Cleasby-Thompson moved off.

At 1600 hours the Battalion moved into Beja, R Company taking over the French sector covering the roads running from Sidi N'Sir and Medjez-el-Bab (Sheet 5 5834) into Beja. Battalion HQ was established in the slaughter house. Field Ambulance in the local hospital.

T Company completed the salvage work at Souk-el-Arba. The 2 i/c and IO attended the funeral of Private Webster who was buried with full military honours by the French in the cemetery.

Lieutenant Clements and 4 ORs returned to base by train with all salvage at 1800 hours at which time the remainder of the company entrained for Beja leaving Lieutenant Mackay to continue with his recce. The train arrived at Beja at 2030 hours and troops remained entrained overnight.

The 2 i/c and IO contacted Major des Voeux at French HQ.

During the early afternoon a Spitfire and a Hurricane landed on Souk-el-Arba aerodrome.

Wednesday 18th November 1942. 2 i/c contacted CO at dawn. T Company was moved into Battalion reserve in Battalion HQ area. The CO attended several conferences with the French. The information they gave was that the enemy was holding the river line to the east of Medjez-el-Bab with a force of some 300 men. They had made no attempt to cross the river. The French declared that they would not open fire on the Germans unless fired upon.

1 Squadron Derbyshire Yeomanry arrived (commanded by Major Inglefield) and went forward to investigate the situation in Medjez-el-Bab

At 1500 hours the CO ordered 1 Platoon of S Company (Lieutenant Wandless) to report to Major Inglefield at Medjez and to place himself at his disposal. Their role was to take up a position on the bridge at Medjez and to force the enemy to fire if they attempted to cross the bridge.

Major Cleasby-Thompson's column arrived back at Beja at 2000 hours with one enemy recce car and prisoners.

One Battery anti-tank guns and one Battery 3.7 howitzers arrived at Beja.

Thursday 19th November 1942. O Group was called at Battalion HQ at 0300 hours and the CO informed them that the situation at Medjez was deteriorating. The enemy had issued an ultimatum to the French which expired at 0700 hours. The Battalion was to be at immediate notice to move up. The Germans, however, made no move at 0700 hours.

At 1100 hours R Company was ordered to move to Medjez to stiffen French resistance. The Company moved out at 1300 hours.

The CO visited Colonel Hull OC Blade Force regarding the Medjez crisis. It was then decided to move the battalion to the village. The Battalion embussed for Medjez at 2300 hours.

Friday 20th November 1942. The Battalion reached Oued Zarga (Sheet 5 4135) at 0200 hours under command of Major Pearson who was met by the CO and informed that the enemy had crossed the river in several places and that it was not possible to move into Medjez. The French and Americans had already commenced to withdraw from the river line. The 2 i/c was ordered to withdraw S Company to Beja in Derbyshire Yeomanry vehicles, and T Company to the French positions 10 kilometres back from Oued Zarga on the Oued Zarga-Beja road. T Company was to cover the Battalions withdrawal.

The CO then moved forward with all available transport to extricate R Company. The Americans lifted Lieutenant Wandless's (S Company) Platoon.

By 0600 hours the Battalion was clear of the French position to the north of Beja and arrived at the village itself at 0700 hours. One Company of the Northamptonshire Regiment took over R Company's position in the Beja sector. The Battalion rested the remainder of the day.

Saturday 21st November 1942. The French reported that an enemy armoured column was moving west on Sidi N'Sir. The CO ordered S Company to move at 1400 hours to assist the French. On arriving at Sidi N'Sir at 1600 hours, Major Cleasby-Thompson, OC S Company, was informed by the French Commandant that Italian lorried infantry

The old road near Sidi N'Sir looking north. (James Macrae)

The old road near Sidi N'Sir looking south. (James Macrae)

supported by tanks had attacked his positions that mornining. All of the tanks had been destroyed by his guns and the infantry dispersed after suffering severe casualties. The situation was well in hand and no assistance was required. This information was passed to the CO who ordered the Company back to Beja.

Before leaving, the French Commandant informed OC S Company that there was an enemy tank harbour about 12 kilometres up the railway line between Sidi N'Sir and Mateur.

At 1500 hours the CO ordered R Company to reinforce the French holding the bridge at Oued Zarga.

The East Surreys took over from the Northants at Beja.

Sunday 22nd November 1942. Battalion at rest in Beja. Captain Maude visited Sidi N'Sir to arrange with the French Commandant an interview for the CO with regard to the tank harbour on the following day. Maude brought back two men of S Company who had been left behind on the previous visit.

Monday 23rd November 1942. At 0900 hours the CO, Major Cleasby-Thompson and Captain Maude visited the French Commandant at Sidi N'Sir, being machine-gunned by Me 109s on route. Information was given by a discharged French sailor who had been wounded by the British at Oran and who lived in the area, that an Italian force, strength about 300 with 17 to 20 tanks, harboured every night eight or nine miles down the railway line. They did not put out outposts or pickets.

The CO decided to attack the position that nigh with the Battalion less R Company with 1 detachment French Senegalese. The CO returned to Beja at 1330 hours. Major

General Eveleigh OC 78th Division with Brigadier Case arrived at Battalion HQ at 1500 hours. He informed the CO that he intended to attack Medjez the following day and granted the CO permission to carry out the night attack on the Italians.

Battalion O Group was briefed for battle at 1500 hours. Zero hour was advanced to 0300 hours. The Battalion embussed in light order at 1800 hours arriving at Sidi N'Sir 2000 hours.

Tuesday 24th November 1942. The Battle of Gué Hill (Tunisia 1/20,000 Sheet 2). The enemy positions were located in the neighbourhood of Djebel es Soudid (4868). The plan was that 1 Platoon T Company and a composite Platoon from Battalion HQ under the commands of Captain Coxen and Lieutenant Lloyd were to attack from the west. 1 Platoon of T Company was to attack from the south. Two Platoons S Company with the CO and HQ S Company were to attack from the east. The remaining Platoon of S Company was to move round the east of the position and attack some anti-aircraft guns reported on the high ground north west of the position. The mortars were to put down a concentration of HE from a position by the bridge south of the river. They would fire from Z to Z+4.

The Senegalese would help in carrying the mortars and bombs and would then come into reserve. RE's were to mine the road to the east.

The Battalion moved by march route in single file guided by the French sailor. About one kilometre from the enemy the Battalion split into its assault group and were in position by Z-20. At Z-15 three heavy explosions were heard at the RE forming up point. Firing then started to the east of the position followed by spasmodic firing from several places. At Zero the mortar concentration came down. It was later discovered that the enemy had vacated the target area.

The enemy it was now found were only about 60-70 strong with a preponderance of MGs. Their main position on the summits of the hills were well prepared. The Platoon of Lieutenant Wandless cleared one hill with great élan and gallantry. There were some small enemy tanks in hull down positions with a pill-box on one hill. These were attacked by the CO who captured the crew and destroyed one tank with bombs. While moving to the second he was severely wounded.

Enemy resistance ended at about Z+90. The Senegalese were in action for the first time and were a little nervous. They were well led by their French officer.

It was impossible to estimate enemy casualties with accuracy. Many severely wounded Germans (the machine gunners were all Germans) and Italians had to be left with their dead. Italian medical orderlies were assisted and left behind. Some Italian walking wounded wanted to return with the Battalion as prisoners and were most reluctant to stay behind. They were far too weak however to be taken, although one Italian kept up for about four miles before collapsing. Our own wounded were lifted in two captured Italian tricycles down the railway or on handcarts pulled by Italian prisoners who worked willingly and well. There were about fifteen enemy dead, including two German officers, left on the position. One Italian officer and 25 German and Italian ORs were taken prisoner.

T Company covered the withdrawal which was organised by Major Pearson. The locality was cleared by 0543 hours.

Our casualties were:-

CO and Adjutant severely wounded
3 ORs killed and 3 ORs wounded
Captain Geary RE was killed and 2 RE officers and 15 ORs RE missing.

Last elements of the Battalion arrived at Beja at 1530 hours. 1 Platoon of S Company took over the road block from the East Surreys on the Oued Zarga road.

Major Pearson assumed command of the Battalion with Major Cleasby-Thompson as 2 i/c. Lieutenant O'Brien Adjutant and Captain Maude assumed command of S Company.

The CO met Colonel Hull at Blade Force HQ at 1730 hours and was informed that the Battalion was to prepare to move to a position in the Mateur area with one Battery anti-tank guns under command. The CO arranged to meet OC Blade Force at his HQ east of Sidi N'Sir at 1400 hours the following day with O Group.

Wednesday 25th November 1942. 0530 hours Beja bombed. Warning order issued to Battalion to move to new locality after dark. CO and O Group moved off to meet Colonel Hull and recce new positions at 1315 hours. Dive-bombed *en route*. The CO was informed that one Company was to move to Sidi N'Sir that night. The remainder of the Battalion was to stay in present location. O Group recced position in area road junction (Sheet 2 5659).

Thursday 26th November 1942. Beja bombed during the morning. German prisoner reported 24 British parachutists had been taken prisoner. It was assumed that these were the missing REs and Captain Stewart and his patrol. At 1000 hours CO visited Colonel

Looking in a north-easterly direction from Coxen's Farm, towards some German positions which were attacked by the 1st Parachute Battalion on 1st December 1942. (James Macrae)

A present day picture of Coxen's Farm. (James Macrae)

Hull who ordered the Battalion to new location to guard Blade Force tank harbour. The CO was ordered to contact Lieutenant Colonel Hamilton Russell of the 17/21 Lancers. The Battalion was to move by daylight in TCVs with air cover and occupy positions by sunset. The CO returned to Beja at 1300 hours leaving again with O Group at 1400 hours to make recce. Battalion under command Major Cleasby-Thompson left Beja at 1400 hours in TCVs. R Company arrived at RV at road junction (Sheet 2 5659) at 16600 hours, and took up positions relieving company of Rifle Brigade. S Company and Battalion HQ bombed and machine-gunned *en route* (8 killed 13 wounded S Company). In position area (Sheet 2 5663). Battalion HQ established in farm (5763). 1 Platoon T Company prepared ambush at Zamak Pass (5859). Patrol under Captain Coxen recced farm 6665 (Coxen's Farm).

Friday 27th November 1942. CO met Captain Coxen at Zamak Pass at 0700 hours. He reported the farm unoccupied. OC 17/21 Lancers made a section of carriers available to Battalion to lift T Company to Coxen's Farm. One section of T Company was ambushed by German parachutists who wounded six ORs. The enemy, four in number, were all killed. Colonel Hull authorised R Company to support T Company in Coxen's Farm. R Company lifted by 17/21 Lancers' carriers.

S Company took over R Company positions.

Saturday 28th November 1942. The day was uneventful. 1 Troop anti-tank guns moved into Coxen's Farm during the night. Information from Blade Force that 2nd Battalion Lancashire Fusiliers would be taking over from the Battalion during the night.

The CO met the CO 2 LF, Major Kelly (their CO Lieutenant Colonel L Manly had been killed in action a few days previously) at midnight and it was arranged that they would not take over until daylight. The LF were weak having lost 9 officers and over 200 ORs at the Battle of Medjez-el-Bab. Coxen's Farm force commenced patrolling. LF informed us that they had buried Captain Stewart and 5 ORs at Oued Zarga.

Lieutenant Perrin-Brown carried out a most successful patrol.

Sunday 29th November 1942. The CO moved to Coxen's Farm for the day and spent the night with T Company. S Company was brought into reserve behind Battalion HQ. Battalion HQ LF moved into the farm buildings next to our RAP. An uneventful day.

Monday 30th November 1942. At 0400 hours a small enemy patrol attacked the left forward company of the LF killing one Fusilier, wounding another and taking a wounded man prisoner. Two enemy dead were found at dawn and in the evening a further three dead Huns were found by a Fusilier patrol. Lieutenant Gammon took out a recce patrol to observe enemy activity in the Coxen's Farm area.

Contact was made with 2nd Battalion The Parachute Regiment who had dropped in the Depienne area on the 29th November through 1st Parachute Brigade W/T. Lieutenant Wandless took a small escort to arrest an Italian farmer suspected of liaising with the enemy in Mateur. Unfortunately the bird had flown.

The night patrols had little to report. Lieutenant Mellor's patrol had a brush with an enemy armoured car which escaped. Mellor himself moved to within 3½ miles of Mateur where he met some Huns at a road block. The enemy opened fire and perforated his tin hat with a bullet.

Tuesday 1st December 1942. An eventful day. A Spitfire pilot shot down in Battalion area was entertained to lunch. M. Borge arrived from MOISB as Arabic interpreter. The Battle of Coxen's Farm, as follows:

Action at Coxen's Farm 1st December 1942.

During the preceding days it had become apparent that the enemy had been increasing his strength in the hills to the north east of Coxen's Farm. It was obvious that unless the high ground in this sector was taken and held, the enemy would dominate the farm which would become untenable.

Except that increased activity on the part of the enemy both here and in the Battalion HQ sector had been noticed, little was known concerning them. An attack on these positions had therefore been contemplated.

On the morning of 1st December 1942 a conference was held at 1st Battalion HQ at which Major Kelly, 2nd Battalion Lancashire Fusiliers and Major French Blake 17/21 Lancer attended. It was decided that the attack would be launched by R Company 1st Parachute Battalion supported by C Squadron 17/21 Lancers that afternoon.

During the morning information that a strong enemy attack was heading towards Tebourba (Sheet 5 7755) was received. This, it was appreciated, might necessitate the move of C Squadron to that front and thereby seriously reduce the strength of the force covering the all important Sidi-N'Sir-Mateur road junction. It was then decided that if the enemy were found in strength on the hills, the garrison at the farm would be withdrawn to Battalion HQ area. At 1300 hours the attacking force assembled at Coxen's Farm and final instructions given.

The first phase of the attack commenced at 1515 hours with an assault on a small farm south east of Coxen's Farm. Three Valentine tanks carrying one section of T Company moved out. After preliminary machine-gunning by the tanks, the section entered the farm which was found to have been evacuated. The section returned to Coxen's Farm and the tanks rejoined their Squadron.

At 1550 hours the tanks machine-gunned the main German positions and then laid an excellent smoke screen to cover R Company then formed up on the start line – then running north and south of the farm. R Company advanced at 1600 hours and by 1615 hours was well up the first hill in spite of heavy enemy LMG fire. Heavy machine guns and mortars opened up on Coxen's Farm.

R Company's mortar detachment came into action against a located enemy MG which was temporarily silenced. The enemy then opened counter mortar fire. At 1700 hours the attack was held by heavy fire from six or seven unlocated machine guns and Coxen's Farm was subjected to a concentration of mortar and shell fire setting it alight in several places. Light began to fail at 1730 hours and at 1800 hours R Company commenced withdrawing to Coxen's Farm carrying the wounded. The dead, Lieutenant Fogarty and two ORs had to be left.

The Company reached the farm at 1845 hours, packed up and then withdrew to Battalion HQ arriving at 2200 hours.

Our casualties were three killed and seven wounded.

The strength of the enemy was probably one company supported by nine or ten machine guns, mortars and an infantry gun. Their positions were well dug-in and very difficult to see. The tank gunners could locate very few machine gun posts and very little help could be given them by our troops. No estimate of casualties inflicted on the enemy could be made.

Wednesday 2nd December 1942. R Company moved into Rest Farm some three miles south west of Battalion HQ on the Sidi N'Sir road. S Company recce patrols in the Coxen's Farm area reported slight enemy activity. A report was received that lorry-borne infantry had debussed about a mile from the Battalion sector on the Mateur road. A fighting patrol (Lieutenant Mellor and 1 Platoon S Company) were taken in carriers supplied by the Fusiliers to investigate. The enemy opposition was stronger than anticipated and the action had to be broken off. The carriers had to be abandoned. We lost one wounded believed killed and two missing. The enemy suffered casualties.

At 2000 hours an LO arrived from 78th Division with orders for the Battalion to move to Medjez-el-Bab on being relieved by an American motorised company. The order was cancelled later.

Thursday 3rd December 1942. GSO1 78th Division visited Battalion HQ and gave us the war situation (very vague).

Friday 4th December 1942. The Battalion had an uneventful day. We witnessed an air battle in which 6 Bisleys [Blenheims] and 4 Spitfires were shot down by 2 Messerschmitts in two minutes within two miles of us. A truly horrible spectacle. The only survivors –

Pilot Officer Holloway (RAF observer), Sub Lieutenant Wallace (RNVR) (he was with us on the *Arundel Castle*), Gunner Paster RAF and Sergeant Short RAF, were entertained by our officers. They promised to drop some tobacco for the IO and a clean pair of pants for the 2 i/c in return for our hospitality – none of which materialised.

Blade Force, somewhat depleted, returned to their old harbours.

Saturday 5th December 1942. Little activity on either side. A patrol under Lieutenant Gammon sent to ambush enemy on the Mateur road about six miles from the Battalion area could not get into position as the enemy had now covered the road from Sidi el Kai (Sheet 2 5766). A few enemy aircraft over. The enemy mortared the left forward company of the LF without effect.

Sunday 6th December 1942. M. Borge donned battledress. He and Lieutenant O'Brien left to patrol the Chouigi district (Sheet 5 7462). The day was quiet.

Monday 7th December 1942. Early in the morning the enemy wasted some mortar bombs on an unoccupied farm a mile north of the Battalion lines. M. Borge and Lieutenant O'Brien returned from Chouigi and reported little activity. Farms reported to be held by the enemy were unoccupied. There was heavy shelling in the Tebourba area. Arabs in bands of three or four hundred had been looting French farms and villages.

Tuesday 8th December 1942. Very heavy rain. Cold and miserable. Companies under cover but most uncomfortable. Captain Coxen took patrol to the scene of the Battle of Gué Hill, but saw no signs of the enemy. Captain Maude took out patrol to shoot up Arab looters, but found that LF had been before him and had already executed a brace. One Arab was arrested, condemned to death and shot. The night patrols had nothing to report.

Wednesday 9th December 1942. Lieutenant O'Brien, M. Borge and Sergeant Floyd went out to arrest Eli, the bandit chief, chief of the looters – he escaped. The Corps Commander visited the LF and saw the CO. He said that there might be a general withdrawal. A number of Frenchmen who had escaped from Mateur *en route* for Beja reported that there were few enemy in Mateur. Lieutenant Perrin-Brown attempted to take some French saboteurs (MOISB) through the enemy lines. The French developed heart attacks and were so exhausted that they had to return.

Mud damnable.

Thursday 10th December 1942. A strong German patrol arrived at the French village in which a section of S Company were located to protect it from Arab looters. The section was forced to withdraw. The REs under Lieutenant Mackay visited the house of Eli, the bandit chief and blew it up.

Warning order from Blade Force to withdraw in the night 11th December 1942. A patrol under Lieutenant Gammon did not contact the enemy. A patrol under Lieutenant Mellor dropped visiting cards on a 88 mm enemy gun position, killed a few Huns and brought home five prisoners. They were very young. One became drunk on a small tot of rum. They answered all questions put to them by the IO Captain O'Brien. Lieutenant Wandless carried out a long distance patrol.

Friday 11th December 1942. At first light the enemy attacked the left forward company of the LF. At 0930 hours the LF reported enemy infiltration round the flank to the right of the Battalion's sector. The 2 i/c Major Cleasby-Thompson, ordered Lieutenant Gammon's Platoon into this area, the CO at that time being at Blade Force HQ.

The enemy, of strength about one company, commenced a general attack about 1030 hours. S Company was moved up to the high ground in front of Battalion HQ by the 2 i/c and the attack was held. Four tanks from 17/21 Lancers were brought up which silenced the enemy machine guns. Major Pearson arrived in the forward area at about 1100 hours and launched an immediate counter-attack in conjunction with the left forward company of the LF. The 2 i/c and IO had some quiet sniping to themselves, each adding another entry in the vermin column of their respective game books.

There was little or no enemy opposition. They lost a few killed and several wounded, who were tended on the battlefield. They had to be left behind as the Battalion was then without transport. One officer and 15 ORs were taken prisoner. Our casualties were one killed and one wounded. We took our leave, rather sadly, of M. Turville, our farmer host at 1800 hours when the Battalion withdrew to Sidi N'Sir by march route. R Company was left as rearguard to cover the Battalion's and LF's withdrawal and joined the Battalion later. One of our Italian trucks was ambushed on the road but the driver, Corporal Whittingham was unhurt. Corporal Whittingham rushed the hill on which the enemy was located, firing his revolver. The enemy withdrew. Lieutenant Wandless with his Platoon was despatched to deal with this party of enemy at about 1200 hours, but did not make contact.

The Battalion reached Sidi N'Sir at 2350 hours and embussed in TCV for the Brigade rest area at Souk-el-Khemis arriving in the early hours of the morning.

Appendix V

Report on S Company Column activities 17th/18th November 1942 by Major P. Cleasby, Thompson Force Commander

Reference Map Tunisia Sheet 2.

17th November 1942. The CO 1st Battalion Parachute Regiment issued a warning order to OC S Company that a column of 2 Platoons S Company, 2 Sections RE and 1 detachment of 3" mortars under command of OC S Company would move by transport into the area of Mateur (J5978) at 1000 hours 17th November 1942. The column was to be ready to move at about 1200 hours. The role of the column was to attack and harass enemy lines of communication between Mateur and Sidi N'Sir (J4159). If contact was not made with the enemy within 48 hours a strong fighting patrol was to attack enemy outposts round Mateur. It was emphasised that prisoners were required. Little information was available regarding the enemy.

At 1200 hour the column moved from Beja (J2038) arriving at Sidi N'Sir at 1400 hours where the Force Commander briefed his command after lunch. Liaison was made with the French Commander who would not allow the French vehicle drivers through the minefield on the Sidi N'Sir pass. At 1530 hours the column again moved off in the vehicles now driven by our own drivers. Two of the four vehicles broke down before reaching the pass and minefield. The 2 i/c, Captain Maude was ordered to take the heavy stores and one Platoon to a harbour about 10 kilometres down the Sidi N'Sir-Mateur road. The remainder of the force continued by march route.

Captain Maude found an excellent hiding up place 9 kilometres from Sidi N'Sir in some Arab houses just off the road. Here he obtained a sheep, bread and eggs from the Arabs who were most helpful and pro-British. During the evening plans were made for operations on the following day. All ranks were very tired having had little or no sleep for three nights.

It was decided that a patrol would move up to within 5 kilometres of Mateur the following day and lay an ambush or attack the outposts if the former appeared unproductive. The remainder of the force was to prepare an ambush 10 kilometres from Mateur. The Force fed and slept well in spite of diverse itches due to the local inhabitants.

At about 0700 hours **18th November 1942**, an enemy column consisting of three heavy eight-wheeled armoured cars and three light recce cars passed the harbour *en route* for Sidi N'Sir. They were fired on by our sentries but took no notice. It was later learnt from the French Commandant at Sidi N'Sir that the German commander complained that he had been fired upon. The vehicles had to return by the same route so an ambush was prepared and was ready by 0730 hours. The force had been lectured on ambush techniques by the commander at Sidi N'Sir. At about 1030 hours the enemy were seen returning. Their order of march was armoured car, scout car, armoured car, two scout cars, armoured car. Distance between vehicles was about 40 yards.

No fire was opened until the first vehicle struck the mines which had been laid by the REs. This was the signal for the battle to commence. Gammon bombers led by Lieutenants Mellor and Kellas quickly immobilised two of the armoured cars. The scout cars with their occupants were quickly put out of action.

The enemy who were not killed or wounded in the first five vehicles quickly surrendered. The armoured car at the rear of the column opened fire with machine gun and sub machine gun but was driven into the ambush by accurate 3" mortar fire directed by Corporal Tucker. The crew of this car fought with gallantry until all were killed or wounded. The action lasted about 20 minutes. The prisoners were searched and the wounded tended to. Our casualties were Sergeant Steadman wounded in the face and leg. The enemy lost six killed, five wounded and eight prisoners. The vehicles were searched and equipment, documents etc removed. One scout car was mobilised and driven back to Beja with Sergeant Steadman and a badly wounded Hun.

The force then moved back to Sidi N'Sir via the hills after destroying the enemy vehicles and burying the 3" mortar and certain explosives. The local Arabs were bribed and promised to hide the equipment and look after the four enemy wounded who could not walk. These were given food, water, cigarettes and morphia. The heavy stores were left behind because the remaining two vehicles could not be started and it was assumed that the enemy column had wirelessed their HQ at Mateur.

The force reached Sidi N'Sir at 1500 hours.

A French car was then obtained and the MO Captain Haggie, Lieutenant Mellor and the Mortar Corporal, Corporal Tucker returned to the scene of the battle and collected the Battalion wounded and stores and mortar. The Arabs had looted the cars and the enemy dead had been stripped naked.

Appendix VI

Report on Patrols 18th-20th November 1942, Lieutenant Wandless, 1st Parachute Battalion

18th November 1942. In a defensive position at Beja. Received the following orders from Lieutenant Colonel Hill – proceed with my platoon by transport to the west side of Medjez-el-Bab where I would meet Major Inglefield of the Derbyshire Yeomanry, under whose orders I would be. Then, supported by armoured cars of the DY, I would take up a defensive position covering the bridge of Medjez-el-Bab, preferably on the east bank of the river.

Arrived at Medjez-el-Bab at 1700 hours and met Major Inglefield who gave me the following information – about 300 Germans were in position on the high ground east of the town. French troops were in positions of defence, but there had been no fighting. German officers visited the town daily under a flag of truce, and had twice demanded

Men of the 1st Parachute Battalion marching near Medjez-el-Bab. (Imperial War Museum)

to occupy it. A French liaison officer explained that the attitude of the Commandant at Medjez-el-Bab was that he was trying to delay the Germans by parley until a British force arrived and so far resisted the German demands by threatening to fight. The Germans apparently wanted to come in peacefully and avoid incidents with the French.

On being informed that one platoon and some armoured cars comprised the total British force, the French Commandant tactfully refused permission to enter the town and after a further conference I was ordered by Major Inglefield to withdraw to Oued Zarga, where I arrived at approx 2100 hours.

19th November 1942. I received orders through Major Inglefield to take up a position in reserve astride the road at Dir el Gueria (J4934). Arrived at this position at about 1000 hours and contacted French officers who were constructing defensive positions. Soon after the area was dive-bombed and machine-gunned, French AA guns retaliated and we opened fire on low flying aircraft with Brens and saw the tracer bullets enter three of the aircraft. Took up a position on the right of the French positions on the high ground at Sidi Ahmed (J504341).

At about 1300 hours received a message from Colonel Hill to proceed to a position on the north bank of the river (559316) and contact a battery of 6 pdr anti-tank guns of the US Army and arrange for their local protection. Arrived at about 1600 hours and dug defensive positions. No enemy seen.

20th November 1942. 0400 hours message arrived to Battery Commander to evacuate position immediately. We withdrew riding on the limbers as far as a point 5 kilometres north of Oued Zarga, where I was ordered by an American Colonel to debuss. I then found R Company and stayed with them and returned to Beja at about 1500 hours.

Appendix VII

Report on operations between 19th and 25th November 1942 by R Company detached from 1st Battalion Parachute Regiment

19th November 1942. Orders were issued by CO 1st Parachute Battalion to OC R Company to move the company to Medjez-el-Bab (5934) area which was then held by a small combined French and American Force. R Company was to come under command of French HQ situated some 6 kilometres west of Medjez-el-Bab. The detachment left Beja (2038) at 1100 hours arriving at French HQ at 1245 hours. The column was attacked *en route*, one man being severely wounded and two vehicles damaged by enemy aircraft.

The French commander instructed Major Conron (detachment commander) to provide units to defend a battery of French 75s acting in an anti-tank role north of the road 2 kilometres west of Medjez-el-Bab and also an American gun on the opposite side of the road.

Two Platoons were then detailed to cover the French battery and one Platoon the American gun. These Platoons were dug in by 2000 hours when the French HQ demanded 30 men to assist the French in Medjez itself. Accordingly one Platoon was left to guard the American gun, the remainder moved into the village arriving at 2330 hours and rested.

20th November 1942. At 0500 hours the Company relieved the troops holding the Medjez bridge. The day was quiet. A patrol of one officer (Lieutenant Fogarty) and 10 ORs was sent at 2239 hours and returned at 0200 hours. Its role was to investigate reported enemy movement across the river. The enemy were encountered attempting to cross. The enemy lost two killed, whose bodies were searched. They were identified as parachutists. At 0345 hours OC Detachment received orders that Medjez-el-Bab was to be evacuated and that he was to move to a position west of Oued Zarga (4136) some 6 kilometres away. This position was held until 1500 hours when the Company withdrew to Beja.

21st November 1942. The Company was ordered to move to Oued Zarga to reinforce the French holding the bridge. OC liaison with the French at their HQ 5 kilometres west of the village and then moved to the bridge arriving at 2045 hours. The French company was holding a position west of the bridge which was mined and covered by machine gun fire from a range of about 700 yards. OC R Company decided to move forward of the bridge to thick cover south of the road. The Company was dug in by 2345 hours.

22nd November 1942. At 0200 hours a patrol of one officer (Lieutenant Gammon) and 10 ORs was ordered to recce the line of the road Oued Zarga-Medjez-el-Bab. This patrol contacted the enemy at 0215 hours only 300 yards from the Company position. The enemy of about one platoon in strength appeared to be pushing either an armoured car or gun down the road. There were more enemy further down the road. One enemy, probably a connecting file, was captured and a motorcycle combination was destroyed with a No 6 grenade. Two enemy were killed. The prisoner, a parachutist, was escorted to Beja and the patrol returned to the Company at about 0800 hours.

Forward elements of the enemy contacted the Company's forward defence line at about 0230 hours and were driven back after a short fight. They then brought up to within 70 yards of the forward defence lines a gun of approx caliber .500 and opened fire on the bridge. At 0300 hours this gun was withdrawn some 700 yards and a mortar opened up on the Company locality. An attack was made on one section north of the road which was forced to withdraw. The enemy were driven off by a counter-attack by 2LF who had arrived at 0330 hours and taken over defended localities in the area of the bridge.

At dawn the enemy were seen digging in 700 yards in front of the Company position. Enemy artillery opened up on the bridge and the LF positions. The Company area was periodically mortared until 0730 hours then the enemy withdrew. The remainder of the day was uneventful. Our casualties were four wounded. The enemy's strength during the nights fighting appeared to be about 80 with supporting arms. Two enemy dead were found opposite the Company sector.

23rd November 1942. At 1000 hours the Company moved out two miles south east of their position at the request of OC 2LF in order to distract the enemy's attention while 2 Companies of the LF moved to the high ground to the north overlooking Medjez-el-Bab. No contact was made with the enemy and the Company withdrew at 1230 hours. During the night the Company sent out local patrols but no contact was made with the enemy.

24th November 1942. One Platoon moved into the French sector at the request of 2LF as the French had withdrawn. This Platoon remained in position until 1700 hours. At 1000 hours at the request of OC 2LF a patrol of one officer (Captain Stewart) and ten ORs from the Company and a section from 2LF moved out by MT towards Medjez covered by carriers. This patrol contacted the enemy and none returned. Captain Stewart's body was recovered several days later and it must be assumed that all were casualties. [Author's note: in spite of this report stating that Captain J.R.C. Stewart's body was recovered, it must be assumed that soon afterwards his body or grave was lost as he is currently commemorated on panel or face 33 of the Medjez-el-Bab Memorial to the Missing. He was formerly of 8th Battalion The King's Regiment (Liverpool) and No. 2 Commando, 11th Special Air Service Battalion, been awarded a Mention in Dispatches and was aged 23.]

25th November 1942. The Company was withdrawn to Beja. The day was uneventful.

Appendix VIII

Patrol Report by Lieutenant C. Perrin-Brown (1st Parachute Battalion), Night 27th/28th November 1942

A patrol of one officer (Lieutenant Perrin-Brown) and one section was ordered to locate enemy positions in the area of the bridge at Sidi Mansour (6469). The patrol left Battalion HQ at 0015 hours and moved down the west bank of the River Oude Tine. First contact with the enemy was made at Point 53 (6466) where he was digging in. The patrol continued towards the bridge and from the scrub at the south corner of the bridge a sentry was located. While carrying out the recce of the bridge an enemy detachment of 25-30 men moving down the road surprised the action.

Lieutenant Perrin-Brown and one OR opened fire with sub machine gun and rifle fire, following up with grenades. An enemy section on the bridge opened fire without effect. The patrol scattered and made its own way back to the Battalion area in two groups according to instructions. No traces of enemy were found on the way back. Corporal Cottrell remained behind to observe and reported that the enemy buried about ten of their dead.

Estimated strength of the enemy holding the bridge and including the digging party at Point 53 was one company.

Appendix IX

Report on action at Coxen's Farm 1st December 1942

At about 1045 hours on 1st December 1942 I was asked by CO 1st Parachute Battalion, Major Pearson, to support an attack on an enemy position 1 mile north east of the farm.

I ordered the Squadron to be ready to move at 1145 and accompanied CO Parachute Battalion to his HQ for more information. The Squadron was ready by 1145 but did not move off until 1215 or 1230. We arrived in preliminary assembly area 1 mile west of Coxen's Farm at about 1340. I went forward and met Major Conron and had a discussion with him in sight of the ground.

It was decided to attack the feature in two phases; the first an attack on the first ridge of sand, followed by a reforming and a second attack on a higher scrub hill behind. In addition, a preliminary operation was to be carried out to clear a small farm 1 mile to the south, in which an enemy mortar had been located in the morning.

During the advance to Coxen's Farm, information came in from my RHQ that there was a strong enemy attack towards Tebourba, which was being successful. This rather altered the nature of our operation, but after consultation with Major Kelly and Lancs Fusiliers, it was decided to continue, but if the enemy was found in strength on the heights, Major Pearson was to withdraw from Coxen's Farm altogether. To this end he ordered all kit etc. to be packed and loaded. The effect of this was slightly to delay the zero hour which was decided to be at 1600, the preliminary operation against the small farm to the south at 1515.

The latter was carried out successfully without incident, no enemy being found. At 1545 my Valentines were on the start line for their advance to the first enemy position. At 1556 I started a smoke screen, and ordered my Crusader Troop which was at the north end of the village, to engage a located enemy MG post on the left in a small mound. At 1600 hours R Company went forward. The smoke was effective, conditions being fortunately perfect. An enemy mortar also opened up from the mound on the left and shelled the north end of the village. I silenced it with HE temporarily. At about 1630 I went forward to the first position and found Major Conron. He took me to a Sergeant who showed me a MG position which I silenced with HE. My wireless was now out of order. The two Valentine Troops were in action on the right but found extreme difficulty in locating targets. The enemy were very well concealed and there was no movement. Even when smoke or flash was seen it was hard to indicate to tank gunners. The parachute troops were not in my opinion aware of the difficulty and did not attempt to point out targets to tank commanders. At the same time, the latter, although inexperienced, did not realise the necessity of asking the infantry, so the result was a lack of co-operation until the latter stages of the battle when this was rectified. At about 1655 the right platoon were still held up and Major Conron arrived, said he would bring up two more platoons and attack at about 1720. I said I was not sure whether it would do any good taking the higher feature and that I would go down and get Major Pearson's opinion and wireless it back (my set being repaired). Conron agreed and I went down to the farm which was being heavily shelled by a large mortar or small gun. Buildings were on fire and had to be evacuated. I then heard from my first troop leader that Major Pearson was at his set and wanted to speak to me. He gave me the order to tell his Company in the farm to withdraw plus transport and anti-tank guns. I passed this order to a Sergeant who I believed passed it on without going first to the Company Commander. This caused confusion which was subsequently rectified.

Two platoon Lancs Fusiliers arrived and were told the order to evacuate had been given. I then arranged for the extraction of the anti-tank guns in co-operation with their Troop Leader. I then found Captain Coxen and confirmed the order to withdraw. I ordered 1st and 2nd Troop to cover and assist R Company's withdrawal and to rally afterwards. I then searched the village for wounded and had wounded CSM of Parachute Company put on my tank. I searched the village for abandoned equipment but found practically nothing. I ordered the German KW IV to be destroyed by 6 pounder gun which was done effectively and the tank burnt out. I then rallied the Squadron and returned to harbour lifting the 2 Platoons Lancs Fusiliers.

One anti-tank gun was irreparably damaged on route back. Some tanks were bogged or broke tracks, but all were in harbour by 1230 hours today 2nd December 1942. I consider the enemy strength to have been at least one company. I myself located 5 MGs, 2 mortars and 1 heavy mortar or infantry gun. In view of their position I imagine there must have been more behind, and I consider that it would not have been practicable to hold the position had the second objective been taken. The effect would have been to have weakened seriously the garrison of the farm and to have made withdrawal difficult. Had the enemy been weak, the objective would have been of great value as an approach to raid his L of C over the Chouigi Pass. As it was a strong enemy force, there was no point in my opinion of losing men or endangering the security of the area of the T-roads where 1st Parachute Battalion HQ now is.

The enemy MG fire was not very accurate, but their positions were extremely well concealed and no movement was visible.

ffrench Blake, Major.
Commanding C Squadron 17/21 Lancers.
2nd December 1942.

Appendix X

Synopsis of patrol activity, T Company, 1st Parachute Battalion, 25th November-8th December 1942

25th November 1942. Recce patrol to Gué (scene of raid) by Lieutenant Perrin-Brown, Sergeant Thornton and Corporal Sparks. Enemy outpost encountered. Motorcycle salvaged from Metteheni Station.

26th November 1942. Patrol to Coxen's Farm. Captain Coxen and 8 Section. Farm deserted. Mines and bobby traps located.

27th November 1942. Patrol to bridge Sidi Mansour. Lieutenant Perrin-Brown and 7 Section. Encounter with enemy patrol after locating positions. Private Davis missing.

29th November 1942. Lieutenant Perrin-Brown, Sergeant Whitby and Private Livesey, daylight recce patrol Sidi Mansour. Enemy positions located. Patrol of Chouigi Pass area Sergeant Thornton and No 2 Section.

30th November 1942. Lieutenant Perrin-Brown and No 9 Section daylight patrol to Sidi Mansour. Encounter with enemy transport. Patrol machine gunned by enemy when returning.

2nd December 1942. Recce patrol area Coxen's Farm. Captain Coxen and two men.

3rd December 1942. Recce patrol area Coxen's Farm. Sergeant Parker and 7 Section.

3rd/4th December 1942. Recce patrol area Coxen's Farm. Sergeant Sawyer and 2 Section.

4th/5th December 1942. Recce patrol area Coxen's Farm. Sergeant Nairn and 3 Section.

5th December 1942. Recce patrol area Coxen's Farm. Sergeant John and 9 Section.

Recce patrol Sidi Bou Assid. Lieutenant Perrin-Brown.

Fighting patrol. Sidi Belhai. Captain Coxen and 3 Section. Enemy encountered and five wounded.

6th December 1942. Standing patrol. Piccadilly Circus. Sergeant Parker and 7 Section.

7th December 1942. Standing patrol. Piccadilly Circus. Sergeant Taylor and 7 Section. Recce patrol to Kueniga. Lieutenant Perrin-Brown and 9 Section.

8th December 1942. Recce patrol Gué. Captain Coxen and 3 men.

Appendix XI

Report by Lieutenant Wandless, 7 Platoon, S Company, 1st Parachute Battalion, December 1942

3rd December 1942. I was ordered to take out a fighting patrol consisting of two sections of No 7 Platoon and one section of LF's to attack a small number of enemy reported to be occupying Tabouna Farm 5969. As a subsidiary task if time allowed, I was also to patrol to Sidi Bou Aoid 579688. If Tabouna Farm contained no enemy I was to make a thorough search of the place for signs of enemy occupation.

Left Battalion HQ at 2300 hours and proceeded along the track running north east. Crossed stream midway between Tabouna Farm and Sidi Bou Aoid. Crossing difficult because of thick mass of undergrowth which covers the stream on both banks. Reached high ground north of farm and advanced in extended order. Entered farm without opposition. An Arab said the farm belonged to Italians who had gone to Mateur five days ago. Stated there had been no soldiers in the place. We entered and searched the farm buildings and the area around about and found no trace of military occupation.

Completed this task at 0445 hours and gathered patrol together. Left at 0500 hours and proceeded along track to Sidi Bou Aoid and when about 800 yards off Bou Aoid turned off to the right and approached under cover of a plantation and got into the farmyard behind a haystack. Detailed section tasks for clearing area and at 0530 hours entered the farm. Challenged by two German sentries who were shot. Enemy then appeared at various places and were completely surprised and shot up. A number were soon running in the direction of the Mateur road. From reports of section commanders it is estimated 17 enemy were killed or wounded. At 0600 hours as dawn was breaking I decided that time would not allow us to make a thorough search of the farm and I withdrew. Two enemy prisoners, both wounded, could not travel very well and had to be left. Enemy identified as parachutists by their dress and estimated number about 30. They had no arrangements for local protection outside the area of the farm buildings. We had no casualties. Private Reed abandoned his Bren gun and his section and withdrew on his own. Returned to Battalion HQ at 0930 hours.

11th December 1942. Took out a patrol consisting of No 7 Platoon. Left lines at 1000 hours with the following orders - proceed to Sidi Bou Aoid and try to take some prisoners.

Proceeded via Tabouna Farm. Midway between Tabouna and Sidi Bou Aoid heard two blank rounds fired from the direction of Tabouna Farm. Approached Bou Aoid from north-west and when about 100 yards from the farm I fell over a trip wire and a can rattled. L/Corporal soon after hit another wire and exploded a mine which fortunately caused no casualties. Three grenades were then thrown from the right flank landing about 20 yards from the right hand section. Being thus caught in open ground with no cover, withdrew about 300 yards and reformed platoon. MG fire opened up but did not come near us. More grenades were thrown apparently at random, and a gun believed to be an anti-tank gun fired one round from the Farm, which was presumed to be a signal.

Decided that position was probably too strong for a fighting patrol and withdrew a further 800 yards towards Tabouna and laid an ambush hoping a patrol would be sent out. Laid up for one hour. Heard what was thought to be a patrol passing eastwards along south bank of stream. Crossed stream and proceeded to about 500 yards from Tabouna without hearing anything further, and it was then 0530 hours, returned to our lines.

Appendix XII

Report from Lieutenant P.E.M. Mellor (1st Parachute Battalion) fighting patrol along north and south road to Mateur (ref 56 and 57) Bizerta map Sheet 2 1/200,000, 29th November 1942

Information received of possible road blocks on north south road to Mateur. Fighting patrol sent out on night of 29th November 1942 to get prisoners. Time to be back – first light, i.e. not later than 0600 hours.

Two 15 cwts were put at our disposal, but there was no information about minefields. These were thought to be a possibility.

Strength of possible road blocks not known.

The patrol set off in the two trucks at 2000 hours along the Mateur road. After going about two miles we came to a position where the right half of the road was cratered. This seemed the possible start of a minefield so the trucks were turned round and the rest of the job was done on foot. It should be mentioned here that previous to this the two farms to the right and left of the road north of our position had been searched and no enemy found.

The patrol proceeded in two single files, one on each side of the road. It was very dark and there was no moon. At 0043 hours we were opened fire on by automatic and LMG fire from the left of the road. We engaged the fire and tried to encircle it but on closing in and a bomb, having been thrown, the enemy, possibly three in number, ran to a scout or armoured car that was ticking over and made off before the situation was fully appreciated in the darkness.

As it was now after 0100 hours and the patrol had to be back before 0600 hours and the car would obviously raise the alarm on return, and the distance away of further enemy dispositions was unknown, I sent the force back (one platoon and I went on towards Mateur to see what the situation was).

At about point 5874 (about three miles from Mateur) while making my way along to the right of the road I was fired at by a sentry on the road. It is impossible to estimate the strength of the position and it was still very dark and the road here curved up and round. Rifle and LMG were fired and a Verey light put up.

No other enemy were encountered during the return to base.

Time out : 2000 hours. Time back : 0400 and 0645 hours.

Appendix XIII

Report on Medjez-el-Bab patrol, 1st Parachute Battalion and Lancashire Fusiliers, 24th November 1942

Patrol made up as follows: 1st Parachute Battalion – Captain Stewart and 18 ORs. LF – One Officer with 2 Bren Carriers and 23 ORs. Total in patrol 43.

The patrol moved off from Oued Zarga at approx. 1230 hours; intention – to contact the enemy and bring back prisoners and information. We proceeded down the main road; the Bren Carriers going forward scouting.

The first signs of the enemy were five miles from Medjez-el-Bab, where we passed into a cutting where the enemy had concealed themselves very effectively; in other words we dropped into an ambush. The first shot fired was from a 20mm German anti-tank gun. On this shot being fired I saw the two Bren Carriers move off, one to the left, the other to the right, as I thought, to tackle the flanks of the enemy. Instead, they moved off one to each flank, turned completely round and went out of the scrap altogether without the permission of the patrol leader.

The enemy next opened up with MGs, mortars and anti-tank guns, and with what we discovered afterwards to be a four-gun 75mm artillery battery. The issue as to whether we should stay or go was decided by an anti-tank shell through the first lorry. Captain Stewart's orders were "Come on boys, we came to fight, so let's give 'em hell!" We debussed and took up defensive positions in a scattered Arab farm.

On debussing the Bren gunner dropped into a ditch with the Bren gun, opened up on the anti-tank gun up the road and the gunner (Private Watton) in spite of the fact that he got two MG bullets in his chest, carried on firing until being killed ten minutes later by a 20mm shell. Captain Stewart reached out for the Bren and managed to get it back.

About this time I had opened up with a German MG 34, which we had captured two days before, and managed to clear up the MG on our right flank, situated near a haystack on a hillside farm. As it was then my turn to get out of the ditch at the roadside (which was necessary owing to the enemy fire which was coming straight down the road) I picked up my gun, spare box of ammunition, and received my first wound. I told the Skipper I was hit. He said, "Get back out of it." I managed to find a better position where I finished off the remainder of the German ammunition and then took up my Sten gun. The next thing I saw was a mortar shell that burst right on top of Captain Stewart. On taking a look I found that his face had been blown right away. He was dead. I checked up, found most of the boys had been hit, but we still had plenty of ammunition.

The Germans now showed signs of making their first assault by putting up a heavy mortar barrage, which came about five minutes after our check up and change of positions. We beat off the first assault with Stens, Brens, pistols and grenades. Very little hand-to-hand fighting took place. We could not counter-attack owing to the lack of numbers, so we settled down to wait and snipe, hoping that the Bren Carriers would be bringing reinforcements along.

These did not materialise and over came Jerry with his second assault. By this time our numbers had been reduced to 17 men, including the men of the LF, and although we managed to beat off the second assault, we found it a much stiffer job than the last time. I checked the ammunition state and found we were running very low. I had five Sten magazines left myself and only one Jerry grenade; and most of the boys were in a similar plight as regards ammunition. The third assault took place, in which we had our first hand-to-hand fighting. Everything was used – feet, fists, pistols and knives. Jerry retired for the third time, but as his third lot retired, up came a fourth lot. Ammunition was exhausted; only five men were on their feet, so we stood up so as to get the job over quicker, as we fully expected the Germans to give no quarter. However, we were told to put our hands up, we refused, but contrary to expectations, we were not shot out of hand, but taken back into the enemy lines, fed and had our wounds dressed.

Captain Stewart's coolness during the initial stages of the action and his encouraging remarks were a great example to the boys who fought that action. The Parachute Battalion survivors of the patrol regret his death very much indeed. One of the highlights of the action was in the third assault, in which Private Higgins of our Company tackled his man with a fighting knife, relieved him of his automatic weapon, and did a good job of work in slaughtering a number of Huns with their own ammunition. Corporal Bourne and Private Dreezer were also taken prisoner and are now in Italy.

I am very proud and pleased to say that right throughout this action not a man lost his head and never at any time was there any hesitation in tackling the enemy when he came to close quarters. Perhaps it is a good thing the CO's batman did not try keeping the tea warm for an hour as we had instructed him!

W Cook
CQMS
1st Parachute Battalion

Appendix XIV

Report on operations between 19th and 25th November 1942 by R Company detached from 1st Battalion Parachute Regiment

19th November 1942. Orders were issued by CO 1st Battalion Parachute Regiment to OC R Company to move the company to Medjez-el-Bab (5934) area which was then held by a small combined French and American force. R Company was to come under command of French HQ situated some six kilometres west of Medjez-el-Bab. The detachment left Beja (2038) at 1100 hours arriving at French HQ at 1245 hours. The column was attacked *en route*, one man being severely wounded and two vehicles damaged by enemy aircraft. The French commander instructed Major Conron (Detachment Commander) to provide units to defend a battery of French 75s acting in an anti-tank role north of the road 2 kilometres west of Medjez-el-Bab and also an American gun on the opposite side of the road. Two platoons were then detailed to cover the French battery and one platoon the American gun. These platoons were dug in by 2000 hours when French HQ demanded 30 men to assist the French in Medjez itself. Accordingly one platoon was left to guard the American gun, the remainder moved into the village arriving at 2330 hours and rested.

20th November 1942. At 0500 hours the Company relieved the troops holding the Medjez bridge. The day was quiet. A patrol of one officer (Lieutenant Fogarty) and 10 ORs was sent at 2359 hours and returned at 0200 hours. Its role to investigate reported enemy movement across the river. The enemy were encountered attempting to cross. The enemy lost two killed, these bodies were searched. They were identified as parachutists.

At 0345 OC Detachment received orders that Medjez-el-Bab was to be evacuated and that he was to move to a position west of Oued Zarga (4136) some 6 kilometres. This position was held until 1500 hours when the Company withdrew to Beja.

21st November 1942. The Company was ordered to move to Oued Zarga to reinforce the French holding the bridge. OC liaison with the French at their HQ five kilometres west of the village and then moved to the bridge arriving at 2045 hours. The French company was holding a position west of the bridge which was mined and covered by MG fire from a range of about 700 yards. OC R Company decided to move forward of the bridge to thick cover south of the road. The Company was dug in by 2345 hours.

22nd November 1942. At 0200 hours a patrol of one officer (Lieutenant Gammon) and 10 ORs was ordered to recce the line of the road Oued Zarga-Medjez-el-Bab. This patrol contacted the enemy at 0215 hours only 300 yards from the Company position. The enemy of about a platoon in strength appeared to be pushing either an armoured car or gun down the road. There were more enemy further down the road. One enemy, probably a connecting file, was captured and a motorcycle combination was destroyed with a No 6 grenade. Two enemy were killed. The prisoner, a parachutist, was escorted to Beja and the patrol returned to the Company at about 0800 hours.

Forward elements of the enemy contacted the Company's forward defence lines at about 0230 hours and were driven back after a short fight. They then brought up to within 70 yards of the FDLs a gun of approx .500 calibre and opened fire on the bridge. At 0300 hours this gun was withdrawn some 700 yards and a mortar opened up on the Company locality. An attack was made on one section north of the road which was forced to withdraw. The driven off by a counter-attack by 2nd Lancs Fusiliers who had arrived at 0330 hours and taken over defended localities in the area of the bridge.

At dawn the enemy were seen digging in 700 yards in front of the Company position. Enemy artillery opened up on the bridge and LF positions. The Company position was periodically mortared until 0730 hours then the enemy withdrew. The remainder of the day was uneventful. Our casualties were four wounded. The enemy's strength during the nights fighting appeared to be about 80 with supporting arms. Two enemy dead were found opposite the Company sector.

23rd November 1942. At 1000 hours the Company moved out two miles south east of their position at the request of OC 2LF in order to distract the enemy's attention while two Companies of the LF moved to the high ground to the north overlooking Medjez-el-Bab. No contact was made with the enemy and the Company withdrew at 1230 hours. During the night the Company sent out local patrols but no contact was made with the enemy.

24th November 1942. One platoon moved into the French sector at the request of OC 2LF as the French had withdrawn. This platoon remained in position until 1700 hours. At 1000 hours at the request of 2LF a patrol of one officer (Captain Stewart) and 10 ORs from the Company and a section from 2LF moved out by MT towards Medjez, covered by carriers.

This patrol contacted the enemy and none returned. Captain Stewart's body was recovered several days later and it must be assumed that all were casualties.

25th November 1942. The Company was withdrawn to Beja. The day was uneventful.

Appendix XV

Gué Hill report by Lieutenant Wandless, 1st Parachute Battalion

23rd November 1942. When at approx 497673 I was leading 7 Platoon of S Company, Colonel Hill gave me the following orders – stated that enemy were on the hill point 163 4967 and 7 Platoon would get up on the north eastern side and snipe the enemy on the hill. I gained the foot of the hill on the north-east side and deployed the Platoon with 7 Section on the right, 8 in the centre and 9 on the left. Proceeded to climb the hill in extended order and soon came under MG fire from the top of the hill. Moved platoon forward into dead ground and stopped to try and locate positions.

Large numbers of grenades were then thrown down so I sent 7 Section round to the right to create a diversion and moved quickly with the remaining two Sections to the south east side of the hill and proceeded to advance up the hill. On this side there was more cover such as boulders. Soon after we again came under MG fire, this time very heavy and more grenades, but I was able to identify one MG position. Giving this as a target to the nearest Bren gunner, we advanced in short bounds covered by the Bren, until we were within throwing distance of the nearest MG. Threw some grenades and advanced to the top of the hill and immediately gave rapid fire onto the position and

The northern side of Gué Hill, note that in 1942 the lake was not there. (James Macrae)

then walked forward in line firing as we went. By this time all the enemy on the hill were killed or wounded. Before the final assault I had shouted to 7 Section to come round behind us which they did. They had got pinned down by fire on the right and were working their way to the left when they heard us shouting. There was one casualty, Private Shirley, Platoon Runner, who was hit by a grenade. L/Corporal Colville gave him attention under fire.

There was a MG 34 on a heavy mounting and a Breda LMG on the hill. There were five enemy dead including a German corporal and eight wounded. An Italian corporal who had run away was later taken prisoner. While in the process of consolidating and searching bodies I received an order to withdraw immediately to the road at 494678, subsequently returning to Sidi N'Sir.

Appendix XVI

Report by Lieutenant P. Mellor, 1st Parachute Battalion, on fighting patrol to Sidi Belhai (5967) Bizerte map Sheet 2 1/200,000 – 2nd December 1942

Information was received that a lorry was seen to stop at a farm to the right of the road about 1½ miles north of our position and about 20 men seen to get out and be making their way in the direction of Mateur. Two carriers and a Section of 10 men were sent to head them off and if possible take prisoners.

We worked our way well round to the right at first, then while sweeping round to the left to come on them unawares, we saw 4 or 5 Germans on the south slope of Sidi Belhai. We opened fire at once and one carrier moved round to the left of the hill. The ground here was very rocky. Two of our men at once started to lead one of the wounded Germans back to base as a prisoner. At the same the force, in two parties, engaged the enemy up on the two high points each of which seemed to be held by about one section with LMGs, small arms and stick grenades. As the object of the raid (i.e. a prisoner) had now been accomplished, and the position could not be taken owing to being outnumbered and commanded by the strongpoints, the force withdrew. One carrier was bellied on the rocks and could not be got going again and the other had a broken track and was out of action.

On arriving back at base it was discovered that the two men with the prisoner were missing, and it was assumed that they were captured on the way back.

Enemy casualties estimated about 5 dead and wounded. Our casualties 1 dead (Private Ballard), 2 wounded and 2 missing.

Time out: 1430. Time back: 1700

[Author's note. In spite of much searching of databases I have been unable to find any member of the 1st Parachute Battalion with the name Ballard being killed on this day. I can only assume he was severely wounded and not expected to survive and somehow the fact that he had been killed entered the report.]

Appendix XVII

Report by Lieutenant Colonel J.D. Frost MC commanding 2nd Parachute Battalion, 29th November-4th December 1942

29/11/1942

Emplaning
The Battalion emplaned at Maison Blanche aerodrome in 44 C47 aircraft. There was considerable confusion over the emplaning and loading of the containers owing to the markings of the aircraft, a last minute change in the number of aircraft available, the order in which the aircraft formed up being different from that which it was expected they would form up and heavy rain turning the aerodrome into thick mud.

The Mission
The Battalion was briefed as follows:- it was to drop near Pont du Fahs (J8/06) destroy enemy aircraft, stores and petrol there; then proceed to Depienne (J9717) where another landing ground was to be attacked; then on to Oudna (K0636) and finally strike north west to St Cyprien (J9048) where contact was to be made with armoured elements of 1st Army.

On the morning of 29/11/1942 information was received that the enemy was not using Pont du Fahs therefore the mission was altered to a drop at Depienne, an attack on the landing ground at Oudna and a link up with the 1st Army at St Cyprien.

The Flight
The flight was uneventful – the leading aircraft took off at 11.30 hours but owing to various delays the whole force was not airborne until 12.30 hours. Long range Hurricanes, Lightnings and Spitfires from Le Kef were escort. The aircraft flew high to clear the mountains and the temperature dropped to zero. No great discomfort was felt, however, though some men in the rear aircraft were sick. Approx 30 miles from Depienne the aircraft came down to 600 feet and approached the DZ at this level.

The Drop
First aircraft dropped its section at 4.50 hours. The pilot of the leading aircraft chose the DZ which was mostly plough. A large water course crossed the middle which considerably delayed some sections in reaching their containers. A number of sticks were dropped some distance from the main body. A total area over which the men and containers were dropped being 1½ miles by ½ mile. A number of containers failed to come off and some

container chutes failed to open. There were some casualties on landing including one dead.

Action on landing

Battalion HQ was immediately established in some ruins north of Depienne. A Company was ordered to hold the area north of the DZ to block the road leading north and to prevent any local inhabitants from leaving and to commandeer all transport. B Company were ordered to occupy Depienne and to commandeer all transport. C Company were ordered to take up positions south of the DZ, to block the road running east and salvage parachutes and containers from the DZ. Major Teichman, the Battalion 2 i/c was sent into the village to arrange for storage of parachutes with the Gendarmes and also to arrange for transport. There was no MT available but a number of mule carts were impressed.

The injured were driven to Depienne by a local French official and were placed in the schoolhouse there. The local French were very friendly and helpful. I was informed that the Germans had been in occupation until three days before but had withdrawn to the north, that there were many Italian civilians in the neighbourhood and that there were German detachments in the area Djebel Oust (J9923).

At approx 16.00 hours three armoured cars from the Yeomanry appeared on the road running north from Depienne. The commander informed me that he was patrolling north as far as Cheylus (K0228) where a German roadblock was suspected. He returned at 17.00 hours with information that there was a roadblock east of Djebel Oust and that he could not go as far as Cheylus. He said he would report us and would arrange to evacuate the injured from Depienne as soon as possible.

Lieutenant Charteris was sent forward with a small patrol to recce routes forward. Orders were given at 22.00 hours. The Battalion was to be formed up by the road by midnight in the following order:- C Company, Advanced Battalion HQ, B Company, Rear Battalion HQ, Mortars, Signals, A Company. Lieutenant Buchanan was to remain at Depienne to complete arrangements for salvage, evacuate the injured and collect a section of his platoon which was thought to have dropped some distance to the south. He was then to move north by the hills to contact the Battalion south of Oudna.

30/11/1942

The Battalion moved off as ordered at 00.15 hours. A certain amount of mortar equipment and ammunition was loaded on mule carts also wireless sets and RE stores. In spite of this considerable fatigue was felt by the RE and mortar personnel and incidentally by the mules. Our route was by the road for one mile, then by tracks across the hills into the Djebel St Dou Jadjessa. The track was fairly well defined but very steep and rough in parts so that progress was slow. No local inhabitants were encountered but the barking of dogs showed the presence of native dwellings not far from our route. After covering approx 12 miles the Battalion was halted. Pickets were put out and at 04.30 hours the men were allowed to sleep. It was bitterly cold so that very little real rest could be had. The Battalion stood to at 06.00 hours. At approx 07.00 hours 2 German aircraft flew over but we were not observed.

At 07.15 hours orders were given. B Company were to act as advance guard to the Battalion. They were to move in bounds and halt in area Prise de l'Eau (map Oudna

Sheet 28). A Company were to picket the hills between the axis of advance and the main Oudna-Depienne road. Battalion HQ and C Company were to follow B Company. Communications were maintained by WS18 sets and the move was carried out without incident. Again it was apparent that the men were far too heavily loaded and the Mortar Platoon was unable to keep up with Battalion HQ.

By 11.00 hours the Battalion was established in position at Prise de l'Eau, A Company forward on the left. B Company disposed centrally round the well. Battalion HQ immediately east of the road and C Company on the left with positions facing the rear.

There were a number of Arabs in the area but it was not possible to stop all movement of them; all mules, donkeys and horses were commandeered. Local Arabs informed us that the landing ground at Oudna was not being used by the Axis and that all the enemy troops were withdrawing to Tunis. The landing ground could be plainly seen from our positions and one crashed aircraft was observed on the centre. Otherwise there was no activity of any kind apart from the sound of bombing or artillery fire well to the north. The men were given permission to brew tea, fill water bottles and wash. By this time it was fairly hot. A Company reported an enemy patrol consisting of armoured cars and lorries moving south along the road Oudna-Depienne.

At 12.30 hours the following orders were given:- A Company were to move forward by the most direct route towards Oudna with the object of making a complete recce of and with the object of occupying the landing ground. B Company were to move around to the right of Henchir Oudna, a dominating feature. C Company were to move along either side of the main ridge of the Djebel St Bou Hadjeba with Battalion HQ and Mortar Platoon. At 13.15 hours A Company moved off and by 13.30 hours the whole Battalion was on the move.

At 14.30 hours the sound of mortar and machine gun fire was heard to the north and a message was received from A Company that they were being fired upon from a low ridge near St Bon Sakouma. They had suffered a few casualties and requested assistance on their left; I ordered C Company forward on the left and B Company to close in behind as reserve and pushed on myself with a skeleton HQ. I also sent a message to the Mortar Platoon to follow as fast as they possibly could. By the time I was in a position to read the battle, A Company had moved forward again. The Company was very skilfully handled by Major Ashford and by 15.30 hours the enemy had withdrawn to the north of the landing ground and A Company were in position on the ridge at St Bon Sakouma, while a Platoon under Lieutenant Rendell had occupied Oudna Railway station. By 16.00 hours C Company were well on their way forward and at 16.15 hours had occupied the farm Tete Amont de Siphon.

It was now possible to confirm beyond all doubt that the enemy were not using the landing ground. There were four native tents on the open ground south of the railway, which it was thought might contain stores. They were found however to be hayricks. At 16.30 hours five German heavy tanks appeared on the west of the landing ground and began to shell and machine gun C Company's positions; Lieutenant Morrison was killed. Gammon bombs were thrown at one tank but it was not possible to estimate damage. The tanks made no attempt to approach our position but were able to dominate the situation.

At 16.30 Messerschmitt fighters (Me 109s) came over the area, they made several low flights over our forward positions and then began several low flying machine gun attacks. Although no casualties were caused they paralyzed movement. Owing to the vital importance of conserving ammunition I had given orders that the enemy aircraft were not to be fired at. Our camouflage smocks and nets made it almost impossible to observe us and most of their attacks were made at unoccupied ground.

At 17.00 hours a flight of six Stukas passed overhead but dropped no bombs. Now as the whole object of the mission had been to destroy aircraft etc on Oudna and there were no aircraft to destroy, I made plans for moving westward to link up with the 1st Army. I had been informed that an armoured thrust was to be made on Tunis but from our positions no sign of any battle or large-scale movement could be seen and I decided to withdraw during darkness to our positions at Prise de l'Eau. Our positions near Oudna were very insecure, the enemy had had time to make a thorough recce of our probable dispositions and by this time I knew the enemy had considerable armoured forces in the area.

C Company were withdrawn to the hills behind B Company at dusk and a Platoon from B Company was sent forward to conform with the area held by A Company. At about 19.00 hours elements of C Company withdrawing became engaged with the enemy. Two of the hayricks had been set alight by fire from the tanks and there were sounds which indicated that the enemy were blowing up a dump of ammunition in the area. I considered sending B Company forward to obtain more exact information and destroy any enemy in the area but by now it became imperative to reorganise and rest A and C Companies. At 21.00 hours I ordered a withdrawal to the same positions as we held in the morning astride the road Prise de l'Eau. By 22.00 the withdrawal was completed; again the night was bitterly cold and it was not possible to get much sleep.

1/12/1942

During the morning I received a wireless message informing me that the armoured thrust on Tunis had been postponed. I appreciated that this made my position untenable and in fact precarious. I knew the enemy had considerable armoured forces on the plains, that he had a considerable number of lorried infantry, that all the roads in the area were frequently patrolled by armoured cars, that Zaghouan in my rear was occupied, that I was only 15 miles from Tunis and 30 to 40 miles from the nearest points which I knew to be held by our own troops i.e. Medjez-el-Bab and Tebourba.

For the moment my own position was fairly secure. We were in positions for all round defence. We had water and I was confident that we could hold out against anything but a full scale attack from a force of all arms. I decided therefore to remain where I was until noon, then to move into the hills and secure positions from which I could move across the plains at night. An ambush was arranged in the bottleneck south of Prise de l'Eau and all ranks were ordered not to fire at any enemy vehicles coming up the road until this bottle neck was reached.

At approx 10.00 hours a force consisting of two tanks, two armoured cars and lorries drawing guns was seen approaching from the north. They halted about 1,200 yards from our positions and one armoured car came forward alone. Unfortunately this car surprised a small party filling water bottles at the well. An Italian officer leaning out of the turret was shot and a Gammon bomb was thrown but missed and the car was able to escape and rejoin his force. This then deployed and began shelling our positions from 1,200 yards. The mortars were brought into action and the enemy withdrew leaving a number of bodies behind (believed 6). They halted after moving approx a mile and appeared to be reorganising. It is thought that they suffered a number of casualties as a result of our mortar fire, several bombs were seen to fall amongst them.

At approx 11.00 hours a force consisting of two armoured cars and one tank appeared on the road from the south. The leading AFV displayed two yellow triangles which deceived the NCO in charge of the anti-tank rifle crew covering the road. The NCO went forward waving his own yellow triangle and was taken prisoner. He was made to walk in front of the AFV which went up to the remainder of the crew and captured them. The NCO was then sent to Battalion HQ with a demand from the Germans to surrender as the position was surrounded. A party was sent around the hill to the rear to cut them off but before they could be reached the enemy opened fire and made off. During the time the enemy were halted they were in a deep depression, which could not be reached by any of our anti-tank weapons, except that which we had captured. The enemy then began desultory shelling of our positions from long range.

At 12.00 hours the Battalion started moving to new positions in the hills, B Company picqueting to the right and C Company to the left with A Company as rearguard. All wounded were sent to a farm near Prise de l'Eau under Lieutenant McGavin RAMC. By 14.30 hours the Battalion was in new positions in the hills called Djebel St Bon Hadjeba (map reference K 050270). There was a spring in the Battalion area and good observation could be had of the plain. Considerable enemy activity was noted. Columns of AFVs and light artillery were moving north to south.

At 15.00 hours enemy lorried infantry was seen moving up to attack in half-tracked vehicles, tanks were also seen and our positions were shelled and mortared. B Company were ordered to push forward onto the hill overlooking the houses but were unable to do so. At the same time enemy were seen approaching on all sides. No further manoeuvre was attempted and it became a matter of holding on until dark. The enemy put their maximum effort against C Company who beat off all infantry attacks, but they suffered very heavy casualties from mortars which were behind the farm houses. The tank at Y was knocked out by Gammon bombs and anti-tank rifle fire but those at W could not be silenced. A section of B Company knocked out one at X and immobilised the other two, but could not get near enough to destroy them. At 17.00 hours Messerschmitt fighters appeared and flew low over our positions, later they were seen diving and opening fire on enemy locations. Not once did they fire at any of our positions. Towards dusk the attack tailed off, the shelling ceased and the enemy appeared to withdraw.

I decided to split up into Company groups and RV in the morning at Massicault. In my original instructions I was told to make for St Cyprien in order to link up with the armoured thrust; this I knew had been postponed and probably had not taken place. On the way to Massicault we would pass the Djebel el Mengoub which offered distinct possibilities as a place to lie up in should Massicault be in enemy hands. Lieutenant Playford was ordered to remain with his Platoon to collect the wounded and take them to the farm at Prise de l'Eau where they could be attended to, he was then to move south towards Depienne and attempt to meet the recce patrol operating in that area. The order for withdrawal was B Company, Battalion HQ and mortars, followed by A Company with remnants of C Company. The signal for beginning the withdrawal was given by myself on a hunting horn. I estimate the dead and wounded at this stage to be 150 killed and wounded from the time the Battalion dropped.

The withdrawal of B Company proceeded and I then followed with Battalion HQ, we allowed B Company to get well ahead. The route to the plains was very steep and difficult in the dark. I led the Battalion HQ group with Lieutenant Charteris, we checked as soon as we reached the foothills and found all HQ present, we marched on a bearing of 312 degrees. The going was in the main difficult, large fields of plough had to be crossed and all ranks were feeling exhausted. We had had no real rest for 48 hours and had been moving over mountainous country all that time; also very heavy loads had to be carried. The rough ground was responsible for a number of cases of sore feet and as there had been no time to attend to these, a few cases of septicaemia had set in. There were two deep riverbeds which had to be crossed and the River Milane also. Water bottles were filled from the river, the water was brackish and only just drinkable.

2/12/1942

A halt was called at 01.00 hours and we slept till 02.30 hours. At this halt it was noticed Major Teichman the 2 i/c and Captain Short, the Adjutant were missing. The march continued at 03.00 hours, rain fell, no local inhabitants were encountered. On one occasion a shot was fired from some distance away. By 06.00 hours we were north-east of, and about a mile from Djebel el Mengoub (J3536) and I decided to halt until daylight, then to look for water, rest and information. At 07.30 hours Lieutenant Charteris went with a small party to recce a farm approx half a mile to the north, he returned at 08.00 hours and reported that the farm was inhabited by friendly Arabs, that plenty of shelter and water was available. He had obtained information that Massicault was occupied by the enemy but that Furna was occupied by Allied Forces. Battalion HQ then moved to the farm. A picket was placed on the hill behind, overlooking the farm and the surrounding country, the men cooked breakfast and washed.

At 09.30 hours an Arab brought information that another party of British were in a farm about half a mile to the east. Contact was made and at approx 10.00 hours Major Ashford arrived. He reported that his company had arrived safely in the area, that the owners of the farm in which his company were billeted were French who had warned him that the area was frequently patrolled by German armoured cars and that both farms were visited by enemy patrols. I then decided to concentrate at the Battalion HQ farm (which will be called el Fedja). A Company were sent for and I made plans for defence. I decided that the enemy would not be able to launch a strong attack until fairly late in the day and that provided we could hold out till dark we would then be able to move about the country again.

At about 11.30 hours I saw a German motor cycle combination on a ridge about one and a half miles away which appeared to be making a reconnaissance of el Fedja. 'Stand To' positions were ordered. Lieutenant Charteris and two men were sent to Furna to contact Allied Forces alleged to be there, he was to return as soon as possible and not later than dark. At 12.00 hours A Company arrived and were placed in position. At 13.30 hours a column of armoured cars was seen moving slowly to the south about two miles away. At 14.00 hours enemy infantry were observed setting up machine guns and mortars on and behind a ridge to the north. By this time there was very little ammunition left and orders were given that no enemy would be engaged at more than

50 yards. Otherwise there was to be no movement or noise in the farm area, the silence on our part seemed to mystify the enemy.

At approx 15.00 hours they opened fire with machine guns and mortars, the mortar fire was concentrated on the orchard near the farm but only one casualty was caused. The farm buildings were not hit; towards dusk the machine gun fire became more intense, most of it was very high and it appeared that some machine guns were firing at each other. So much so that at one time we thought Allied units were on the hills to the south and some of the more imaginative men fancied they heard words being shouted in English.

Very careful observation was kept on the road running east past the hayricks as I intended to move out by this route in the dark. An enemy machine gun was located in this area at 16.00 hours but it moved after firing a number of bursts at the farm. Towards dusk the enemy became very bold and a party with two officers approached within 5 yards of the cactus hedge surrounding the orchard at A. They were killed with grenades and Sten fire. I gave orders that when I blew my hunting horn everyone was to leave his position, run past Battalion HQ and out to the south east passing near the hayricks and so out into Djebel el Mengoub where they would rally. We had not sufficient ammunition left to fight another battle and I estimated that the enemy were approx 4 to 1 stronger in numbers. Lieutenant Charteris had not returned so I presumed that we were still a long way from other British forces.

At about 18.00 hours the enemy attacked, their main effort coming in at B; this was beaten back and a number of Germans killed or wounded. Similarly a party of enemy approached near A and the whole party were killed or wounded with grenades and Sten gun fire. At 16.15 hours the signal for withdrawal was given and the Battalion moved off according to plan. The enemy made no further attack. It was however difficult to collect everyone in the dark. All had been told to make for Medjez-el-Bab. Battalion HQ and A Company mustered approx 100 when a halt was called in the hills, the remainder had been seen moving further to the south with Captain Vernon and the REs. At first I intended to strike north west to join the main Tunis-Medjez road, but when we reached a secondary road at Bou Khail (J8539). I decided to move towards Medjez along it; we stopped to fill water bottles at a well along the route. At midnight a halt was called for one hour.

3/12/1942

The march continued. At approx 03.00 hours some inhabitants of a farm were roused for information and they confirmed my suspicion that enemy armoured units were in the area. Almost immediately after leaving this position we joined forces with Captain Vernon's party who had arrived on the same road by a different route. By this time 04.00 hours all ranks were feeling extreme fatigue and we decided to lay up until dawn at the next farm. This happened to be at a road and track junction (J7837), the inhabitants were French, very friendly and helpful. By 05.00 hours the men were all under cover, sentries were posted and rest was obtained. At 06.00 hours 'Stand To' was ordered and some tea was made.

The French warned me that an Arab known to be pro-German had left to inform the enemy of our whereabouts. I decided to move back towards the high ground near Ksar Tyr (J7531) which was thought to be held by British units. During the move an

Arab who appeared to be taking undue interest in our movements was fired at. When the high ground near Ksar Tyr was reached Medjez and the main road could be seen and I decided to move across the open ground in open formation. There were sounds of a battle coming from the direction of Tebourba. There were a number of orchards between us and Sidi Medien (J7133) where I decided to join the main road. An Arab informed us that Ksar Tyr and Sidi Medien contained small numbers of enemy but that Medjez-el-Bab was strongly held by the Allies. We halted in the last orchard in St Medien to eat a meal. At 12.00 hours an unidentified armoured car was observed leaving St Medien and later another. I learned that the enemy had just vacated St Medien (i.e. 2 armoured cars).

Shortly after reaching the main road an American armoured patrol was observed approaching across country from the north, they joined us on the road and gave me, the walking wounded and a small party a lift into Medjez-el-Bab. We arrived at about 16.00 hours. The wounded were taken to a dressing station and billets and rations were arranged for the Battalion. At 17.00 hours I met the CRE 78th Division who took me to Divisional HQ at Oued Zarga. There I reported to General Eveleigh; Captain Moore who was Liaison Officer to 1st Army was there and arrangements were made for an armoured patrol to search the country over which we had been moving on the following morning. The patrol was to leave Medjez-el-Bab at 07.00 hours. I then returned to Medjez-el-Bab.

4/12/1942

At 05.00 hours an Officer arrived at my HQ and informed me that a heavy bombing attack was expected at first light, followed by German parachute troops. The Battalion was roused and positions were taken up outside and to the west of the town. The attack did not materialise. At 08.00 hours the Battalion was lifted in TCVs to Sloughia (J5126). The day was spent in resting and washing. At 14.00 hours Major Ross and a small party arrived. A defence plan was coordinated with the French at Sloughia and the Battalion was moved into Arab houses for the night. The French were very helpful and friendly; the night passed without incident.

Appendix XVIII

Report on failure of some Field Ambulance Personnel to accompany 2nd Battalion Parachute Regiment on Sunday 29th November 1942

To Lieutenant Colonel MacEwan DFC TD OC 16 Parachute Field Ambulance
Personnel left behind:- 1 Officer, 7 Other Ranks
Surgical Team:- Lieutenant Longland, Private Howe, Private Keates, Private Roberts, Private Thompson and Private Sykes
No 2 Section:- S/Sergeant Lewis and Corporal Dewey
Containers left behind:- 5
Numbers 37, 0, I, II and IIII
Container 36 IIII was also left behind but was found to be empty.
Planes concerned:-
6 S/Sergeant Lewis and Cpl Dewey Container 37 0
14 Container 37 I
44 Lieutenant Longland and Private Howe
46 Private Keates, Private Roberts, Private Thompson and Private Sykes Containers 37 III and IIII

Sequence of events

At the briefing on Saturday evening 28.11.42 numbers of planes on which Field Ambulance personnel were to travel and their allocation of Field Ambulance men and containers were given by OC 2nd Battalion. On Sunday morning 29.11.42 the containers were taken to the aerodrome early by a baggage party.

The remainder of the Field Ambulance Section and the Surgical Team with their personal haversacks followed in a truck detailed for them, arriving at Maison Blanche at about 11.05 a.m.

Personal haversacks were put in the containers which were in the hangar used that morning. It was then found that there were no metal bands for the cradles for many of the containers. The medical personnel were the last to arrive at the airfield and their containers were the last to be filled with personal haversacks. By the time this had been done the supply of metal bands had been exhausted and had to be improvised. Because of the delay S/Sergeant Lewis and Corporal Dewey missed plane 6 which took off soon after 11.30 a.m.

Four men of the Surgical Team found their plane (46) but were told by the pilot that he could only take two men, not four men and two containers as allocated, because he feared overloading. There were insufficient parachutes for the men; who in any case could not take their equipment. They did not emplane, the aircraft taking off shortly afterwards.

Myself and Private Howe found our plane, 44, drew chutes from the nearby lorry and fitted them. We were unable to pack our personal haversacks in the containers being loaded on to the plane, which were full to capacity and took them into the plane with us.

The plane took off after some delay, apparently due to uncertainty about loading the containers, about 12.45 and headed eastwards. After crossing the range of mountains the pilot decided to return because he was unable to see any other planes of the formation, and had no fighter protection. In my own view it would have been feasible to fly much further east to continue the search, but the pilot would not agree to this point of view and landed at Maison Blanche about 13.15 hours.

Summary.
The lorry taking the Section to the airfield arrived too late.
There were insufficient bands for the cradles.
In one case the pilot would not accept the men and containers allocated to him.
C. Longland
Lieutenant
In the Field 30.11.42

Appendix XIX

Memories of Andrew Young, 2nd Parachute Battalion, regarding the Oudna Airfield mission November 1942

The 2nd Battalion, Parachute Regiment sailed from Greenock on 1st November 1942 and my Company (C Company) sailed on the *Strathmore*, accompanied by several other ships. We were bound for Algeria, arriving at Algiers on 12th November 1942. Under the command of Lieutenant Colonel John Frost, the battalion marched approximately 10 miles from Algiers to Maison Blanche and used a school there as a base until Lieutenant Colonel Frost received orders for an operation in Tunisia. Our mission was to destroy German aircraft at Oudna airfield, then to move off to the northwest and join up with the armoured forces of the 1st Army in the St. Cyprien area.

The battalion of 530 men boarded approximately 40 American Dakotas at midday on the 29th November 1942 and we took off from the airfield at Maison Blanche. We flew over the Atlas Mountains before descending to a height of 600ft in preparation for being dropped near Depienne. Lieutenant Colonel Frost was in the leading Dakota and he dropped first, followed by the rest of the battalion. During the landing one man was killed when his parachute failed to open and a few were injured. Major John Ross led C Company, and we were tasked with securing the area to the south of the drop zone, including the road leading southeast to Zaghouan. We also had to recover the parachutes and weapons containers.

Lieutenant Buchanan of C Company was tasked with gathering together men who had jumped south of the drop zone and hadn't yet joined up with the battalion at Depienne. Once these men had been grouped, they were to evacuate those injured during the landing that were being cared for at a school in Depienne, and then rejoin the rest of the battalion. As things turned out, Lieutenant Buchanan and his men were attacked by German forces and, after an exchange of fire during which many paras were wounded, they were forced to surrender, hopelessly outnumbered by the Germans. I remember hearing that after the paras surrendered a German captain handed them over to the Italian Army and they were led to a nearby farmhouse. A jeep carrying a high-ranking German officer approached and he ordered the Italians to shoot the paras. They were lined up against a wall and were about to be shot when an armoured car pulled up. A commander of a German *Fallschirmjäger* (Parachute Regiment) got out the car and had an angry discussion with the high-ranking officer. The commander eventually turned to the paras and told them that they were prisoners of war and would be treated as such – he basically saved their lives.

In 1942 the airfield at Oudna was located behind the line of trees in the middle of the photograph. (James Macrae)

In the early hours of 30th November, C Company led the battalion on the way to Oudna. We took a route through the hills and the march was very difficult due to the terrain. After approximately 12 miles we stopped for a rest, but it was a cold night and the decision was made to set off again just after 07.00 hours with B Company leading the way this time. By late morning we reached a plain overlooking Oudna airfield and we stopped again whilst Lieutenant Colonel Frost considered his options. He decided that A Company should move towards Oudna and occupy the airfield. However, in the process of carrying out this manoeuvre they came under attack at Sidi Bou Sakouma and suffered casualties. C Company was moved to join up with A Company and assisted to recover the position, with the Germans retreating northwards. Not long after 16.00 hours, C Company took over a farmhouse at Tete Amont de Siphon, whilst another part of the battalion moved to occupy Oudna railway station. When A Company eventually reached Oudna airfield they found that there were no aircraft there to be destroyed.

As we were awaiting further orders at the farmhouse at Tete Amont de Siphon, German tanks approached from the west and attacked us with heavy shell and machine gun fire. Then we came under air attack from two Messerschmitt 109s that appeared on the scene and made several passes at low-level with their machine guns firing. We were ordered not to fire at the fighter planes, as we had to conserve our ammunition. During one of the low-level passes made by the Me 109s, I was shot in the right leg and later captured by a Romanian soldier of the German *Fallschirmjäger*.

After being captured, I was transferred to what I can only describe as a dungeon, somewhere in Italy, where I remained for 3 months. I was then admitted to a military hospital as the wound in my leg hadn't been treated properly and gangrene was beginning to set in. I was hospitalised for almost 1 year and have the skill of an Italian doctor to thank for saving my leg. After being released from hospital, I was transferred to a POW camp in Germany where I remained for almost 2 years until the end of the war.

In the days that followed after I was captured, the battalion, particularly C Company, suffered heavy casualties as they fought their way to the safety of the British 1st Army positions at Medjez-El-Bab. In total, 16 officers and 250 soldiers, many of them Scots, were killed, injured or captured during the operation. It had been badly planned and based on inaccurate information that resulted in us being dropped into an area surrounded by German and Italian forces backed with armoured support. The fact that there were no aircraft at Oudna airfield meant that the operation had been completely unnecessary.

Appendix XX

My memories of the drop at Depienne by Lieutenant P. Stainforth, 1st Parachute Squadron RE

The crew compartment door opened, all the bodies sprawled in the seats shook themselves awake and began to fidget with their jumping equipment. The crew chief entered wearing steel helmet and rip cord parachute and worked his way carefully aft over the static lines. "We've crossed the frontier, men!" he said. "Twenty minutes to go! Those of you who aren't hooked-up had better get ready. We may run into trouble from a bunch of Krauts any minute now!"

I came to with a start. The crew chief's words suddenly focused the full reality of our position on a brain which had been eager to forget it, and I felt horribly sick for the first time during the flight. In some embarrassment I called hastily for the bucket and parted company with the early breakfast I had eaten at Maison Carre, nine hours before. I felt better immediately, but at the same time most annoyed that I should have to fight on an empty stomach. The flight had been most dumpy during the whole of the past two and a half hours, but my mind had been so absorbed in the landscape that I had hardly noticed the air pockets, the yawning, the up currents rocking the wings, and the plane slowing, trying desperately to maintain our packed formation. Many of the men however, had suffered misery from airsickness.

Soon after taking off we had begun to climb, exchanging the rolling farmland of the coastal belt for the wild uplands which make of the foothills of the Atlas round Bouira. Algiers faded behind the mist hanging like muslin over the bay, and all at once we were above a tangled wilderness of rock and thorn, too uninviting for even the Arabs to attempt to till. The country grew wilder as we flew on, until gradually losing the last traces of vegetation, it became desolate world of saw-tooth ridges and scar-like ravines, hills, valleys, peaks and spurs, all heaped together in a chaos of earth and rock.

We stole in on the mountains, so that I was unaware of their presence until we were right amongst them. The lumps of rock grew bigger, more wild and fierce, and heaved themselves hungrily at our wings as we passed. Then a sandstone giant appeared beside us, reached out a jagged spur to knock us out of the sky, and turned his back on us as we flew on. After that the mountains were on every side, rearing terrible peaks high above the formation. Conscious of our own insignificance, we threaded our way carefully through their midst, following a natural pass.

The sight was so awe inspiring that it baffles description. It was gigantic, terrible, wonderful and savage, all together – at times I felt as though we were trespassing upon nature. Huge buzzards wheeled and volplaned round the peaks, angry and defiant that their long solitude had been disturbed by a flock of winged creatures so much larger than themselves. They screamed their disapproval, but no one heard. The mountains bared their sandstone teeth and promised us a rocky grave at the bottom of a thousand foot abyss if we dared to go too close.

There was something so fascinating about the fierceness of their beauty that one felt lonely and frustrated when we flew out on the other side of the range on to low foothills and then rolling country covered with olive groves. The pigmy world of primitive cultivation below us, sandy cart tracks, haphazard clusters of crude Arab dwellings, all appeared so futile and worthless beside the immortal mountains. My mind was still trying to retain something of their grandeur, even though it was now invaded by man's squalor. Then, to complete the transition from dreams to reality, there was the crew chief picking his way down the fuselage, shouting above the roar of engines that battle lay ahead only twenty minutes ahead.

We took some little time to get each other hooked up. My next door neighbour passed me in the end of my static line over my right shoulder. I gave it a tug and pulled about six foot out of the parachute pack. I was unusually clumsy all of a sudden and had difficulty in fastening the safety pin which seared the snap hook. Measures came round and checked our equipment. "You all right?" he enquired, bending over me. I fingered my quick release box, checked the snap hook and strop and nodded in reply.

"How do you feel?" I asked him. "Ok so far! I'll feel a lot happier when it's all over! Look! There go the Spitfires! Whew! What a superb sight!"

I looked out of my foot-square Perspex window and saw three dark furies rushing over the surface of the plain. They banked as one and rose silently to meet us, fast as shooting stars.

"Five minutes to go! Stand up!" Measures shouted. We clambered awkwardly to our feet, fidgeted with our length of hanging static line, then crowded up in line behind number one who crouched in the doorway. We clung to the sides of the fuselage – the plane was bucking all over the sky in trying to keep formation – and waited for the red warning light. Everyone was silent, and there was an electric tension in the air. The seconds went by slowly. Then the red winked on and shone like an evil eye.

A few seconds later, number one had plunged out, and his static line cracked against the rear edge of the door. The line surged towards the tail and melted before the square of sunlight. Almost before I knew what had happened I was scrambling for the aperture and lunged outwards into space.

I stood up, slipped out of my parachute harness and jumping jacket, then slipped a thirty round magazine on to my Sten machine gun.

Everywhere other figures were getting to their feet and moving across the dropping zone. The last flight of three aircraft came over and dropped their bouquet of coloured parachutes, followed by the train of men. The canopies sank earthwards gently in the hot afternoon and joined the harvest of mottled parachutes already abandoned on the ground.

We had landed in a field of hard plough divided by a muddy stream. About three hundred yards away lay a large Arab farm surrounded by a high cactus hedge, and a dusty road, marked by a row of telephone poles, ran north and south. We were in the middle of a plain of sun scorched earth, broken only by cactus hedges and clumps of camel thorn. All round the open country there ran a wall of rocky hills, rising steadily in a jumbled mess. In the south-east towered a massive needle of sandstone, the Djebel Zaghouan, the highest mountain in Tunisia – over seven thousand feet. After the warmth of colour and rich fertility of Algeria, this fizzled landscape looked a desert.

Sapper Madden joined me a moment later, and we hurried off to look for our container. We found it at last among the reeds, lying half under water in the stream. Two or three men with containers in a similar plight came and gave us a hand, and we dragged it to dry land by the rigging lines. The contents were fairly dry thanks to their protective coverings.

C Company Headquarters and rendezvous was marked by a white star on a large red sheet. The wireless section was installed in a ditch beneath a cactus hedge and was reporting to battalion headquarters. Most of the infantry had already arrived, and the platoons had taken up defensive positions around the farm.

The rest of my section came along in a moment. Two of my men were missing, together with half a platoon of C Company, with whom they had been. We heard that their plane had become bogged down in the mud at Maison Blanche and had been unable to take off. My wireless set had been smashed in the drop, and our trolley too, was in bits, as its parachute had failed to open.

The Battalion had suffered about fifteen to twenty injuries, mostly 'concussions' and sprained ankles and wrists, from heavy landings in gullies and plough. But there was a fatal accident, due, in parachuting jargon, to a 'Roman candle'. One of Dennis's (Captain Vernon's) sappers had been killed by rigging lines getting thrown over the canopy, causing it to stream out like a wind-sock, too hopelessly entangled to develop. Sapper Craighan, the dead man, had swapped the parachute he drew from the stores with Cpl Halliwell, because he was superstitious and it had been numbered 13.

The landing ground was not occupied by the enemy. In fact, there was little evidence that the airfield had ever existed. Intelligence seemed to be very much in fault, and we had drawn a blank at our first foray.

We were operating on Greenwich Mean Time – two hours behind 1st Army time – and it would be quite dark by four o'clock. In the two hours of daylight that remained we collected our parachutes and containers into the barns, and foraging parties went round all the neighbouring farms to procure mules and carts for our march to Oudna. Meanwhile our Padre, Murdo Macdonald, officiated at a short burial service of our dead comrade at the place where he had fallen to his death.

We left our dropping casualties in the care of friendly French farmers in Depienne. Buchanan of C Company – whose half-platoon it was that had not arrived stayed to protect the injured with the rest of his men, to await our advance guard from Pont-du-Fahs.

Meanwhile we had received a report from one of our armoured car patrols that the Germans had a roadblock about four miles up the road in the direction of Tunis. But our 1:50,000 maps showed a track leading to Oudna through the hills to the north east of us, and, in consultation with the company commanders, the colonel decided that we should take this. It was decided, too, that we should not start till ten o'clock. Our intentions would be obvious if we left as soon as it was dark; we should stand a better chance by giving the impression that we were staying there for the night and then slipping away quietly when the countryside had settled down. The men could have a meal and some rest before the next phase, for they were now very tired after their long day and the strain of the jump.

The temperature dropped suddenly after sun down. We were, of course, only lightly clad under our smocks and were thankful for the parachutes we had salvaged during the afternoon. We wrapped ourselves in the heaps of silk, to snatch what was to be the last real sleep for four days and nights.

When we moved out of cover shortly before ten and formed up on the road facing north, a wonderful array of Arab carts, donkeys and mules had been added to our cavalcade; and on to these we bundled our heavy explosive and incendiary packs, our mortars, anti-tank rifles and wireless sets. Major Ross, OC C Company, gathered all his officers together and pointed out our route on the map with the aid of a shielded torch. I totted up the kilometres and reckoned the distance to be about eighteen miles.

The column moved off. We marched in silence, and except for the occasional of jingling of harness and creak of carts there was nothing audible save the dull murmur of a thousand padding feet.

Soon we turned off up a broad and well-trodden track, and the column straggled out into single file. Our numbers quickly faded with the background, and it now seemed that I was alone with two or three companions among the rocks and scrub. Occasionally, there would be the rustle of clothing close at hand and the slither of feet as though the hills were peopled with ghosts. The moon came up about midnight, and we could see the tail of our column winding like a snake far below, whilst above us the advance-guards had just topped the ridge and were moving like flies across the skyline. In the silvery half-light there appeared to be no end to our force.

The moon did not help us much, for the track rapidly got worse and sometimes petered out altogether. Marching became impossible over the layers of rock and stone, and the men swore, floundering and slipping at every step. Animals heaved and grunted as they dragged the creaking carts over boulders and scrub. Often they would be jerked to a stop, as wheels jammed in a crevice or stuck on a rock edge, and the carts would have to be man-handled forward to an accompaniment of shouts and curses. The work became heavier as the hours went by and the track deteriorated further. Every cart had to be hauled up the steep hills and this added to the exhaustion which had already laid its hold on the battalion. When a halt was called we lay face downwards in the heather and sobbed for breath, until the night air dried our sweat and chilled our bodies, and we were glad to be on the move again. When the track disappeared we plunged straight through the undergrowth in front of us, too tired to look for a better way. Progress was intolerably slow, and sometimes it seems as though we floundered in quick sand, getting nowhere but merely sapping our strength. The hills were bewitched that night.

By four o'clock in the morning when the moon was beginning to wane, we estimated that we had come ten miles; neither men nor animals were in any such condition to go further. We had put the worst of our march behind us, so the colonel called a halt until dawn. We dragged our carts off the track until the undergrowth and lay down on the cold earth, falling asleep immediately.

Appendix XXI

Roll of Honour for the 2nd Battalion Group for the Oudna operation (29th November-6th December 1942) with their date of death and grave location or commemoration on a memorial to the missing

29th November 1942
Sergeant D. Grieve MM Enfidaville CWGC Cemetery 2A2
Private E. Harrison NKG Medjez-el-Bab Memorial to the Missing
Private G. Jenkins Enfidaville CWGC Cemetery 6B22
Sergeant A. Prentice NKG Medjez-el-Bab Memorial to the Missing

Massicault CWGC Cemetery, where some of the 2nd Parachute Battalion who fell in the Oudna operation are buried. (James Macrae)

Headstones at Massicault for seven of the 2nd Parachute Battalion casualties. (James Macrae)

30th November 1942
L/Corporal N. Ashcroft NKG Medjez-el-Bab Memorial to the Missing
Private R. Astley Enfidaville CWGC Cemetery 2A3
Private T. Bowers NKG Medjez-el-Bab Memorial to the Missing
Private E. Brookes NKG Medjez-el-Bab Memorial to the Missing
Lieutenant The Hon K. Cecil NKG Medjez-el-Bab Memorial to the Missing
Major H. Cleaver Massicault CWGC Cemetery 3L19
Private C. Coombes Enfidaville CWGC Cemetery 2A4
L/Corporal J. Diamond NKG Medjez-el-Bab Memorial to the Missing
Private J. Dickson NKG Medjez-el-Bab Memorial to the Missing
Private R. Falconer Massicault CWGC Cemetery 3L19
Private J. Fletcher Massicault CWGC Cemetery 3L19
Private A. Heron NKG Medjez-el-Bab Memorial to the Missing
Private S. Hughes NKG Medjez-el-Bab Memorial to the Missing
Private H. Lucas Massicault CWGC Cemetery 3L19
Corporal S. Lyon Massicault CWGC Cemetery 3L19
Sergeant W. MacFarlane NKG Medjez-el-Bab Memorial to the Missing
L/Corporal H. Matkin NKG Medjez-el-Bab Memorial to the Missing
Lieutenant K. Morrison Enfidaville CWGC Cemetery 6B21
L/Corporal D. Murdoch NKG Medjez-el-Bab Memorial to the Missing
Private J. Rose RAMC Massicault CWGC Cemetery 4B9
Private W. Wain MiD Massicault CWGC Cemetery 3L19

Private H. Young Massicault CWGC Cemetery 3L19

1st December 1942
Corporal S. Duncan Massicault CWGC Cemetery 3H5
Sergeant L. Holmes NKG Medjez-el-Bab Memorial to the Missing

2nd December 1942
L/Corporal F. Berryman Massicault CWGC Cemetery 3A19

3rd December 1942
Lieutenant E. Charteris MC Massicault CWGC Cemetery 2A20
Private J. Spilsbury Medjez-el-Bab CWGC Cemetery 7H10

30th November 1942 to 4th December 1942
Corporal R. Scott NKG Medjez-el-Bab Memorial to the Missing

1st December 1942 to 5th December 1942
Major P. Teichman Massicault CWGC Cemetery 4A9

6th December 1942
Private T. Worlock Dely Ibrahim CWGC Cemetery 3J9

Appendix XXII

2nd Battalion Parachute Regiment Admin Order No 1, 23rd November 1942

2nd Battalion Parachute Regiment Admin Order No 1. Secret.
In the Field.
23-11-1942.
The following has been decided upon as operational dress:

1. Not to be taken.
   Respirator, groundsheet, gas cape, toggle rope, binocular case, parachutist gloves, AB Parts I & II or documentation whatsoever i.e. letters, bills etc.
2. The man will wear identity disc, string vest, shirt, pants, jumping trousers, socks, gaiters, boots, airborne smock (with scrimmage not as a scarf), equipment, jumping jacket and helmet parachutist.
3. In the airborne smock he will carry:
   Inside pocket right – identity cloth, tea ration in ration bag.
   Inside pocket left – beret and badge, water purifying outfit.
   Outside top left hand pocket – 1 tin dripping, 2 cheese and 2 boxes matches (ration).
   Outside top right hand pocket – 1 tin dripping, 2 cheese and 1 anti mosquito cream.
   Outside bottom left pocket – 1 grenade & 2 lbs plastic.
   Outside bottom right pocket – 1 grenade & Gammon bomb fuse.
4. In the trousers parachutist he will carry:-
   First field dressing pocket – First field dressing and emergency ration.
   Large pocket – 1 spare pair socks.
5. Contents of haversack:- 2 halves mess tins, 2 tins bully beef, 2 tins biscuits, shaving and washing kit and 2 spirit burners.
6. Where the fighting knife is carried is optional.
7. Respirators will be stacked in Company bulk at Company stores, they should be marked with number, rank and name.
8. 1 Officer and 10 ORs from the base party will proceed to the aerodrome with the Battalion and act as rear party. The Officer will ensure that he has available 10 empty sandbags for a final check on documents or any other surplus gear.

Appendix XXIII

Report on Operation of 3rd Parachute Battalion on Green Hill 5th/6th January 1943

Herewith a report on the activities of 3rd Parachute Battalion during its attachment for operations to 36th Infantry Brigade.

The experience gained was invaluable and the Battalion rendered valuable assistance to the Brigade even though the object of the operation was not attained. The fighting qualities of all ranks was magnificent as one would naturally expect, but the method of their employment left much to be desired. The Battalion was split up from the time of its attachment and never got an opportunity of fighting as a Battalion, or even as more than one company. Nevertheless, one Company (B) got within an ace of achieving what the 5th Buffs had failed to do, and that was the seizure of the top of Green Hill.

The failure of 5th Buffs to carry their objective on the first night, resulted in the Battalion (less two Companies) being thrown into the battle at night at a strange objective and at short notice. The enemy was on his toes as consequence of the Buffs attack and probably reinforced since that attack.

An alternative view of Green Hill (right-hand side of the picture) with Sugar Loaf Hill in front of it. (Imperial War Museum)

I cannot speak too highly of the work of B Company in their attack. No recce was possible as the Buffs guide (the IO) was unable to locate the Buffs Company which should have been in position on the line of approach for B Company. The Buffs had not completed their reorganisation and no support was available from them.

The only other troops in a position to render any assistance were A Company who were holding a position to the west end of the flat top of the hill. This Company was under orders of 5th Buffs and was earmarked for action with the Buffs the following day, consequently it could only be used for creating a diversion by fire.

By the time the Battalion (less two Companies) had arrived at Green Hill it was already beginning to get dark and orders had to be given at once. Nothing could be pointed out on the ground. The artillery concentration was first class and B Company's attack went in as arranged – the Company Commander was unfortunate in having to carry out a most difficult operation with one Platoon Commander who had only had his Platoon for a short time (being a reinforcement replacement of a casualty), another Platoon Commander who had only recently received returned to his Platoon from hospital and who had not led it in any previous patrols etc., while the third had no officer at all (due to casualties in the previous position and insufficient reinforcements). His regular second-in-command was lost on the outward flight and the acting one, though first class, naturally has not yet got the experience of the original officer.

The enemy were in very strong dug-in positions on top of the hill, he also had the advantage of a daylight knowledge of the ground and had arranged his fixed lines to cover all likely approaches. It is almost certain that he had numerical superiority – the German habit of firing tracer at night was of assistance to B Company whose actions were based on drawing fire (thus locating the posts) and then the stalking and grenading of them by small parties. Many deeds of individual heroism were performed by personnel of this Company and it known that seven posts were destroyed, it is thought that there were at least fourteen machine gun posts on the hill.

C Company were unlucky in that their role was purely static and they had no contact throughout.

General

The strength of the enemy on these two hills would seem to have been seriously underestimated and too much reliance was placed in the effect of heavy artillery fire on prepared positions. The artillery fire was not very effective (although extremely accurate) as the enemy positions were well dug in and the ground was hard and rocky.

The splitting up of the Battalion in such a way that the commander had nothing left to command was, of course, an absurdity.

Had it been possible to give the role of attacking Green Hill to the Battalion as a whole, or even to have released either A or C Companies, from their commitments, there is no doubt that the hill would have been captured and held. The enemy will certainly further strengthen his hold on Green Hill now and it is considered that nothing less than a Battalion attack would hope to succeed.

Casualties during the attachment were:-

A Company

Killed 1 officer (Lieutenant Elton-Tuckett) and 3 ORs.

Wounded 11 ORs.

Missing Nil.

B Company
Killed 1 officer (Lieutenant Blewitt) and 4 ORs.
Wounded 9 ORs.
Missing 9 ORs.

RAMC
Wounded 1 OR.

Total
Killed 2 officers and 7 ORs.
Wounded 21 ORs.
Missing 9 ORs.

Appendix XXIV

Report by Major Terrell OC A Company, 3rd Parachute Battalion, covering period during which his Company was under command 5th Buffs for the action on Green Hill, 5th/6th January 1943

Commanding Officer's Note

At the time A Company was placed under orders CO 5th Buffs, it was understood that the role of the Company was to act as reserve Company with the possibility of being employed for mopping up. 3rd Parachute Battalion was under orders to carry out an attack on another large feature (Bald Hill) on the day following the attack by 5th Buffs on Green Hill. This attack, had it materialised, would have required the full strength of the Battalion. It will be seen from the following account that A Company did considerably more than the original arrangement visualised and it is extremely unlikely that it could have been withdrawn from Green Hill to enable it to have taken part in the attack with its own Battalion the following day.

2nd January 1943.

1400 Left Souk-el-Khemis with remainder of O Group for HQ 36th Infantry Brigade. Informed that A Company was to be under command 5th Buffs for attack on objective. Reported to CO 5th Buffs and made recce with him and senior FOO, watched artillery registering on Green and Bald Hills. Company arrived in area by TCVs in small hours of the morning. Spent night in tunnel area with remainder of Battalion.

3rd January 1943.

0900 Attended administrative conference held by CO 5th Buffs.

1345 CO 5th Buffs gave out orders for the attack (CO 3rd Parachute Battalion present). Pouring with rain all day, tracks very muddy, MT in difficulties even on the roads.

1500 Took Company 2 i/c forward to OP and showed him the route for the Company. Company now known as F Company 5th Buffs.

2000 Information reached me that the attack had been postponed for 24 hours owing to the rain.

4th January 1943.
1115 Took Lieutenant Elton-Tuckett (who was to act as guide) to the forward OP and pointed out features, route etc.

2100 Company moved off from tunnel area and was met by Lieutenant Elton-Tuckett at RV and led by him to assembly position.

5th January 1943.
0145 Moved off for assembly position with CO 5th Buffs, found all Companies in no state to move off and not closed up as ordered. Considerable delay in getting them closed up.

0300 Companies started to move off (An hour and a quarter late), Battalion led by IO, moved very slowly owing to slippery going. Rate of advance not more than half a mile an hour, carried out in single file in pitch dark.

0445 CO 5th Buffs halted Battalion and sent for IO, to take stock of the situation – found Battalion was still half a mile from start line. CO 5th Buffs ordered Companies to assemble where they were and launch themselves independently on their objectives. B Company (5th Buffs) found to be lost and search failed to find them. A Company then ordered to assume B Company's role. Battalion HQ, FOO and self (CO 5th Buffs ordered me to move with Battalion HQ and not with my Company) moved eastwards towards Green Hill.

0615 Arrived at foot of Green Hill, found only two Platoons of my Company had arrived as the remainder of the Company had been placed at the end of the column and part of this column had taken a wrong turning. Ordered these two Platoons to dig in and went forward to see if position was better, found it was, so moved the two Platoons forward and ordered them to dig in there. Battalion HQ was also moved forward to this area and established themselves in a cave (after Lieutenant Thesiger had removed some Arabs from it). My two Platoons used for local defence of Battalion HQ.

0645 Firing could be heard on Green Hill, CO 5th Buffs asks for the barrage to be continued a little longer to cover the late arrival of Battalion.

0730 Report received to effect that there was a sniper up the hill on the left, CO 5th Buffs ordered me to investigate and deal with this – went forward with Lieutenant Elton-Tuckett and his Platoon, found enemy machine guns in position but no sniper. Saw no traces of attack Companies of 5th Buffs and had difficulties and casualties in getting back off the top of the hill under the machine gun fire. Reported to CO 5th Buffs who ordered me to take the whole Company (they were all present by this time) and hold the western end of Green Hill. Carried out this order under cover of fire from my own mortar detachments, who fired 40 bombs under direction of Mortar Officer 5th Buffs. Found meanwhile that Lieutenant Elton-Tuckett had rallied seven Buffs who were pinned on top of the hill and managed to get them back to a position of cover. He had also brought back Captain Goulding their Officer, who was seriously wounded. Lieutenant Elton-Tuckett later brought in a German prisoner to Company HQ. This prisoner had given himself up and appeared to have been demoralised by the artillery fire around his position, he stated when questioned by Lieutenant Thesiger that the number of enemy on the hill was "Eine Kompanie" (180 men).

1115 Reported my Company in position on the west end of the top of Green Hill. Artillery fire on the east end of Green Hill (point 396) continued accurately but one shell fell short amongst my Company and killed one man. Enemy mortared us at irregular intervals. Digging in very difficult because of the rocky nature of the ground. Went down hill and reported to CO 5th Buffs who informed me that an attack was going in on point 396 at 1415 following an artillery barrage. Suggested putting down 18 rounds of smoke from my mortars at the end of the barrage. CO 5th Buffs agreed. No attack seemed to materialise. CO 5th Buffs informed me that B Company (3rd Parachute Battalion) was coming up to attack point 396 tonight.

1730 Went down to HQ 5th Buffs and saw CO (Para) and OC B (Para). Told them position as far as I knew it. Listened to orders for attack by CO 3rd Parachute Battalion then returned to top of the hill.

Note – It was arranged that I should assist B Company's attack by firing from 0100 to 0120 at the right flank of point 396.

6th January 1943.

0130 Heard much small arms firing and assumed B Company's attack to be going in. Enemy used a large amount of tracer and firing was almost continuous for about an hour and a half.

0300 Two stragglers came into my lines and said OC B Company (Para) was shouting for OC A Company. Sent them down to HQ 5th Buffs. One of my own men wounded by small arms fire during B Company's attack. No information as to success or otherwise of B Company's attack by dawn. My wireless not working.

0800 Went down to HQ 5th Buffs to find out the situation. Ammunition and ration situation getting serious in my own position.

1100 Heard from runner that Lieutenant Elton-Tuckett had been wounded. Also found that three Sections (of different Platoons) were pinned by machine gun fire from point 396 – arranged with FOO for 15 minutes concentration on point 398 at 1200. Found that Elton-Tuckett had gone forward with an anti-tank rifle (presumably to try and get a machine gun post about which he had previously complained) – six anti-tank rounds were fired but this brought several machine guns onto our positions and Elton-Tuckett and nine others were wounded. Lieutenant Elton-Tuckett fell in a very exposed position and efforts to bring him in resulted in failure. He was later hit again and killed.

1200 Barrage came down as arranged and enemy machine gun fire ceased. My 2 i/c (Captain Ellis), the Buffs Mortar Officer, Lieutenant Thesiger and self ran and brought in the wounded. Could not find Lieutenant Elton-Tuckett's body but certain he was killed as Corporal Rogers (RAMC) had crawled out to him before the concentration came down.

1230 Reported to CO 5th Buffs. Medical arrangements very good throughout despite difficult conditions (stretchers had to be carried down nearly 1,000 feet of steep rocky scrub). Intermittent mortar fire on our positions for the rest of the day, a 3" mortar and Bren gun being smashed by direct hits.

1400 Went down to conference with CO 5th Buffs and learned details of withdrawal for tonight.

1445 Gave out orders to my O Group.

2000 Withdrawal from Green Hill – my Company acting as rear party.

Appendix XXV

Report by Major Dobie OC B Company, 3rd Parachute Battalion, covering period during the night 5th/6th January 1943

2000 hours 4th January 1943 to 1400 hours 5th January 1943.
B Company in position in 5th Buffs former area – front 354765 to 344743.

5th January 1943.
1400 hours received one hour's notice to move to RV at track junction 362777.
1545 hours moved off (less mortars). Fighting strength 90 all ranks.
1715 hours met CO at 372770

1745 hours received orders to make night attack on Point 396, darkness complete on orders being finished. Impossible to make any recce or even see ground approach. Information about enemy very sketchy. Machine guns and snipers reported (learned later that Major Terrell had information from prisoner that enemy had one company 180 strong supported by 4 inch mortars and machine guns – enemy were parachutists). A Company were in position at the west end of Green Hill about 374766. Made plan

An alternative view of Green Hill and Sugar Loaf Hill. (Imperial War Museum)

David Dobie, who commanded B Company of the 3rd Parachute Battalion, and Derek Bentham, one of his platoon commanders, pictured during a quiet period. David Dobie is wearing a captured German cap. (R. Pine-Coffin)

to climb hill northwards from 373770 to northern ridge then swing eastwards to find enemy's right flank. Approach to as near as possible under the barrage, which was from 0030 hours to 0100 hours.

1830 to 2300 rested Company.

2330 Company moved off in order of 6 Platoon, Company HQ, 4 Platoon and 5 Platoon.

6th January 1943.

0030 hours about 300 yards short of enemy's right flank. Barrage commenced. Worked Company forward to within 200 yards until 4 shorts fell within 20 – 30 yards of the Company (position O).

0100 hours barrage ceased. Worked forward. Going was worst possible, very thick scrub making silence impossible. Night darkest possible.

0110 hours A Company fired a few shorts which went close to us, just afterwards enemy opened up on us from at least four machine gun positions on their right flank. They had no doubt heard our approach through the scrub (machine guns firing from D, H, G and A).

0120 hours changed plan ordering Lieutenant Blewitt (6 Platoon) to take left flank. Lieutenant Bentham (5 Platoon) to take right flank. Company HQ to take centre. Zero from start lines 0145 hours. Platoons had to get to – 6 Platoon to Q, Company HQ and 4 Platoon to P and 5 Platoon to O.

0150 hours more machine guns firing, two from 396, also rifle fire and heavy machine gun fire.

Action by 6 Platoon

0145 hours Lieutenant Blewitt and Sergeant Kerr with 2 ORs stalked heavy machine gun at A. Machine gun post neutralised by grenades. They were then fired at by machine guns from B and C at 20 yards, proceeded to stalk post B. Lieutenant Blewitt received a full burst in chest, Sergeant Kerr shot the machine gunner but he himself received a grenade between his legs and was wounded in five places in the legs and head. Nevertheless he succeeded in getting a grenade into the position which was neutralised. One section under Sergeant Lawson had been sent to position approx A to cover other two sections stalking positions. Another section could not get at machine gun post C and suffered casualties – the ground was bare on that side, they were pinned down and could not get back onto high ground and took no part in the action on top of the hill.

Action by 5 Platoon

0145 Started from O, objectives machine gun posts at H, G and Point 396, Lieutenant Bentham and Sergeant McDonnel got one light machine gun, but on throwing grenades, four machine guns opened up, catching the Platoon in the open, the first burst killed one section commander and seriously wounded a second, besides a number of other casualties. Some personnel were pinned down and others scattered. Lieutenant Bentham managed to regain high ground but with only one man, remainder unable to regain high ground and took no part in the action on top of the hill.

Action by Company HQ and 4 Platoon

0145 hours I started forward from P and was soon under direct fire from 40 yards from post D, also others at C and F, detailed Sergeant Hughes and anti-tank section, to assault it with grenades, he proceeded forward, one man killed, one seriously wounded and pinned down. L/Corporal Hillyard-Todd went on his own by right flank, crawled up and found it was a sunken post with only slit openings and an iron roof; he had to push his hand inside slit and drop grenade in. Post neutralised. Company HQ then advanced to D about 0245 hours.

0245 hours very heavy machine gun fire coming from E 30 yards away, Sergeant Copling with two men detailed to grenade, they crawled forward and neutralised the post. By this time the enemy had started to mortar us, they were also using hand grenades in large numbers. Another post at F was attacked by Sergeant Copling who was shot in the head and wounded, his riflemen however, managed to shoot the enemy and neutralised the post.

0300 hours H and G had been neutralised by Sergeant Baynes and his Section, using light machine gun fire and grenades. Only one post on Furze Hill by this time was left firing, it was extremely well sited with all-round protection and contained a heavy and a light machine gun and several riflemen. Several attempts to neutralise failed with several casualties inflicted, the ground being very bare on that side. However every machine gun on 396 was bringing a terrific amount of fire down on us. Mortars were

APPENDIX "A"

Report by Major DOBIE, OC "B" COY
covering period during night 5/6th Jan 43

Explanatory plan of top of "Green Hill" (not to scale)

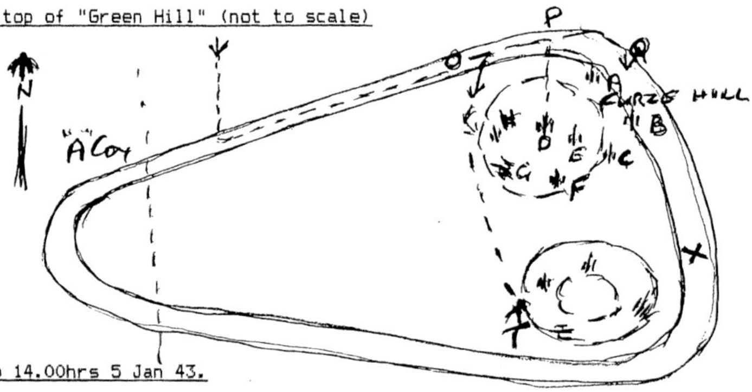

20.00hrs 4 Jan 43 to 14.00hrs 5 Jan 43.

"B" Coy in position in 5 Buffs former area - front 354765 to 344753

5 Jan 43 14.00hrs Received one hours notice to move to RV at track junct, 362777
15.45hrs Moved off (less mortars). Fighting strength 90 all ranks.
17.15hrs Met CO at 372770.
17.45hrs Received orders to make night attack on Pt 396, darkness complete on orders being finished: impossible to make any recce or even see ground approach: Information about enemy very sketchy: MGs and snipers reported (learned later that Major Terrell had information from prisoner that enemy had one Company 180 strong supported by 4" mortars and MGs- enemy were Parachutists) "A" Coy were in position WEST end of "Green Hill" about 374766: Made plan to climb hill Northwards from 373770 to northern ridge then swing eastwards to find enemy's right flank: Approach to as near as possible under barrage, which was from 00.30hrs to 01.00hrs.
18.30hrs to 23.00hrs, rested Company.
23.30hrs Company moved off in order of 6Pln, Coy HQ, 4Pln, 5Pln.

6 Jan 43 00.30hrs About 300yds short of enemy's right flank: Barrage commenced: Worked Coy forward to within 200yds until 4 "shorts" fell within 20 - 30yds of the Coy (Position at "O").
01.00hrs Barrage ceased: Worked forward: Going was worst possible, very thick scrub making silence impossible: Night darkest possible.
01.10hrs A Coy fired a few shorts which went close to us, just afterwards enemy opened up on us from at least four MG positions on their right flank; They had no doubt heard our approach through the scrub (MGs firing from D, H, G and A).
01.20hrs Changed plan ordering Lieut Blewitt (6Pln) to take left flank, Lieut Bentham (5Pln) to take right flank, Coy HQ to take centre, Zero from start lines 01.45hrs; Plns had to get to:- 6 Pln to "Q" Coy HQ and 4 Pln to "P", 5 Pln to "O".
01.50hrs More MGs firing, two from 396, also rifle fire and heavy MG fire.

Major Dobie's original sketch map that accompanied this report. (Airborne Assault Duxford) also firing strongly. I decided to dig in and gave orders for this to be done, I had realised the enemy were at least a company strong on the two hills. Despite my signaller's efforts there was no wireless communication. Enemy appeared from X where infantry mortars were situated and advanced in line, strength appeared to be about 80. Terrific volume of fire from Point 396, enemy infantry chanted as they advanced and my men were forced to give ground under the terrific concentration of fire from machine gun and Schmeisser automatics. I managed to rally them and we then counter-attacked regaining the line by a bayonet charge, Sten, grenades and covered by light machine guns, the enemy broke and retired leaving approx 20 casualties. I realised there must be nearly two enemy companies there and during the lull that followed this attack I started to dig in again and hoped to hold onto Furze Hill. I took stock of the situation, found I had approx 30 fighting effectives left, No 5 Platoon cut off and No 6 Platoon cut off and firing weakly from my left flank.

0330 hours the lull was broken by an increase in machine gun fire from 396, also a line of enemy advanced from X towards Q and from T toward O. We opened fire on them – they widened their sweep and were obviously making a pincer movement to our rear. I could only spare about three men to each flank. I then noticed another line approaching on the same line as before (but not chanting this time), these were supported by a creeping barrage of infantry mortars governed by small Verey lights – I suffered casualties from the mortar fire, we managed to check their advance but the three Bren guns I had left had practically run out of ammunition, there were no grenades left and practically all the Sten gun ammunition was exhausted. We managed to use one German machine gun which was conveniently sited.

0345 hours by this time I realised that I could not possibly hold the ground, I had numerous casualties so I gave the order to evacuate them out – I divided the remainder into two parties of about ten each and withdrew by bounds after giving a signal of three whistles for "reorganise on me". We got our party to the edge of the thick scrub on our original start line – an exchange of fire took place and they went to ground. The party advancing across the top opened up again with machine guns, so I gave orders to withdraw down the hill. We were fired on fairly heavily the whole time downwards. I left the top line of scrub at 0400 hours. When I reached HQ I had 40 missing. The final figures were 5 known killed, 9 wounded and 9 missing. Germans killed on Furze Hill, known 28, with at least 30 killed in counter-attack.

0600 hours regained HQ.

Conclusions.

The enemy appeared to be about a company strong when we arrived – the first counter-attack was obviously not planned, whilst the second was a masterpiece, a company (probably of full strength 180) with 2 inch mortars in support took part.

Observations.

Our men fought an extremely gallant action, they gave no quarter and pressed home each assault in the fiercest fire I have ever seen with the greatest of courage. I am convinced it would have been a difficult Battalion task, we had no reinforcements at all to call upon. Considering also the fact that we had not any idea what the ground was like nor where the enemy posts were situated, the amount accomplished was great.

Appendix XXVI

3rd Parachute Battalion Roll of Honour 5th-6th January 1943

5th-6th January 1943

Private J. Hughes NKG Medjez-el-Bab Memorial to the Missing
Private F. Skinner NKG Medjez-el-Bab Memorial to the Missing

6th January 1943

Lieutenant W. Blewitt Tabarka Ras Rajel CWGC Cemetery 1E22
Private D. Carney NKG Medjez-el-Bab Memorial to the Missing
Lieutenant J. Elton-Tuckett NKG Medjez-el-Bab Memorial to the Missing
Private F. Graham NKG Medjez-el-Bab Memorial to the Missing
Private F. Holliday NKG Medjez-el-Bab Memorial to the Missing
Private H. Jones NKG Medjez-el-Bab Memorial to the Missing
L/Corporal S. Keegans NKG Medjez-el-Bab Memorial to the Missing
L/Sergeant C. McIntyre NKG Medjez-el-Bab Memorial to the Missing
Private G. Morgan NKG Medjez-el-Bab Memorial to the Missing
Private E. Wood NKG Medjez-el-Bab Memorial to the Missing

Appendix XXVII

Major-General Browning's diary of visit to North Africa December 1942 and associated report appendices

Permission was obtained for Major-General F.A.M. Browning, CB, DSO, Group Captain Sir Nigel Norman (commanding 38 Wing RAF) and Lieutenant Colonel A.G. Walch OBE (GSO1 Airborne Division) to visit the theatre of operations in North Africa in December 1942. General Eisenhower and General Smith kindly authorised the American Army Air Force to convey these officers by aircraft from England and back again. The final arrangements were made by General McClure, United States Army HQ in London.

1200 hours 2nd December. Information received from General McClure's office that General Browning, Group Captain Norman and Lieutenant Colonel Walch should be at Portreath airfield by the evening of 8th December to take-off for North Africa in a Fortress aircraft. Total weight per passenger, including himself, to be 350 lbs but to be as little as possible within that.

8th December. Party left Netheravon in Vega Gull and Oxford aircraft, all the baggage being in the Oxford and General Browning, Group Captain Norman and Lieutenant Colonel Walch being in the Vega. The Vega arrived all right at Portreath, but the weather was very bad and clouds very low and the Oxford aircraft crashed just before landing on the airfield and was completely smashed up. Luckily none of the crew were seriously injured and all the baggage was rescued intact or nearly so. The party was due to take-off for Gibraltar next morning but the trip was postponed at 1800 hours, owing to the weather. All three officers spent the night at Fowey.

9th to 17th December. The weather was very bad throughout this period and the flight was impossible. We stayed at Truro in the Red Lion Hotel and spent many disturbed nights during which the proposed flight for the next day was cancelled at any time between 2000 and 0400 hours. Brigadier Cazenove at HQ Cornwall Coastal Area was extremely hospitable. Various defences were visited and criticised from the point of view of attacks by airborne forces and the whole party became extremely bored.

18th December. Breakfast at Portreath airfield at 0445 hours. Took-off in Fortress at 0805 hours. Arrived at Gibraltar 1445 after a good and uneventful trip. Stayed night at

Gibraltar. General Browning at Government House and Group Captain Norman and Lieutenant Colonel Walch at Rock Hotel.

19th December. Left Gibraltar in C53 aircraft at 0915 hours. Made landfall at Cap Tenes. Arrived at Maison Blanche airfield near Algiers at 1300 hours. There we met Colonel Mann who took us to the St George's Hotel in Algiers. This is Allied HQ. Met General Clark, General Spaatz (commanding 12th Air Force), General McClure, General Eaker and various other officers. Dined with Air Vice Marshal Robb and American Air Force officers at Air Force Mess. General Browning spent the night at St Georges, while Group Captain Norman and Lieutenant Colonel Walch stayed at Foyer Feminine (taken over by the Americans).

20th December. Group Captain Norman ill and stayed in the British Hospital at Algiers. General Browning and Lieutenant Colonel Walch left St Georges at 1015 hours for Maison Blanche airfield. Took-off for Bone at 1235 hours in C47 aircraft, escorted by two Hurricanes. Arrived at Bone at 1430 hours, where we saw 21 C47 passing over Bone from Oran for the south. Left by car provided by 1st Army for Constantine at 1500 hours, arriving there at 1915 hours. This is the HQ of 1st Army.

General Browning stayed the night at Hotel Trans-Atlantique. Lieutenant Colonel Walch stayed the night at the Sirta Hotel.

21st December. Left 0910 hours by car, passed Guelma at 1210 hours, having spent 90 minutes over lunch and passed Souk Arhas at 1500 hours. Broke down with loose wheel at 1520 hours and restarted at 1535 hours. Held by burning ammunition lorry at 1620 hours and passed it while it was still burning at 1635 hours. The remainder of the convoy on both sides was being held up.

Arrived at Souk-el-Khemis at 1845 hours and stayed night there with HQ V Corps. As we arrived we met Major Cleasby-Thompson taking a party of 1st Parachute Brigade up to their new RV near Beja.

22nd December. Left for 1st Parachute Brigade by car 0945 hours, arriving there (5 miles north east of Beja) at 1100 hours. Saw Brigadier Flavell, Lieutenant Colonels Frost and Pine-Coffin at Brigade HQ. Lunched at Brigade HQ. During afternoon visited by car Le Kef, Treboursouk and Thiba (where we met Major Pilkington who was in charge of the Press Correspondents) and returned to HQ V Corps, where General Anderson had arrived. Two French Generals, Juin and Carré, were also at HQ that evening. Again stayed night here.

23rd December. Visited 1st Parachute Brigade again in the morning and lunched with them. Visited all Battalions of the Brigade. After lunch visited HQ 1st Guards Brigade (Brigade includes 3rd Grenadier, 2nd Coldstream and 2nd Hampshires) south-east of Medjez. Saw Brigadier Copeland-Griffiths who had just been attacked by German aircraft. Visited 3rd Grenadiers who had attacked the night before. There was an American Combat Team on their right and 2nd Coldstreams were on their left. 2nd Coldstreams had just attacked successfully at Djebel Asmara and Company from 3rd Grenadiers had just occupied Crick. Returned to HQ V Corps after dark, taking two and a half hours and found that Group Captain Norman had arrived there, having come to Bone by air and having visited 1st Parachute Brigade during the afternoon. We all stayed at HQ V Corps for the night, General Anderson also being there.

24th December. Group Captain Norman left for Bone to try and get to Algiers as soon as possible. General Browning and Lieutenant Colonel Walch visited 1st Parachute Brigade again and particularly the Field Squadron and Field Ambulance. Returned to HQ V Corps for dinner and night. General Eisenhower and General Anderson were both present and General Eisenhower was called back to Algiers urgently after dinner because of Admiral Darlan's assassination.

25th December. Attended Christmas Day communion service at HQ V Corps at 0730 hours, the service being taken by Lieutenant Colonel Victor Pike – Senior Chaplain to the Forces. Left by car for 1st Army Command Post at Ame Semour at 0950 hours, arriving there, having had lunch *en route* at 1400 hours. Heard King's speech at 1500 hours. Saw General Anderson and picked up his report for CIGS. Dined and wined and stayed night.

26th December. Left for Constantine at 1000 hours. Arrived, having had lunch *en route* at 1545 hours. Stayed night.

27th December. Left Constantine with General Anderson at 0750 hours for Telegma airfield, where we arrived at 0845 hours. Took-off in Fortress for Algiers at 1100 hours, arriving Maison Blanche at 1215 hours. Met Group Captain Norman who had flown in Beaufighter from Bone on 25th December. Lunched at Rear HQ 1st Parachute Brigade with Major Yeldham. Visited first reinforcements 1st Parachute Brigade and then the hospital at Beni Msus. Saw Lieutenant Colonel Hill, Captain Rob RAMC, Lieutenant Crawley and Sergeant Duffy RE. Visited Allied HQ at Hotel St Georges. All returned for night to Rear Brigade HQ at Rouiba.

28th December. General Browning visited General Clark at 0845 hours at St George's. Stood by to take-off in Fortress aircraft from Maison Blanche from 1030 hours, but owing to magneto trouble flight had to be cancelled for that day. Again stayed night at Rouiba. In the meantime Brigade Rear HQ had moved to near Blida airfield, which is about thirty miles west of Rouiba.

29th December. Take-off in Fortress from Maison Blanche at 1015 hours. Arrived Gibraltar 1330 hours. Went shopping and stayed night at Gibraltar.

30th December. Took-off from Gibraltar 0830 hours with a large load of local produce. Arrived Portreath, Cornwall at 1530 hours. Stayed night at Truro.

31st December. Left Portreath in Hudson piloted by Group Captain Cooper at 1100 hours. Arrived Netheravon at 1200 hours.

An interesting appendix to this report are brief comments about the equipment and weapons used by the 1st Parachute Brigade in the early days in North Africa.

1. No 75 grenades. Useful. Should be included on G1098 in unit reserve.
2. No 6 grenades (Gammon bombs). By far the best light infantry anti-tank weapon. Successful on only occasion so far used against tanks. Effective against armoured cars. Also highly effective anti-personnel weapon at close range when attacker is under cover. More heads and detonators are required urgently as plastic is not available in reasonable quantities in North Africa.
3. Fighting knife. 1st Parachute Brigade are very doubtful if this is really required. It should be kept on until we have more experience but it should be carried somewhere other than at it is at present as, when going uphill, it catches in the side of the knee.
4. .45 Colt. Better than the.38 revolver. No complaints.
5. Stens. Considerable trouble with jamming, chiefly owing to dirt.
6. No 4 rifle. Bolt inclined to jam and aperture sight to fill with sand, both due to bad weather conditions and lack of proper care.
7. Scales of ammunition. Satisfactory with present experience, except that 75 grenades should be included.
8. Tracer. Germans use tracer very considerably and much more than our present scales allow. The morale effect is very great. It does not give away the position of the firer to any serious extent. Recommended that we should increase our scales very greatly, for all types of ammunition.
9. Vickers machine gun. There is a general demand throughout 1st Army for the reintroduction of the Vickers machine gun and there is no doubt that this weapon would be extremely valuable in the Airborne Division both for airlanding and parachute troops. The problem is how and where to include it.
10. Welbike. Has not yet been dropped. Has been found useful and suitable on roads but cannot cope with the very thick mud -very few vehicles can. Should carry more petrol as in practice the tank does not hold more than a safe average of 25 miles. Suggest a 2 gallon petrol can, be dropped in the container with the motorcycle and an attachment for it provided on the motorcycle. It might also be possible to run a feed pipe from the petrol can to the tank.
11. Folding trolleys. Have been found very useful for administrative purposes as well as operations. The difficulties of taking them across country are well known and have not altered. They remain the best article of its type at present in production but something better is required. Prototype of the Polish 'motor-mover' vehicle should be hastened and tried out.
12. Camouflage smocks. Have been an outstanding success and are much envied by the rest of the Army. They would be better if more waterproofing is possible. They require a belt of some kind if worn without equipment on patrol as they are loose-fitting but string tied round the waist is good enough. Elastic at waist stretches a lot and becomes very loose, so strap of some kind should be added.
13. Brinje vests. Reports are good on the whole. A few men have complained that they are inclined to ruck up around the waist and then chafe. There have also been a few complaints that they are a little drafty under the bosom. They are easy to wash and unlikely to get lousy. The shoulder strap of the vest should be a little broader. 1st Battalion dropped at Souk el Arba wearing brinje vests and camouflaged smocks

without battle dress blouse. This dress is suitable for special occasions but should not be regarded as normal.

14. Lining of large trouser pockets. Chammy leather is not really necessary and it takes a long time to dry when once wet. Suggest that pockets be lined with thin canvas (as per battle dress blouse) in future.
15. Berets. Excellent in every respect. A lot lost and more replacements and reserve wanted.
16. Jumping jacket. New type very good. Brigade dislike the idea of discarding it on landing as it is useful as a garment as well as a jumping jacket.
17. Dubbin and brush. Should be included in men's personal kit.
18. Anti-flea powder. None issued. Definitely required.
19. Socks. The value of wearing two pairs of socks both fitting fairly loosely has again been proved.
20. The Brigade has had no cases of pneumonia although the remainder of the 1st Army has suffered to some extent in this way. It is suggested that the loose clothing provided for parachute personnel has a great deal to do with this.
21. Canvas water bags. Very useful.
22. Sun compasses. None issued and not required at present. May well be very useful later on. Should be investigated.
23. 3" mortar harnesses. Good. No 1 Commando has also adopted it.
24. Torches. Flat type provided proved very flimsy. Ordinary hooded type as issued to the rest of the Army not a very suitable shape. Best type is American bent over cylindrical torch with a clip to fit on the belt.
25. Smoke. No aircraft available for laying or dropping smoke. No opposition on landing, so no 2" mortar bombs (smoke) used for immediate cover on landings. As it happened, therefore no special report on the value of smoke can be made.
26. Container lighting sets. No drops made at night, so not used.
27. Folding stretchers. Very good.
28. Gas respirators. 1st Battalion dropped at Souk el Arba with them. 2nd Battalion dropped at Depienne without them.
29. Supply baskets. Very satisfactory. No daisy-chaining done as no aircraft allotted only for supplies. So far, only method has been to drop two baskets with stick of 14 men, by just pushing them put. No rollers necessary for that. Compo rations dropped in baskets very successfully.
30. Men will often have to carry more than 48 hours rations on them. 2nd Battalion carried 4 days when dropping at Depienne. Must be capable of distributing on person.
31. 18 set. Much better than expected. Have maintained average good range of 7 to 8 miles, but up to 14 miles on occasions. 20 foot aerial makes all the difference. Still too heavy to be the final answer for airborne troops.
32. 38 set. Is good but not so simple as it first appears. Considerable training is required to get the best out of it. 1st Battalion say that mortars do not require it but this is not yet confirmed by the remainder of the Brigade. Heavy for its capabilities.
33. 65 set. Excellent. Stands a dropping well. Has worked very well up to 400 miles.
34. Visual signalling lamps. Good and very useful.
35. Ground-air strips. Very effective for very simple messages on pre-arranged code.

36. The identification of airborne forces equipment at port of disembarkation was satisfactory. The packages containing the parachutes were not quite strong enough to stand the journey and burst in several cases. They are a little bit too big and too heavy and should be reduced by about one third in size and weight. Their water and air-tight qualities were satisfactory. It is absolutely necessary, as was done on this occasion, to pack them operationally.
37. It would be better if all equipment, both Army and RAF, could be sent out in one consignment under one service. The RAF staff provided in this case was hardly large enough to deal by themselves with all the equipment they had to look after and, in any case, they had no transport in which to move it.
38. Drying and packing parachutes. All except a very few parachutes arrived in good order after sea voyage and were not repacked before use in first three drops. There are now available in North Africa nearly two complete sets of parachutes for the whole Brigade plus the reserve sent out after the Brigade. Parachutes are being dried in a laundry at Algiers and packed in a shed at Rouiba (near Algiers) until mobile parachute section arrives. Arrangements have been good enough as a temporary measure but there are considerable other demands for the laundry, and, of course, if the Brigade is required to operate from somewhere else, local resources may not be so good there.
39. The Mobile Parachute Unit would have been of the utmost value and still will be, although facilities were obtained in and near Maison Blanche aerodrome for both

The RAF Mobile Parachute Packing Unit in action at an unknown location in Tunisia. It could be assumed they are just checking this parachute for broken and missing rigging lines and tears in the canopy. (Imperial War Museum)

drying and packing parachutes, they were not so good as the facilities offered by the Mobile Parachute Section. They are totally immobile. Equally good facilities are unlikely to exist at any of the other bases which the Parachute Brigade might have to use.

40. 64 Group dropped 1st Battalion. 64 and 62 Groups dropped 2nd Battalion. 60 Group have left their bomb racks behind to come by sea from England and are only just getting them now. It is unfortunate that 60 Group who received the most training in parachute operations in England were thus situated, whilst the two other Groups had their equipment but had not been trained in England.
41. The supporting arms to the Battalions i.e. RE, Royal Signals and RAMC have proved their worth and their equipment on the whole has been a very great success. At present there are no suggestions or alterations of the Field Squadron or Signals Sections and the few minor alterations in the medical equipment are included at Appendix C (see Chapter 11). Although these units may seem to be rather expensive in their personnel and equipment this is not really so and their use in operations has confirmed this. The equipment of the Signals Section and the Field Ambulance has proved of great use to other formations and even by HQ 1st Army itself and has pulled them out of several awkward situations when their own resources were inadequate.
42. A minimum scale of administrative transport is essential for the Parachute Brigade overseas and must be under their own command and travel with them. This minimum scale is being worked out by 1st Parachute Brigade now but present suggestions are included in the notes by Major Yeldham at Appendix E to this report [Author's note: not included here]. The present system whereby 1st Parachute Brigade has had to borrow transport from many units at the expense of these units is most unsatisfactory to everyone.
43. Salvage of equipment. About 90 'expendable' stores e.g. parachutes, containers and baskets recovered from drops by 1st and 3rd Battalions. Circumstances of 2nd Battalion drop necessarily resulted in complete loss.

The report also contains a useful annex in which it lists the casualties suffered by the Brigade up to midnight 23rd December 1942. Regretfully whilst it gives names of the Officers, it just gives numbers for the Other Ranks.

Divisional HQ
Wounded Major des Voeux

1st Battalion
Killed Captain Stewart and Lieutenant Fogarty and 18 ORs.
Wounded Lieutenant Colonel Hill, Captain Whitlock and Lieutenant Kellas and 39 ORs.
Missing 15 ORs.

2nd Battalion
Killed Major Cleaver, Lieutenant Morrison and Lieutenant Buchanan and 16 ORs.
Wounded Lieutenant Crawley and 3 ORs.
Missing Major Teichman, Captain Measures, Captain Reverend McDonald, Captain Short, Lieutenant The Hon Cecil, Lieutenant Charteris, Lieutenant Naoumoff, Lieutenant Playford and Lieutenant Rendell and 256 ORs.

3rd Battalion
Killed 1 OR.
Missing Lieutenant Sharman, Lieutenant Clementson and Lieutenant Davies and 17 ORs.

Royal Engineers
Killed Captain Geary and 2 ORs.
Wounded Lieutenant Birkett and 1 OR.
Missing Major Dorman, Lieutenant White and Lieutenant Holland and 21 ORs.

Field Ambulance
Missing Lieutenant McGavin and 24 ORs.

Signals
Killed 1 OR.

Totals:

	Killed	Wounded	Missing	Total
Officers	6	6	17	29
ORs	38	43	333	414
Totals	44	49	350	443

Appendix XXVIII

Report from the 1st Parachute Battalion regarding Djebel Mansour, 1st-5th February 1943

1st February 1943

On the night of 1st February 1943 the CO received orders from the Brigade Commander that the Battalion was to attack and capture Djebel Mansour and if possible El Alliliga on the night of 2nd/3rd February. The object of the attack was to capture and hold these positions to allow other troops to push through. The attack would be supported by the 17th Field Regiment RA. The CO was also informed that units of the 6th Armoured Division were going to push down the Bou Arada-Pont du Fahs road and then swing south behind Djebel Mansour. A mule column was put under command to supply the Battalion when the position was taken. The CO asked if any assistance could be obtained from the Foreign Legion and the Brigade Commander said he would arrange for the 2nd Company under Captain Faveau to be put under command.

The CO pointed out that it might not be possible to capture El Alliliga the same day as Djebel Mansour but it would be done on the following night. If the position was

Djebel Alliliga from the west. (James Macrae)

to be held against a determined counter-attack reinforcements would have to be sent up, as one Battalion was not strong enough to hold both Djebel Mansour and El Alliliga.

CO then returned to Battalion HQ and issued a preliminary warning order to Company Commanders to move the following day to lying up area and that the Battalion would be organised as follows for the attack:-

Rifle Companies less Mortar Detachments

Battalion HQ

Mortar Platoon

Each Company would send 5 mortar men to Mortar Platoon to act as ammunition carriers, remainder would remain with Companies to carry reserve .303 ammunition.

2 i/c and Adjutant would remain at supply point to organise mule train and supplies. Anti-Tank Platoon would remain with 2 i/c to provide necessary protection for mule train.

2nd February 1943

At 0800 CO went to see Major Robinson of 17th Field Regiment to discuss the artillery plan. Major Robinson informed him that he had to go to a conference and he was not sure what the situation regarding support was going to be.

At 0900 Battalion moved from Toutla position by march route to lying up positions in area 665952.

CO visited Captain Proileau of the Mule Transport Company to make arrangements for mules to move as soon as possible to S'Arifa 6595.

Lieutenant Perrin-Brown was sent to liaise with Captain Faveau OC 2nd Company Foreign Legion and get any further information regarding the enemy and inform him that he would be under the command of the Battalion for the forthcoming attack.

At 1200 CO met Captain Faveau who informed him that he had received no instructions from his CO that he was to cooperate in the attack. An immediate message was sent to him asking for his permission. Colonel Bouchier replied that he had not received the necessary permission from higher authority but that he would ask for it and let Captain Faveau know as soon as possible.

The Battalion by this time had arrived at the lying up position, had a meal and were getting down to rest. O Group had been called to come forward to receive orders at 1400.

CO held a conference with Captain Faveau regarding guides and route to start line and the composition and armament of his Company, if permission was received to use them. At 1330 a message was received from Brigade that the CO was to report at 1430. 2 i/c was ordered to take O Group and all officers to go forward to let them examine and study the ground they were going to operate over.

CO arrived at Brigade where he was informed by Brigade Major that he did not know what he was required for. The journey wasted a valuable 1½ hours. CO informed Brigade Major that French had received no orders to cooperate. Brigade Major then sent an immediate message to Colonel Bouchier ordering him to put one Company under command 1st Parachute Battalion.

At 1600 CO arrived back at French Company HQ. Still no word had been received from Colonel Bouchier so another urgent message was sent out asking if the message had been received from 1st Parachute Brigade. As time was now becoming short CO decided to use Foreign Legion in a role that if permission was not received to use them it would not materially affect the main attack. The role decided on was to create a diversion in El Alliliga between 0430-0530 and to bring down mortar fire on a heavy machine gun position on track between 0430-0500.

At 1700 CO gave out his orders for the attack from a position where O Group could all see the ground. A tape-laying party under Captain Coxen was to move ahead to mark the route to the start line. Guides were to be provided for each Company by the French.

At 1800 Major Robinson 17th Field Regiment arrived and the artillery plan was decided upon and it was arranged that a FOO should move forward with Battalion HQ.

At 1900 CO gave out orders for approach march and administrative orders. A conference was then held with Captain Proileau of the Mule Carrying Company and 2 i/c to decide on the supply situation. It was decided more mules should be made available to carry mortars and ammunition to the extremity of the French lines on approach march to save the mortar men this long carry. A mule column should be loaded with ammunition ready to move from French lines at 0700.

It was also arranged that a 21 set and 18 set should be posted at the French OP. Captain O'Brien would be in charge of these sets.

At 2030 a message was received from Captain Faveau saying that he had just received his orders from Colonel Bouchier and he was under our command and he would be able to carry out the task allotted to him.

At 2200 Brigade Major and Staff Captain arrived. Brigade Major informed CO that 3rd Battalion Grenadier Guards less one Company was moving into our lying-up area and would be available to support and reinforce the positions at first light. He also reported that that it had been reported that there were twenty enemy tanks and some

A local hazard encountered when walking up the Djebel Mansour! (James Macrae)

anti-tank guns in rear of Djebel Mansour. He also said that French 75s were going to take on opportunity targets south of 91 grid line.

3rd February 1943

At 0030 hours the tape-laying party moved off according to plan followed by remainder of Battalion. Guides were picked up and the journey to the start line was uneventful. Somehow S Company managed to miss the tape at the beginning where there was a slight gap and got lost with the result that they never reached the start line and never contacted the main body till the position was taken. It is considered that not sufficient time was left between Companies as there was a lot of long halts on the way as the troops negotiated the long gulley.

Also the time allowed for the approach march was too generous as the Battalion was formed up on the start line less S Company at 0415 hours. It is suspected that a German patrol spotted the tape in one of the gulleys. At 0500 hours leading Companies crossed start line and made their way up the hill. Wireless communication was opened and S Company were contacted who said they were coming up to the start line.

At about 0515 the enemy opened fire with his machine guns and mortars. It was observed that there was a lot of fire from a machine gun post on the left of the Battalion front. It would have been invaluable if the reserve Company had been present as a platoon could have been dispatched to mop this post up as it caused a considerable amount of casualties during the day and to S Company when they were moving up the hill.

At 0530 Battalion Headquarters moved up the hill followed by the Battalion mortars. About half-way up heavy mortar fire came down on to Battalion Headquarters causing casualties to the signallers and protective section. The Commanding Officer with FOO and runner moved with all speed to the top of the hill leaving the IO to bring on Battalion Headquarters as the success signal had gone up from Djebel Mansour at 0540.

The situation on Djebel Mansour was as follows:-

Except for Point 646 the feature was in our hands. T and R Companies were pushing on to Alliliga and the situation was rather confused as there was a lot of firing going on to the left of our front. The mortars very quickly got into position and brought fire to bear on 646 which very quickly fell into our hands. At 0630 the success signal was fired from El Alliliga, but the feature had not been entirely cleared of machine gun posts and there was still a considerable amount of fire coming from it.

There is still a considerable amount of doubt as to just what happened to the various Platoons in the assault owing to most of the Platoon Commanders being wounded, but the following facts have been ascertained. T Company ran into heavy machine gun fire 200 yards from the start line which caused casualties. Due to wounded and prisoners T Company had two platoons left by the time the initial assault was completed. T Company then advanced along Djebel Mansour mopping up machine gun posts *en route*. They suffered a few casualties and took further prisoners. The Company was halted at the end of Mansour and reorganised into two storming parties to attack Alliliga encountering in the woods one machine gun post and three enemy snipers all of whom were eliminated. Emerging from the woods at the top of the hill the Company suffered three casualties from machine gun fire. The post was rushed and taken. The Company was then held up by very heavy machine gun fire identified as from three guns which could not be silenced. T Company was by this time reduced to 2 officers and about 20 ORs.

R Company early in the assault ran into very heavy machine gun fire which caused heavy casualties to two platoons and a lot of confused fighting on the hillside began which was being swept by machine gun fire from the flank. Company Commander and one platoon reached the top of the hill and went into the attack on Alliliga on the left of T Company. They were subsequently pinned down by fire from the left flank of the Alliliga position.

S Company it appears had gone too far to the right of their objective and ran into a machine gun in a fixed line running down the gully which was knocked out the Company Command and practically the whole of the Company Headquarters. The leading platoon then ran into a booby trap which killed the Platoon Commander and caused casualties. The situation then became rather confused.

At 0700 the situation was as follows:-

S Company and a portion of R Company were in possession of 646 and area. Resistance had completely ceased on Djebel Mansour.

T Company were in possession of El Alliliga though there was considerable machine gun fire still coming from it. Casualties appeared to be heavy. The enemy was bringing a fair amount of mortar and machine gun fire down on Djebel Mansour which restricted movement. Battalion Headquarters and Mortar Platoon were at the top of the gully. All troops were in position in case of immediate counter-attack. Commanding Officer then sent two Mortar Detachments to assist T Company.

By 0800 it was obvious that it was not possible to hold Alliliga and Mansour with the force available and the nature of the ground. Also it was obvious that there was still a lot of machine guns in position on one of the features of Alliliga. Therefore the Commanding Officer ordered T Company to withdraw from Alliliga and take up position covering the track running between the two features with R Company in the centre and S on Point 646.

The remainder of the day was spent in consolidating the position and evacuating the wounded. Digging was commenced immediately to deepen the enemy positions which were shallow and too broad. The ground was extremely hard and stony.

The Commanding Officer sent back a wireless message asking that reinforcements could be sent up as soon as possible. During the day some 105 casualties were evacuated and 35 prisoners. The Battalion was in possession of 10 MG 34's and two enemy mortars all of which were put in position. At 1745 Major Cleasby-Thompson arrived with the mule train which brought up rations, two Vickers machine guns (these were without asbestos packing), 1500 rounds Mk. VIII ammunition and a certain amount of.303. Major Cleasby-Thompson informed the Commanding Officer that a large-scale attack was going to be put on to Alliliga by the Guards with the object of driving down to the Pont Du Fahs road. During the course of the day the FOO had managed to get a 21 set with which he conducted some very good shots. At about 1900 the Company of the Foreign Legion arrived and took up position in the area Point 646 on the Battalion's left flank. A message was received that there was to be no firing on Alliliga that night as the Guards were going to attack. At 2100 a Company of the Guards arrived under Commander Major Tufnell. They said they had started moving at 1300.They were placed in reserve ready to go to assist in the consolidation of Alliliga the following morning. The night was uneventful.

4th February 1943

At 0630 the Commanding Officer despatched the IO to contact Guards on Alliliga. It was found the enemy were still in possession. No information was received till 0730 that the attack had not taken place. This lack of information might have had disastrous results if the enemy had counter-attacked from that direction, as defensive fire was to be brought down on Alliliga by the Gunners in event of a counter-attack and this had to be cancelled owing to the Guards attack. During the morning information was obtained that the Guards were going to attack at 1530 and that Major Tufnell's Company was going to take part. There was a certain amount of shelling and mortar fire during the day. At 1530 hours the Guards attacked and we lost touch completely with them and it was not known whether the attack had been successful or not though there was a considerable amount of machine gun fire still coming onto our position from Alliliga. Every effort was made to get in touch with the Guards through the Brigade net. At 2300 some firing was heard to the east of Djebel Mansour.

5th February 1943

At first light heavy firing broke out from the French positions and it was obvious that the enemy were counter-attacking. The enemy captured Point 646 very quickly and a runner arrived from the French saying that Captain Faveau and his Lieutenant had been badly wounded. The Company was in the hands of the CSM, who very bravely organised a bayonet charge as a counter-attack. By 0715 the French position was in enemy hands. It is assumed that the enemy crawled up during the night and surprised the French on Point 646 which he very quickly took. Once in possession of Point 646 the remainder of the French positions became untenable. By 0715 the enemy was in complete possession of the French positions which overlooked our own. In point of fact he did very little damage to us from this position as he was kept down by accurate machine gun and mortar fire from S Company positions. It has to be pointed out that the French were sent up, as reserve ammunition, .303 which is of no use for the Springfield rifle with which they are armed and they very quickly ran out of ammunition. By this time the enemy had begun to mortar and shell our positions very heavily and it became obvious that without reinforcements it would not be possible to hold the position. At the same time there was a considerable amount of machine gun fire coming from Alliliga and it was obvious that the Guards were not in full possession of it. CO got in touch with Brigade by 22 set and explained the situation. By 0915 mortars were completely out of ammunition and Companies were running very low.

By this time communication had been established with the Guards and they were asked to try and knock out the machine guns on the side of Alliliga which was causing us a certain amount of casualties and restricting all movements. They replied they would try and do this.

The FOO tried to get his guns to fire on the enemy but owing to the height of Mansour it was not possible to do this. At 1000 a wireless message was sent to Brigade giving the situation. At 1045 permission was received to withdraw and a message was sent to Companies telling them to withdraw to the gulley. By this time the enemy was within 30-40 yards of our positions and Companies were completely out of ammunition. Companies withdrew in an orderly manner followed by a hail of machine gun fire from our positions which were now occupied by the enemy. During the evacuation to the French positions several casualties occurred and there was a good deal of shelling. The evacuation of the wounded was greatly assisted by carriers of the Grenadier Guards which did extremely well. The retirement was covered by a concentration of smoke and HE put down on Mansour by the artillery and also by smoke on the foothills put down by tanks.

Casualties

Officers Killed	2
Died of Wounds	1
Wounded	10
Missing	1
Other Ranks Killed	30
Died of Wounds	2
Wounded	122
Missing	15
Total Killed	32
Died of Wounds	3
Wounded	132
Missing	16

Appendix XXIX

Report by Lieutenant Colonel M. MacEwan CO 16 Parachute Field Ambulance RAMC on the operations on 2nd, 3rd, 4th and 5th February 1943

Tuesday, 2nd February 1943

I was notified that 1st Battalion was attacking Djebel Mansour that night. No 1 Section under the Command of Captain D Wright was already attached to the Battalion. The section consisted of Staff Sergeant Clegg, Corporal Hatcher and seventeen other ranks. A road reconnaissance was made and it was found that it would be impossible for ambulances to proceed forward until Djebel Alliliga was taken, and that even then the roads were in such a condition that the going would be both difficult and dangerous. Captain Wright was informed that until the success signal for Djebel Alliliga was given a certain point would be used as an ambulance car post (hereafter referred to as Car Post 'A'). The section went into action carrying very light equipment and stretchers. When the assault on Djebel Mansour took place, and while Battalion Headquarters was waiting for a success signal, a few casualties took place due to machine gun and mortar fire. The casualties were attended by Staff Sergeant Clegg and his bearers, and as casualties were still being caused when Battalion Headquarters moved forward, Captain Wright took Corporal Hatcher and one other bearer only up the hill with Battalion Headquarters, while Staff Sergeant Clegg immediately started evacuating casualties from the bottom of the hill. The ambulance car allotted to 1st Battalion was located at Car Post 'A'. Captain J. Cassidy, ordered another ambulance from Brigade Headquarters to report to Car Post 'A'. I found that owing to the difficult nature of the terrain, the intense mortar and machine gun fire, and the distance to Car Post 'A', that it took ten hours to get a patient from the hill to Post 'A'. Furthermore, stretcher-bearers were dead weary on arriving.

Wednesday, 3rd February 1943

I arranged for the remainder of our ambulance cars to report to Post 'A' where Captain Cassidy was attending to patients, and for the ambulance cars to report to Djelida Station on the Bou Arada – El Arousa road, where an ambulance train, provided by ADMS Armoured Division was waiting to take patients to the Main Dressing Station at Garfour. It was also arranged that as soon as an ambulance car reported at Djelida Station another would immediately be sent forward to replace it at Point 'A'. The time taken from Djelida Station to Garfour was thirty-five minutes, and the time from Point 'A' to Djelida Station just over an hour, but as the roads were improved, this latter time was cut down considerably. I appreciated that if all casualties were to be removed within a reasonable time of being wounded, the whole of the Field Ambulance would have to be thrown in. I ordered Lieutenant (QM) E. Anderson forward to Point 'A' to be responsible for the actual evacuation, while Captain Cassidy attended to the medical side. I immediately gave orders for the Field Ambulance to move forward and, as I wanted to know what conditions were like on Mansour and if there was anything else I could do to help, I took No 4 Section, consisting of Captain A. Percival RAMC, Staff Sergeant Anderson and seventeen bearers on to Mansour, arriving at the top of the hill just about dusk. After reconnoitring the route, I decided to go by carrier from the woods west of the 'woggery' (a term used by British troops meaning native huts) to the first ravine – where the ground was very exposed and covered by mortar and shell fire – and from there to follow the tapes to the left side of the main gully running up Djebel Mansour. This journey, carrying empty stretchers and first aid equipment, took two hours from the 'woggery'. On arrival at Mansour I saw Colonel Pearson and Haggie and arranged that, as there were then several cases still not evacuated, the worst cases would be carried down by No 4 Section, with French guides during the night. I myself with Captain Cassidy, who had accompanied me up the hill went back to arrange for the remainder of the Field Ambulance to go up the hill in the morning. We went back by practically the same route, but kept more to the west to avoid an enemy mortar which had been seen firing from the valley during the evening.

Thursday, 4th February 1943

In the morning I sent twenty men under Staff Sergeant Pruden with Corporal MacKenzie and Private Neil as guides, up the hill to reinforce the stretcher-bearers. I again went forward and reconnoitred the position in the main ravine, where I established an intermediate post with Captain Percival in charge (hereafter referred to as Car Post 'B'), and where I established a forward Car Post with Captain Wright in charge (Ravine Post).

Car Post 'B', Ravine Post and the ground in between was being heavily mortared, and therefore I obtained carriers from the Grenadier Guards to bring patients from the Ravine Post to Car Post 'B'. It now took three hours from the top of Mansour to the Ravine Post if fire was heavy, and two if it was not, then approximately three hours from that point to the Main Dressing Station at Garfour. In this way a shuttle service was arranged using all available personnel of the Field Ambulance except clerks, stores men and cooks. The carry from the top of the hill to the Ravine Post was extremely arduous and constantly under fire and bearers got very tired. In the afternoon the enemy started a continuous and heavy mortar shell fire on the Ravine Post and the plain leading from there to Car Post 'B'. When an apparent lull in the firing took place I called for four volunteer stretcher-bearers and, accompanied by Captain Wright, I went forward to the Ravine Post to see what damage had been done. As soon as we started to cross the open ground the enemy opened up again and the fire became so intense we had to turn back. I sent Captain Wright and the stretcher-bearers back to Post 'B', but as I was very worried about the fate of the Ravine Post, I went forward with my servant, believing that two individuals would not draw their fire as much as a group. In this, however, I was mistaken, but we got through and found the post intact. As I came away from the post the enemy dive-bombed the Ravine, and my servant, Lance Corporal Jermey was wounded. We again went back to the Ravine Post and found it still intact. When I returned to Car Post 'B' I was informed that a Major was lying in the forward 'woggery' where he had been dumped by the driver of a carrier who considered it unsafe for the officer to be lying on top of the carrier whilst the ground was under mortar fire. I got four volunteers and we went back down to the 'woggery' and brought Major Martin, 1st Battalion, back to Car Post 'B'. Finally when everyone was evacuated and as no more wounded came down the hill I withdrew the Ravine Post. My unit had by this time evacuated not only the casualties of the Parachute Battalion but also many casualties from the Grenadier Guards and the French.

Friday, 5th February 1943

Just before dawn every available stretcher-bearer left on the hill carried wounded down, and at 0800 hours all wounded had been evacuated. Immediately after this reports came through that the 1st Battalion had suffered many casualties due to heavy mortar and machine gun fire. I asked for twenty volunteers who went forward under the command of Captain Cassidy and Staff Sergeant Pruden with Corporal MacKenzie acting as guide. Captain Cassidy was halfway up the hill when the order for the evacuation of Mansour was given, but he decided – and quite rightly in my opinion – to go on to the top of the hill and to evacuate all available casualties. Captain Cassidy asked for some form of protection while doing this and it was immediately given by a Platoon Commander of the 1st Battalion, whose name is unknown to myself and Captain Cassidy. Every single casualty which could be found on the hill was evacuated. In the meantime I had sent a signal to my second-in-command to send every remaining member of the Field

The road leading to Djebel Mansour, with the author leading from the back. (Claire Cherry)

On the evocative lower slopes of Djebel Mansour 2010 – the medics at the rear as usual! (Claire Cherry)

Ambulance up except the Quartermaster Sergeant and two men. As the plain was by this time under continuous mortar and machine gun fire and many casualties were obviously taking place, I organised every available man to go forward and search the whole of the plain including the ravines. We found many wounded both parachutists and Grenadier Guards, particularly in the ravines, and brought them in. After this I again went out with another party and searched the plain until night fell.

My parties this time consisted of a mixture of Field Ambulance including clerks and storemen, RASC personnel and cooks. When it was obvious that nothing at all could be done any more and as no more wounded were coming in I withdrew Car Post 'B'.

Casualties evacuated by 16 Para Fd Ambulance

1st Battalion, The Parachute Regiment	129
Grenadier Guards	45
Argyll and Sutherland Highlanders	3
16 Para Fd Amb	1
RASC	2
French	9
German	1
Total	190

The figure does not include quite a few cases of wounded men who died on the way down the hill and were left, neither does it include many cases, particularly on the last day, who were killed by mortar fire after having been carried for some distance.

M. MacEwan
Lieutenant Colonel RAMC
Commanding 16 Parachute Field Ambulance
In the Field
11th February 1943

Appendix XXX

Report by L/Sergeant Cleland from the 1st Parachute Squadron RE on a night patrol undertaken on 17th February 1943

At 2000 on 17/02/1943 I set off on a patrol with L/Corporal Simpkins and Sapper Wright. We were under the command of Lieutenant Dover of the 2nd Battalion, the Parachute Regiment, who had with him six infantrymen.

The subject of the patrol was to discover if the Italians were occupying the Al el Maza ridge and also to investigate a 'woggery' which it was suspected that the Italians were using as an OP (map reference 688906). If the woggery was occupied or held by a small number of the enemy it was to be occupied by us and then booby-trapped.

At 2330 we had travelled along the ridge Al el Maza and reached the top of a gully about 300 yards from the 'woggery' without incident. We had been lying there for a few minutes when we were attacked by rifle fire from a wood about 30 yards east of the woggery. We kept our positions and did not return the fire. Lieutenant Dover decided to go forward to investigate. I was to accompany him. We had travelled about 20 yards to the left in order to proceed up a wadi towards the woggery when his decision was altered by the sound of a rifle being cocked close by. We then lay quiet for 10 minutes and then it was decided that the whole patrol should go forward to occupy the buildings.

We did so without incident and with the few other sappers we booby-trapped the building. During this operation the enemy were plainly heard coughing, talking and moving about. When the job was finished we left the woggery at about 0030 and returned to our own lines without incident.

Appendix XXXI

2nd Parachute Battalion – Standing Orders in defensive positions, 18th February 1943

1. Siting of positions.
   (a) Positions will be sited so as to be capable of all-round defence and so as to support each other by fire. In addition to defensive positions at least one OP per company will be dug separate from battle positions. All OPs must have covered lines of approach to them.
   (b) Bivouac positions will be sited well under cover and as near to defensive positions as is practicable.
2. Digging and wiring.
   (a) All positions will be dug to a depth of 5 feet so as to render their occupants safe should tanks overrun them.
   (b) All positions will be wired and all wire sited tactically. Where wire has to be sited in the open it will consist of single strands of trip wire, fastened to short pickets and interspersed with booby traps and alarms. All nullahs and gulleys leading up to positions and giving covered approaches there to will be well blocked with wire entanglements, booby traps and mines. All wiring will be covered by fire and wired blocks will be also be covered by grenade posts. Wire will be erected at a sufficient distance from main positions so as to be out of enemy range.
   (c) Where positions are liable to enemy observation digging and wiring will be carried out by night. In other cases it will be carried out by day. All digging and wiring parties will be protected by other troops in positions by night.
3. Mining and Booby traps.
   (a) Mining will be carried out to conform with the Battalion policy. Priority of mines is C Company, A Company and B Company.
   (b) All booby trapping will be carried out by troops of 1st Parachute Squadron RE in conformance with the Battalion policy.
   (c) Para 2 (b) of these orders applies to all mining and booby trapping.
4. State of readiness.
   (a) By day.
   OPs only will be manned, each by two soldiers. All remaining troops will keep under cover either on working parties or resting.
   (b) By night.
   Owing to the varying nature of platoon localities, different procedures must be adopted by each company. These will be:-
      (i) A Company.

Positions on forward slopes will be manned by two men of each section with light machine guns throughout the night. Positions on reverse slopes will not be manned: soldiers with positions on reverse slopes will sleep in bivouac areas with double sentries per bivouac area.

(ii) B Company.

Platoon on Yeomanry Hill will sleep in battle positions with double sentries per section. Platoon on Wardles Knoll will have two forward sections sleeping in battle positions. Remaining section will sleep in bivouac area. Double sentries per section. Remaining platoon will sleep in bivouac area with double sentries per section in battle positions.

(iii) C Company.

All platoons will sleep in battle positions. Double sentries per section.

(iv) Battalion mortars and MMGs

Will sleep in battle positions with double sentries per detachment. Where sub-unit positions are far apart intervening ground will be covered either by listening posts or periodical patrols.

(c) Hours of "stand to"

0600-0700 hours and 1800-1900 hours until further notice.

All platoons less A Company platoons and Wardles Knoll platoon will stand to in battle positions. A Company platoon at Wardles Knoll will stand to in bivouac positions with double sentries and light machine guns per section in battle positions. Where platoon positions are exposed platoons will not move into them until halfway through the hour of stand to.

5. 3" Mortars.

Company mortars will have alternative positions prepared in addition to their normal battle positions from which they can bring fire to bear on their own platoon localities in the event of these being overrun. Battalion mortars will be prepared to fire on all company localities.

6. Movement.

Will be kept to a minimum during daylight. Orders will be issued by sub-unit commanders so as to prevent unnecessary movement to and around positions under enemy observation. No transport will be sent to company positions by day unless approach is under cover. Each company will have a point beyond which no WD vehicle may proceed by day and ensure that the orders on this subject are carried out.

7. Range Cards.

Will be prepared for all positions.

8. Track Discipline.

To and around battle positions will be strictly maintained. Where tracks begin to appear leading to exposed battle positions, these will be prolonged away and forward of the positions so that they do not appear to lead to a position and then stop abruptly.

9. Anti-Aircraft.

(a) Companies will organise a system on AA alarm on which all men will remain still, under cover if possible, and not move about. Aircraft sentries only will look up.

(b) Should aircraft attack or swoop low over positions all small arms fire open up against it. Otherwise there will be no firing against aircraft.

10. Ammunition.
Will be held as under per weapon.

	(a) To be carried on man	(b) To be dumped in battle positions
Rifle .303	100 rounds	50 rounds
LMG .303	100 rounds	1000 rounds
Pistols .38 or .45	21 rounds	14 rounds
2" Mortar smoke	6 rounds	6 rounds
A/T .55	50 rounds	50 rounds
Grenades 36	2	nil
3" Mortar HE	nil	102 rounds
Sten 9mm	256 rounds	64 rounds

(c) In addition 100% reserve scale for the Battalion is held by RSM at Battalion HQ.

11. Practice firing.
Will not take place without permission from Battalion HQ.

12. Information.
- (a) Sub- unit commanders will ensure that all soldiers under command knows:
  - (i) All known enemy positions, likely lines of approach to own positions, and considered probable activities and intentions of enemy.
  - (ii) Positions and arcs of fire of neighbouring own troops (right, left, forward and rear) this includes those of supporting arms.
  - (iii) Own particular task (responsibility of observation and conduct in event of attack).
- (b) IO will ensure that companies are kept informed of all latest information concerning enemy and own troops.

13. Action against tanks.
- (a) No one will leave their positions. Should tanks overrun positions, soldiers will get well down in their slit trenches and lob sticky grenades at tanks when the opportunity occurs.
- (b) Provided soldiers keep well down in trenches, they will not be harmed should tanks go over them.
- (c) Supplies of sticky grenades will be kept in positions sited on probable approaches to tank attack.

14. Daily Routine.
- (a) The following routine inspections and checks will be carried out daily under arrangements of and by platoon commanders:-
  Arms, ammunition, foot, skin, picks and shovels.
- (b) All deficiencies will be reported to QM as soon as they occur. Any loss of arms, ammunition, equipment or clothing will always be treated as a Commanding Officer's offence.

(c) Rest will be properly organised on the roster system.

15. Sanitation.

Latrines and rubbish dumps will be inspected daily and re-dug where necessary.

16. Dress.

(a) NO form of head-dress will be worn by day other than steel helmets or berets. Cap comforters may be worn by night. Beret will NOT be worn inside out.

(b) No form of scarf (including face veils) will be worn.

(c) Equipment may be removed during daylight by those not on duty. By night all ranks in company areas will wear equipment including working parties carrying out wiring and digging etc. Working parties will have arms slung or in ready accessible place.

17. Saluting.

Particular attention will be paid to saluting both in and out of the line.

JWB Marshall
Major
2 i/c 2nd Battalion Parachute Regiment
In the field
18.2.1943.

Appendix XXXII

Report from A Troop 1st Parachute Squadron, 26th February 1943

Activity on morning 26th February 1943

At approximately 0600 26th February 1943 sustained machine gun fire was heard in the direction of 3rd Battalion positions. The Troop was turned out. At 0700 a message was received from Major Coxen 1st Battalion via Lieutenant Norton to say that A Troop were to proceed immediately to 3rd Battalion. On reporting to Battalion Headquarters we were guided to B Company.

Major Dobie, B Company commander ordered us to advance onto hill 375 to clear up "small pockets of enemy resistance". A guide was provided in Sergeant Lawson. The Troop were ordered to attack:

1 Section commanded by Captain George in front
2 Section Lieutenant Brown left
3 Section Sergeant Swift reserve
4 Section Lieutenant Mackay right

The Troop moved by bounds first left and swung round right. Lieutenant Mackay occupied 5 Platoon positions and detailed his Bren gunner to give covering fire. The Troop moved through heavy machine gun and rifle fire and mortaring to the centre of the ridge, Sergeant Lawson, Sappers Orton and Richie and Bren gun swung right to attack a machine gun position below by an abandoned enemy truck. During this phase Sergeant Swift was hit across the throat with a bullet but carried on after attention. 1 and 2 Platoons now occupied our position on the edge of the hill and were under fire from above and below. Approximately one section of Germans were seen preparing to attack 5 Platoon positions, they were all shot by riflemen (except one). I then ordered Lieutenant Brown to attack the upward machine gun from the left, he started to go but was shot from above or below. Sniping was continuous at this time from three sides. The machine gun crew above them threw several grenades and prepared to attack but were met by strong rifle and Bren fire at close range. I then ordered four men to attack the post – Sergeant Ellis, L/Sergeant Street and two Sappers, covered by Sappers Griffin and Brown and the machine gun post.

Later two captured MG34 machine guns were organised to cover our position and to cover the wadi below 5 Platoon's position. About this time Sapper Nelson was killed from below and L/Corporal Alexander was also wounded while attending to Lieutenant Brown.

I then moved down the hill covered by Sergeant Swift and then proceeded to attack the enemy position by the truck.

We found Sapper Ritchie badly wounded, Sapper Davies and I carried him out but he died whilst being attended. I had now contacted the infantry on my right and wanted to attack the lower machine gun but was told that we could not advance due to our own mortar fire. Eventually this post was silenced when I contacted Lieutenant Mackay and his Section moved up to occupy the hill.

In the meantime Sergeant Ellis and party on the centre position had cleared the lower slopes and accompanied by an infantry section had cleared the hill by sniping and grenades.

There were two mortar positions discovered on the lower slopes of the hill. From about 1500-1530 the hill was shelled by German artillery but no casualties caused. Sapper Orton was wounded in the foot whilst attacking the lower post and Captain George received a very slight flesh wound about the same time as Lieutenant Brown.

Observations

The Germans used only ball ammunition as it was very difficult to spot their positions as there was practically no smoke and certainly no flash was observed.

Recommendations

I should like to recommend Sergeant Ellis and Sergeant Lawson.

Sergeant Ellis, for his coolness and willingness, as he is always at the front and inflicted great damage by his accurate fire.

Sergeant Lawson, for his initiative and his attack with two men upon a machine gun during which all three were wounded.

Sapper Griffin, for his resource and initiative when using the Bren to cover us. He was always there when required and constantly on the move when under heavy fire.

Results

Captured two MG34s on heavy mounts with telescopic sights. One MG42. One rifle discharger. Two mortars complete and bombs.

Killed and wounded approximately 14.

Prisoners approximately 11 with appropriate rifles etc.

Captain S. George RE

Appendix XXXIII

Report from the 1st Parachute Battalion on actions of the 27th/28th February 1943

27th February

At 0615 hours R Company reported that the Company of the 3rd Battalion on their right was being attacked. Almost simultaneously a battle broke out on 38th Brigade front. Mobile Company was ordered to stand by. Some ten minutes later 1 Platoon of the Mobile Company was ordered to join 3rd Battalion at Argoub, a few minutes after this the remainder of the Mobile Company was ordered to stand by and CO and IO went up to Argoub. At 1000 hours S Company were ordered to join in the party together with Battalion HQ. The CO went forward and contacted CO 3rd Parachute Battalion and it appeared that the enemy had seized the high ground forward of Argoub 375. 725982 had been seized by the enemy. The first platoon of T Company to go up was sent off to reinforce B Company 3rd Battalion in area 466197. The remainder of the company went in on the counter-attack together with A Company 3rd Battalion on 375 and clearing the gully running north-east. They eventually returned with some 60 prisoners. Major Bull was put out of action early in the day when the truck transporting him to battle turned over near the cactus. The cactus was a clump around farm 708998 and was the scene of much lively activity. At dawn, just as the CO and IO arrived at this point three shells landed about 40 yards in front of the car.

R Company had the worst time during the battle as they were not involved in the actual fighting but were heavily shelled and mortared all day. They had eleven casualties but only one man was killed. It was decided to leave the Battalion up in Argoub for the night in case of further activity by the Hun. Toutla, meanwhile was being defended by a Field Park Company RE but as they were short of officers their force was strengthened by the addition of Major Hall and Lieutenant Disney. During the night it rained as hard as it could which did not improve the supply problem which was bad even at the best of times, Ammunition for mortars and small arms and rations had to be got up. Lieutenant Perrin-Brown was sent back to bring these up after dark. The rain made the track so bad that it was obvious our 15cwt trucks fitted with sand tyres would be useless. Major Cleasby-Thompson rang up the Staff Captain to try and get mules and carriers. This was impossible. However the REs lent us a six-wheeled semi-tracked 3 tonne lorry and Lieutenant Perrin-Brown set out at 0230 hours with ammunition. All went well on the journey up but on the way back a track came off and shortly afterwards the other track came off. Then, the trouble started, the lorry ended up in a ditch. The IO walked back leaving the REs to get their own lorry out. The Colonel who had stayed up at Argoub was screaming for his Pick Up.

Having arrived back on foot from the Argoub the IO then set out to get the Pick Up to the Colonel. The track was blocked by the RE lorry, therefore the journey had to be made via the Bou Arada-Pont du Fahs road, which necessitated going through the French minefields and these had to be lifted to get through, then put back. However, eventually the Pick Up arrived at Argoub to find the Colonel just leaving in a Brigade car. It was decided that T Company would remain under command of 3rd Battalion. This was most unsatisfactory as Captain Stevenson who was acting OC was being used as chief muleteer for 3rd Battalion and instead of 3rd Battalion rationing our men, Captain Stevenson had to chase around all 3rd Battalion Companies feeding his odd Platoons. Our guns were busy, heavily shelling and the enemy who replied in a very desultory manner.

Protective patrols were sent out at night.

28th February

Sunday was made a little different by a visit from Padre Watkins who held a church service in the chicken run at Battalion HQ. Followed by a communion service. This was the first service held since Christmas Day. The night was interrupted by a message from Brigade to the effect that the REs were returning to take over the Toutla and Saila positions and that S Company would be moved into reserve in counter-attacking role and as Mobile Company. These REs were due to arrive at 0030 hours. They were met by the Adjutant who put them in the bushes for the night. The major in charge of the REs was our old friend Major Freeston who was the bridge-blowing expert at S'Nasir. A message from T Company informed us that they were coming under our own command tomorrow and were to occupy hill 375.

Appendix XXXIV

Extracts from the war diary of 16 PFA for the Argoub period, 26th-27th February 1943

26th February 1943

0830. Information received that 3rd Battalion Parachute Regiment positions were being heavily attacked and had suffered heavy casualties. Captain Percival, Staff Sergeant and 6 ORs of No 4 Section with two ambulance cars proceeded to the area in order to evacuate casualties.

0930. Captain Percival's party arrived at R Company's position, 1st Battalion Parachute Regiment where Captain's Wright and Logan with 1 Staff Sergeant and 5 ORs already were - Argoub el Hanech (712996) - this position was being heavily shelled. Captain Percival's party then proceeded to RAP 3rd Battalion.

1000. Reported by RMO 3rd Battalion (Captain Rutherford RAMC) that casualties had by this time arrived at the RAP and were immediately evacuated by ambulance cars (2), via Captain Wright's position to Bou Arada.

Captain Wright's two ambulance cars were also sent forward to the RAP and assisted in the evacuation of the wounded.

1100. Sergeant Smith and 3 ORs restocked the RAP with extra dressings.

1400. Sergeant Weatherly and 9 ORs arrived as reinforcement stretcher-bearers.

1630. Heavy rain commenced which stopped evacuation of casualties by ambulance car and eleven casualties were held in the RAP.

1700. It was reported that enemy tanks were in the area north of El Arousa and that a tank attack was expected along the Pont du Fahs-Bou Arada road. The Brigade Commander therefore ordered the Field Ambulance to move to a site further south of Bou Arada. Major Wheatley recced a position while stores were being packed. The site chosen was three miles south of the present position at 615957 in a wood on the west side of the road. The troops in camp marched to the new site. All the stores were transferred in two lorries going backwards and forwards.

The CO remained at Brigade HQ setting up a permanent quarter there with Captain Ridler ADC and 4 ORs.

27th February 1943

The enemy had retired after suffering heavy casualties. The final casualties were evacuated during the day. Total casualties evacuated by this unit to ADS of No 1 Field Ambulance at Bou Arada were:

1st Parachute Battalion	20
3rd Parachute Battalion	28

The 3rd Parachute Battalion took a fair number of prisoners and their RMO, Captain J. Rutherford, had told the rest of the officers that he spoke German. One day this was put to the test – this picture, which was taken at an unknown location, shows him (far right) translating what the A Company commander Major S. Terrell, another barrister, had to ask them. As Lieutenant Colonel Pine-Coffin put it, "the MO enjoyed it all even less than the prisoners as his knowledge of German was not far beyond the 'pen-of-my-aunt' stage." (R. Pine-Coffin)

1st Parachute Squadron RE	2
68 Mortar Company	2
German	15
Total	67

CO ordered Captain Wright and 8 ORs and Captain Percival and 19 ORs to rejoin the unit. They reported in at 1730 and 1830 respectively.

On the 2nd Parachute Battalion front attacks were made by the Italians who suffered heavy losses but no casualties were sustained by that unit. No 3 Section were under shell and mortar fire whilst standing by with the Companies.

Sergeant Weatherby and 9 ORs proceeded to 3rd Parachute Battalion to relieve the men of No 4 Section.

Appendix XXXV

Report by Lieutenant Colonel R. Pine-Coffin, 3rd Parachute Battalion, Argoub Battle, 26th-27th February 1943

Report by Lieutenant Colonel R. Pine-Coffin, 3rd Battalion
Commanding Officer's account of the Argoub Battle
Reference Map Tunisia 1:50,000 Sheet 41 (Djebel Mansour)

On 26th February 1943 the Battalion was in position on the Tagoubet El Araan feature 7096, 7196; it was disposed as follows:-

Point 466 – A Company, Battalion Mortar Platoon (less one detachment) and FOO 13 Battery 17 Field Regiment RA

Point 414 (west) – C Company FOO 26 Battery 17 Field Regiment RA

Point 414 (east) – B Company

A group of Italian prisoners being searched for documents, maps and other useful items. (R. Pine-Coffin)

Point 375 track junction 700976 – Battalion HQ and one detachment Mortar Platoon

A vigorous patrolling policy had been followed from which it had been found that the enemy were occupying positions on the south-east bank of the wadi which runs 711931-720937-722950- O el Krammass-O Zenngou and on and off the Battalion front to the north.

Many machine gun positions and mortar sites were pinpointed from time to time. The enemy constantly shifted these positions and as a result it was difficult to gauge his exact strength or find the areas of responsibility of his sub-units, with any possible gaps between them.

The ground between the Battalion position and the wadi held by the enemy was cut up by a mass of lesser wadis except for a strip of very open ground, about 800 yards wide, immediately on the Battalion's side of the enemy's wadi. These lesser wadis had further tributary wadis leading in and out of them, usually at right angles, and although not so big as the enemy's wadis, they were nevertheless of considerable depth and were mostly scrub covered. They provided perfect cover from view and were naturally continually being searched by my patrols, who soon learned their way about in them. To the east of the Battalion feature the terrain was completely different and although the area of lesser wadis existed, there were fewer of them and the general impression was of very open country. Observation from this flank was very good and patrol routes could be worked out in great detail from OPs. The rest of the Battalion feature was thickly wooded and observation of the foreground was very limited.

Some of the prisoners taken by the 3rd Parachute Battalion being led away to the rear area. (R. Pine-Coffin)

The size of the feature and the thickness of the wood meant many points where the enemy could infiltrate deeply into the position; despite this however my chief worries were the flanks where nasty gaps existed between the Battalion and:-

(a) The French on the right. The left hand French position was at 892956 (except for a very small party of men at 695958)
and
(b) 1st Parachute Battalion (one company only) on the left. This company was on the Argoub feature i.e. just off Sheet 41 to the north of 7298.

I covered the gap on my right by fire, patrolling, wiring and heavy booby traps with a heavy mortar concentration instantly available in the event of a breakthrough (which would have seriously threatened my HQ). The gap on the left was extremely difficult to cover and required medium machine guns but I was unable to obtain any. It was watched by patrols and listening posts and very close liaison was maintained with the company of the 1st Parachute Battalion on the other side of the gap.

Two 6 pounder anti-tank guns were placed to deal with any tanks entering the gap and later an extensive minefield was laid with the object of driving the tanks onto the guns.

These gaps were a permanent headache as a determined enemy thrust at either of them would have been extremely difficult to have countered effectively. The Company areas were all ringed with wire and this was thickened as more wire became available; work however was slow as transport could only visit the Company areas by night and even so was dependent on the weather as the tracks were not negotiable to vehicles after the slightest rain. The rain at this time was almost continuous. It was not possible for the wire to be covered completely by fire owing to the thick nature of the country.

At 0615 on 26th February I received reports from both A and B Companies that they were being attacked. A on their left flank and B on their right. Both attacks were infiltrations which came right into the positions and in each case seriously threatened the Company HQ. Both were driven off by immediate counter-attacks, delivered with great dash by the Sections most easily available. A Company's attack took longer to beat off than B Company's and before A Company had stabilised their situation, B Company again reported trouble in the form of an attack on Point 375.

In the meantime I had contacted the 1st Battalion Company on the Argoub feature (which was not being attacked) and arranged for the Troop of 1st Parachute Squadron RE (which I knew to be with them) to be sent immediately for use as necessary. This was very necessary as the whole Battalion was required to hold the position and no reserve was available to me. I also asked for the Brigade Mobile Reserve which consisted of one Company from the 1st Parachute Battalion and was stationed in the Toutla area 6599. It was agreed that this Company would be sent to me as soon as possible but I had to expect it to arrive by Platoons separately.

The RE Troop arrived at my HQ at 0915 hours and I had to send them straight off to B Company as the situation at Point 375 was then being reported as critical. The situation was that the enemy appeared to have overrun the Platoon of B Company which had been holding this feature and to be in possession of the hill. Communications with this Platoon had gone dead and the 2 i/c of B Company had been killed on his way over to take charge of the situation. The Troop were used for a counter-attack on the feature immediately on arrival in the area. This attack was successful and the enemy was driven off the feature, which was then occupied by the Troop and the regrouped Platoon of B Company, which had been overrun (but one Section of which was later found to have remained in its position on the hill throughout). The enemy withdrew in some disorder to the area of the lesser wadis already referred to; here they attempted to reorganise, but made the mistake of remaining within mortar range. He undoubtedly suffered heavy losses from mortar fire at this stage. During the counter-attack Sergeant McDonnell and three men of B Company performed a series of almost fantastic feats of gallantry on the enemy side of the hill and cleared up many enemy posts on their own; they also followed the retreating enemy into the wadis and increased their casualties and disorder by getting amongst them and firing off the remainder of their ammunition into them at point blank range.

By this time A Company had driven off the enemy after the initial infiltration and reported that the enemy were moving westwards. It appeared that the next attack on this Company would come from the right flank, where the dangerous gap between the French and ourselves existed. In anticipation of this I sent them the first Platoon of the Mobile Reserve Company which had just arrived and ordered OC A Company to try and keep them intact for a counter-attack. This he was able to do.

I then found out that another Platoon of the Mobile Reserve Company had arrived earlier on but had reported direct to B Company, without coming to my HQ at all. Brigade also informed me that the Mobile Reserve was going to be increased and that I should receive two full Companies instead of one but that the second Company could not be expected for some hours – it arrived at my HQ at 1230. In view of this information I sent the third Platoon of the Mobile Reserve Company to A Company and hoped to be able to keep the whole of the second Company in hand for a counter-attack at the right moment.

The enemy made several further attempts on both flanks, but was clearly shaken by his original reception and was beaten off each time with heavy losses to himself. Large numbers of them were killed in the wadis and by 1300 it was clear that he had shot his bolt. A Reserve Company at this stage would have been invaluable but it did not exist and the second Company of the Mobile Reserve had not reached B Company's area (I had sent this Company straight off to the B Company area as soon as it arrived as it seemed the most promising flank from which to launch a counter-stroke). It arrived soon after however and was accompanied by CO 1st Parachute Battalion himself; the counter-attack force, consisting of a full Company and one Platoon (the one that had reported direct to B Company) was sent after the enemy with the minimum delay. They set off within 15 minutes of the 'right' moment for a counter-stroke.

The counter-attack was, in brief, a left-handed clockwise sweep following a frontal attack on the farm at Point 284, 733980 (which had been observed to have been used as a HQ or RAP or both). CO 1st Parachute Battalion followed this sweep and was in communication by 18 set with OC B Company at his OP. OC B Company was in turn in touch with me by line, using his own HQ as a link.

By 1415 the sweep was well advanced and was sending in prisoners at a great rate. I ordered OC A Company at this hour to launch one of the two 1st Parachute Battalion Platoons which he then had with him on a right-handed anti-clockwise sweep from his right flank. This Platoon soon ran into well-placed machine guns and became pinned down and I ordered OC A Company to send out the second Platoon from his left flank.

This second Platoon made slightly more progress than the first but, in due course also became pinned down by machine gun fire.

Meanwhile the force carrying out the wider sweep from the B Company front was beginning to come in through C Company's position so I ordered OC C Company to reorganise them and send them over to A Company's area. The force went out on the same lines as the first Platoon to get pinned down, but made a wider sweep. Somewhat confused fighting took place on this flank for the rest of the day and continued until well after dark. A considerable number of enemy were killed and captured in this action, but not nearly so many as on the other flank. The German troops on the right were found to be from a Jäger battalion and their fighting qualities were definitely superior to the troops on the other flank (T and A Companies).

The action proved an outstanding success for the Battalion and something like 1150 prisoners were taken together with a large amount of equipment and arms etc. Information is not available as to the number killed but there is no doubt that it was very considerable. For the Battalion's first battle (fighting as a whole Battalion) the result was most encouraging. The whole machinery worked extremely well and the fighting ability of all ranks was shown to be exceptional.

The Battalion's casualties were:

Killed 2 Officers (Captain Bromley-Martin and Lieutenant Wilson) and 12 ORs.

Wounded 1 Officer (Lieutenant Benton) and 33 ORs.

Interrogation of prisoners showed that the attack had been carried out by four German Battalions; this was confirmed by identifications obtained from other PoWs. A captured map (marked) gave an indication of the German plan and also showed the positions the Germans had been holding; these positions were exactly along the line that the Battalion intelligence map had them marked. The marked map indicated that the plan was to occupy Point 466 and Point 409 (near Battalion HQ), these points had been ringed on the map and arrows drawn to them were on the line that the original attacks followed. It seemed that the German patrolling had not been so good as ours and that they thought both Points 375 and 414 were unoccupied.

Appendix XXXVI

Roll of Honour for the Argoub fighting, 26th-27th February 1943

All casualties buried at Medjez-el-Bab CWGC Cemetery unless other stated together with grave number.

1st Battalion

26/02/1943

Corporal D. Bolland Massicault CWGC Cemetery 3L14
Private J. Crabtree NKG Medjez-el-Bab Memorial to the Missing
Private H. Gordon 2H11
Private L. Williams 10H13

3rd Battalion

26/02/1943

Captain G. Bromley-Martin 2H1
Private F. Cother NKG Medjez-el-Bab Memorial to the Missing
Corporal D. Guthrie 2H7
L/Corporal W. Hill 2C7
Private D. Millard 2H6
Private A. Moseley 2C15
Private D. Sidlow NKG Medjez-el-Bab Memorial to the Missing
Private T. Stewart 2C16
Private A. Svensson 2H4
L/Corporal F. Tyson Massicault CWGC Cemetery 3L10
Private J. Williams 2H5
Lieutenant L. Wilson 2C14
Private S. Wiseberg (served as Wilby) 2C13
Private E. Worsfold 2C18

27/02/1943

Private J. Birch 2C13

28/02/1943

Corporal A. Towler 9F10

1st Parachute Squadron Royal Engineers

26/02/1943

Lieutenant J. Brown Massicault CWGC Cemetery 3J16

27/02/1943

Sapper L. Nelson 2H3
Sapper D. Ritchie 2H2

28/02/1943
L/Corporal R. Alexander 9F1

Appendix XXXVIII

Roll of Honour for the 2nd Parachute Battalion, Tamera, 8th March 1943

Private A. Bacon Tabarka Ras Rajel CWGC Cemetery 1B16
Private G. Bigsby Tabarka Ras Rajel CWGC Cemetery 1B12
Private E. Donald Tabarka Ras Rajel CWGC Cemetery 1B17
Private J. Jackson Tabarka Ras Rajel CWGC Cemetery 1B9
Private G. Martin Tabarka Ras Rajel CWGC Cemetery 1B14
Private J. Miles Tabarka Ras Rajel CWGC Cemetery 4C9
Captain E. Radcliffe Tabarka Ras Rajel CWGC Cemetery 4C8
Corporal W. Reeves Tabarka Ras Rajel CWGC Cemetery 1B19

It is known that Bert Bacon was killed as a result of an attack by German aircraft, which also wounded a number of other men including Mick Miles and Ron Moon. He was aged 20.

Appendix XXXIX

Roll of Honour for the 3rd Parachute Battalion, Tamera, 8th March 1943

Private V. Alford Tabarka Ras Rajel CWGC Cemetery 4E7
Private W. Blood Tabarka Ras Rajel CWGC Cemetery 4A14
Private L. Chandler Tabarka Ras Rajel CWGC Cemetery 4A1
Lieutenant J. Evans Tabarka Ras Rajel CWGC Cemetery 4E8
Private J. Kitson NKG Medjez-el-Bab Memorial to the Missing
Private J. Lanigan Tabarka Ras Rajel CWGC Cemetery 4A17
Lieutenant F. Norton Medjez-el-Bab CWGC Cemetery 4A10
Private T. Sanderson Tabarka Ras Rajel CWGC Cemetery 4A15
Sergeant D. Storer Tabarka Ras Rajel CWGC Cemetery 4A16
Private D. Utton Tabarka Ras Rajel CWGC Cemetery 8B3

Appendix XL

Roll of Honour for Tamera, 9th March 1943

1st Battalion

Private A. Mason NKG Medjez-el-Bab Memorial to the Missing
Private N. Twaddle Tabarka Ras Rajel CWGC Cemetery 4E6
Sergeant W. Weaving Tabarka Ras Rajel CWGC Cemetery 1A16

2nd Battalion

Corporal A. Clouting Bone CWGC Cemetery 3A5
Private W. Lambirth Tabarka Ras Rajel CWGC Cemetery 1B18

Royal Corps of Signals attached to 1st Parachute Brigade

Signalman J. Marson Tabarka Ras Rajel CWGC Cemetery 3C2

Appendix XLI

Roll of Honour for Tamera, 10th March 1943

1st Parachute Brigade HQ

Captain J. Cassidy RAMC Tabarka Ras Rajel CWGC Cemetery 3C7
Lieutenant J. Battye Royal Corps of Signals Tabarka Ras Rajel CWGC Cemetery 3C14

1st Battalion

Private V. Amey Tabarka Ras Rajel CWGC Cemetery 3C9
Private F. Francis Tabarka Ras Rajel CWGC Cemetery 2C3
Private W. Litchfield Medjez-el-Bab CWGC Cemetery 4A12
Private J. Moore NKG Medjez-el-Bab Memorial to the Missing
Private T. Wilson NKG Medjez-el-Bab Memorial to the Missing

2nd Battalion

L/Sergeant W. Anderson Tabarka Ras Rajel CWGC Cemetery 1B21
Private L. Carroll Tabarka Ras Rajel CWGC Cemetery 2C3
Private S. Dangerfield Tabarka Ras Rajel CWGC Cemetery 3C6
Major G. Rothery Medjez-el-Bab CWGC Cemetery 4A4
Private A. Stevenson NKG Medjez-el-Bab Memorial to the Missing

1st Parachute Squadron RE

Lieutenant A. Mothersill Tabarka Ras Rajel CWGC Cemetery 1A8

Major G. Rothery's grave at Medjez-el-Bab CWGC Cemetery. (N. Cherry)

Appendix XLII

Roll of Honour for Tamera, 11th March 1943

1st Battalion

Private R. Ferguson Tabarka Ras Rajel CWGC Cemetery 3C8
Private N. Johnston Tabarka Ras Rajel CWGC Cemetery 2C4
Private J. Ross Tabarka Ras Rajel CWGC Cemetery 2C6

2nd Battalion

Private G. Burns Tabarka Ras Rajel CWGC Cemetery 2C5
Private J. Byng Tabarka Ras Rajel CWGC Cemetery 4C10
L/Corporal W. Clark NKG Medjez-el-Bab Memorial to the Missing
Private J. Southern Tabarka Ras Rajel CWGC Cemetery 1B1
Private G. Wickwar Tabarka Ras Rajel CWGC Cemetery 1B15

3rd Battalion

Captain J. Ellis Medjez-el-Bab CWGC Cemetery 8B3
Corporal T. Grieve NKG Medjez-el-Bab Memorial to the Missing
L/Corporal J. Murphy MM Medjez-el-Bab CWGC Cemetery 4A18
Corporal A. Picken Tabarka Ras Rajel CWGC Cemetery 3D12
Private S. Sageman Tabarka Ras Rajel CWGC Cemetery 1B20
Private E. Smith Tabarka Ras Rajel CWGC Cemetery 4C22
Corporal J. Webb Tabarka Ras Rajel CWGC Cemetery 1E10

Appendix XLIII

Roll of Honour for Tamera, 27th-30th March 1943

27th March

2nd Battalion

Private I. Adams NKG Medjez-el-Bab Memorial to the Missing
Private B. Arliss Tabarka Ras Rajel CWGC Cemetery 3B13
Private J. Beddo NKG Medjez-el-Bab Memorial to the Missing
Private H. Davis NKG Medjez-el-Bab Memorial to the Missing
Private J. Friel NKG Medjez-el-Bab Memorial to the Missing
Corporal T. Gay NKG Medjez-el-Bab Memorial to the Missing
Private M. Herwood NKG Medjez-el-Bab Memorial to the Missing
Private J. Hines NKG Medjez-el-Bab Memorial to the Missing
Private C. Hoy NKG Medjez-el-Bab Memorial to the Missing
Sergeant C. Huntley Tabarka Ras Rajel CWGC Cemetery 1D18
Sergeant J. Jackson NKG Medjez-el-Bab Memorial to the Missing
Sergeant P. Lenderyou Tabarka Ras Rajel CWGC Cemetery 3B15
Private R. MacDonald Tabarka Ras Rajel CWGC Cemetery 3B14
Private H. McArdle NKG Medjez-el-Bab Memorial to the Missing
Private M. McCarthy Beja CWCG Cemetery 2J2
L/Corporal L. McGrath NKG Medjez-el-Bab Memorial to the Missing
Private R. Page Tabarka Ras Rajel CWGC Cemetery 3B12
Private F. Selman Beja CWGC Cemetery 2H12
Captain R. Spender Tabarka Ras Rajel CWGC Cemetery 3B20
Private R. Stark NKG Medjez-el-Bab Memorial to the Missing
Major M. Wardle Tabarka Ras Rajel CWGC Cemetery 3B19

28th March

1st Battalion

Sergeant C. Baxter NKG Medjez-el-Bab Memorial to the Missing
Private C. Billingsley Beja CWGC Cemetery 2B1
Private W. Brown Beja CWGC Cemetery 2H9
Private L. Day NKG Medjez-el-Bab Memorial to the Missing
Lieutenant K. Gallagher NKG Medjez-el-Bab Memorial to the Missing
Corporal F. Jarrett RAMC attached Beja CWGC Cemetery 2H8
L/Corporal L. McLeod Beja CWGC Cemetery 2A1
Private A. Reid Beja CWGC Cemetery joint grave 2H10/11
Private L. Venn NKG Medjez-el-Bab Memorial to the Missing
Private S. Wall NKG Medjez-el-Bab Memorial to the Missing
Private G. Wood Beja CWGC Cemetery joint grave 2H10/11

3rd Battalion
Private M. Fitch RAMC attached Tabarka Ras Rajel CWGC Cemetery 1D10
L/Corporal F. Lumsden Beja CWGC Cemetery 2J3
1st Parachute Brigade Signal Section
Corporal J. McConney Tabarka Ras Rajel CWGC Cemetery 1N9

29th March
1st Battalion
Private H. Crosby Tabarka Ras Rajel CWGC Cemetery 3B17
Private F. Dodson NKG Medjez-el-Bab Memorial to the Missing

30th March
1st Battalion
Private L. Hayselden NKG Medjez-el-Bab Memorial to the Missing
Private G. Hearnden Tabarka Ras Rajel CWCG Cemetery 1B22
Private C. Mortimer RAMC attached Tabarka Ras Rajel CWGC Cemetery 1B24
Private J. Potter Tabarka Ras Rajel CWGC Cemetery 1D1

Appendix XLIV

Report written for Major-General Browning's visit to North Africa in December 1942 on the activities of 16 Parachute Field Ambulance up to this time from their arrival in November 1942

A. General

Experience in the field under varied conditions, some not even thought of before, have proved that the organisation, battle drill and equipment as worked out by ADMS and ourselves is basically sound. The equipment carried in a parachute action by a section and its surgical team is vastly superior to anything carried by any other unit forward of a CCS. This is justified by:-

(a) We are the first medical unit on the ground.
(b) We treat not only our own casualties but also the casualties of other units, for some time before normal medical help arrives.
(c) We take the surgeon to the patient, not the patient to the surgeon, and our results so far have been extremely satisfactory. Our mortality rate from major surgical interference is .75.

One fact has emerged very clearly as a result of our experience in North Africa and that is that the limiting factor in the amount of equipment carried in a parachute operation will always have to be what men can carry over long distances and not the number of containers available.

Here the atmosphere is rarer than that at home and a man drops much faster. DZ casualties have established that the parachutist with the barest minimum of equipment is best even at the risk of losing containers. One DZ casualty starts a team off at a great disadvantage.

B. Tactical Deployment

We had visualised either the Brigade dropping as a whole, or a Battalion concentrated two or three miles from its objective, forming up – the approach march, followed by the seizure and holding of the objective.

The Brigade has been employed as follows:

(a) One Battalion carrying out an operation as visualised at home.

(b) One Battalion being ordered to drop and take three objectives in succession involving an approach march to the third objective of twenty five miles from the DZ and then returning through enemy country to its base.

(c) The three Battalions in action simultaneously in three different parts of the country. Although this did not materialise we had at one stage to make preparations for it.

(d) Where the Brigade is acting as an Infantry Brigade on the ground and the Field Ambulance goes into action either in support of its own Brigade or as part of the general medical plan.

The very minimum of equipment should be taken. In this type of operation the RAP and ADS must at all times be inside the defensive perimeter of the Battalion. If it is impossible, owing to the tactical situation to carry wounded, dumps of wounded must be formed and the normal Corps proportion of medical orderlies left with them. Transport suitable for the terrain should be requisitioned to carry the wounded. In (c) if each of the three Battalions is carrying out a role where a surgical team can be employed then it is essential that there should be a third surgical team on the establishment.

I was lucky enough to have Major P. Wheatley a graded surgeon, on my establishment, and to have enough experienced men to enable me to form my third surgical team.

In (d) lack of transport is our greatest problem. I feel certain that this phase of Parachute Field Ambulance work must be practised in the future.

C. Answers to questionnaire

1. Has the attachment of a Section of the Field Ambulance to each Battalion worked satisfactorily? Yes.
2. What use has been made of the surgical teams? No 1 Surgical Team under Lieutenant C. Rob performed 162 operations when they dropped with the 1st Battalion. Cases were treated very early and retained until they were fit to travel with the result that out of the 162 cases operated on only one died.

Details of units for those operated on:

1st Parachute Battalion	37
2nd Parachute Battalion	4
Hampshire Regiment	19
US forces	16
R West Kents 1	4
RA	12
E Surreys	8
6 Commando	6
17/21 Lancers	4
RASC	4
Northants Regiment	7
Germans	5
Italians	1
RE	1
A&SH	1
Lancashire Fusiliers	1
Total Military cases	140

Arab and French civilians	22
Total	162

Types of injury of service personnel:
121 single wounds
15 multiple wounds
77 flesh wounds
34 compound fractures
8 abdominal wounds
7 burns
5 chest
4 eye
3 joints
2 simple fractures
1 urethra
1 testicle
1 spine
1 jaw
1 skull and brain
1 peripheral nerves
2 gas gangrene (before surgery)
1 gas gangrene
1 amputation (after surgery)

No complete record of civilians operated on, but the majority were limb wounds. One civilian died. No praise can be too high for the officers and men of this Section. The other teams have been standing by but have not yet functioned.

3. Is the establishment of the Section suitable? Yes (see recommendations for war establishments).
4. Has CO Field Ambulance been in W/T contact with the Sections on operations? Yes, through Battalion and Brigade links.
5. Was the medical equipment found to be satisfactory? Eminently (see recommendations for equipment). I should like here to express my gratitude to Colonel A. Eagger, for his untiring energy put in by himself and the DADMS for all the time devoted.
6. Any items found unnecessary and any items deficient? See recommendations for equipment.
7. Have the stretchers been satisfactory? Yes, absolutely.
8. Comment on the attachment of RAMC personnel to Battalions. Very satisfactory.
9. Has the collection of casualties been satisfactory? See remarks on tactical handling. Casualties have been collected and evacuated rapidly. In the case of the 2nd Battalion casualties were collected by Lieutenant J. McGavin and his Section from all over the hills and taken to a farm which was unfortunately outside the perimeter of defence, with a result that the whole section are now reported missing.
10. Any difficulties on DZ or on approach march? Two types of container drill have been evolved as the result of experience (C47 aircraft).
    (a) Where a Section and its Surgical Team are carried in two aircraft.

This is in my opinion the method of choice. Normal container drill using trolleys which we have found to be very successful, is the order.

Trolleys must have permanent attachments for handling and hauling, and for securing the load. It is absolutely vital that trolley assembly and trolley packing is practised over and over again.

(b) Here the personnel of the Section are distributed among the aircraft of the Battalion. This method is unsatisfactory and should not be used if at all possible. The disadvantages are that containers which would normally be emptied by two or three men have to be emptied by one or two. It slows down the time between the drop and the forming-up point considerably. The disadvantage far override the advantage of having all ones eggs in more than two baskets.

If the operation is a single objective operation a Company should be guarding the DZ until all have landed and DZ casualties can be collected, but if the operation is a more than one objective operation casualties should be dumped and left unless transport is easily available.

On the approach march trolleys must be used or a very light load of equipment carried. Training in endurance carrying heavy loads is of more importance than short fast bursts.

11. What casualties to RAMC personnel have occurred? In No 1 Section one man was accidentally shot and Lieutenant Rob injured his knee whilst dropping but hid this fact and carried on operating for three weeks while he himself aspirated his knee.

    At the end of the mission he had to go into hospital and has unfortunately been evacuated for removal of a cartilage. In No 2 Section Lieutenant McGavin and 16 Other Ranks are missing. 8 Other Ranks of the Battalion medical orderlies are also missing. From No 3 Section Captain Keesey and 2 Other Ranks were in the aircraft which caught fire when taking off from Gibraltar. Fortunately the aircraft landed in the sea and they were able to get out and after spending some time in the sea were picked up and have now joined us.

12. What arrangements have been made for setting up dressing stations when the objective has been reached? Normal arrangements as practised in England. Advantage was taken of every building and hospital available at Bone, Souk-el-Arba and at Beja.

D. Recommendations

1. Dress. Battle dress should always be worn and the smock either rolled or worn. In the back part of the smock, pullover, shirt and socks can be inserted by opening up the lining.

   One basic pouch should hold first aid medical equipment and the other one emergency rations, water sterilising tablets, spare socks and one meal ration (MRS).

2. Rations. The ration is too heavy and not easily divisible into separate meals. I recommend the use of the MRS meal ration.

3. Equipment. Operating lamps. The present type is too heavy and cumbersome and the batteries do not last long enough without being recharged. It is suggested that a petrol lamp should be used. The question on lighting is very important in the theatre. The establishment of spare batteries for headlamps should be increased. Primus stoves. Collapsible type should be devised.

Bedpans. Absolutely essential but are difficult to pack in their present shape.
Sterilized swabs. Suggest that the German pattern of compressed sterilized gauze swab be used.
Sleeping tablets. Tablets of the barbiturate class should be provided for post-operative cases.
Ethyl chloride. General should be substituted for local type.
Omnopon. Tubonics should be of the latest type with the tube enclosed in a mica case.
Binoculars. Suggest the folding monocular type should be provided.
Tannic acid jelly. Has not been used.
Pentothal. All tubes should be one size.
Medical comforts. The present issue is not suitable for packing. It should be provided in compact tins and not in bulk.
General. After more experience has been gained a report will be forwarded giving details of packing and loading tables, Field Surgical Packs and Field Medical Packs. Equipment should be provided as individual items rather than made up from the contents of these panniers. Packs packed operationally could then be stowed in Field Parachute Panniers. Under the present system in order to prepare for a parachute operation many panniers have to be completely broken down. Full report with suggestions on this later.

Appendix XLV

Post-Operational Thoughts on the First Deployment of a Parachute Field Ambulance by Lieutenant Colonel M. MacEwan, April 1943

Introduction

i) Experience in the field, under varied conditions, has proved that the organisation, battle drill and equipment of the Parachute Field Ambulance, as worked up by ADMS Airborne Division and ourselves, are basically sound. The equipment carried in a parachute action is vastly superior to that of any other medical unit forward of the CCS, but this apparent extravagance is justified by the facts that:-

a) We are the first medical unit on the ground.
b) We treat not only casualties of our own Brigade, but also casualties of other units, pending the arrival of normal medical formations.
c) We take the surgeon to the patient – and not the patient to the surgeon – and our results because of this factor have been extremely satisfactory.
d) We must be prepared to treat and **hold**.

I must here express my gratitude to Colonel A.E. Eagger OBE, for his untiring energy in fighting everybody to get us the equipment and for all the time and thought put in on it by himself and Major Courtney RAMC.

ii) Containers must be issued to units and packed, cradled and shackled in unit lines. The stick complete with its containers should then travel to the airfield to be met there by a unit guide who should direct it to its aircraft. Electrical circuits should then be tested and containers loaded. In the same way, chutes should be issued in unit lines, fitted and carried by the individuals concerned to the airfield. This would entail a minimum of time spent on the airfield, which, in a battle zone may tend to be unhealthy.

iii) Field Ambulance medical personnel should be carried in separate aircraft and not distributed among Battalion personnel.

iv) I feel that provisions should be made in the Parachute Brigade establishment for a wireless tentacle to be attached to the Field Ambulance for use with the MDS or ADS. At present communication is through the Brigade and Battalion links, but circumstances have arisen where, in spite of the fact that there is a medical liaison officer at Brigade Headquarters, communications have at times been difficult.

v) If the parachute mission is a single-objective operation, the first company down should guard the DZ until all have landed and DZ casualties have been collected. But if the operation has more than one objective casualties should be collected into dumps and left with the normal Corps proportion of medical orderlies, unless transport is available. Battalion Commanders must co-operate in seizing transport suitable to the terrain, not only for Battalion needs but also to transport their wounded.

Tactical Employment

The tactical employment of a Parachute Field Ambulance must conform very closely to that of its Brigade.

1) During Training in England we had visualised the Brigade going into action as:-
   a) A complete Brigade, either alone or as part of a bigger airborne force to establish a bridgehead allowing our armour to go through unscathed.
   b) A Battalion or Company going into action such as Bruneval, supported by a corresponding number of Field Ambulance personnel.
2) Since our arrival in this country however the Parachute Brigade has either been employed in or earmarked for the following roles:-
   a) 1 Battalion seizing and holding an objective and pushing out aggressive patrols.
   b) 1 Battalion seizing and destroying one objective, then advancing 15 miles to a second objective and finally fighting its way back through enemy territory to our own lines.
   c) The Brigade complete was asked to do an airlanding operation on Sfax. Although this operation did not materialise, every preparation was made for it, loading tables being drawn up and tested out in actual aircraft practice.
   d) 3 Battalions in action simultaneously in different parts of the country, necessitating the provision of 3 surgical teams, although the 3rd Battalion drop did not materialise, the necessary surgical adjustments were made.
   e) The Brigade in action on the ground as an ordinary infantry brigade i) in defence ii) in attack.
   f) A complete Brigade drop. So far such an operation has not been carried out, but I feel sure that we must always keep this in front of us as the peak of our training. When we are asked to do one, I shall, depending, of course, on the operational requirements of the particular mission set up i) 2 ADS's, each with a surgical team while the third section reinforces the stretcher-bearers of the Battalions, or ii) use the framework laid down for our airlanding operation, whether the second party comes in the same flight or on the next day. That is advance Field Ambulance HQ functioning with Parachute Brigade HQ and 2 sections and 2 surgical teams forming the MDS. The remaining section act as stretcher-bearers to evacuate the wounded from the Battalions to the MDS. As can be seen from the loading tables with C47 aircraft more than 13 personnel can be carried without overloading. Thus practically all the SB's of the unit can be taken in the first lift, allowing 1 aircraft for Field Ambulance HQ and 6 aircraft for the rest of the unit.

In 1 a) the basic principles of training at home are, in my opinion, sound. The ADS must be inside the perimeter of defence of the Brigade and cases must be held and treated until the force is relieved. As such an undertaking would lead to shelling and dive-bombing attacks, the ADS must be dug in and slit trenches made.

In 1 b) the factors influencing policy are: – i) whether the operation will be static long enough for a surgical team to function, ii) the type of country, which will influence the equipment to be carried and iii) a Staff picture of expected casualties.

In 2 b) a surgical team cannot function and the equipment carried by the section will be little more than stretchers, blankets, basic pouches and 1 or 2 standard packs. The provision of stretchers is absolutely vital and transport suitable to the terrain must be requisitioned to carry the wounded.

In 2 c) operations once the unit has landed should not differ materially from 1 a) except that equipment can be carried on a large scale.

In 2 d) if the establishment of surgical teams is to remain at 2, at least 200% ORA's and NO's experienced in theatre work should be trained inside the unit, and at least 1 of the ordinary MO's should be a graded surgeon. I now have quite a number of men trained as ORA's over and above my establishment. I further recommend that every officer on the establishment of a parachute field ambulance should be a trained anaesthetist. The FSU has an anaesthetist attached, but the surgical team of a parachute field ambulance has not. I have been using my Dental Officer as anaesthetist.

In 2 e) the following comments are made. In my opinion, so long as our manpower situation remains what it is, parachute troops will, on occasions be called upon to fight as ground troops in whatever theatre of war they are engaged. In this connection, the lack of unit transport out here has been a continuous headache. Whenever heavy equipment has to be carried in an advance or a withdrawal, the Parachute Field Ambulance, unless supplied with its own transport is practically immobile and there is always a grave risk of losing valuable stores.

i) In defence the unit has worked very efficiently in my opinion and, as we are equipped on a better scale than any other medical formation forward of the CCS we are capable of supporting our Brigade on the ground under all circumstances.
ii) In the attack a very careful appreciation of all factors must be made as on that appreciation depends how the personnel are placed, stores to be carried and the chain of evacuation. In attack, as in defence, the ADS must be pushed up as close to the fighting as possible. If the site is well chosen and ordinary elementary precautions taken from the very beginning casualties among Field Ambulance personnel should not be heavy and, at the same time, the Battalion casualties can be, in most cases in the ADS within a very short time of being wounded. Moreover, our men, by reason of their training and close association and liaison as parachutists with their respective Battalions, are more inclined in an ordinary land operation to work much closer to the fighting troops than the personnel of a normal Field Ambulance.

Surgery

The Surgical Teams of 16 Parachute Field Ambulance, working both on parachute missions and in conjunction with ground forces, have performed to date a total of 456 operations – detailed later.

Lieutenant C. Rob MC, working single handed at Beja early in the campaign had to hold all his cases, all of which were evacuated to him by personnel of 16 Parachute Field Ambulance. Major P. Wheatley, Lieutenant C. Longland and Lieutenant A. Lipmann

Kessel were all, however, operating at MDS's other than our own except for a short period when we had our own operating centre at Maison Forestiere. At these MDS's only, the most serious cases were treated and these were for the most part evacuated within 24 hours of operation, although abdominals were as a rule held for 6-10 days.

Thus the mortality rate shown in Appendix 1, although not fictitious, does not give a true picture as results could not always be followed up in the case of those patients evacuated within 24 hours of operation. Some cases operated upon were already almost hopeless, and these operations were, of course, performed by our most experienced surgeon.

The time lag between injury and operating varied from 4 to 36 hours (a small proportion of casualties not being found for some time after injury owing to the nature of the terrain in the battle area). The following table, giving a casual analysis of one series of 150 consecutive cases, is interesting:-

Type:	
Single Wounds	89
Multiple Wounds	61
Total	150
Casual:	
Bullet wounds	46*
Mortar, Shell and Grenade	94
Road Accidents	10
Total	150

*17 of which were accidental GSW.

Gas Gangrene

In my own unit anti-gas gangrene serum is given as a routine at the ADS to any patient with buttock or thigh wounds, or wounds causing great loss or pulping of soft tissues. One case only developed gas gangrene, which was not fatal. In five other cases gas gangrene was diagnosed clinically and was fatal in each case. In only two of these cases were typical local changes present i.e. sainous [serous] fluid, gas and brick-red dead muscle (at 36 hours). Excision of the initial wound at 8 hours had been inadequate and death followed amputation. In a third case the systemic toxaemia was accompanied by an apparently healthy wound, but at 40 hours clostridia were demonstrated microscopically in smears; death again followed amputation, the initial excision having been wide at 5½ hours. In a fourth there were no local signs, primary excision at 7 hours had been radical and no clostridia were obtained from the excised edges post-mortem (26 hours after wound). In the fifth case wide excision of a calf wound at 9 hours did not prevent death at 26 hours, despite anti-gas gangrene serum intravenously in full doses from the time of operation. Post-mortem examination showed a healthy wound [with] retro-peritoneal gas cellulitis, which had spread, by the femoral canal on the side of the wound.

Despite the widest early excision and full use of anti-gas gangrene serum there are occasional cases in which the infection is early and overwhelming. Cases developing later, after the patient has left the MDS, are probably more benign.

Anaesthetics

a) Choice of Anaesthetics. Normally either pentothal or ether with an induction by ethyl chloride was used. In 4 cases out of a series of 150 endo-tracheal anaesthetic was absolutely essential and the addition to the equipment of Magill's Tubes is considered necessary.

b) Proportion of Anaesthetics used.
Ether inducted by ethyl chloride42%
Pentothal 40%
Local 6%
Chloroform and ether followed by ether7%
Pure chloroform5%

c) Anaesthetic apparatus.

1. Ether. The Ogsden's mask was used in preference to the Schimmelbusch, owing to the necessity for conserving ether. On the average three patients required 1lb of ether. In view of the ever-present likelihood of the patient's collapse on the operating table the absence of oxygen and carbon dioxide presents an acute problem. It is recommended that a light cylinder and inhaler, as supplied to airman and rescue parties, might be included without adding greatly either to the weight or bulk of the stores.
2. Pentothal anaesthesia. Although a large serum needle can be used for mixing purposes, a cannula would be an improvement. The average expenditure of pentothal was found to be 1½ gram per patient.

Plasma and Plaster

Plasma. This was used in considerable quantity in the resuscitation of patients, both prior to, and during operations. Its use enabled many severely wounded cases to be 'got fit' for operations and to withstand major operative procedures. These cases otherwise would have been inoperable.

Amount used per 100 cases – approximately 50 pints.
About 10% of the cases needed transfusion and each case usually required 3 pints.
Plaster. 4 inch, 6 inch and 24 inch (Collona Slab) bandages were used.
Amounts per 100 cases:
40 inch x 4 inch 80
6 inch 60
24 inch (slab) 2
About 40% of the cases required plaster.

A Parachute Field Ambulance in an Airlanding Operation

a) Personnel.

The loading caters for the War Establishment (less first reinforcements) of RAMC and AD Corps (less one Corporal and one Private left at base with stores), eleven Other Ranks RASC, five cooks ACC, one Padre and his batman. The total personnel are 11 Officers and 109 Other Ranks. 10 additional men may be added according to requirements without overloading aircraft. The RASC personnel consist of a CSM, 2 Fitters and 8 drivers their object being to operate captured vehicles.

b) Organisation.
The personnel are organised into:-
(i) Advance HQ or CO's party with 1 Surgical Team.
(ii) Rear HQ or 2 i/c's party with QM and second Surgical Team.
(iii) 3 Sections – each consisting of 1 MO, 19 ORs RAMC and 1 driver RASC.
Twelve planes are allotted and each section is self-contained in two planes. Advanced HQ occupies two planes and Rear HQ four planes.
Each section is capable of setting up an independent ADS or 2 sections can combine with HQ and set up an MDS which can operate on, and retain patients. The organisation is flexible and can be adapted to circumstances. The following is an example, which has been visualised:-
The Brigade lands in two separate lifts at the same place on consecutive days. With the first lift Advance HQ and 2 sections land. Advance HQ with its surgical team and 1 section set up a dressing station and prepares the site for the MDS. The other section evacuates casualties from the RAPs to the MDS. With the next lift Rear HQ and the remaining section arrive. They reinforce the skeleton MDS already formed.

c) Equipment.
The equipment is designed to treat 600 casualties of whom 200 can be operated on by the two surgical teams. Sufficient equipment is taken to set up either one large dressing station or two small ones, each with a surgical team. It is designed on the expectation of working for a fortnight and to remain as a unit in the forward area.
The normal equipment for a parachute operation is taken, although the packs can be put into baskets for convenience and additional equipment which it would be impossible to carry on a parachute operation is also taken. For example, each section has two panniers containing ward equipment and each surgical team has a pannier containing heavy articles such as electrolyte and a pelvis rest. Advance HQ takes two folding motorcycles, light office equipment, light cooking and sanitary equipment. Rear HQ carries further office, cooking and sanitary equipment and the QM Stores, which includes complete reserve section equipment, a complete reserve surgical team equipment and reserve expendable medical stores to supply RMOs. Certain reserve equipment such as blankets and stretchers, are spread over the section planes.
Standard equipment in each plane includes 5 boxes of Compo rations, 4 gallons of water, 1 pick, 5 shovels and 2 airborne trolleys.

(d) Loading.
Experimental loading has been carried out for a section and it has been found that in the C47 aircraft, of which the maximum load is 4,500 lbs. there is ample space for all the stores and personnel detailed above.
The airborne trolleys can be emplaned and deplaned with ease and much saving of time when they are fully loaded, but care must be taken to leave the strop line at the side of the plane clear when loading.

Recommendations for the use of Parachute Surgical Teams in Land Operations

Personnel

An officer, dental or medical, with anaesthetic experience in the management of lists of surgical operations, in cases of all grades of severity, is necessary for full time work as an anaesthetist with each team. 5 Other Ranks are sufficient.

Equipment

Additions to the equipment used for parachute missions are necessary for convenience (thereby adding to efficiency) and for prolonged periods of work done. The equipment dropped initially on a parachute action is designed only for work lasting a few days, whereas the parachute surgical team may well be expected to function, in the role of a Field Surgical Unit after the land forces have made contact with the airborne troops. If the parachute surgical team possessed additional equipment for use in land operations this could then be brought up to augment its original resources.

Suggested additions as 'land equipment':

1 operating table (as issued to land field ambulances)
2 Mayo overtables (instrument as issued to FSUs)
1 arm table
4 Primus stoves
4 6 feet folding tables to accommodate stores, stoves etc
1 1-kilowatt lighting set complete
1 heater for the theatre (free from danger of other explosion)
1 sterilizer, fish kettle type
3 lids for instrument trays (2 for trays 15" x 11" 1 for tray 11" x 9")
5 enamel jars with lids 1 pint capacity
2 nail brush dishes (enabling brushes to be kept in antiseptic)
6 small grab drums (300 swabs each)
1 bath galvanised (approx. 30" length)
2 buckets galvanised
1 broom soft

General Notes

Operating Table. The present airborne table is not as satisfactory as the standard type in that the Trendelenburg position cannot be easily used – a point of great importance. Modifications of the present design to overcome this difficulty are suggested. In any event a collapsible type of light structure is unlikely to be as robust as the usual type and should be only used for dropping.

Instrument Tables. An overtable which fits into a suspension bar and a table 15" x 27" raised to operating table height have been made to accommodate instruments and the latter is also used for supporting the arm in operations on the upper limb. Mayo overtables would be more satisfactory but an arm table is also needed.

Theatre Heater. Heating of the patient is frequently essential. A 'Valor' paraffin stove or a primus stove under the operating table are efficient, but both need protection on the Davy miners' lamp principle.

Lids. Instrument trays and ligature jars need lids, since most improvised theatres are dusty. We have made some from wood, lined with tin, but enamelled iron would be preferable.

Swab Drums. Swab containers in which swabs can be autoclaved and necessary for maintaining supplies of swabs. Gun cotton boxes are being used at present.

Bath. A galvanised iron bath is required for laundry and for the cleaning of rubber sheeting and jaconet.

Method of working as a land unit attached to a Field Ambulance

With the foregoing additions and amendments a Parachute Surgical Team can work indefinitely given the following conditions:-

(i) Adequate theatre accommodation.

(ii) A Resuscitation Unit capable of preparing patients for operation from the shock standpoint.

(iii) Beds and nursing facilities for severe cases after operation.

The presence of a Field Surgical Unit ensures theatre accommodation (marquee) and beds; the nursing can be done by personnel of the Field Ambulance to which the team is attached. Resuscitation, in the absence of a Transfusion Unit is also done by the Field Ambulance, but better results are obtained by an officer engaged wholly in this work.

A Parachute Surgical Team can therefore, it seems, be best employed to provide a relief shift (and, if necessary, a second table for a FSU) but if beds and tents or buildings are available the Parachute Team can, in fact do the actual work of a FSU.

Packing for land transport

It has been found that large webbing packs are not suitable for the conveyance of surgical equipment, except when in containers for parachute operations. Ammunition boxes (Bofors, 40mm AA ammunition) have been found extremely useful for packing of the smaller items. 4-gallon petrol containers are required for the storage of water.

General Recommendations on Equipment

Ordnance Items.

Operating Lamps. The present type of operating lamp is too heavy and cumbersome for a parachute operation. The lamp can of course still be carried if trolleys are available, but the batteries do not last long enough without being recharged and recharging facilities may not always be available. We have been using Tilley (pressure-paraffin) lamps but it is suggested that a petrol lamp should be evolved. The present operating lamp is extremely good for an airlanding or land operating, where recharging facilities are available, but more spare bulbs should be provided. The seals of spare batteries for headlamps and Orilux torches should also be increased.

Primus Stoves. A collapsible type of primus stove should be devised.

Bed Pans. These are absolutely necessary but difficult to pack in their present shape.

Medical Items

I.1248 Equipment. Should be provided as individual items and panniers should be supplied in which standard and basic packs can be stored and carried.

Tablets. All tablets should always be carried in tins.

Ethyl Chloride. The general anaesthetic should be substituted for the local type.

Pentothal. Should be 1 gram size only, as no dose less than 1 gram is ever given, and the packing should be improved as the tubes are inclined to break.

Barbiturates. Tablets of the barbiturate class should be provided for post-operative cases.

RASC Supplies

48 hour rations. This is too heavy and not easily divisible into separate meals. I recommend the use of the MRS meal ration or of the American type.

Medical Comforts. These should be provided in compact tins and not in bulk. The tea, sugar and milk elements should be separate as it is not always possible to have fires going continuously and tea mixed with milk cannot be kept satisfactorily in a Thermos flask.

Candles. A few candles can with advantage be included in the contents of each standard pack.

Clothing and Personal Equipment

It has been found that the pullover, together with spare shirt, socks, etc. can be conveniently carried in the airborne smock by opening up the lining. One basic pouch should hold first aid medical equipment and the other emergency rations, water sterilising outfit, spare socks and one meal ration MRS. If the personal haversack is lost the man is then able to exist some time without undue hardship.

Conclusion

Whilst it would appear from the various suggestions and comments regarding War Establishment, equipment, training, etc. made in this report and in the appendices that I am recommending many departures from our original organisation, this is not actually so. As I have mentioned earlier in the report the principles of our training and organisation as originally laid down still hold good, and my proposed alterations are no more than variations of the same theme, suggested in the light of experience gained during a hard testing period under actual battle conditions.

That we have not only survived this testing period, but have emerged from it with such creditable achievements is, I feel, a tribute in itself to the early organisation and battle drill. And in conclusion, I would like to thank Lieutenant Colonel Kohane, RAMC for his selflessness in sending out to me as reinforcements such a good type of officer and man, whom I found well up to the proven standards of my original personnel.

Appendix – Casualties treated and evacuated by 16 Parachute Field Ambulance from 12th November 1942 to 14th April 1943

Battle	A	B	C	D	E	F	G	H	I	J	K
Bone				12			24	2			38
Beja		37	4				74	16	25	6	162
Depienne			130								130

Djebel Mansour		129				2	50		9	11	201
Djebel El Kramaissia									3	2	5
Argoub		20	6	28	2		2			18	76
Tamera	8	123	113	65	9	2	179		11	44	554
Viaduct			11								11
Pimple		2								2	4
Sedjenane		29	58	14	3	3	15		10	38	170
31/3/43 to 14/4/43		7	4	1			4		2		18
Total	8	347	326	120	14	7	348	18	60	121	1369

Key:
A 1st Parachute Brigade HQ
B 1st Parachute Battalion
C 2nd Parachute Battalion
D 3rd Parachute Battalion
E Parachute Squadron RE
F Parachute Field Ambulance
G Other Units
H Americans
I French
J Enemy
K Total

Appendix – Record of operations performed by surgeons of 16 Parachute Field Ambulance while serving with the unit from 16th November 1942 to 14th April 1943

	A	B	C	D	E	Total
1	119	22	84	25		250
2	36	5	61	99	5	206
3	77			44		121
4	34		17		3	54
5	8	4	14	7	1	34
6			19			19
7	5	1	7	13		26
8			1			1
9				4		4

10	4					4
11			10	15		25
12	3		8			11
13	2					2
14	13	21	49	31		114
15	2		6			8
16	2		3			5
17	2			3		5
18	1		1	2		4
19	1		6	2	1	10
20	1	1	4	3		9
21	7		1			8
22	1					1
23	1		4			5
24	319	54	295	248	10	926

Key – Letters denote the location and name of surgeon and anaesthetist respectively and the figures the type of operation.

A Beja, Lieutenant C. Rob and Captain D. Wright
B Robaa, Lieutenant C. Longland and Captain D. Ridler
C Gafour-Tabarka and Maison Forestiere, Lieutenant C. Longland and Captain D. Ridler
D Tabarka, Lieutenant A. Lipmann Kessel and Captain D. Ridler
E Robaa and Maison Forestiere, Major P. Wheatley and Captain D. Ridler
1 Single wounds
2 Multiple wounds
3 Flesh wounds
4 Compound fractures
5 Abdominal wounds
6 Hands and feet
7 Chest intrathoracic
8 Vessels
9 Larynx and Pharynx
10 Eye
11 Severe muscle wounds
12 Joints
13 Simple fractures
14 Miscellaneous
15 Amputations
16 Peripheral nerves

17 Genitalia
18 Spine
19 Jaw and face
20 Skull and brain
21 Burns
22 Gas gangrene before surgery
23 Gas gangrene after surgery
24 Totals

Appendix – Battle Casualties sustained by 1st Parachute Brigade Medical Personnel

16 Parachute Field Ambulance

Location	Killed	Wounded	Missing	POW	Total
Gibraltar		3			3
Beja		1			1
Depienne			5	12	17
Djebel Mansour	1	2			3
Tamera	2	4			6
Sedjenane	1	3			4
Total	4	13	5	12	34

Battalion Medical Personnel

Unit	Killed	Wounded	Missing	POW	Total
1st Parachute Battalion	3	3	1		7
2nd Parachute Battalion		1	6		7
3rd Parachute Battalion	1	4			5
Total	4	8	7		19

Appendix XLVI

Conclusions and suggestions from Colonel MacEwan, 16 Parachute Field Ambulance RAMC, written in 1943 after the experiences of North Africa

Loading Table for Parachute Field Ambulance in an Airlanding Operation.
Summary of Aircraft:

Plane No	Plane Title	Officers	RAMC	AD Corps	RASC	ACC	Inf	Summary
1	A	1	9		1			M
2	B		10					N
3	C	2	6		2	1		O
4	D	1	8		1	1		P
5	E	1	9		1			Q
6	F		10					R
7	G	1	9		1			S
8	H		10					T
9	I	2	5	1	2	1		U
10	J	1	8		1	1		V
11	K	1	4		1	1		W
12	L	1	3		1		1	X
Total		11	91	1	11	5	1	Total 120

Key:

A No 1 Section A
B No 1 Section B
C Advance HQ Commanding Officer's Party
D Advance HQ No 1 Surgical Team
E No 2 Section A
F No 2 Section B
G No 3 Section A
H No 3 Section B
I Rear HQ 2 i/c Party

J Rear HQ No 2 Surgical Team
K Rear HQ QM A
L Rear HQ QM B
M ½ Section
N ½ Section
O 1 Motor Cycle Fitter's Tools ½ Surgical Team
P ½ Surgical Team 1 Motor Cycle Sanitary and Cooks
Q ½ Section
R ½ Section
S ½ Section
T ½ Section
U Office Dental ½ Surgical Team
V ½ Surgical Team Cooks
W ¼ Section (Reserve Surgical Team) Reserve Stores Anti-Gas Stores
X ¼ Section (Reserve Surgical Team) Reserve Stores Anti-Gas Stores Disinfector

Loading of a Section:

Plane No	Contents of Plane	Weight in lb
1, 5, 7 (each)	Personnel:	
	Medical Officer	
	Corporal RAMC	
	8 Privates RAMC	
	1 Driver RASC	
	Total 1 Officer 10 Other Ranks	2,200
	Personal Equipment including parachutes at 75lb	825
	Standard Stores:	
	2 Trolleys at 75lb	150
	3 Boxes Composite Rations at 65lb	195
	4 Gallons water at 11lb	44
	1 Shovel GS	5
	1 Pick complete	6
	Total	400
	½ Normal Parachute Section Equipment contained in 1 Basket and 3 Bundles	350
	Additional Equipment:	
	Ward Pannier	70
	6 Stretchers at 15lb	90
	10 Blankets at 5lb	50
	5 Groundsheets at 4lb	20
	Total weight	4,005

Plane No	Contents of Plane	Weight in lb
2, 6, 8 (each)	Personnel:	
	S/Sergeant RAMC	
	9 Privates RAMC	
	Total 10 Other Ranks	2,000
	Personal Equipment including parachutes at 75lb	750
	Standard Stores:	
	2 Trolleys at 75lb	150
	3 Boxes Composite Rations at 65lb	195
	4 Gallons water at 11lb	44
	1 Shovel GS	5
	1 Pick complete	6
	Total	400
	½ Normal Parachute Section Equipment contained in 1 Basket and 4 Bundles	350
	Additional Equipment:	
	Ward Pannier	70
	6 Stretchers at 15lb	90
	10 Blankets at 5lb	50
	5 Groundsheets at 4lb	20
	Total weight	3,730

Loading of Advance HQ:

Plane No	Contents of Plane	Weight in lb
3	Personnel:	
	Commanding Officer	
	1 Medical Officer	
	1 S/Sergeant	
	1 Clerk	
	2 Batmen	
	2 Privates RAMC (Nursing Orderlies)	
	1 Cook ACC	
	1 Fitter RASC	
	1 Driver RASC	
	Total 2 Officers 9 Other Ranks	2,200
	Personal Equipment including parachutes at 75lb	750
	Standard Stores (as detailed in tables above showing Loading of a Section)	400
	Additional Equipment:	
	1 Folding Motor Cycle	70
	2 Gallons petrol and oil mixed	22

Plane No	Contents of Plane	Weight in lb
3	Personnel:	
	1 Fitter's box	50
	1 table, 1 stool, 1 stationery box	65
	½ normal Parachute Surgical Team Equipment	200
	1 Accumulator	52
	1 Additional box Plasma	70
	Total weight	3,954

Plane No	Contents of Plane	Weight in lb
4	Personnel:	
	Graded Surgeon	
	2 ORAs	
	4 Nursing Orderlies	
	1 Batman	
	1 Sanitary Sergeant	
	1 Corporal	
	1 Cook ASC	
	Total 1 Officer 10 Other Ranks	2,200
	Personal Equipment including parachutes at 75lb	825
	Standard Stores (as detailed in tables above showing Loading of a Section)	400
	Additional Equipment:	
	1 additional pannier Surgical Team Equipment	100
	½ normal Parachute Surgical Team Equipment	276
	1 Additional box Plasma	70
	1 Accumulator	52
	1 Folding Motor Cycle	70
	2 gallons petrol and oil mixed	22
	1 pannier sundry Sanitary and Cook's Equipment	100
	Total weight	4,115

Loading of Rear HQ:

Plane No	Contents of Plane	Weight in lb
9	Personnel:	
	Second in Command	
	Dental Officer	
	RSM	

Plane No	Contents of Plane	Weight in lb
9	Personnel:	
	Sergeant Clerk	
	1 Corporal Dental Clerk Orderly	
	1 Nursing Orderly	
	2 Batmen	
	1 Cook ACC	
	1 Fitter RASC	
	1 Driver RASC	
	Total 2 Officers 9 Other Ranks	2,200
	Personal Equipment including parachutes at 75lb	825
	Standard Stores (as detailed in tables above showing Loading of a Section)	400
	Additional Equipment:	
	Office Equipment – 1 table, 2 stools, 2 stationery boxes, 1 typewriter and 2 crates	150
	Dental Equipment – 2 panniers and 1 dental chair	200
	½ normal Parachute Surgical Team Equipment	200
	1 Accumulator	52
	1 Additional box Plasma	70
	1 Fitter's Box	50
	1 Container 6 gallons	50
	Petrol 6 gallons	66
	1 Basket – sundry HQ G1098 Equipment	100
	Total weight	4,363

Plane No	Contents of Plane	Weight in lb
10	Personnel:	
	Graded Surgeon	
	2 ORA's	
	4 Nursing Orderlies	
	1 Clerk	
	1 GD Orderly	
	1 Cook ACC	
	1 Driver RASC	
	Total 1 Officer 10 Other Ranks	2,200
	Personal Equipment including parachutes at 75lb	825
	Standard Stores (as detailed in tables above showing Loading of a Section)	400
	Additional Equipment:	
	½ normal Parachute Surgical Team Equipment	200
	1 Additional pannier containing Surgical Equipment	100
	1 Additional box Plasma	70
	1 Accumulator	52
	1 Cooker No 1 (less baffle plates)	60
	1 Container 6 gallon	50
	1 Pannier - Cook's Equipment	100
	1 Basket – sundry G1098 Equipment	100
	Petrol 6 gallons	66
	Total weight	4,223

Plane No	Contents of Plane	Weight in lb
11	Personnel:	
	Quartermaster	
	Ration Corporal	
	Batman	
	Carpenter	
	Barber	
	1 Cook ACC	
	1 Driver RASC	
	Total 1 Officer 6 Other Ranks	1,400
	Personal Equipment including parachutes at 75lb	525

Plane No	Contents of Plane	Weight in lb
11	Personnel:	
	Standard Stores (as detailed in tables above showing Loading of a Section)	400
	Additional Equipment:	
	½ normal Parachute Surgical Team Equipment plus additional equipment (as in Section Plane 1)	580
	½ Surgical Team Stores plus additional Plasma and accumulator (see Plane 5)	322
	2 Baskets – Reserve expendable Medical Equipment	200
	1 Basket – Reserve Comforts	150
	2 Baskets – sundry G1098 Equipment	200
	1 Pannier – Anti-gas stores	100
	1 Pannier Officers' Mess Equipment	80
	1 Box Carpenter's Tools	100
	Petrol 6 gallons	66
	Kerosene 2 gallons	22
	Total weight	4,145

Plane No	Contents of Plane	Weight in lb
12	Personnel:	
	Padre	
	QMS	
	Storeman (RAMC)	
	1 Private RAMC	
	1 Driver RASC	
	1 Batman (Infantry)	
	Total 1 Officer 5 Other Ranks	1,200
	Personal Equipment including parachutes at 75lb	450
	Standard Stores (as detailed in tables above showing Loading of a Section)	400
	Additional Equipment:	
	½ normal Parachute Surgical Team Equipment plus additional equipment (as in Section Plane 2)	580

Plane No	Contents of Plane	Weight in lb
12	Personnel:	
	½ Surgical Team Stores plus additional Pannier, Box of Plasma and Accumulator (see Plane 4)	495
	2 Baskets – Reserve expendable Medical Equipment	200
	2 Baskets – sundry G1098 Equipment	200
	1 Pannier – Soaps and Expendable Sundries	100
	1 Pannier – Anti-gas Stores	100
	1 Pannier – Sergeants' Mess Equipment	80
	Disinfector	100
	Petrol 6 gallons	66
	Kerosene 4 gallons	44
	Total weight	4, 015

Note: It would appear that Colonel MacEwan's recommendation that the medical personnel travel together in their own aircraft was adopted certainly at Arnhem where 16 and 133 PFA flew in 6 Dakotas each. They were not spread about, as had been the case on previous operations.

Appendix XLVII

Awards to RAMC personnel 1st Parachute Brigade for the North African Campaign 1942-43

Distinguished Service Order
Colonel M. MacEwan OBE DFC TD
Lieutenant Colonel P.R. Wheatley
Captain J. Logan
Major A. Young

Officer of the British Empire
Colonel M. MacEwan DSO DFC TD

Bar to Military Cross
Captain R. Gordon

Military Cross
Captain J. Rutherford
Captain M. Heggie
Captain D. Ridler
Lieutenant C. Rob
Lieutenant D. Wright

Distinguished Conduct Medal
S/Sergeant E. Stevens

Military Medal
CSM Rowe
S/Sergeant E. Stevens
Corporal G. McKenzie
Corporal E. Hardie
Corporal R. Jermey
Private S. Tynan

British Empire Medal
Sergeant J. Bellamy
Corporal E. Sirrell

Mentioned in Despatches

Captain J. Cassidy
Captain A. Percival
S/Sergeant E. Pruden
S/Sergeant R. Clegg
Corporal A. Hatcher
Corporal Jarrett
Corporal McIntosh
Private J. Etherington
Private R. Godden
Private S. Harris
Private E. Hewitt
Private A. Hope
Private S. Kirk
Private G. Neal
Private R. Pick
Private G. Stanners
Private L. Swift
Private S. Tynan

American Silver Star

Private G. Neal

Appendix XLVIII

Awards to the 1st Parachute Brigade for North Africa 1942-43

Note that the rank was the substantive one at the time of award and not any acting or temporary one.

Distinguished Service Order
11/02/1943 Major S. Hill 1st Battalion
11/02/1943 Captain J. Frost 2nd Battalion
11/02/1943 Captain J. Ross 2nd Battalion
22/04/1943 Brigadier E. Flavell GOC 1st Parachute Brigade
22/04/1943 Captain D. Dobie 3rd Battalion
04/05/1943 Major A. Pearson 1st Battalion
15/06/1943 Captain H. Coxen 1st Battalion
15/06/1943 Captain J. Logan RAMC RMO 1st Battalion
11/11/1943 Colonel M. MacEwan OBE, DFC, TD 16 PFA RAMC

Bar to the Distinguished Service Order
18/05/1943 Major A. Pearson 1st Battalion

Officer of the British Empire
23/09/1943 Major M. MacEwan DFC, TD

Military Cross
11/02/1943 Captain R. Ashford 2nd Battalion
11/02/1943 Captain M. Haggie RAMC RMO 1st Battalion
11/02/1943 Lieutenant J. Brayley 2nd Battalion
11/02/1943 Lieutenant T. Livesey 1st Parachute Squadron RE
11/02/1943 Lieutenant P. Mellor 1st Battalion
11/02/1943 Lieutenant C. Rob 16 PFA RAMC
11/02/1943 Lieutenant S. Wandless 1st Battalion
22/04/1943 Lieutenant G. Street 3rd Battalion
18/05/1943 Captain J. Hall 3rd Battalion
18/05/1943 Captain H. Lloyd 1st Battalion
01/06/1943 Lieutenant J. Timothy 2nd Battalion
15/06/1943 Lieutenant W. Anderson 1st Battalion
15/06/1943 Lieutenant H. Burwash 3rd Battalion
15/06/1943 Lieutenant R. Ellis 3rd Battalion
15/06/1943 Lieutenant R. Stark 2nd Battalion
23/09/1943 Captain P. Cleasby-Thompson 1st Battalion

23/09/1943 Captain H. Coxen DSO 1st Battalion
23/09/1943 Captain D. Crawley 2nd Battalion
23/09/1943 Captain D. Murray 1st Parachute Squadron RE
23/09/1943 Captain A. Pearson 1st Battalion
23/09/1943 Captain R. Pine-Coffin 3rd Battalion
23/09/1943 Captain D. Wright 16 PFA RAMC
23/09/1943 Lieutenant C. Perrin-Brown 1st Battalion
23/09/1943 Lieutenant C. Vernon 1st Parachute Squadron RE

Bar to the Military Cross
11/02/1943 Captain R. Gordon RAMC RMO 2nd Battalion

Distinguished Conduct Medal
18/04/1943 Sergeant H. Howells 1st Battalion
22/04/1943 Sergeant J. McDonnell 3rd Battalion
22/04/1943 Sergeant R. McDougall 3rd Battalion
18/05/1943 WOII R. Richards 1st Battalion
15/06/1943 S/Sergeant E. Stevens 16 PFA RAMC

Military Medal
11/02/1943 Sergeant J. Ryan 1st Battalion
11/02/1943 L/Corporal H. Bainbridge 1st Battalion
11/02/1943 L/Corporal R. Morgan 1st Battalion
11/02/1943 Private W. McDermott 2nd Battalion
11/02/1943 Private J. Meadows 1st Battalion
11/02/1943 Private D. Miller 2nd Battalion
11/02/1943 Private F. Welsh 2nd Battalion
11/02/1943 Private F. Wright 2nd Battalion
22/04/1943 WOII J. Donbavand 3rd Battalion
22/04/1943 Sergeant J. Branthwaite 3rd Battalion
22/04/1943 Sergeant C. Eveleigh 3rd Battalion
22/04/1943 L/Corporal J. Grabham 3rd Battalion
22/04/1943 L/Corporal J. Murphy 3rd Battalion
22/04/1943 L/Corporal I. Royles 3rd Battalion
18/05/1943 Sergeant A. Clements 1st Battalion
18/05/1943 Private M. Crowe 1st Battalion
18/05/1943 Private A. Lloyd 1st Battalion
01/06/1943 Sergeant W. Cloves 2nd Battalion
01/06/1943 Sergeant W. Fleming 2nd Battalion
01/06/1943 Private J. Hacking 2nd Battalion
15/06/1943 Sergeant L. Curtis 1st Battalion
15/06/1943 Sergeant V. Padureano 1st Battalion
15/06/1943 Sergeant A. Vedeniapine 3rd Battalion
15/06/1943 Corporal L. Bradley 1st Battalion
15/06/1943 Corporal T. Griffiths 2nd Battalion
15/06/1943 Corporal E. Hardie 16 PFA RAMC

15/06/1943 Private C. Lamb 1st Battalion
15/06/1943 Private M. McAllister 2nd Battalion
15/06/1943 Private H. Parker 3rd Battalion
15/06/1943 Private R. Weller 3rd Battalion
26/08/1943 Sergeant W. Bailey 3rd Battalion
23/09/1943 WOII M. Forsyth 2nd Battalion
23/09/1943 WOII S. Steadman 1st Battalion
23/09/1943 Sergeant A. John 1st Battalion
23/09/1943 Sergeant W. Kerr 1st Battalion
23/09/1943 Sergeant J. Lawson 2nd Battalion
23/09/1943 L/Sergeant J. Copling 3rd Battalion
23/09/1943 L/Sergeant G. Strong 1st Battalion
23/09/1943 Corporal J. Bennett 1st Battalion
23/09/1943 Corporal W. Westripp 1st Battalion
23/09/1943 L/Corporal W. Westwood 1st Battalion
23/09/1943 L/Corporal E. Larner 1st Battalion
23/09/1943 Private J. Colville 1st Battalion
23/09/1943 Private E. Harris 1st Battalion
23/09/1943 Private D. Wilson 3rd Battalion
23/09/1943 Private H. Bartley 1st Battalion

Bar to the Military Medal
23/09/1943 Sergeant J. Sharp MM 2nd Battalion

Mentioned in Despatches
All gazetted 23/09/1943
Captain J. Bull 1st Battalion
Captain J. Cassidy RAMC RMO HQ 1st Parachute Brigade
Captain A. Percival 16 PFA RAMC
Lieutenant W. Blewitt 3rd Battalion
Lieutenant J. Brayley 2nd Battalion
Lieutenant G. Bromley Martin 3rd Battalion
Lieutenant A. Clements 1st Battalion
Lieutenant J. Elton-Tuckett 3rd Battalion
Lieutenant A. Kellas 1st Battalion
Lieutenant J. Richey 1st Battalion
Lieutenant R. Stark 2nd Battalion
Lieutenant J. Stewart 1st Battalion
S/Sergeant T. Anderson 16 PFA RAMC
S/Sergeant R. Clegg 16 PFA RAMC
Sergeant J. Baynes 3rd Battalion
Sergeant C. Eveleigh MM 3rd Battalion
Sergeant J. Hetherington 3rd Battalion
Sergeant J. Rainnie 1st Battalion
Sergeant A. Watson 3rd Battalion
Corporal L. Kidman 1st Battalion

Corporal J. Newton 3rd Battalion
Corporal F. Tucker HQ 1st Parachute Brigade
Corporal J. Webb 3rd Battalion
L/Corporal J. Murphy MM 3rd Battalion
L/Corporal W. Simpson 1st Parachute Squadron RE
Private M. Bromnick HQ 1st Parachute Brigade
Private H. Fisher HQ 1st Parachute Brigade
Private E. Hewitt RAMC 1st Battalion
Private D. Humphrey HQ 1st Parachute Brigade
Private T. Jones 1st Battalion
Private A. Mackie 2nd Battalion
Private W. Wain 2nd Battalion

Foreign Decorations Awarded

France

Croix de Guerre

Captain E. O'Brien 1st Battalion
Sergeant Heyhow 2nd Battalion
L/Corporal Thirkell 2nd Battalion
Private F. Wright MM 2nd Battalion

United States of America

Distinguished Service Cross

C/Sergeant R. Allen 3rd Battalion

Silver Star

Captain E. Yeldham 3rd Battalion
Captain A. Rutherford 2nd Battalion
L/Corporal W. Simpson 1st Parachute Squadron RE
Private G. Neal 16 PFA RAMC
Private M. Peters

Soldier's Medal

Sergeant A. Powell 16 PFA RAMC

Appendix XLIX

Lessons from the Tunisian Campaign – the 1st Parachute Battalion's view

Report originally titled 'Lessons from the present campaign'.

1. General

It is as well if we take stock of our tactical shortcomings which have come to light during the last six weeks. A great many of the points mentioned below were considered and practised in England during training. The tempo of the advance to begin with, combined with the fact that being shot over is a new experience to a great many, has made us forget some of the elementary teaching. I would therefore ask all commanders to impress on all ranks the importance of this question, for unless this is done the result can only lead to unnecessary loss of life.

2. Information

On the whole information has not been coming back to the Divisional HQ with the result that, in many cases, the Divisional Commander has been forced to take decisions on information which is as much as four hours out of date. The chief reasons for this failure are, I think, as follows:-

(a) Commanders are so engrossed in fighting the battle that they sometimes forget to pass back information. This is understandable at the beginning of a campaign but it must not continue.

(b) Vital information is not always being sent back by duplicate means.

(c) The means of communication for a Commander, particularly a Brigade Commander, are not always been as good as they might have been. If a Brigade HQ has not the resources in its own hand, then they must be supplemented by loans from Division and Corps.

(d) Sufficient forethought is not always given as to the correct positioning of an HQ, and this makes all the difference.

(e) Liaison Officers are often being used as DRs instead of in their proper role. For particular operations their number may have to be increased if units can stand the strain.

(f) The organisation within an HQ has in some cases been such that the information coming in cannot be easily collated and digested. In other cases too it has been noticed that the staff officer is so hampered by visitors and others seeking information that he cannot concentrate on his job.

3. Co-ordination

(a) At the outset of this campaign speed was very important and as a result some bad habits crept in. That period has now passed and we must be sure that we take every step to ensure that if an operation is proposed, no stone is left unturned to provide that operation with the best co-ordinated support available. Initially, decentralised artillery became the rule – and quite rightly so. But now we must make sure that our attacks are supported by the maximum use of co-coordinated artillery, mortar, and other supporting fire.

Often an artillery group commander will be incapable of co-ordinating the fire of the number of units involved. In such cases the CRA must prepare, at short notice, to transfer his allegiance to a Brigadier in order to arrange proper support, for he alone can provide the necessary signal communications.

(b) Cases have occurred in which the policy for the anti-tank layout has not been laid down by the commander, and the layout has been left to the anti-tank commander. This has resulted in the employment of too many guns in a primary anti-tank role. If the control of artillery is to be properly centralised, then obviously too many field guns must not be used in an anti-tank role. When the whole lay-out has been co-ordinated by the anti-tank commander it has usually been very successful. In this case the anti-tank commander should also control the layout of the 2 pounders.

4. Digging

The importance of digging has already been proved several times. Directly a position is taken digging must commence forthwith, however tired the men are. Moreover slit trenches must be dug to such a depth that if the position is attacked by tanks the occupants are safe at the bottom of the trenches. Shallow trenches may mean that the occupants are crushed by tanks. At present the Germans are more energetic and more cunning than we are at digging. We must rectify this by sweat.

5. Concealment

Concealment is neglected in some cases. Trenches dug in regular formation are extremely obvious to the air and should be avoided.

We are still not careful enough to avoid disclosing our main position to enemy aircraft by movement, lighting of fires, hanging out of washing, etc. Where possible the aim should be to occupy an alternative position, and only to move to the battle position when the commanding officer judges the time to be ripe.

The German is an artist at concealing his weapons in defiladed positions. We realise the importance of this tactical teaching, but in practice the number of weapons that one sees defiladed is very small. The question must be tackled with more realism.

6. Size of Localities

There is still a tendency for localities to be too widespread. We agreed during training that:

(a) Sections should be within 60 yards of their platoon commander.
(b) A company locality should fit inside a circle of 1000 yards diameter.

(c) That within a battalion layout companies should be within small arms range for supporting fire.

There may be occasionally obviously be exceptions to the above, but they are good rough rules on which to work, and have been grossly ignored in some cases.

7. Anti-tank mines

Counter-attack by tanks is one of our chief dangers after the capture of a position. The antidote is the quickest organisation of anti-tank defence, combined with the quick putting down of minefields. It is the latter practice in which we have got to quicken up. Lessons from Libya have already told us that failure to produce quick minefields may mean disaster.

Some battalions in this country now make practice of carrying 75 grenades on every man, and I would urge commanders to encourage this practice for certain operations, for it does ensure that mines are available quickly and the problem of trying to bring them forward is obviated.

8. Mopping up

As in other theatres of war the enemy here is making use of concealed machine guns and light automatics which lie low when overrun and then come to life again. This does emphasize the importance of mopping up, for which purpose troops must always be allotted. The length of time for this operation is not always realised.

9. Road movement

In spite of the fact that transport moving by day has been shot up, there is still much unnecessary movement by day on the roads. Commanders will take steps to ensure, by disciplinary action when necessary, that unnecessary movement by day is eliminated.

At the same time when it is necessary to move vehicles or a column by day, every step should be taken to provide maximum anti-aircraft protection within that column. If a column is attacked then we must produce sufficient fire to make that attack not worthwhile as being too expensive. Low flying attacks on German columns are considered by the RAF not to be worthwhile as being too expensive. We must use our anti-aircraft weapons so as to produce the same results against the enemy. Unprotected vehicles must move at really wide spacing by day – at least 250 yards between vehicles.

10. Action against enemy aircraft

(a) Being dive bombed is an unnerving experience and has a great effect initially on the morale of young troops. The casualties inflicted by dive bombing are very light and every opportunity should be taken to point this out to the troops who will eventually realise the truth of this statement.

(b) Whenever troops are, or are not told, to engage enemy aircraft should be laid down by a commander. It may well be that if we wish to hide our dispositions from the enemy aircraft, that it is better not to disclose them by firing at enemy recce aircraft. This does not alter the fact, however, that once it is clear that enemy aircraft have located our troops and begin to take offensive action against them, we must use every weapon we have against the attacking aircraft.

(c) The habits of enemy aircraft should be studied, for the enemy is a creature of habit. Where he carries out offensive action against roads at regular timings and against the same locality, it may easily be possible to arrange an ambush by well-sited anti-aircraft guns hidden in positions.

11. Protection of guns

It is still not realised in all cases that artillery must be so placed that it is protected against action by enemy infantry at night. If its position is not so protected then it may be necessary to move the guns at night so that they are actually within infantry localities.

12. ST grenades and 68 grenades

The organisation for the distribution of ST and 68 grenades within battalions still requires improvement. Instances have occurred where tanks have got into infantry positions and where ST grenades were not available although they would have been invaluable.

13. Observation Posts (artillery and infantry)

It should be a point of honour that the occupant of an OP makes himself fully acquainted with every detail of his landscape as soon as possible. This is not being done with the result that golden opportunities of inflicting casualties on the enemy are lost, owing to the time required to identify the position of the target. In addition accurate information of enemy movement cannot be given unless the officer at the OP really does know his bit of country. When own troops are advancing OPs must be fully operative before it gets light.

14. Rumours

Loose talk has taken place and in a few cases has definitely done harm. It nearly always takes the form of exaggerating casualties, or painting a picture more blackly than is justified. This again is no new practice and has happened in every theatre of war.

It is imperative, however, that it be stopped, and all ranks will demand from the originator of such statement the source of his information. If it proves to be dangerous and hearsay only, disciplinary action will be taken forthwith. It is only by the active co-operation of all ranks that this can be done.

There is nothing new in anything that is mentioned above. With experience all these points become automatic. It is vital, however, that we relearn well-known lessons by bitter experience as seldom as possible.

Bibliography

Unpublished sources

War Diaries:
HQ 1st Parachute Brigade
1st Parachute Battalion
2nd Parachute Battalion
3rd Parachute Battalion
1st Parachute Squadron Royal Engineers
16 Parachute Field Ambulance RAMC
1st Parachute Brigade Signal Section

Published sources

Arthur, M., *Men of the Red Beret: Airborne Forces 1940-1990* (London: Hutchinson, 1990)

Cherry, N., *Red Berets and Red Crosses: Story of the Medical Services in the 1st Airborne Division in World War II* (Renkum: R. Sigmond, 1999, 2nd Revised Ed.)

Cherry, N., *Striking Back: Britain's Airborne and Commando Raids 1940-1942* (Solihull: Helion, 2009)

Curtis, R., *Churchill's Volunteer: A Parachute Corporal's Story* (London: Avon Books, 1995)

Otway, Lt Col T.B.H. (comp.), *Airborne Forces* (London: War Office, 1951)

Peatling, R., *Without Tradition: 2 Para 1941-45* (Wimborne Minster: R. Peatling, 1994)

Thompson, J., *Ready for Anything: The Parachute Regiment at war 1940-1982* (London: Weidenfeld & Nicolson, 1989)

Index

Index of People

Index of Places

Index of Military Units

Corps

Divisions

Brigades

Regiments